Visit classzone.com and get connect

Online resources provide instruction, p and learning support correlated to your

- **Misconceptions database** provides solutions for common student misconceptions about science and their world.

- **Professional development links,** including SciLinks, offer additional teaching resources.

- **Animations and visualizations** help improve comprehension.

- **Math Tutorial** helps strengthen students' math skills.

- **Flashcards** help students review vocabulary.

- **State test practice** prepares students for assessments.

You have immediate access to *ClassZone's* teacher resources.

MCDTCOWDMSSZ

Use this code to create your own username and password.

Also visit *ClassZone* to learn more about these innovative and updated online resources.

- eEdition Plus Online
- eTest Plus Online
- EasyPlanner Plus Online
- Content Review Online

Now it all clicks!™

 CLASSZONE.COM

McDougal Littell

TEACHER'S EDITION

McDougal Littell Science

Earth's Atmosphere

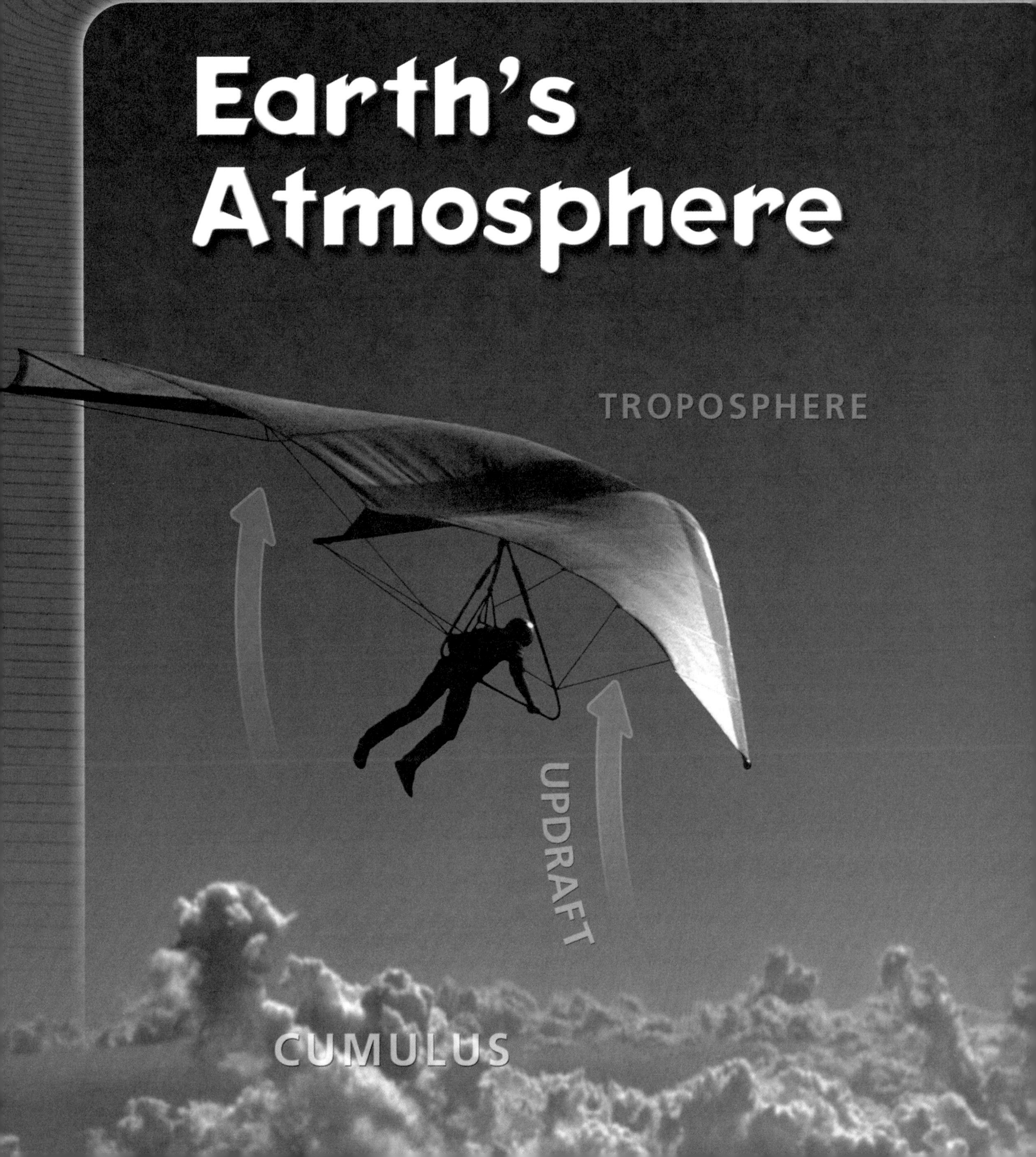
TROPOSPHERE
UPDRAFT
CUMULUS

Credits
5B Illustration by Stephen Durke; **39B** Illustration by Richard Bonson/Wildlife Art Ltd.; **113B** Illustration by Chris Forsey/MCA;**113C** Mapquest.

Acknowledgements
Excerpts and adaptations from National Science Education Standards by the National Academy of Sciences. Copyright © 1996 by the National Academy of Sciences. Reprinted with permission from the National Academies Press, Washington, D.C.

ISBN: 0-618-33416-5   1 2 3 4 5 6 7 8 VJM 08 07 06 05 04

Internet Web Site: http://www.mcdougallittell.com

McDougal Littell Science

Effective Science Instruction Tailored for Middle School Learners

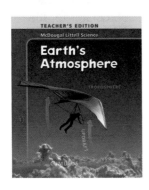

Earth's Atmosphere
Teacher's Edition
Contents

Science Consultants

Chief Science Consultant

James Trefil, Ph.D. is the Clarence J. Robinson Professor of Physics at George Mason University. He is the author or co-author of more than 25 books, including *Science Matters* and *The Nature of Science.* Dr. Trefil is a member of the American Association for the Advancement of Science's Committee on the Public Understanding of Science and Technology. He is also a fellow of the World Economic Forum and a frequent contributor to *Smithsonian* magazine.

Rita Ann Calvo, Ph.D. is Senior Lecturer in Molecular Biology and Genetics at Cornell University, where for 12 years she also directed the Cornell Institute for Biology Teachers. Dr. Calvo is the 1999 recipient of the College and University Teaching Award from the National Association of Biology Teachers.

Kenneth Cutler, M.S. is the Education Coordinator for the Julius L. Chambers Biomedical Biotechnology Research Institute at North Carolina Central University. A former middle school and high school science teacher, he received a 1999 Presidential Award for Excellence in Science Teaching.

Instructional Design Consultants

Douglas Carnine, Ph.D. is Professor of Education and Director of the National Center for Improving the Tools of Educators at the University of Oregon. He is the author of seven books and over 100 other scholarly publications, primarily in the areas of instructional design and effective instructional strategies and tools for diverse learners. Dr. Carnine also serves as a member of the National Institute for Literacy Advisory Board.

Linda Carnine, Ph.D. consults with school districts on curriculum development and effective instruction for students struggling academically. A former teacher and school administrator, Dr. Carnine also co-authored a popular remedial reading program.

Donald Steely, Ph.D. serves as principal investigator at the Oregon Center for Applied Science (ORCAS) on federal grants for science and language arts programs. His background also includes teaching and authoring of print and multimedia programs in science, mathematics, history, and spelling.

Sam Miller, Ph.D. is a middle school science teacher and the Teacher Development Liaison for the Eugene, Oregon, Public Schools. He is the author of curricula for teaching science, mathematics, computer skills, and language arts.

Vicky Vachon, Ph.D. consults with school districts throughout the United States and Canada on improving overall academic achievement with a focus on literacy. She is also co-author of a widely used program for remedial readers.

Content Reviewers

John Beaver, Ph.D.
Ecology
Professor, Director of Science Education Center
College of Education and Human Services
Western Illinois University
Macomb, IL

Donald J. DeCoste, Ph.D.
Matter and Energy, Chemical Interactions
Chemistry Instructor
University of Illinois
Urbana-Champaign, IL

Dorothy Ann Fallows, Ph.D., MSc
Diversity of Living Things, Microbiology
Partners in Health
Boston, MA

Michael Foote, Ph.D.
The Changing Earth, Life Over Time
Associate Professor
Department of the Geophysical Sciences
The University of Chicago
Chicago, IL

Lucy Fortson, Ph.D.
Space Science
Director of Astronomy
Adler Planetarium and Astronomy Museum
Chicago, IL

Elizabeth Godrick, Ph.D.
Human Biology
Professor, CAS Biology
Boston University
Boston, MA

Isabelle Sacramento Grilo, M.S.
The Changing Earth
Lecturer, Department of the Geological Sciences
Montana State University
Bozeman, MT

David Harbster, MSc
Diversity of Living Things
Professor of Biology
Paradise Valley Community College
Phoenix, AZ

Richard D. Norris, Ph.D.
Earth's Waters
Professor of Paleobiology
Scripps Institution of Oceanography
University of California, San Diego
La Jolla, CA

Donald B. Peck, M.S.
Motion and Forces; Waves, Sound, and Light;
Electricity and Magnetism
Director of the Center for Science Education (retired)
Fairleigh Dickinson University
Madison, NJ

Javier Penalosa, Ph.D.
Diversity of Living Things, Plants
Associate Professor, Biology Department
Buffalo State College
Buffalo, NY

Raymond T. Pierrehumbert, Ph.D.
Earth's Atmosphere
Professor in Geophysical Sciences (Atmospheric Science)
The University of Chicago
Chicago, IL

Brian J. Skinner, Ph.D.
Earth's Surface
Eugene Higgins Professor of Geology and Geophysics
Yale University
New Haven, CT

Nancy E. Spaulding, M.S.
Earth's Surface, The Changing Earth, Earth's Waters
Earth Science Teacher (retired)
Elmira Free Academy
Elmira, NY

Steven S. Zumdahl, Ph.D.
Matter and Energy, Chemical Interactions
Professor Emeritus of Chemistry
University of Illinois
Urbana-Champaign, IL

Susan L. Zumdahl, M.S.
Matter and Energy, Chemical Interactions
Chemistry Education Specialist
University of Illinois
Urbana-Champaign, IL

Safety Consultant

Juliana Texley, Ph.D.
Former K–12 Science Teacher and School Superintendent
Boca Raton, FL

English Language Advisor

Judy Lewis, M.A.
Director, State and Federal Programs for reading proficiency
and high risk populations
Rancho Cordova, CA

Research-Based Solutions for Your Classroom

The distinguished program consultant team and a thorough, research-based planning and development process assure that *McDougal Littell Science* supports all students in learning science concepts, acquiring inquiry skills, and thinking scientifically.

Standards-Based Instruction

Concepts and skills were selected based on careful analysis of national and state standards.

- National Science Education Standards
- Project 2061 Benchmarks for Science Literacy
- Comprehensive database of state science standards

Standards and Benchmarks

Each chapter in **Earth's Atmosphere** covers some of the learning goals that are described in the *National Science Education Standards* (NSES) and the Project 2061 *Benchmarks for Science Literacy*. Selected content and skill standards are shown below in shortened form. The following National Science Education Standards are covered on pages xii–xxvii, in Frontiers in Science, and in Timelines in Science, as well as in chapter features and laboratory investigations: Understandings About Scientific Inquiry (A.9), Understandings About Science and Technology (E.6), Science and Technology in Society (F.5), Science as a Human Endeavor (G.1), Nature of Science (G.2), and History of Science (G.3).

Content Standards

1 Earth's Changing Atmosphere

National Science Education Standards

D.1.h The atmosphere
- is a mixture of the gases nitrogen and oxygen
- has small amounts of water vapor and other gases
- has different properties at different heights

F.3.b Human activities can produce hazards and affect the speed of natural changes.

Project 2061 Benchmarks

4.B.6 The atmosphere can change suddenly when a volcano erupts or when Earth is struck by a huge rock from space. A small change in the substance of the atmosphere can have a big effect if the change lasts long enough.

4.E.3 Heat energy can move by the collision of particles, by the motion of particles, or by waves through space.

2 Weather Patterns

National Science Education Standards

D.1.f Water
- evaporates from Earth's surface
- rises, cools, and condenses in the atmosphere
- falls to the surface as rain or snow

D.1.i Clouds form when water vapor condenses. Clouds affect the weather.

D.1.j Global patterns have an effect on local weather and weather patterns.
- Global patterns of air motion affect the local weather.
- Oceans affect the weather patterns of a place.

Project 2061 Benchmarks

4.B.7 Water is important in the atmosphere. Water
- evaporates from Earth's surface
- rises and cools
- condenses into rain or snow
- falls back to the surface

4.B.4 Sunlight falls more intensely on different parts of Earth, and the pattern changes over the year. The differences in heating of Earth's surface produce seasons and other weather patterns.

x Unit: Earth's Atmosphere

CHAPTER

1 Earth's Changing Atmosphere

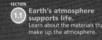
the **BIG** idea

Earth's atmosphere is a blanket of gases that supports and protects life.

What will make this kite soar?

Key Concepts

SECTION
1.1 Earth's atmosphere supports life.
Learn about the materials that make up the atmosphere.

SECTION
1.2 The Sun supplies the atmosphere's energy.
Learn how energy from the Sun affects the atmosphere.

SECTION
1.3 Gases in the atmosphere absorb radiation.
Learn about the ozone layer and the greenhouse effect.

SECTION
1.4 Human activities affect the atmosphere.
Learn about pollution, global warming, and changes in the ozone layer.

Internet Preview

CLASSZONE.COM

Chapter 1 online resources: Content Review, two Visualizations, two Resource Centers, Math Tutorial, Test Practice

have caused these changes?

Internet Activity: Atmosphere

Go to ClassZone.com to learn about Earth's atmosphere.

Observe and Think How does the thickness of the atmosphere compare with the height of a mountain or the altitude of the space shuttle in orbit?

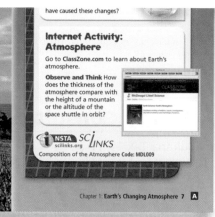

NSTA SCiLINKS
scilinks.org
Composition of the Atmosphere Code: MDL009

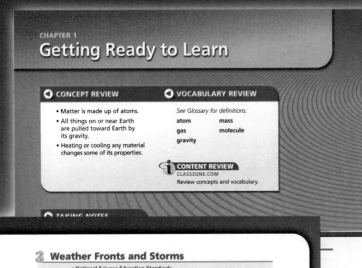

CHAPTER 1
Getting Ready to Learn

● CONCEPT REVIEW
- Matter is made up of atoms.
- All things on or near Earth are pulled toward Earth by its gravity.
- Heating or cooling any material changes some of its properties.

● VOCABULARY REVIEW
See Glossary for definitions.
atom   mass
gas   molecule
gravity

(i) CONTENT REVIEW
CLASSZONE.COM
Review concepts and vocabulary.

● TAKING NOTES

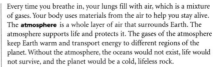

Effective Instructional Strategies

McDougal Littell Science incorporates strategies that research shows are effective in improving student achievement. These strategies include

- Notetaking and nonlinguistic representations (Marzano, Pickering, and Pollock)
- A focus on big ideas (Kameenui and Carnine)
- Background knowledge and active involvement (Project CRISS)

Robert J. Marzano, Debra J. Pickering, and Jane E. Pollock, *Classroom Instruction that Works; Research-Based Strategies for Increasing Student Achievement* (ASCD, 2001)

Edward J. Kameenui and Douglas Carnine, *Effective Teaching Strategies that Accommodate Diverse Learners* (Pearson, 2002)

Project CRISS (Creating Independence through Student Owned Strategies)

VOCA
atmosp
altitude
density
cycle p.

VOCABULARY
Remember to make a frame game diagram for the term *atmosphere*.

The atmosphere makes life on Earth possible.

Every time you breathe in, your lungs fill with air, which is a mixture of gases. Your body uses materials from the air to help you stay alive. The **atmosphere** is a whole layer of air that surrounds Earth. The atmosphere supports life and protects it. The gases of the atmosphere keep Earth warm and transport energy to different regions of the planet. Without the atmosphere, the oceans would not exist, life would not survive, and the planet would be a cold, lifeless rock.

Even though the atmosphere is very important to life, it is surprisingly thin. If the solid part of Earth were the size of a peach, most of the atmosphere would be no thicker than the peach fuzz surrounding the fruit. The atmosphere is a small but important part of the Earth system.

CHECK YOUR READING How does the atmosphere make life possible? Find three examples in the text above.

Chapter 1: Earth's Changing Atmosphere **9** **A**

Comprehensive Research, Review, and Field Testing

An ongoing program of research and review guided the development of *McDougal Littell Science.*

- Program plans based on extensive data from classroom visits, research surveys, teacher panels, and focus groups
- All pupil edition activities and labs classroom-tested by middle school teachers and students
- All chapters reviewed for clarity and scientific accuracy by the Content Reviewers listed on page T5
- Selected chapters field-tested in the classroom to assess student learning, ease of use, and student interest

Content Organized Around Big Ideas

Each chapter develops a big idea of science, helping students to place key concepts in context.

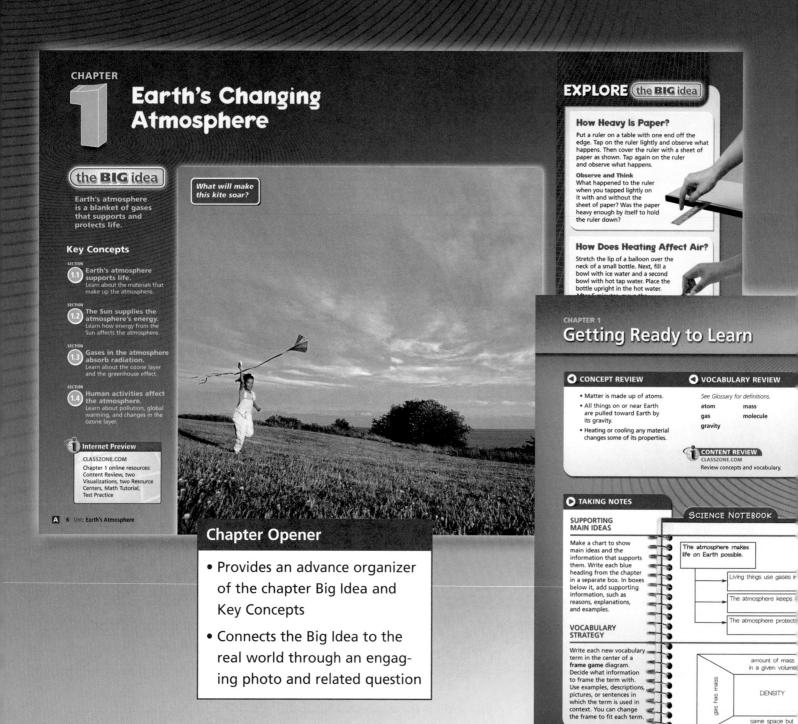

CHAPTER

1 Earth's Changing Atmosphere

the **BIG** idea

Earth's atmosphere is a blanket of gases that supports and protects life.

Key Concepts

SECTION

1.1 Earth's atmosphere supports life.
Learn about the materials that make up the atmosphere.

SECTION

1.2 The Sun supplies the atmosphere's energy.
Learn how energy from the Sun affects the atmosphere.

SECTION

1.3 Gases in the atmosphere absorb radiation.
Learn about the ozone layer and the greenhouse effect.

SECTION

1.4 Human activities affect the atmosphere.
Learn about pollution, global warming, and changes in the ozone layer.

Internet Preview

CLASSZONE.COM
Chapter 1 online resources: Content Review, two Visualizations, two Resource Centers, Math Tutorial, Test Practice

A 6 Unit: Earth's Atmosphere

What will make this kite soar?

EXPLORE the **BIG** idea

How Heavy Is Paper?
Put a ruler on a table with one end off the edge. Tap on the ruler lightly and observe what happens. Then cover the ruler with a sheet of paper as shown. Tap again on the ruler and observe what happens.

Observe and Think
What happened to the ruler when you tapped lightly on it with and without the sheet of paper? Was the paper heavy enough by itself to hold the ruler down?

How Does Heating Affect Air?
Stretch the lip of a balloon over the neck of a small bottle. Next, fill a bowl with ice water and a second bowl with hot tap water. Place the bottle upright in the hot water.

CHAPTER 1
Getting Ready to Learn

CONCEPT REVIEW

• Matter is made up of atoms.
• All things on or near Earth are pulled toward Earth by its gravity.
• Heating or cooling any material changes some of its properties.

VOCABULARY REVIEW

See Glossary for definitions.

atom   mass
gas   molecule
gravity

CONTENT REVIEW
CLASSZONE.COM
Review concepts and vocabulary.

TAKING NOTES

SUPPORTING MAIN IDEAS

Make a chart to show main ideas and the information that supports them. Write each blue heading from the chapter in a separate box. In boxes below it, add supporting information, such as reasons, explanations, and examples.

VOCABULARY STRATEGY

Write each new vocabulary term in the center of a **frame game** diagram. Decide what information to frame the term with. Use examples, descriptions, pictures, or sentences in which the term is used in context. You can change the frame to fit each term.

See the Note-Taking Handbook on pages R45–R51.

A 8 Unit: Earth's Atmosphere

SCIENCE NOTEBOOK

The atmosphere makes life on Earth possible.

Living things use gases in

The atmosphere keeps

The atmosphere protects

amount of mass in a given volume

DENSITY

same space but more mass = dens

Chapter Opener

• Provides an advance organizer of the chapter Big Idea and Key Concepts

• Connects the Big Idea to the real world through an engaging photo and related question

Visual Summary

- Summarizes Key Concepts using both text and visuals
- Reinforces the connection of Key Concepts to the Big Idea

Section Opener

- Highlights the Key Concept
- Connects new learning to prior knowledge
- Previews important vocabulary

Chapter Review

the BIG idea
Earth's atmosphere is a blanket of gases that supports and protects life.

CONTENT REVIEW
CLASSZONE.COM

KEY CONCEPTS SUMMARY

1.1 Earth's atmosphere supports life.

The **atmosphere** is a thin layer surrounding Earth. Gases in the atmosphere provide substances essential for living things. Natural **cycles** and sudden changes affect the atmosphere.

VOCABULARY
atmosphere p. 9
altitude p. 10
density p. 10
cycle p. 12

1.2 The Sun supplies the atmosphere's energy.

Energy from the Sun moves through Earth's atmosphere in three ways.

Density and temperature change with altitude. The layers, from top to bottom, are
- thermosphere
- mesosphere
- stratosphere
- troposphere

radiation
convection
conduction

VOCABULARY
radiation p. 17
conduction p. 18
convection p. 19

1.3 Gases in the atmosphere absorb radiation.

Ozone molecules in the stratosphere absorb harmful ultraviolet radiation.

Greenhouse gases in the

VOCABULARY
ultraviolet radiation p. 23
infrared radiation p. 23
ozone p. 23
greenhouse effect

1.4 Human activities affect the

Human activities have added pollutants and ozone-destroying chemicals to the atmosphere.

ozone

A 36 Unit: Earth's Atmosphere

Reviewing Vocabulary

Draw a word triangle for each of the vocabulary terms listed below. Define the term, use it in a sentence, and draw a picture to help you remember the term. A sample is shown below.

The air is warm near the ceiling because of air convection.

Convection: movement of energy by a heated gas or liquid

1. conduction   5. altitude
2. atmosphere   6. radiation
3. density   7. cycle
4. air pollution   8. particulate

Reviewing Key Concepts

Multiple Choice *Choose the letter of the best answer.*

9. Which of the following represents a sudden change in Earth's atmosphere?
   a. the carbon cycle   c. a rain shower
   b. the nitrogen cycle d. a dust storm

10. The gas that makes up the largest percentage

...ide
...ygen gas
...cycle
...cycle
...th's

...cycle

Thinking Critically

Use the photographs to answer the next two questions.

cold water   hot water

In the demonstration pictured above, hot water has been tinted red with food coloring, and cold water has been tinted blue. View B shows the results after the divider has been lifted and the motion of the water has stopped.

20. **OBSERVE** Describe how the hot water and the cold water moved when the divider was lifted.

21. **APPLY** Use your understanding of density to explain the motion of the water.

22. **CALCULATE** The top of Mount Everest is 8850 meters above sea level. Which layer of the atmosphere contains the top of this mountain? Use the information from page 20 and convert the units.

23. **APPLY** Why is radiation from Earth's surface and atmosphere important for living things?

24. **PREDICT** Dust is often light in color, while soot from fires is generally dark. What would happen to the amounts of solar radiation reflected and absorbed if a large amount of light-colored dust was added to the air? What if a large amount of dark soot was added?

25. **IDENTIFY EFFECT** When weather conditions and sunlight are likely to produce smog, cities may ask motorists to refuel their cars at night instead of early in the day. Why would this behavior make a difference?

26. **COMPARE** How are the processes in the diagram on page 19 similar to those in the illustration below?

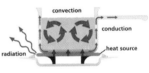
convection
conduction
heat source
radiation

27. **CONNECT** Give an example from everyday life that shows that the atmosphere has substance.

28. **EVALUATE** If you had a choice between burning natural gas to cook or using electricity from a power plant, which would you choose? Explain the issues involved. **Hint:** Where does the power plant get energy?

the BIG idea

29. **SYNTHESIZE** Write one or more paragraphs describing the specific ways that the atmosphere supports and protects life. In your description, use each of the terms below. Underline each term in your answer.

carbon dioxide	solar radiation
water	ozone
oxygen	stratosphere
cycle	

30. Look again at the photograph on pages 6–7. Now that you have finished the chapter, how would you change or add details to your answer to the question on the photograph?

UNIT PROJECTS

If you are doing a unit project, make a folder for your project. Include in your folder a list of the resources you will need, the date on which the project is due, and a schedule to track your progress. Begin gathering data.

A 38 Unit: Earth's Atmosphere

KEY CONCEPT

1.1 Earth's atmosphere supports life.

BEFORE, you learned
- Living things need food, water, and air
- Matter can be solid, liquid, or gas

NOW, you will learn
- Why the atmosphere is important to living things
- What the atmosphere is made of
- How natural cycles affect the atmosphere

VOCABULARY
atmosphere p. 9
altitude p. 10
density p. 10
cycle p. 12

EXPLORE Air Resistance

How does air affect falling objects?

PROCEDURE
1. Drop the washer from shoulder height.
2. Tape the metal washer to the center of the coffee filter. The filter will act as a parachute.
3. Drop the washer with the parachute from shoulder height.

MATERIALS
- metal washer
- coffee filter
- tape

WHAT DO YOU THINK?
- What difference did the parachute make?
- What do your results tell you about air?

VOCABULARY
Remember to make a frame game diagram for the term *atmosphere.*

The atmosphere makes life on Earth possible.

Every time you breathe in, your lungs fill with air, which is a mixture of gases. Your body uses materials from the air to help you stay alive. The **atmosphere** is a whole layer of air that surrounds Earth. The atmosphere supports life and protects it. The gases of the atmosphere keep Earth warm and transport energy to different regions of the planet. Without the atmosphere, the oceans would not exist, life would not survive, and the planet would be a cold, lifeless rock.

Even though the atmosphere is very important to life, it is surprisingly thin. If the solid part of Earth were the size of a peach, most of the atmosphere would be no thicker than the peach fuzz surrounding the fruit. The atmosphere is a small but important part of the Earth system.

CHECK YOUR READING How does the atmosphere make life possible? Find three examples in the text above.

Chapter 1: Earth's Changing Atmosphere 9 A

The Big Idea Questions

- Help students connect their new learning back to the Big Idea
- Prompt students to synthesize and apply the Big Idea and Key Concepts

T9

Many Ways to Learn

Because students learn in so many ways, *McDougal Littell Science* gives them a variety of experiences with important concepts and skills. Text, visuals, activities, and technology all focus on Big Ideas and Key Concepts.

Integrated Technology

- Interaction with Key Concepts through Simulations and Visualizations

- Easy access to relevant Web resources through Resource Centers and SciLinks

- Opportunities for review through Content Review and Math Tutorials

Considerate Text

- Clear structure of meaningful headings

- Information clearly connected to main ideas

- Student-friendly writing style

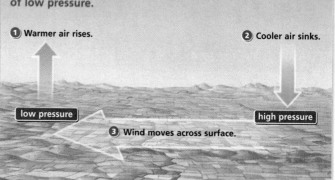

VISUALIZATION
CLASSZONE.COM
View an animation of the Coriolis effect.

How Wind Forms

Wind moves from an area of high pressure toward an area of low pressure.

① Warmer air rises.

② Cooler air sinks.

low pressure

high pressure

③ Wind moves across surface.

The illustration above shows a common pattern of air circulation caused by uneven heating of Earth's surface:

① Sunlight strongly heats an area of ground. The ground heats the air. The warm air rises, and an area of low pressure forms.

② Sunlight heats an area of ground less strongly. The cooler, dense air sinks slowly, and an area of high pressure forms.

③ Air moves as wind across the surface, from higher toward lower pressure.

When the difference in pressure between two areas is small, the wind may move too slowly to be noticeable. A very large pressure difference can produce wind strong enough to uproot trees.

CHECK YOUR READING What factor determines the strength of wind?

The distance winds travel varies. Some winds die out quickly after blowing a few meters. In contrast, **global winds** travel thousands of kilometers in steady patterns. Global winds last for weeks.

Uneven heating between the equator and the north and south poles causes global winds. Notice in the illustration at left how sunlight strikes Earth's curved surface. Near the equator, concentrated sunlight heats the surface to a high temperature. Warm air rises, producing low pressure.

In regions closer to the poles, the sunlight is more spread out. Because less of the Sun's energy reaches these regions, the air above them is cooler and denser. The sinking dense air produces high pressure that sets global winds in motion.

Sunlight is concentrated near the equator because it strikes the surface directly.

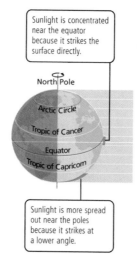

North Pole

Arctic Circle

Tropic of Cancer

Equator

Tropic of Capricorn

Sunlight is more spread out near the poles because it strikes at a lower angle.

Earth's rotation affects wind direction.

If Earth did not rotate, global winds would flow directly from the poles to the equator. However, Earth's rotation changes the direction of winds and other objects moving over Earth. The influence of Earth's rotation is called the **Coriolis effect** (KAWR-ee-OH-lihs). Global winds curve as Earth turns beneath them. In the Northern Hemisphere, winds curve to the right in the direction of motion. Winds in the Southern Hemisphere curve to the left. The Coriolis effect is noticeable only for winds that travel long distances.

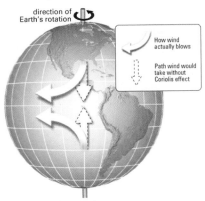

direction of
Earth's rotation

How wind
actually blows

Path wind would
take without
Coriolis effect

Because the Coriolis effect causes global winds to curve, they cannot flow directly from the poles to the equator. Instead, global winds travel along three routes in each hemisphere. These routes, which circle the world, are called global wind belts.

 CHECK YOUR READING In which direction do winds curve in the Northern Hemisphere?

INVESTIGATE Coriolis Effect

How does Earth's rotation affect wind?

PROCEDURE

1. Blow up a balloon and tie it off.

2. Have a classmate slowly rotate the balloon to the right. Draw a line straight down from the top of the balloon to the center as the balloon rotates.

3. Now draw a line from the bottom of the balloon straight up to the center as the balloon rotates.

WHAT DO YOU THINK?

- How did the rotation affect the lines that you drew?
- How does this activity demonstrate the Coriolis effect?

CHALLENGE How might changing the speed at which the balloon is rotated affect your results? Repeat the activity to test your prediction.

SKILL FOCUS
Modeling

MATERIALS
- round balloon
- felt-tip pen

TIME
10 minutes

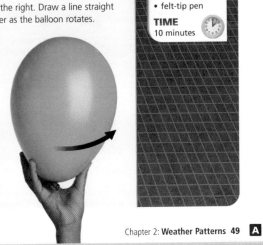

Visuals that Teach

- Information-rich visuals directly connected to the text
- Thoughtful pairing of diagrams and real-world photos
- Reading Visuals questions to support student learning

Hands-on Learning

- Activities that reinforce Key Concepts
- Skill Focus for important inquiry and process skills
- Multiple activities in every chapter, from quick Explores to full-period Chapter Investigations

Differentiated Instruction

A full spectrum of resources for differentiating instruction supports you in reaching the wide range of learners in your classroom.

1.1 INSTRUCT

INVESTIGATE Gas in the Air

PURPOSE To predict the presence of different gases in the air

TIPS *10 min.* Bromthymol blue can be used as a substitute for limewater—it turns yellowish in the presence of carbon dioxide. Mix enough limewater for the class ahead of time, then suggest the following:

• Keep the limewater in a covered container until ready for use.

• Do not touch or drink the limewater.

WHAT DO YOU THINK? *The limewater in the first jar stayed clear. The limewater in the jar that contained exhaled breath turned cloudy. The exhaled breath reacted with the limewater in the second jar, indicating the presence of carbon dioxide. The limewater in the other jar did not react, indicating that the change was due to the exhaled breath and not just air.*

CHALLENGE *Sample answer: A burning candle could test the presence of oxygen.*

R Datasheet, Gas in the Air, p. 20

Technology Resources

Customize this student lab as needed or look for an alternative. Print rubrics to assess student lab reports.

Lab Generator CD-ROM

EXPLORE (the BIG idea)

Revisit "How Heavy Is Paper?" on p. 7. Have students explain their results.

Ongoing Assessment

PHOTO CAPTION Answer: The air is less dense at that altitude, so there are fewer oxygen molecules to breathe.

A 10 Unit: **Earth's Atmosphere**

Characteristics of the Atmosphere

In 1862 two British balloonists reached the highest **altitude**, or distance above sea level, any human had ever reached. As their balloon rose to 8.8 kilometers (5.5 mi), one balloonist fainted and the other barely managed to bring the balloon back down. They found that the air becomes thinner as altitude increases.

The thickness or thinness of air is measured by its density. **Density** is the amount of mass in a given volume of a substance. If two objects take up the same amount of space, then the object with more mass has a greater density than the one with less mass. For example, a bowling ball has a higher density than a soccer ball.

The atmosphere's density decreases as you travel upward. The air on top of a mountain is less dense than the air at sea level. A deep breath of mountain air fills your lungs but contains less mass—less gas—than a deep breath of air at sea level. Higher up, at altitudes where jets fly, a breath of air would contain only about one-tenth the mass of a breath of air at sea level. The air farther above Earth's surface contains even less mass. There is no definite top to the atmosphere. It just keeps getting less dense as you get farther from Earth's surface. However, altitudes 500 kilometers (300 mi) or more above Earth's surface can be called outer space.

The decrease of density with greater altitude means that most of the mass of the atmosphere is close to Earth's surface. In fact, more than 99 percent of the atmosphere's mass is in the lowest 30 kilometers (20 mi).

INFER This climber has reached the top of Mount Everest, 8850 m (29,000 ft) above sea level in Nepal. Why does he need an oxygen mask?

INVESTIGATE Gas in the Air

How do you know that air has different gases?
PROCEDURE

1. Put a spoonful of limewater into each jar. Limewater is clear, but turns milky in the presence of carbon dioxide.

2. Cover one jar. Add extra carbon dioxide to the second jar by exhaling gently into it before you cover it. Tighten the lids carefully to seal the jars.

3. Predict what will happen, then shake each jar.

WHAT DO YOU THINK?

• What happened to the limewater in each jar?

• How do you know that air is made of different gases?

CHALLENGE How would you test a different gas in the air?

SKILL FOCUS
Predicting

MATERIALS
• limewater
• 2 jars
• spoon

TIME
10 minutes

A 10 Unit: **Earth's Atmosphere**

Gases of Earth's Atmosphere

Close to Earth's surface, nitrogen, oxygen, and other atmospheric gases are completely mixed together. A sample of the atmosphere taken from anywhere on Earth would contain about the same percentages of gases shown in the graph.

Percentages of Gases in Dry Air

argon, carbon dioxide, and other gases 1%

oxygen 21%

nitrogen 78%

The percentage of water vapor in the atmosphere, not included on this graph, varies from 0% to 4%.

READING VISUALS INTERPRET How do the graph and the photograph show, in two different ways, that the atmosphere has substance?

Materials in the Atmosphere

Most of the materials in the atmosphere are gases. However, the atmosphere also contains tiny particles of solid or liquid material such as dust, sea salt, and water droplets. Perhaps you have sat by an open window and noticed some of these particles on the window sill.

If you were to write a recipe for air, you would include nitrogen gas as the main ingredient. In dry air, about 78 percent of the gas is nitrogen. The next most common ingredient is oxygen gas, which makes up about 21 percent of the atmosphere. Argon, carbon dioxide, and other gases make up about 1 percent of the atmosphere. Unlike the amounts of nitrogen and other gases, the amount of water vapor varies a great deal. In some places at some times, water vapor can make up as much as 4 percent of the air.

The atmosphere's gases provide materials essential for living things. Nitrogen promotes plant growth and is an important ingredient in the chemicals that make up living things. Oxygen is necessary for animals and plants to perform life processes. Plants use carbon dioxide and water to make food.

READING TIP As you read about the amounts of gases, find each gas on the graph above.

CHECK YOUR READING Which gas is the most common material in the air around you?

Chapter 1: **Earth's Changing Atmosphere** 11 **A**

DIFFERENTIATE INSTRUCTION

? More Reading Support

A What is density? *the amount of mass in a given volume*

B What happens to the atmosphere's density as you travel upward? *it decreases*

English Learners English learners may have difficulty using the words *affect* and *effect* correctly. Explain that *affect* is a verb and *effect* is a noun. A common trick for remembering the difference is that *affect* begins with the letter a. A verb is an action, which also begins with the letter a.

DIFFERENTIATE INSTRUCTION

? More Reading Support

C Nitrogen makes up what percentage of air? *about 78 percent*

D What is the second most common gas in air? *oxygen*

Additional Investigation To reinforce Section 1.1 learning goals, use the following full-period investigation:

R **Additional INVESTIGATION**, Oxygen in the Air, A, B, & C, pp. 71–79, 284–285 (Advanced students should complete Levels B and C.)

Advanced Have students explain why the percentage of water vapor in the atmosphere varies. *Water evaporates from bodies of water, so wet regions have more water vapor.*

R Challenge and Extension, p. 19

Teacher's Edition

• More Reading Support for below-level readers

• Strategies for below-level and advanced learners, English learners, and inclusion students

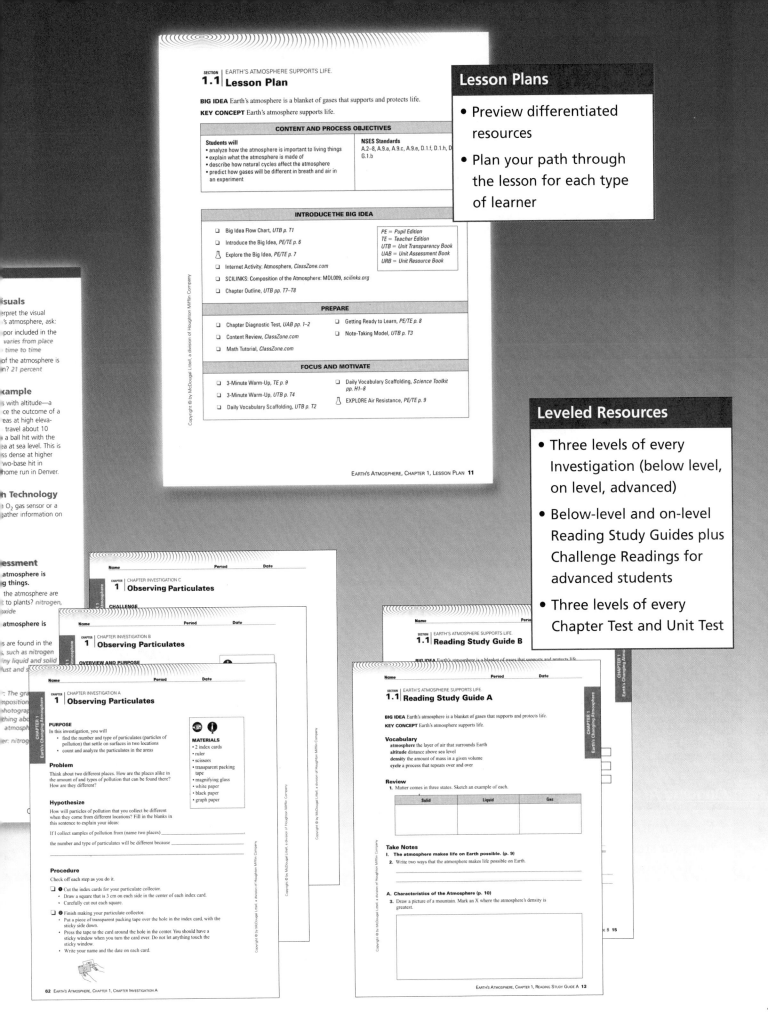

SECTION | EARTH'S ATMOSPHERE SUPPORTS LIFE.
1.1 | Lesson Plan

BIG IDEA Earth's atmosphere is a blanket of gases that supports and protects life.

KEY CONCEPT Earth's atmosphere supports life.

CONTENT AND PROCESS OBJECTIVES

Students will
- analyze how the atmosphere is important to living things
- explain what the atmosphere is made of
- describe how natural cycles affect the atmosphere
- predict how gases will be different in breath and air in an experiment

NSES Standards
A.2–8, A.9.a, A.9.c, A.9.e, D.1.f, D.1.h, D
G.1.b

INTRODUCE THE BIG IDEA

- ☐ Big Idea Flow Chart, *UTB p. T1*
- ☐ Introduce the Big Idea, *PE/TE p. 6*
- ⚗ Explore the Big Idea, *PE/TE p. 7*
- ☐ Internet Activity: Atmosphere, *ClassZone.com*
- ☐ SCILINKS: Composition of the Atmosphere: MDL009, *scilinks.org*
- ☐ Chapter Outline, *UTB pp. T7–T8*

PE = Pupil Edition
TE = Teacher Edition
UTB = Unit Transparency Book
UAB = Unit Assessment Book
URB = Unit Resource Book

PREPARE

- ☐ Chapter Diagnostic Test, *UAB pp. 1–2*
- ☐ Content Review, *ClassZone.com*
- ☐ Math Tutorial, *ClassZone.com*
- ☐ Getting Ready to Learn, *PE/TE p. 8*
- ☐ Note-Taking Model, *UTB p. T3*

FOCUS AND MOTIVATE

- ☐ 3-Minute Warm-Up, *TE p. 9*
- ☐ 3-Minute Warm-Up, *UTB p. T4*
- ☐ Daily Vocabulary Scaffolding, *UTB p. T2*
- ☐ Daily Vocabulary Scaffolding, *Science Toolkit pp. H1–8*
- ⚗ EXPLORE Air Resistance, *PE/TE p. 9*

EARTH'S ATMOSPHERE, CHAPTER 1, LESSON PLAN **11**

Lesson Plans

- Preview differentiated resources
- Plan your path through the lesson for each type of learner

Leveled Resources

- Three levels of every Investigation (below level, on level, advanced)
- Below-level and on-level Reading Study Guides plus Challenge Readings for advanced students
- Three levels of every Chapter Test and Unit Test

---

isuals

erpret the visual
's atmosphere, ask:

por included in the
varies from place
time to time
of the atmosphere is
n? *21 percent*

xample

s with altitude—a
ce the outcome of a
eas at high eleva-
travel about 10
a ball hit with the
ea at sea level. This is
ss dense at higher
wo-base hit in
home run in Denver.

h Technology

O₂ gas sensor or a
ather information on

essment

atmosphere is
g things.

the atmosphere are
t to plants? *nitrogen,*
oxide

atmosphere is

s are found in the
, such as nitrogen
ny liquid and solid
ust and s

: The gra
mposition
photograp
thing abo
atmosph

er: nitrog

Name _____ Period _____ Date _____

CHAPTER | CHAPTER INVESTIGATION C
1 | **Observing Particulates**

CHALLENGE

Name _____ Period _____ Date _____

CHAPTER | CHAPTER INVESTIGATION B
1 | **Observing Particulates**

OVERVIEW AND PURPOSE

Name _____ Period _____ Date _____

CHAPTER | CHAPTER INVESTIGATION A
1 | **Observing Particulates**

PURPOSE
In this investigation, you will
- find the number and type of particulates (particles of pollution) that settle on surfaces in two locations
- count and analyze the particulates in the areas

MATERIALS
- 2 index cards
- ruler
- scissors
- transparent packing tape
- magnifying glass
- white paper
- black paper
- graph paper

Problem
Think about two different places. How are the places alike in the amount of and types of pollution that can be found there? How are they different?

Hypothesize
How will particles of pollution that you collect be different when they come from different locations? Fill in the blanks in this sentence to explain your ideas:

If I collect samples of pollution from (name two places) _____

the number and type of particulates will be different because _____

Procedure
Check off each step as you do it.

☐ ❶ Cut the index cards for your particulate collector.
- Draw a square that is 3 cm on each side in the center of each index card.
- Carefully cut out each square.

☐ ❷ Finish making your particulate collector.
- Put a piece of transparent packing tape over the hole in the index card, with the sticky side down.
- Press the tape to the card around the hole in the center. You should have a sticky window when you turn the card over. Do not let anything touch the sticky window.
- Write your name and the date on each card.

62 EARTH'S ATMOSPHERE, CHAPTER 1, CHAPTER INVESTIGATION A

Name _____ Period _____ Date _____

SECTION | EARTH'S ATMOSPHERE SUPPORTS LIFE.
1.1 | **Reading Study Guide B**

BIG IDEA Earth's atmosphere is a blanket of gases that supports and protects life.

Name _____ Period _____ Date _____

SECTION | EARTH'S ATMOSPHERE SUPPORTS LIFE.
1.1 | **Reading Study Guide A**

BIG IDEA Earth's atmosphere is a blanket of gases that supports and protects life.
KEY CONCEPT Earth's atmosphere supports life.

Vocabulary
atmosphere the layer of air that surrounds Earth
altitude distance above sea level
density the amount of mass in a given volume
cycle a process that repeats over and over

Review
1. Matter comes in three states. Sketch an example of each.

Solid	Liquid	Gas

Take Notes
I. **The atmosphere makes life on Earth possible. (p. 9)**
2. Write two ways that the atmosphere makes life possible on Earth.

_____

A. **Characteristics of the Atmosphere (p. 10)**
3. Draw a picture of a mountain. Mark an X where the atmosphere's density is greatest.

EARTH'S ATMOSPHERE, CHAPTER 1, READING STUDY GUIDE A **13**

Effective Assessment

McDougal Littell Science incorporates a comprehensive set of resources for assessing student knowledge and performance before, during, and after instruction.

Diagnostic Tests

- Assessment of students' prior knowledge
- Readiness check for concepts and skills in the upcoming chapter

Ongoing Assessment

READING VISUALS *Sample answer: In the second image, a dust cloud covers the blue of the ocean, and the white clouds in the upper left of the first image are gone.*

Reinforce (the BIG idea)

Have students relate the section to the Big Idea.

Reinforcing Key Concepts, p. 21

1.1 ASSESS & RETEACH

Assess

Section 1.1 Quiz, p. 3

Reteach

Have students role-play the gases, materials, and living things involved in the carbon cycle. The room itself can represent the atmosphere. Two students can each represent an oxygen atom, one student can represent a carbon atom, one an animal, and one a plant. Station the plant and the animal ten feet apart. Have the two oxygen atoms and the carbon atom start together as a carbon dioxide molecule that the animal has just exhaled. All three should walk over to the plant. Remind students that in photosynthesis the plant takes in carbon dioxide and releases oxygen. See if students can guess what their next move should be. The carbon atom should remain with the plant, and the oxygen atoms should continue in a circular motion back to the animal. Other students can get involved in the cycle at any time as new oxygen or carbon atoms. Try modeling the water cycle and the nitrogen cycle in this manner.

Technology Resources

Have students visit ClassZone.com for reteaching of Key Concepts.

- CONTENT REVIEW
- CONTENT REVIEW CD-ROM

A 14 Unit: Earth's Atmosphere

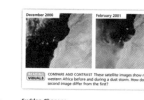

READING VISUALS COMPARE AND CONTRAST These satellite images show northwestern Africa before and during a dust storm. How does the second image differ from the first?

December 2000 | February 2001

Sudden Changes

In addition to ongoing processes, dramatic events may cause changes in the atmosphere. When sudden events occur, it takes time before the atmosphere is able to restore balance.

SUPPORTING MAIN IDEAS Record information about the events that cause sudden changes in the atmosphere.

- **Volcanic Eruptions** Volcanoes shoot gases and huge amounts of ash into the atmosphere. Certain gases produce a haze that may affect the air for many months and lower temperatures worldwide.
- **Forest Fires** When forests burn, the carbon that makes up each tree combines with oxygen and enters the atmosphere as carbon dioxide. Wood ash also enters the atmosphere.
- **Dust Storms** Wind, water, or drought can loosen soil. Powerful windstorms may then raise clouds of this eroded soil, as in the second picture above. These storms add huge amounts of particles to the air for a time.

1.1 Review

KEY CONCEPTS
1. How is the atmosphere important to living things?
2. What substances make up air?
3. Draw a diagram to show how one natural cycle affects the atmosphere.

CRITICAL THINKING
4. **Apply** Give three examples from everyday life of how the atmosphere supports and protects life.
5. **Predict** How would the atmosphere in your area change if a disease killed all the plants?

CHALLENGE
6. **Compare** Carbon dioxide enters the oceans from the air. Some carbon becomes stored in shells, and then in rocks. Eventually, it can be released back into the air by volcanoes in the form of carbon dioxide. How are these slow processes similar to the cycles shown on page 13?

A 14 Unit: Earth's Atmosphere

ANSWERS

1. It transports energy to different regions of Earth. It allows oceans to exist and life to survive.

2. nitrogen, oxygen, argon, carbon dioxide, water vapor, and other gases

3. Diagram should be similar to one of the diagrams on p. 13.

4. People need oxygen from the air to stay alive. Plants need air to make food. Birds need air to fly.

5. There would be more carbon dioxide and less oxygen in the air.

6. These processes also involve a constant and complete cycle involving the atmosphere.

Reviewing Vocabulary

Draw a word triangle for each of the vocabulary terms listed below. Define the term, use it in a sentence, and draw a picture to help you remember the term. A sample is shown below.

The air is warm near the ceiling because of air convection.

Convection: movement of energy by a heated gas or liquid

1. conduction   5. altitude
2. atmosphere   6. radiation
3. density   7. cycle
4. air pollution   8. particulate

Reviewing Key Concepts

Multiple Choice *Choose the letter of the best answer.*

9. Which of the following represents a sudden change in Earth's atmosphere?
   - a. the carbon cycle   c. a rain shower
   - b. the nitrogen cycle   d. a dust storm

10. The gas that makes up the largest percentage of the atmosphere's substance is
    - a. nitrogen   c. water vapor
    - b. oxygen   d. carbon dioxide

11. Which of the cycles below involves oxygen gas?
    - a. the carbon cycle   c. the density cycle
    - b. the water cycle   d. the argon cycle

12. What process moves energy from Earth's surface to high in the troposphere?
    - a. solar energy   c. convection
    - b. conduction   d. the nitrogen cycle

13. In which of the atmosphere's layers does temperature decrease as the altitude increases?
    - a. the troposphere and the stratosphere
    - b. the troposphere and the mesosphere
    - c. the stratosphere and the mesosphere
    - d. the stratosphere and the thermosphere

14. What keeps Earth's surface warm?
    - a. conduction   c. convection
    - b. the ozone layer   d. the greenhouse effect

15. Which gas absorbs ultraviolet radiation?
    - a. carbon dioxide   c. ozone
    - b. methane   d. water vapor

16. Which type of pollution includes harmful droplets?
    - a. particulate   c. dust
    - b. gas   d. smoke

Short Answer *Write a short answer to each question.*

17. Explain why ozone is helpful to life in the stratosphere but harmful in the troposphere.

18. Describe three of the ways human activities affect the atmosphere.

19. Write a brief paragraph describing how the photograph below provides evidence that Earth's atmosphere is in motion.

ging Atmosphere 37 **A**

Ongoing Assessment

- Check Your Reading questions for student self-check of comprehension
- Consistent Teacher Edition prompts for assessing understanding of Key Concepts

Section and Chapter Reviews

- Focus on Key Concepts and critical thinking skills
- A full range of question types and levels of thinking

Leveled Chapter and Unit Tests

- Three levels of test for every chapter and unit
- Same Big Ideas, Key Concepts, and essential skills assessed on all levels

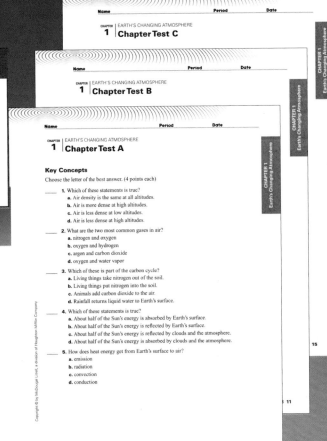

Name ___ Period ___ Date ___

CHAPTER | EARTH'S CHANGING ATMOSPHERE
1 | **Chapter Test C**

Name ___ Period ___ Date ___

CHAPTER | EARTH'S CHANGING ATMOSPHERE
1 | **Chapter Test B**

Name ___ Period ___ Date ___

CHAPTER | EARTH'S CHANGING ATMOSPHERE
1 | **Chapter Test A**

Key Concepts

Choose the letter of the best answer. (4 points each)

_____ 1. Which of these statements is true?
   a. Air density is the same at all altitudes.
   b. Air is more dense at high altitudes.
   c. Air is less dense at low altitudes.
   d. Air is less dense at high altitudes.

_____ 2. What are the two most common gases in air?
   a. nitrogen and oxygen
   b. oxygen and hydrogen
   c. argon and carbon dioxide
   d. oxygen and water vapor

_____ 3. Which of these is part of the carbon cycle?
   a. Living things take nitrogen out of the soil.
   b. Living things put nitrogen into the soil.
   c. Animals add carbon dioxide to the air.
   d. Rainfall returns liquid water to Earth's surface.

_____ 4. Which of these statements is true?
   a. About half of the Sun's energy is absorbed by Earth's surface.
   b. About half of the Sun's energy is reflected by Earth's surface.
   c. About half of the Sun's energy is reflected by clouds and the atmosphere.
   d. About half of the Sun's energy is absorbed by clouds and the atmosphere.

_____ 5. How does heat energy get from Earth's surface to air?
   a. emission
   b. radiation
   c. convection
   d. conduction

EARTH'S ATMOSPHERE, CHAPTER 1, CHAPTER TEST A **7**

15

11

Thinking Critically

Use the photographs to answer the next two questions.

A

cold water   hot water

B

In the demonstration pictured above, hot water has been tinted red with food coloring, and cold water has been tinted blue. View B shows the results after the divider has been lifted and the motion of the water has stopped.

20. OBSERVE Describe how the hot water and the cold water moved when the divider was lifted.

21. APPLY Use your understanding of density to explain the motion of the water.

22. CALCULATE The top of Mount Everest is 8850 meters above sea level. Which layer of the atmosphere contains the top of this mountain? Use the information from page 20 and convert the units.

23. APPLY Why is radiation from Earth's surface and atmosphere important for living things?

24. PREDICT Dust is often light in color, while soot from fires is generally dark. What would happen to the amounts of solar radiation reflected and absorbed if a large amount of light-colored dust was added to the air? What if a large amount of dark soot was added?

25. IDENTIFY EFFECT When weather conditions and sunlight are likely to produce smog, cities may ask motorists to refuel their cars at night instead of early in the day. Why would this behavior make a difference?

26. COMPARE How are the processes in the diagram on page 19 similar to those in the illustration below?

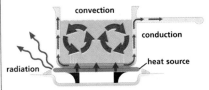

convection

conduction

radiation

heat source

27. CONNECT Give an example from everyday life that shows that the atmosphere has substance.

28. EVALUATE If you had a choice between burning natural gas to cook or using electricity from a power plant, which would you choose? Explain the issues involved. **Hint:** Where does the power plant get energy?

the BIG idea

29. SYNTHESIZE Write one or more paragraphs describing the specific ways that the atmosphere supports and protects life. In your description, use each of the terms below. Underline each term in your answer.

carbon dioxide	solar radiation
water	ozone
oxygen	stratosphere
cycle	

30. Look again at the photograph on pages 6–7. Now that you have finished the chapter, how would you change or add details to your answer to the question on the photograph?

Rubrics

- Rubrics in Teacher Edition for all extended response questions
- Rubrics for all Unit Projects
- Alternative Assessment with rubric for each chapter
- A wide range of additional rubrics in the Science Toolkit

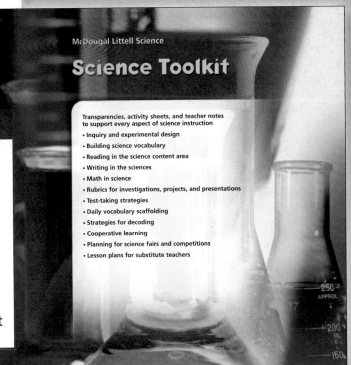

McDougal Littell Science

Science Toolkit

Transparencies, activity sheets, and teacher notes to support every aspect of science instruction

- Inquiry and experimental design
- Building science vocabulary
- Reading in the science content area
- Writing in the sciences
- Math in science
- Rubrics for investigations, projects, and presentations
- Test-taking strategies
- Daily vocabulary scaffolding
- Strategies for decoding
- Cooperative learning
- Planning for science fairs and competitions
- Lesson plans for substitute teachers

McDougal Littell Science Modular Series

McDougal Littell Science lets you choose the titles that match your curriculum. Each module in this flexible 15-book series takes an in-depth look at a specific area of life, earth, or physical science.

- Flexibility to match your curriculum

- Convenience of smaller books

- Complete Student Resource Handbooks in every module

Life Science Titles

A ▶ Cells and Heredity
1. The Cell
2. How Cells Function
3. Cell Division
4. Patterns of Heredity
5. DNA and Modern Genetics

B ▶ Life Over Time
1. The History of Life on Earth
2. Classification of Living Things
3. Population Dynamics

C ▶ Diversity of Living Things
1. Single-Celled Organisms and Viruses
2. Introduction to Multicellular Organisms
3. Plants
4. Invertebrate Animals
5. Vertebrate Animals

D ▶ Ecology
1. Ecosystems and Biomes
2. Interactions Within Ecosystems
3. Human Impact on Ecosystems

E ▶ Human Biology
1. Systems, Support, and Movement
2. Absorption, Digestion, and Exchange
3. Transport and Protection
4. Control and Reproduction
5. Growth, Development, and Health

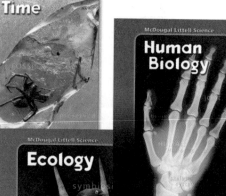

Earth Science Titles

A ▶ **Earth's Surface**
1. Views of Earth Today
2. Minerals
3. Rocks
4. Weathering and Soil Formation
5. Erosion and Deposition

B ▶ **The Changing Earth**
1. Plate Tectonics
2. Earthquakes
3. Mountains and Volcanoes
4. Views of Earth's Past
5. Natural Resources

C ▶ **Earth's Waters**
1. The Water Planet
2. Freshwater Resources
3. Ocean Systems
4. Ocean Environments

D ▶ **Earth's Atmosphere**
1. Earth's Changing Atmosphere
2. Weather Patterns
3. Weather Fronts and Storms
4. Climate and Climate Change

E ▶ **Space Science**
1. Exploring Space
2. Earth, Moon, and Sun
3. Our Solar System
4. Stars, Galaxies, and the Universe

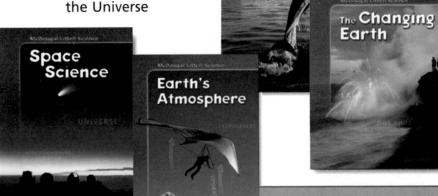

Physical Science Titles

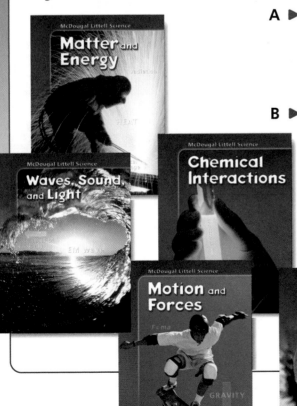

A ▶ **Matter and Energy**
1. Introduction to Matter
2. Properties of Matter
3. Energy
4. Temperature and Heat

B ▶ **Chemical Interactions**
1. Atomic Structure and the Periodic Table
2. Chemical Bonds and Compounds
3. Chemical Reactions
4. Solutions
5. Carbon in Life and Materials

C ▶ **Motion and Forces**
1. Motion
2. Forces
3. Gravity, Friction, and Pressure
4. Work and Energy
5. Machines

D ▶ **Waves, Sound, and Light**
1. Waves
2. Sound
3. Electromagnetic Waves
4. Light and Optics

E ▶ **Electricity and Magnetism**
1. Electricity
2. Circuits and Electronics
3. Magnetism

Teaching Resources

A wealth of print and technology resources help you adapt the program to your teaching style and to the specific needs of your students.

Book-Specific Print Resources

Unit Resource Book provides all of the teaching resources for the unit organized by chapter and section.

- Family Letters
- *Scientific American Frontiers* Video Guide
- Unit Projects
- Lesson Plans
- Reading Study Guides (Levels A and B)
- Spanish Reading Study Guides
- Challenge Readings
- Challenge and Extension Activities
- Reinforcing Key Concepts
- Vocabulary Practice
- Math Support and Practice
- Investigation Datasheets
- Chapter Investigations (Levels A, B, and C)
- Additional Investigations (Levels A, B, and C)
- Summarizing the Chapter

Unit Assessment Book contains complete resources for assessing student knowledge and performance.

- Chapter Diagnostic Tests
- Section Quizzes
- Chapter Tests (Levels A, B, and C)
- Alternative Assessments
- Unit Tests (Levels A, B, and C)

Unit Transparency Book includes instructional visuals for each chapter.

- Three-Minute Warm-Ups
- Note-Taking Models
- Daily Vocabulary Scaffolding
- Chapter Outlines
- Big Idea Flow Charts
- Chapter Teaching Visuals

Unit Lab Manual

Unit Note-Taking/Reading Study Guide

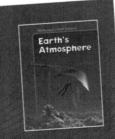

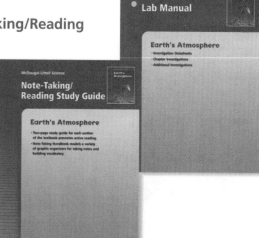

McDougal Littell Science

Unit Resource Book

Earth's Atmosphere

- Family Letters (English and Spanish)
- *Scientific American Frontiers* Video Guides
- Unit Projects (with Rubrics)
- Lesson Plans
- Reading Study Guides (Levels A and B and Spanish)
- Challenge Activities and Readings
- Reinforcing Key Concepts
- Vocabulary Practice and Decoding Support
- Math Support and Practice
- Investigation Datasheets
- Chapter Investigations (Levels A, B, and C)
- Additional Investigations (Levels A, B, and C)

Program-Wide Print Resources

Process and Lab Skills

Problem Solving and Critical Thinking

Standardized Test Practice

Science Toolkit

City Science

Visual Glossary

Multi-Language Glossary

English Learners Package

Scientific American Frontiers Video Guide

How Stuff Works Express
This quarterly magazine offers opportunities to explore current science topics.

Technology Resources

Scientific American Frontiers **Video Program**
Each specially-tailored segment from this award-winning PBS series correlates to a unit; available on VHS and DVD

Audio CDs Complete chapter texts read in both English and Spanish

Lab Generator CD-ROM
A searchable database of all activities from the program plus additional labs for each unit; edit and print your own version of labs

Test Generator CD-ROM

eEdition CD-ROM

EasyPlanner CD-ROM

Content Review CD-ROM

Power Presentations CD-ROM

Online Resources

   ClassZone.com

   Content Review Online

   eEdition Plus Online

   EasyPlanner Plus Online

   eTest Plus Online

Correlation to National Science Education Standards

This chart provides an overview of how the five Earth Science modules of *McDougal Littell Science* address the National Science Education Standards.

A Earth's Surface
B The Changing Earth
C Earth's Waters
D Earth's Atmosphere
E Space Science

A. Science as Inquiry
	Book, Chapter, and Section
A.1– A.8 **Abilities necessary to do scientific inquiry** Identify questions for investigation; design and conduct investigations; use evidence; think critically and logically; analyze alternative explanations; communicate; use mathematics.	All books (pp. R2–R44) All Chapter Investigations, All Think Science features
A.9 Understandings about scientific inquiry Different kinds of investigations for different questions; investigations guided by current scientific knowledge; importance of mathematics and technology for data gathering and analysis; importance of evidence, logical argument, principles, models, and theories; role of legitimate skepticism; scientific investigations lead to new investigations.	All books (pp. xxii–xxv) A1.4, B1.4, C1.1, D3.3, E3.2

B. Physical Science
	Book, Chapter, and Section
B.1 **Properties and changes of properties in matter** Physical properties; substances, elements, and compounds; chemical reactions.	A2.2, B1.1, C3.1, D1.1 (Connecting Sciences), D1.4, D2.1
B.2 **Motions and forces** Position, speed, direction of motion; balanced and unbalanced forces.	C3.4, C4.1, C4.3, E2.1, E2.2, E2.3
B.3 **Transfer of energy** Energy transfer; forms of energy; heat and light; electrical circuits; sun as source of Earth's energy.	D1.2, D1.3, E1.2, E4.1, E4.2, E4.3, E4.4, B5.3

C. Life Science
	Book, Chapter, and Section
C.3 **Plants**	E1.4 (Connecting Sciences)
C.4 **Populations and ecosystems** Populations; ecosystems; producers, consumers, and decomposers; food webs; energy flow; population size and resource availability; population growth.	B5.1 (Connecting Sciences), C4.1, C4.2, C4.3
C.5 **Diversity and adaptations of organisms** Unity and diversity; similarities in internal structures, chemical processes, and evidence of common ancestry; adaptation and biological evolution; extinction and fossil evidence.	A5.3 (Connecting Sciences), B4.1, B4.2, B4.3

D. Earth and Space Science
	Book, Chapter, and Section
D.1 **Structure of the earth system** Lithosphere, mantle, and core; plate movement and earthquakes, volcanoes, and mountain building; constructive and destructive forces on landforms; soil, weathering, and erosion; water and water cycle; atmosphere, weather, and climate; living organisms in earth system.	A1.1, A2.3, A3, A4, A5, B1.1, B1.2, B1.3, B1.4, B2.1, B2.2, B2.3, B3.1, B3.2, B3.3, C1.1, C1.2, C1.3, C3.1, C3.2, D1.1, D1.2, D1.3, D2.2, D2.3, D2.4, D3.1, D3.2, D3.3, D4.1, D4.2, E3.2
D.2 **Earth's history** Continuity of earth processes; impact of occasional catastrophes; fossil evidence.	A4.3, A5.1, 5.4, B1.2, B2.1, B3.1, B4, D1.1, D4.3, E3.2, E3.4, E (Frontiers in Science)

		Book, Chapter, and Section
D.3	**Earth in the solar system** Sun, planets, asteroids, comets; regular and predictable motion and day, year, phases of the moon, and eclipses; gravity and orbits; sun as source of energy for earth; cause of seasons.	A1.1, B5.1, B5.3, C1.1, C1.2, C3.4, D1.2, D1.3, D2.2, D4.4, E1.1, E2.1, E2.2, E2.3, E3.1, E3.2, E3.3, E3.4

E. Science and Technology

		Book, Chapter, and Section
E.1– E.5	**Abilities of technological design** Identify problems; design a solution or product; implement a proposed design; evaluate completed designs or products; communicate the process of technological design.	A5.1, B1.4, B2.3, B5.2, C1.1, C1.3, C4.1, C4.2, D3.4
E.6	**Understandings about science and technology** Similarities and differences between scientific inquiry and technological design; contributions of people in different cultures; reciprocal nature of science and technology; nonexistence of perfectly designed solutions; constraints, benefits, and unintended consequences of technological designs.	All books (pp. xxvi–xxvii) All books (Frontiers in Science, Timelines in Science) A1.1, A1.2, A1.3, A1.4, B5.3, C3.4

F. Science in Personal and Social Perspectives

		Book, Chapter, and Section
F.1	**Personal health** Exercise; fitness; hazards and safety; tobacco, alcohol, and other drugs; nutrition; STDs; environmental health.	C2.2, D1.3, D1.4, D4.3
F.2	**Populations, resources, and environments** Overpopulation and resource depletion; environmental degradation.	B5.1, B5.2, B5.3, C1.2, C2.1, C2.2, C2.3, C4.1, C4.2, C4.3, D1.4, D4.3
F.3	**Natural hazards** Earthquakes, landslides, wildfires, volcanic eruptions, floods, storms; hazards from human activity; personal and societal challenges.	A1.1, A5.1, B2.3, B3.1, B3.2, B3.3, B4.3, C2.1, C2.2, C4.1, C4.3, D1.1, D1.4, D3.2, D3.3, D4.3, E3.4
F.4	**Risks and benefits** Risk analysis; natural, chemical, biological, social, and personal hazards; decisions based on risks and benefits.	B2.3, B3.3, B5.1, B5.2, B5.3, C2.1, C2.2, C2.3, C4.1, C4.2, C4.3, D1.1, D3.1, D3.2, D3.3, E (Frontiers in Science)
F.5	**Science and technology in society** Science's influence on knowledge and world view; societal challenges and scientific research; technological influences on society; contributions from people of different cultures and times; work of scientists and engineers; ethical codes; limitations of science and technology.	All books (Timelines in Science) A1.1, A1.2, A1.4, C2.3, C4.2, C4.3, D4.3, E1.2, E1.3, E1.4

G. History and Nature of Science

		Book, Chapter, and Section
G.1	**Science as a human endeavor** Diversity of people w.orking in science, technology, and related fields; abilities required by science	All books (pp. xxii–xxv; Frontiers in Sciences)
G.2	**Nature of science** Observations, experiments, and models; tentative nature of scientific ideas; differences in interpretation of evidence; evaluation of results of investigations, experiments, observations, theoretical models, and explanations; importance of questioning, response to criticism, and communication.	B4.1, B4.2, E1.2, E1.3, E4.4
G.3	**History of science** Historical examples of inquiry and relationships between science and society; scientists and engineers as valued contributors to culture; challenges of breaking through accepted ideas.	All books (Frontiers in Science; Timelines in Science), B1.2, B4.3, E1.3

Correlations to Benchmarks

This chart provides an overview of how the five Earth Science modules of *McDougal Littell Science* address the Project 2061 Benchmarks for Science Literacy.

A Earth's Surface
B The Changing Earth
C Earth's Waters
D Earth's Atmosphere
E Space Science

1. The Nature of Science	Book, Chapter, and Section
	The Nature of Science (pp. xxii–xxv); A1; Scientific Thinking Handbook (pp. R2–R9); Lab Handbook (pp. R10–R35); Think Science Features: A1.4, B1.4, C1.1, D3.3, E3.2

3. The Nature of Technology	Book, Chapter, and Section
	The Nature of Technology (pp. xxvi–xxvii); A1, D3.4, E.1.2, E.1.3, E1.4; Timelines in Science Features

4. The Physical Setting	Book, Chapter, and Section

4.A THE UNIVERSE

4.A.1 The Sun is a medium-sized star on the edge of a disk-shaped galaxy; galaxies contain billions of stars; the universe contains billions of galaxies.	E1.1, E4.1, E4.3, E4.4
4.A.2 Light from the Sun takes a few minutes to reach Earth; some galaxies are so far way that their light takes several billion years to reach Earth.	E1.2, E4.1, E4.3, E4.4
4.A.3 Nine planets of very different size, composition, and surface features move around the Sun in nearly circular orbits.	E2.2, E3.2
4.A.4 Chunks of rock orbiting the Sun sometimes impact Earth's atmosphere and sometimes reach Earth's surface.	E (Frontiers in Science), E3.1, E3.4

4.B THE EARTH

4.B.1 We live on a relatively small planet, the third from the Sun in the only system of planets definitely known to exist.	E3.1, E3.2
4.B.2 Three-fourths of Earth's surface is covered by a relatively thin layer of water; the entire planet is surrounded by a relatively thin blanket of air.	A1.1, A3.1, C1.1, E3.2, E3.3
4.B.3 Everything on or anywhere near the Earth is pulled toward the Earth's center by gravitational force.	E2.1
4.B.4 Because Earth's axis is tilted, sunlight falls more intensely on different regions during the year, producing Earth's seasons and weather patterns.	D2.2, E2.1, E3.2
4.B.5 The moon's orbit around Earth changes what part is lighted by the Sun and how much of that part can be seen from Earth—the phases of the Moon.	E2.3
4.B.6 Climates have sometimes changed abruptly; even small changes in atmospheric or ocean content can have widespread effects on climate.	A3.1, B1.2, B3.3, B4.1, B4.3, C3.2, D1.1, D1.4, D4.3, E3.4
4.B.7 The cycling of water in and out of the atmosphere plays an important role. Water evaporates, rises and cools, condenses, falls again to the surface.	A5.3, C1, D1.1, D2.3, D2.4, D3.1, D3.2, D3.3, D4.1
4.B.8 Fresh water, limited in supply, is essential for life and industry. Rivers, lakes, and groundwater can be depleted or polluted.	B5.1, B5.2, C2.1, C 2.2, C2.3

4.B.9 Heat energy carried by ocean currents has a strong influence on climate around the world.	C3.2, D3.1, D3.2, D4.1
4.B.10 Ability to recover minerals is as important as how abundant or rare they are; as they are used up, obtaining them becomes more difficult.	A2.3, B5.1, B5.2
4.B.11 Benefits of Earth's resources can be reduced by using them wastefully; the atmosphere and oceans have limited capacity to absorb waster and recycle materials naturally; cleaning up pollution can be very difficult and costly.	B5.1, C2.2, C2.3, C4.3, D1.4, D2.4, D4.3
4.C PROCESSES THAT SHAPE THE EARTH	
4.C.1 Earth's interior is hot. Heat flow and movement of material within Earth cause earthquakes, volcanic eruptions, create mountains, and ocean basins.	B1, B3.3, C3.1, D1.1
4.C.2 Some changes in Earth's surface are abrupt (earthquakes, volcanic eruptions) while other changes happen very slowly (motion of wind, water).	A5, B1, B2, B3, B4.3
4.C.3 Sand, smaller particles, and dissolved minerals form solid rock.	A2, A3.3, B3.1
4.C.4 Rock bears evidence of the minerals, temperatures, and forces that created it in the rock cycle.	A3.4
4.C.5 Successive layers of sedimentary rock confirm the history of Earth's changing surface and provide evidence of changing life forms.	B4.1, B4.2, B4.3
4.C.6 Soil composition, texture, fertility, and resistance to erosion are influenced by plant roots, debris, and organisms living in the soil.	A4.2, A5.1, A5.2, A5.3, A5.4, A5.5
4.C.7 Human activities can change Earth's land, oceans, and atmosphere, sometimes rendering the environment unable to support some life forms.	A4.3, B5.1, C2.2, C2.3, C4.1, C4.3, D1.4, D4.3
4.E ENERGY TRANSFORMATIONS	B1.2, B5.1, C3.4, D1.2, E1.2, E2.3, E3.1, E4.1
4.F MOTION	B2.2, E1.2
4.G FORCES OF NATURE	A5.1, C3.4, E1.1, E2, E3.1
5. The Living Environment	**Book, Chapter, and Section**
5.D INTERDEPENDENCE OF LIFE	C1.2
5.E FLOW OF MATTER AND ENERGY	A4.2, D1.1
5.F EVOLUTION OF LIFE	B4.1, B4.2, B4.3
8. The Designed World	**B5**
9. The Mathematical World	**All Math in Science Features; A1.2**
10. Historical Perspectives	**E1, E2.3, E3.1, E4.2**
12. Habits of Mind	**Book, Chapter, and Section**
12.A VALUES AND ATTITUDES	Think Science Features: A1.4, B1.4, C1.1, D3.3, E3.2
12.B COMPUTATION AND ESTIMATION	All Math in Science Features, Lab Handbook (pp. R10–R35)
12.C MANIPULATION AND OBSERVATION	All Investigates and Chapter Investigations
12.D COMMUNICATION SKILLS	All Chapter Investigations, Lab Handbook (pp. R10–R35)
12.E CRITICAL-RESPONSE SKILLS	Think Science Features: A1.4, B1.4, C1.1, D3.3, E3.2; Scientific Thinking Handbook (pp. R2–R9)

Planning the Unit

The Pacing Guide provides suggested pacing for all chapters in the unit as well as the two unit features shown below.

Frontiers in Science

- Features cutting-edge research as an engaging point of entry into the unit
- Connects to an accompanying *Scientific American Frontiers* video and viewing guide
- Introduces three options for unit projects.

Timelines in Science

- Traces the history of key scientific discoveries
- Highlights interactions between science and technology.

Earth's Atmosphere Pacing Guide

The following pacing guide shows how the chapters in **Earth's Atmosphere** can be adapted to fit your specific course needs.

	TRADITIONAL SCHEDULE (DAYS)	BLOCK SCHEDULE (DAYS)
Frontiers in Science: Dust in the Air	1	0.5
Chapter 1 Earth's Changing Atmosphere		
1.1 Earth's atmosphere supports life.	2	1
1.2 The Sun supplies the atmosphere's energy.	2	1
1.3 Gases in the atmosphere absorb radiation.	2	1
1.4 Human activities affect the atmosphere.	3	1.5
Chapter Investigation	1	0.5
Chapter 2 Weather Patterns		
2.1 The atmosphere's air pressure changes.	2	1
2.2 The atmosphere has wind patterns.	2	1
2.3 Most clouds form as air rises and cools.	2	1
2.4 Water falls to Earth's surface as precipitation.	3	1.5
Chapter Investigation	1	0.5
Chapter 3 Weather Fronts and Storms		
3.1 Weather changes as air masses move.	2	1
3.2 Low-pressure systems can become storms.	2	1
3.3 Vertical air motion can cause severe storms.	2	1
3.4 Weather forecasters use advanced technologies.	3	1.5
Chapter Investigation	1	0.5
Timelines in Science: Observing the Atmosphere	1	0.5
Chapter 4 Climate and Climate Change		
4.1 Climate is a long-term weather pattern.	2	1
4.2 Earth has a variety of climates.	2	1
4.3 Climates can change suddenly or slowly.	3	1.5
Chapter Investigation	1	0.5
Total Days for Module	**40**	**20**

Planning the Chapter

Complete planning support precedes each chapter.

Previewing Content

- Section-by-section science background notes
- Common Misconceptions notes

CHAPTER

1 Earth's Changing Atmosphere

Earth Science
UNIFYING PRINCIPLES

PRINCIPLE 1	PRINCIPLE 2	PRINCIPLE 3	PRINCIPLE 4
Heat energy inside Earth and radiation from the Sun provide energy for Earth's processes.	Physical forces, such as gravity, affect the movement of all matter on Earth and throughout the universe.	Matter and move amon rocks and s atmosphere and living t	

Unit: Earth's Atmosphere
BIG IDEAS

CHAPTER 1 Earth's Changing Atmosphere	CHAPTER 2 Weather Patterns	CHAPTER 3 Weather Fronts and Storms
Earth's atmosphere is a blanket of gases that supports and protects life.	Some features of weather have predictable patterns.	The interaction of air masses causes changes in weather.

CHAPTER 1 KEY CONCEPTS

SECTION 1.1	SECTION 1.2	SECTION
Earth's atmosphere supports life.	**The Sun supplies the atmosphere's energy.**	**Gases in the absorb radia**
1. The atmosphere makes life on Earth possible.	1. Energy from the Sun heats the atmosphere.	1. Gases can off radiati
2. Natural processes modify the atmosphere.	2. The atmosphere moves energy.	2. The ozone life from h
	3. The atmosphere has temperature layers.	3. The green keeps Eart

 The Big Idea Flow Chart is available on p. T1 in the **UNIT TRANSPARENCY BOOK**

Previewing Content

Previewing Content

SECTION
(1.1) Earth's atmosphere supports life. pp. 9–15

1. The atmosphere makes life on Earth possible.
The **atmosphere** is a whole layer of air that surrounds Earth. It supports and protects life in several ways, such as by
- absorbing harmful radiation
- maintaining Earth's temperature
- providing elements essential for life

SECTION
(1.2)

1. Ene
Mos
take
Rad
elect
sola

Previewing Content

SECTION
(1.3) Gases in the atmosphere absorb radiation, pp. 22–26

1. Gases can absorb and give off radiation.
Different gases in the atmosphere absorb and emit different types of radiation. In the stratosphere, ozone absorbs **ultraviolet radiation,** which has more energy per wave than visible light. In the troposphere, the following gases absorb and emit **infrared radiation,** which has less energy per wave than visible light:
- carbon dioxide
- methane
- water vapor
- nitrous oxide

2. The ozone layer protects life from harmful radiation.
Ozone (O_3) is a gas with molecules made of three oxygen atoms. In the stratosphere, ozone and atmospheric oxygen (O_2) break apart and form again in a complex, yet balanced, cycle. The ozone layer protects life on Earth by absorbing harmful ultraviolet (UV) rays. Exposure to UV radiation can cause sunburn, skin cancer, and damaged eyesight. The radiation can also harm crops and materials such as plastic or paint.

3. The greenhouse effect keeps Earth warm.
Water vapor, carbon dioxide, methane, nitrous oxide, and certain other gases keep Earth warm by absorbing and giving off infrared radiation. This process is known as the **greenhouse effect,** even though greenhouses are different because they mostly prevent convection. The gases themselves are collectively known as **greenhouse gases.** The greenhouse effect, which takes place mainly in the troposphere, involves the following steps:
- Solar radiation heats Earth's surface, which grows warm and emits infrared radiation.
- Greenhouse gases absorb some of this infrared radiation and allow the rest to pass into space.
- Greenhouse gases then emit infrared radiation. Some is absorbed by the ground, while some is lost to space.

SECTION
(1.4) Human activities affect the atmosphere. pp. 27–35

1. Human activity can cause air pollution.
Air pollution consists of smoke and other harmful materials that are added to the air. The two components of air pollution are gases and particulates. The gases include methane, ozone, carbon monoxide, sulfur oxides, and nitrogen oxides. **Particulates** are tiny particles or droplets that are mixed in the air; they include dust, dirt, pollen, and sea salt. Air pollution can come from natural sources, such as volcanoes, or from human activities, such as the burning of fossil fuels. **Fossil fuels** are energy sources formed from the remains of ancient plants and animals. Air pollution can cause health problems and environmental damage.

2. Human activities are increasing greenhouse gases.
When levels of greenhouse gases increase, global temperatures increase. The burning of fossil fuels and other human activities have increased atmospheric carbon dioxide. Increased greenhouse gases may lead to global warming, which is an increase in Earth's temperatures.

3. Human activities produce chemicals that destroy the ozone layer.
Chlorofluorocarbons (CFCs) are chemicals that were once widely used in cooling systems, spray cans, and foam packing. CFCs react with sunlight and release chlorine, which destroys ozone. Substitute chemicals used today destroy ozone more slowly than chlorine.
The chemical reactions in the stratosphere that produce and destroy ozone depend on weather. Much of the ozone over the South Pole is destroyed in certain seasons, resulting in the so-called ozone hole. Ozone is also destroyed in other locations, though less dramatically.

Common Misconceptions

OZONE LAYER Students may hold the misconception that there are huge holes or gaps in the ozone layer. In fact, it is more correct to say that the ozone layer is thinning. Although not technically a "hole," this thinning still allows harmful ultraviolet rays to reach Earth's surface.

 This misconception is addressed on p. 32.

 MISCONCEPTION DATABASE
CLASSZONE.COM Background on student misconceptions

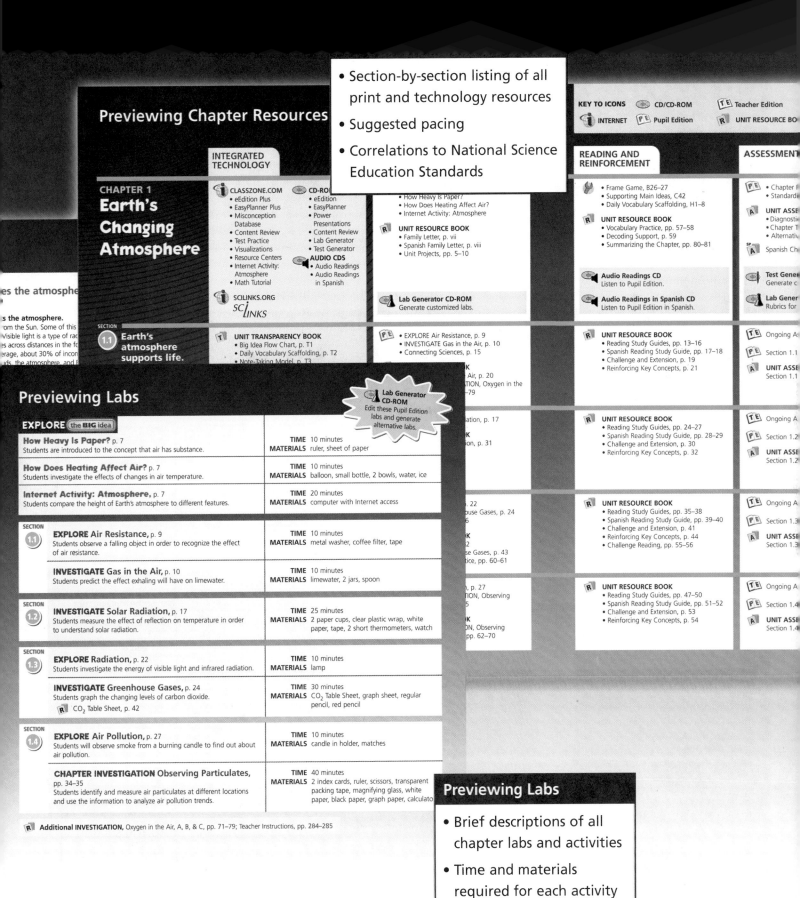

Previewing Chapter Resources

- Section-by-section listing of all print and technology resources
- Suggested pacing
- Correlations to National Science Education Standards

KEY TO ICONS CD/CD-ROM **TE** Teacher Edition
 INTERNET **PE** Pupil Edition **R** UNIT RESOURCE BOOK

	INTEGRATED TECHNOLOGY			READING AND REINFORCEMENT	ASSESSMENT
CHAPTER 1 **Earth's Changing Atmosphere**	**CLASSZONE.COM** • eEdition Plus • EasyPlanner Plus • Misconception Database • Content Review • Test Practice • Visualizations • Resource Centers • Internet Activity: Atmosphere • Math Tutorial **SCILINKS.ORG** SC*i*LINKS	**CD-ROM** • eEdition • EasyPlanner • Power Presentations • Content Review • Lab Generator • Test Generator **AUDIO CDS** • Audio Readings • Audio Readings in Spanish	• How Heavy Is Paper? • How Does Heating Affect Air? • Internet Activity: Atmosphere **UNIT RESOURCE BOOK** • Family Letter, p. vii • Spanish Family Letter, p. viii • Unit Projects, pp. 5–10 **Lab Generator CD-ROM** Generate customized labs.	• Frame Game, B26–27 • Supporting Main Ideas, C42 • Daily Vocabulary Scaffolding, H1–8 **R UNIT RESOURCE BOOK** • Vocabulary Practice, pp. 57–58 • Decoding Support, p. 59 • Summarizing the Chapter, pp. 80–81 **Audio Readings CD** Listen to Pupil Edition. **Audio Readings in Spanish CD** Listen to Pupil Edition in Spanish.	**PE** • Chapter • Standardi **A** UNIT ASSE • Diagnosti • Chapter T • Alternativ **SP A** Spanish Ch **Test Gene** Generate c **Lab Gener** Rubrics for
SECTION 1.1 Earth's atmosphere supports life.	**UNIT TRANSPARENCY BOOK** • Big Idea Flow Chart, p. T1 • Daily Vocabulary Scaffolding, p. T2 • Note-Taking Model, p. T3		**PE** • EXPLORE Air Resistance, p. 9 • INVESTIGATE Gas in the Air, p. 10 • Connecting Sciences, p. 15	**R UNIT RESOURCE BOOK** • Reading Study Guides, pp. 13–16 • Spanish Reading Study Guide, pp. 17–18 • Challenge and Extension, p. 19 • Reinforcing Key Concepts, p. 21	**TE** Ongoing As **PE** Section 1.1 **A** UNIT ASSE Section 1.1

Previewing Labs

Lab Generator CD-ROM
Edit these Pupil Edition labs and generate alternative labs.

EXPLORE the **BIG** idea

How Heavy Is Paper? p. 7
Students are introduced to the concept that air has substance.
TIME 10 minutes
MATERIALS ruler, sheet of paper

How Does Heating Affect Air? p. 7
Students investigate the effects of changes in air temperature.
TIME 10 minutes
MATERIALS balloon, small bottle, 2 bowls, water, ice

Internet Activity: Atmosphere, p. 7
Students compare the height of Earth's atmosphere to different features.
TIME 20 minutes
MATERIALS computer with Internet access

SECTION 1.1
EXPLORE Air Resistance, p. 9
Students observe a falling object in order to recognize the effect of air resistance.
TIME 10 minutes
MATERIALS metal washer, coffee filter, tape

INVESTIGATE Gas in the Air, p. 10
Students predict the effect exhaling will have on limewater.
TIME 10 minutes
MATERIALS limewater, 2 jars, spoon

SECTION 1.2
INVESTIGATE Solar Radiation, p. 17
Students measure the effect of reflection on temperature in order to understand solar radiation.
TIME 25 minutes
MATERIALS 2 paper cups, clear plastic wrap, white paper, tape, 2 short thermometers, watch

SECTION 1.3
EXPLORE Radiation, p. 22
Students investigate the energy of visible light and infrared radiation.
TIME 10 minutes
MATERIALS lamp

INVESTIGATE Greenhouse Gases, p. 24
Students graph the changing levels of carbon dioxide.
R CO_2 Table Sheet, p. 42
TIME 30 minutes
MATERIALS CO_2 Table Sheet, graph sheet, regular pencil, red pencil

SECTION 1.4
EXPLORE Air Pollution, p. 27
Students will observe smoke from a burning candle to find out about air pollution.
TIME 10 minutes
MATERIALS candle in holder, matches

CHAPTER INVESTIGATION Observing Particulates, pp. 34–35
Students identify and measure air particulates at different locations and use the information to analyze air pollution trends.
TIME 40 minutes
MATERIALS 2 index cards, ruler, scissors, transparent packing tape, magnifying glass, white paper, black paper, graph paper, calculato

R Additional **INVESTIGATION,** Oxygen in the Air, A, B, & C, pp. 71–79; Teacher Instructions, pp. 284–285

Previewing Labs

- Brief descriptions of all chapter labs and activities
- Time and materials required for each activity

Planning the Lesson

Point-of-use support for each lesson provides a wealth of teaching options.

1. Prepare

- Concept and vocabulary review
- Note-taking and vocabulary strategies

2. Focus

- Set Learning Goals
- 3-Minute Warm-up

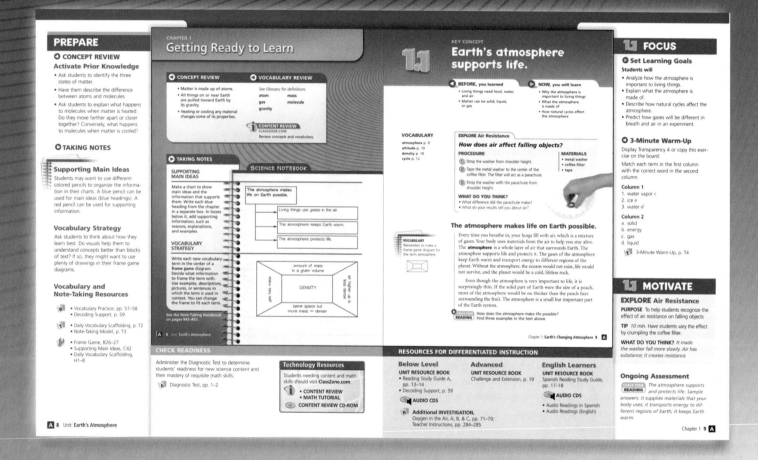

3. Motivate

- Engaging entry into the section
- Explore activity or Think About question

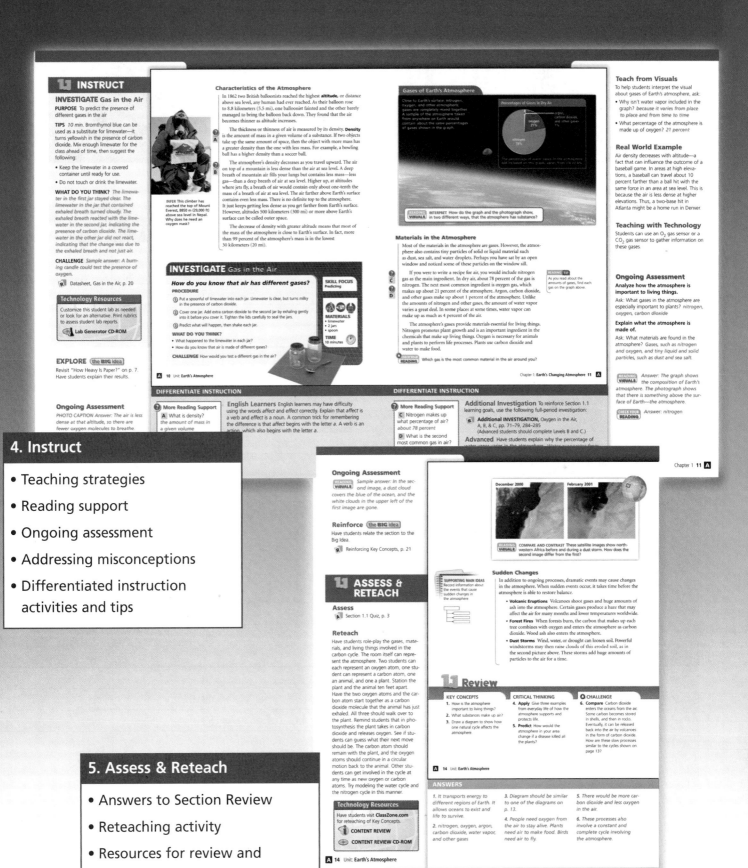

4. Instruct

- Teaching strategies
- Reading support
- Ongoing assessment
- Addressing misconceptions
- Differentiated instruction activities and tips

5. Assess & Reteach

- Answers to Section Review
- Reteaching activity
- Resources for review and assessment

Lab Materials List

The following charts list the consumables, nonconsumables, and equipment needed for all activities. Quantities are per group of four students. Lab aprons, goggles, water, books, paper, pens, pencils, and calculators are assumed to be available for all activities.

Materials kits are available. For more information, please call McDougal Littell at 1-800-323-5435.

Consumables

Description	Quantity per Group	Explore *page*	Investigate *page*	Chapter Investigation *page*
aluminum foil, 10 cm x 20 cm	1	92		
balloon	2		45, 49	
bottle, plastic, 1 liter	1		67	
bottle, plastic, 1 liter with cap	1		59	
candle, tea light	1	27		
cardboard, 12 cm x 12 cm	4		94	
cardboard, 20 cm x 20 cm	1		81	
cardboard tube, paper towel	1	117		
carton, milk, pint	1			64
cloth, heavy cotton, 6" x 6"	1			64
coffee filter, basket	1	9		
cup, paper	2		17	
cup, clear plastic	4		81, 90	
cup, Styrofoam	7		94, 119	
egg, hard-boiled	1	43		
food coloring, red	1 bottle		81, 94	
food coloring, blue	1 bottle		94	
gravel	1/2 lb		67	
ice	1 1/2 cups	79	90	
index card	2			34
limewater	2 tbs		10	
marker, permanent black	1		49, 67	
match, wood	5	27, 43	59	
paper, black, 4 cm x 4 cm	2	117		
paper, black, 8.5" x 11"	1			34
paper, graph, 8.5" x 11"	2			34, 104
paper, tissue, white	1 sheet		133	
paper, white, 6" x 6"	1		17	
paper, white, 8.5" x 11"	1			34
pencil, red	1		24	

Description	Quantity per Group	Explore page	Investigate page	Chapter Investigation page
plastic wrap	200 cm	79	17	
rubber band, large	4		45	64
rubber eraser	1	92		
salt, table	20 mL		81, 90	
soil, potting	1/2 lb		119	
spoon, plastic	1		10	
stirring straw	1		45	
tape, transparent	1 roll	9	17, 45, 133	
tape, transparent packing	20 cm			34
thumbtack, flat-headed	1	92		
tray, polystyrene (plastic foam), medium	1	92		
weather map, newspaper	1	98		

Nonconsumables

Description	Quantity per Group	Explore page	Investigate page	Chapter Investigation page
beaker, 100 mL	1		81	
beaker, 500 mL	1		81	
bottle, glass	1	43		
bowl, large plastic	1			64
bowl, small plastic	3	79		
can, metal, 8–14 oz	1		45	
candle holder	1	27		
compass	1			104
eyedropper	1		94	
fabric, wool, 30 cm x 30 cm	1	92		
flashlight with batteries	1	47		
globe	1	47		
hand lens	1			34
jar, baby food with lid	2		10	
lamp, gooseneck desk	1	117	22, 119	

Description	Quantity per Group	Explore *page*	Investigate *page*	Chapter Investigation *page*
light bulb, incandescent, 60 watt	1	117	22, 119	
measuring spoon, tablespoon	1		59	
mirror, hand	1	56		
pan, glass, 10" x 14"	1		94	
ruler, metric	1	47	45, 67, 119	34, 64
scissors	1		67, 81	34, 64
shoe box, cardboard	3	79		
stopwatch	1		17	
thermometer	2	117	17, 119, 133	64, 104, 130
toy top	1	87		
washer, metal 1"	1	9		

Unit Resource Book Datasheets

Description		Explore *page*	Investigate *page*	Chapter Investigation *page*
Greenhouse Gases datasheet			24	
Relative Humidity Table			64	

McDougal Littell Science

Earth's Atmosphere

TROPOSPHERE

UPDRAFT

CUMULUS

EARTH SCIENCE

A ▶ Earth's Surface
B ▶ The Changing Earth
C ▶ Earth's Waters
D ▶ Earth's Atmosphere
E ▶ Space Science

PHYSICAL SCIENCE

A ▶ Matter and Energy
B ▶ Chemical Interactions
C ▶ Motion and Forces
D ▶ Waves, Sound, and Light
E ▶ Electricity and Magnetism

LIFE SCIENCE

A ▶ Cells and Heredity
B ▶ Life Over Time
C ▶ Diversity of Living Things
D ▶ Ecology
E ▶ Human Biology

ISBN: 0-618-33415-7   1 2 3 4 5 6 7 8 VJM 08 07 06 05 04

Internet Web Site: http://www.mcdougallittell.com

Science Consultants

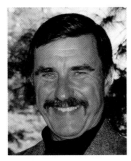

Chief Science Consultant

James Trefil, Ph.D. is the Clarence J. Robinson Professor of Physics at George Mason University. He is the author or co-author of more than 25 books, including *Science Matters* and *The Nature of Science.* Dr. Trefil is a member of the American Association for the Advancement of Science's Committee on the Public Understanding of Science and Technology. He is also a fellow of the World Economic Forum and a frequent contributor to *Smithsonian* magazine.

Rita Ann Calvo, Ph.D. is Senior Lecturer in Molecular Biology and Genetics at Cornell University, where for 12 years she also directed the Cornell Institute for Biology Teachers. Dr. Calvo is the 1999 recipient of the College and University Teaching Award from the National Association of Biology Teachers.

Kenneth Cutler, M.S. is the Education Coordinator for the Julius L. Chambers Biomedical Biotechnology Research Institute at North Carolina Central University. A former middle school and high school science teacher, he received a 1999 Presidential Award for Excellence in Science Teaching.

Instructional Design Consultants

Douglas Carnine, Ph.D. is Professor of Education and Director of the National Center for Improving the Tools of Educators at the University of Oregon. He is the author of seven books and over 100 other scholarly publications, primarily in the areas of instructional design and effective instructional strategies and tools for diverse learners. Dr. Carnine also serves as a member of the National Institute for Literacy Advisory Board.

Linda Carnine, Ph.D. consults with school districts on curriculum development and effective instruction for students struggling academically. A former teacher and school administrator, Dr. Carnine also co-authored a popular remedial reading program.

Donald Steely, Ph.D. serves as principal investigator at the Oregon Center for Applied Science (ORCAS) on federal grants for science and language arts programs. His background also includes teaching and authoring of print and multimedia programs in science, mathematics, history, and spelling.

Sam Miller, Ph.D. is a middle school science teacher and the Teacher Development Liaison for the Eugene, Oregon, Public Schools. He is the author of curricula for teaching science, mathematics, computer skills, and language arts.

Vicky Vachon, Ph.D. consults with school districts throughout the United States and Canada on improving overall academic achievement with a focus on literacy. She is also co-author of a widely used program for remedial readers.

Content Reviewers

John Beaver, Ph.D.
Ecology
Professor, Director of Science Education Center
College of Education and Human Services
Western Illinois University
Macomb, IL

Donald J. DeCoste, Ph.D.
Matter and Energy, Chemical Interactions
Chemistry Instructor
University of Illinois
Urbana-Champaign, IL

Dorothy Ann Fallows, Ph.D., MSc
Diversity of Living Things, Microbiology
Partners in Health
Boston, MA

Michael Foote, Ph.D.
The Changing Earth, Life Over Time
Associate Professor
Department of the Geophysical Sciences
The University of Chicago
Chicago, IL

Lucy Fortson, Ph.D.
Space Science
Director of Astronomy
Adler Planetarium and Astronomy Museum
Chicago, IL

Elizabeth Godrick, Ph.D.
Human Biology
Professor, CAS Biology
Boston University
Boston, MA

Isabelle Sacramento Grilo, M.S.
The Changing Earth
Lecturer, Department of the Geological Sciences
Montana State University
Bozeman, MT

David Harbster, MSc
Diversity of Living Things
Professor of Biology
Paradise Valley Community College
Phoenix, AZ

Richard D. Norris, Ph.D.
Earth's Waters
Professor of Paleobiology
Scripps Institution of Oceanography
University of California, San Diego
La Jolla, CA

Donald B. Peck, M.S.
*Motion and Forces; Waves, Sound, and Light;
  Electricity and Magnetism*
Director of the Center for Science Education (retired)
Fairleigh Dickinson University
Madison, NJ

Javier Penalosa, Ph.D.
Diversity of Living Things, Plants
Associate Professor, Biology Department
Buffalo State College
Buffalo, NY

Raymond T. Pierrehumbert, Ph.D.
Earth's Atmosphere
Professor in Geophysical Sciences (Atmospheric Science)
The University of Chicago
Chicago, IL

Brian J. Skinner, Ph.D.
Earth's Surface
Eugene Higgins Professor of Geology and Geophysics
Yale University
New Haven, CT

Nancy E. Spaulding, M.S.
Earth's Surface, The Changing Earth, Earth's Waters
Earth Science Teacher (retired)
Elmira Free Academy
Elmira, NY

Steven S. Zumdahl, Ph.D.
Matter and Energy, Chemical Interactions
Professor Emeritus of Chemistry
University of Illinois
Urbana-Champaign, IL

Susan L. Zumdahl, M.S.
Matter and Energy, Chemical Interactions
Chemistry Education Specialist
University of Illinois
Urbana-Champaign, IL

Safety Consultant

Juliana Texley, Ph.D.
Former K–12 Science Teacher and School Superintendent
Boca Raton, FL

English Language Advisor

Judy Lewis, M.A.
Director, State and Federal Programs for reading proficiency
and high risk populations
Rancho Cordova, CA

Teacher Panel Members

Carol Arbour
Tallmadge Middle School,
Tallmadge, OH

Patty Belcher
Goodrich Middle School,
Akron, OH

Gwen Broestl
Luis Munoz Marin Middle School,
Cleveland, OH

Al Brofman
Tehipite Middle School,
Fresno, CA

John Cockrell
Clinton Middle School,
Columbus, OH

Jenifer Cox
Sylvan Middle School,
Citrus Heights, CA

Linda Culpepper
Martin Middle School,
Charlotte, NC

Kathleen Ann DeMatteo
Margate Middle School,
Margate, FL

Melvin Figueroa
New River Middle School,
Ft. Lauderdale, FL

Doretha Grier
Kannapolis Middle School,
Kannapolis, NC

Robert Hood
Alexander Hamilton Middle School,
Cleveland, OH

Scott Hudson
Coverdale Elementary School,
Cincinnati, OH

Loretta Langdon
Princeton Middle School,
Princeton, NC

Carlyn Little
Glades Middle School,
Miami, FL

Ann Marie Lynn
Amelia Earhart Middle School,
Riverside, CA

James Minogue
Lowe's Grove Middle School,
Durham, NC

Joann Myers
Buchanan Middle School,
Tampa, FL

Barbara Newell
Charles Evans Hughes Middle School,
Long Beach, CA

Anita Parker
Kannapolis Middle School,
Kannapolis, NC

Greg Pirolo
Golden Valley Middle School,
San Bernardino, CA

Laura Pottmyer
Apex Middle School,
Apex, NC

Lynn Prichard
Booker T. Washington Middle Magnet
School, Tampa, FL

Jacque Quick
Walter Williams High School,
Burlington, NC

Robert Glenn Reynolds
Hillman Middle School,
Youngstown, OH

Theresa Short
Abbott Middle School,
Fayetteville, NC

Rita Slivka
Alexander Hamilton Middle School,
Cleveland, OH

Marie Sofsak
B F Stanton Middle School,
Alliance, OH

Nancy Stubbs
Sweetwater Union Unified School District,
Chula Vista, CA

Sharon Stull
Quail Hollow Middle School,
Charlotte, NC

Donna Taylor
Okeeheelee Middle School,
West Palm Beach, FL

Sandi Thompson
Harding Middle School,
Lakewood, OH

Lori Walker
Audubon Middle School & Magnet Center,
Los Angeles, CA

Teacher Lab Evaluators

Jill Brimm-Byrne
Albany Park Academy,
Chicago, IL

Gwen Broestl
Luis Munoz Marin Middle School,
Cleveland, OH

Al Brofman
Tehipite Middle School,
Fresno, CA

Michael A. Burstein
The Rashi School,
Newton, MA

Trudi Coutts
Madison Middle School,
Naperville, IL

Jenifer Cox
Sylvan Middle School,
Citrus Heights, CA

Larry Cwik
Madison Middle School,
Naperville, IL

Jennifer Donatelli
Kennedy Junior High School,
Lisle, IL

Paige Fullhart
Highland Middle School,
Libertyville, IL

Sue Hood
Glen Crest Middle School,
Glen Ellyn, IL

Ann Min
Beardsley Middle School,
Crystal Lake, IL

Aileen Mueller
Kennedy Junior High School,
Lisle, IL

Nancy Nega
Churchville Middle School,
Elmhurst, IL

Oscar Newman
Sumner Math and Science Academy,
Chicago, IL

Marina Penalver
Moore Middle School,
Portland, ME

Lynn Prichard
Booker T. Washington Middle Magnet
School, Tampa, FL

Jacque Quick
Walter Williams High School,
Burlington, NC

Seth Robey
Gwendolyn Brooks Middle School,
Oak Park, IL

Kevin Steele
Grissom Middle School,
Tinley Park, IL

Earth's Atmosphere

eEdition

Unit Features

1 Earth's Changing Atmosphere   6

the BIG idea

Earth's atmosphere is a blanket of gases that supports and protects life.

2 Weather Patterns   40

the BIG idea

Some features of weather have predictable patterns.

What weather conditions do you see in the distance?
page 40

What types of weather can move a house?
page 76

Features

Visual Highlights

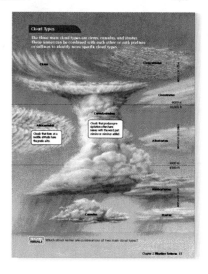

Internet Resources @ ClassZone.com

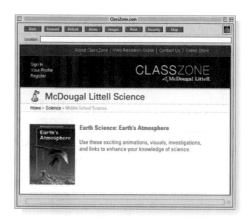

INVESTIGATIONS AND ACTIVITIES

Each chapter in **Earth's Atmosphere** covers some of the learning goals that are described in the *National Science Education Standards* (NSES) and the Project 2061 *Benchmarks for Science Literacy.* Selected content and skill standards are shown below in shortened form. The following National Science Education Standards are covered on pages xii–xxvii, in Frontiers in Science, and in Timelines in Science, as well as in chapter features and laboratory investigations: Understandings About Scientific Inquiry (A.9), Understandings About Science and Technology (E.6), Science and Technology in Society (F.5), Science as a Human Endeavor (G.1), Nature of Science (G.2), and History of Science (G.3).

Content Standards

1 Earth's Changing Atmosphere

National Science Education Standards

D.1.h | The atmosphere
- is a mixture of the gases nitrogen and oxygen
- has small amounts of water vapor and other gases
- has different properties at different heights

F.3.b | Human activities can produce hazards and affect the speed of natural changes.

Project 2061 Benchmarks

4.B.6 | The atmosphere can change suddenly when a volcano erupts or when Earth is struck by a huge rock from space. A small change in the substance of the atmosphere can have a big effect if the change lasts long enough.

4.E.3 | Heat energy can move by the collision of particles, by the motion of particles, or by waves through space.

2 Weather Patterns

National Science Education Standards

D.1.f | Water
- evaporates from Earth's surface
- rises, cools, and condenses in the atmosphere
- falls to the surface as rain or snow

D.1.i | Clouds form when water vapor condenses. Clouds affect the weather.

D.1.j | Global patterns have an effect on local weather and weather patterns.
- Global patterns of air motion affect the local weather.
- Oceans affect the weather patterns of a place.

Project 2061 Benchmarks

4.B.7 | Water is important in the atmosphere. Water
- evaporates from Earth's surface
- rises and cools
- condenses into rain or snow
- falls back to the surface

4.B.4 | Sunlight falls more intensely on different parts of Earth, and the pattern changes over the year. The differences in heating of Earth's surface produce seasons and other weather patterns.

3 Weather Fronts and Storms

National Science Education Standards

D.1.j | Global patterns of air motion and heat energy from oceans both have big effects on weather.

F.3.a | Processes of the Earth system, such as storms, can cause hazards that affect humans and wildlife.

Project 2061 Benchmarks

3.A.2 | Technologies are important in science because they let people gather large sets of data, put them together, analyze them, and share data and ideas.

11.B.1 | Models are often used to think about processes that cannot be observed directly or that are too vast or too dangerous to be changed directly. Models can be displayed on a computer and then changed to see what happens.

4 Climate and Climate Change

National Science Education Standards

D.1.j | The global patterns of motion in the atmosphere and the oceans affect the weather in different places.

D.2.a | The Earth processes we see today are similar to those that occurred in the past. Earth history is sometimes affected by catastrophes, such as the impact of an asteroid.

Project 2061 Benchmarks

4.B.6 | In the past, weather patterns have changed suddenly from events such as a volcano erupting or a large rock from space hitting Earth. Weather patterns around the world can be affected by even a small change in the atmosphere, if the change lasts long enough.

4.B.9 | Currents in the oceans move heat energy from place to place, so they affect the weather patterns in different locations.

Process and Skill Standards

National Science Education Standards

A.2 | Design and conduct a scientific investigation.

A.3 | Use appropriate tools and techniques to gather and interpret data.

A.4 | Use evidence to describe, predict, explain, and model.

A.5 | Use critical thinking to find relationships between results and interpretations.

A.7 | Communicate procedures, results, and conclusions.

A.8 | Use mathematics in scientific investigations.

E.2 | Design a solution or product.

E.3 | Implement the proposed solution.

E.4 | Evaluate the solution or design.

Project 2061 Benchmarks

12.B.5 | Estimate distances and travel times from maps.

12.C.3 | Using appropriate units, use and read instruments that measure length, volume, weight, time, rate, and temperature.

12.D.1 | Use tables and graphs to organize information and identify relationships.

12.D.2 | Read, interpret, and describe tables and graphs.

12.D.4 | Understand information that includes different types of charts and graphs, including circle charts, bar graphs, line graphs, data tables, diagrams, and symbols.

12.E.4 | Recognize more than one way to interpret a given set of findings.

Introducing Earth Science

Scientists are curious. Since ancient times, they have been asking and answering questions about the world around them. Scientists are also very suspicious of the answers they get. They carefully collect evidence and test their answers many times before accepting an idea as correct.

In this book you will see how scientific knowledge keeps growing and changing as scientists ask new questions and rethink what was known before. The following sections will help get you started.

What Is Earth Science?

Earth science is the study of Earth's interior, its rocks and soil, its atmosphere, its oceans, and outer space. For many years, scientists studied each of these topics separately. They learned many important things. Recently, however, scientists have started to look more and more at the connections among the different parts of Earth—its oceans, atmosphere, living things, and rocks and soil. Scientists have also started to learn more about other planets in our solar system, as well as stars and galaxies far away. Through these studies they have learned more about Earth and its place in the universe.

The text and pictures in this book will help you learn key concepts and important facts about earth science. A variety of activities will help you investigate these concepts. As you learn, it helps to have a big picture of earth science as a frame-work for this new information. The four unifying principles listed below will give you this big picture. Read the next few pages to get an overview of each of these principles and a sense of why they are so important.

- **Heat energy inside Earth and radiation from the Sun provide energy for Earth's processes.**

- **Physical forces, such as gravity, affect the movement of all matter on Earth and through-out the universe.**

- **Matter and energy move among Earth's rocks and soil, atmosphere, waters, and living things.**

- **Earth has changed over time and continues to change.**

Each chapter begins with a big idea. Keep in mind that each big idea relates to one or more of the unifying principles.

Heat energy inside Earth and radiation from the Sun provide energy for Earth's processes.

The lava pouring out of this volcano in Hawaii is liquid rock that was melted by heat energy under Earth's surface. Another, much more powerful energy source constantly bombards Earth's surface with energy, heating the air around you, and keeping the oceans from freezing over. This energy source is the Sun. Everything that moves or changes on Earth gets its energy either from the Sun or from the inside of our planet.

What It Means

You are always surrounded by different forms of energy, such as heat energy or light. **Energy** is the ability to cause change. All of Earth's processes need energy to occur. A process is a set of changes that leads to a particular result. For example, **evaporation** is the process by which liquid changes into gas. A puddle on a sidewalk dries up through the process of evaporation. The energy needed for the puddle to dry up comes from the Sun.

Heat Energy Inside Earth

Underneath the cool surface layer of rock, Earth's interior is so hot that the solid rock there is able to flow very slowly—a few centimeters each year. In a process called **convection,** hot material rises, cools, then sinks until it is heated enough to rise again. Convection of hot rock carries heat energy up to Earth's surface, where it provides the energy to build mountains, cause earthquakes, and make volcanoes erupt.

Radiation from the Sun

Earth receives energy from the Sun as **radiation**—energy that moves in the form of certain types of waves. Visible light is one type of radiation. Radiation from the Sun heats Earth's surface, making bright summer days hot. Different parts of Earth receive different amounts of radiation at different times of the year, causing seasons. Energy from the Sun also causes winds to blow, ocean currents to flow, and water to move from the ground to the atmosphere and back again.

Why It's Important

Understanding Earth's processes makes it possible to

- know what types of crops to plant and when to plant them
- know when to watch for dangerous weather, such as tornadoes and hurricanes
- predict a volcano's eruption in time for people to leave the area

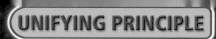
Physical forces, such as gravity, affect the movement of all matter on Earth and throughout the universe.

The universe is everything that exists, and everything in the universe is governed by the same physical laws. The same laws govern the stars shown in this picture and the page on which the picture is printed.

What It Means

What do galaxies, stars, the solar system, and Earth have in common? For one thing, they are all made of matter. **Matter** is anything that has mass and takes up space. Rocks are matter. You are matter. Even the air around you is matter. Matter is made of tiny particles called **atoms** that are too small to see through an ordinary microscope.

Everything in the universe is also affected by the same physical forces. A **force** is a push or a pull. Forces affect how matter moves everywhere in the universe.

- One force you experience every moment is **gravity,** which is the attraction, or pull, between two objects. Gravity is pulling you to Earth and Earth to you. Gravity is the force that causes objects to fall downward toward the center of Earth. Gravity is also the force that keeps objects in orbit around planets and stars.

- **Friction** is the force that resists motion between two surfaces that are pressed together. Friction can keep a rock on a hillside from sliding down to the bottom of the hill. If you lightly rub your finger across a smooth page in a book and then across a piece of sandpaper, you can feel how the different surfaces produce different frictional forces. Which is easier to do?

- There are many other forces at work on Earth and throughout the universe. For example, Earth has a magnetic field. A compass needle responds to the force exerted by Earth's magnetic field. Another example is the contact force between a rock and the ground beneath it. A contact force occurs when one object pushes or pulls on another object by touching it.

Why It's Important

Physical forces influence the movement of all matter, from the tiniest particle to you to the largest galaxy. Understanding forces allows people to

- predict how objects and materials move on Earth
- send spacecraft and equipment into space
- explain and predict the movements of Earth, the Moon, planets, and stars

Matter and energy move among Earth's rocks and soil, atmosphere, waters, and living things.

When a wolf eats a rabbit, matter and energy move from one living thing into another. When a wolf drinks water warmed by the Sun, matter and energy move from Earth's waters into one of its living things. These are just two examples of how energy and matter move among different parts of the Earth system.

What It Means

Think of Earth as a huge system, or an organized group of parts that work together. Within this system, matter and energy move among the different parts. The four major parts of Earth's system are the

- **atmosphere,** which includes all the air surrounding the planet
- **geosphere,** which includes all of Earth's rocks and minerals, as well as Earth's interior
- **hydrosphere,** which includes oceans, rivers, lakes, and every drop of water on or under Earth's surface
- **biosphere,** which is made up of all the living things on Earth

Matter in the Earth System

It's easy to see how matter moves within the Earth system. When water in the atmosphere falls as rain, it becomes part of the hydrosphere. When an animal drinks water from a puddle, the water becomes part of the biosphere. When rainwater soaks into the ground, it moves through the geosphere. As the puddle dries up, the water becomes part of the atmosphere again.

Energy in the Earth System

Most of the energy you depend on comes from the Sun and moves among the four major parts of the Earth system. Think again about the puddle that is drying up. Sunlight shines through the water and heats the soil, or geosphere, beneath the puddle. Some of this heat energy goes into the puddle, moving into the hydrosphere. As the water evaporates and becomes part of the atmosphere, it takes the energy that came from the Sun with it. The Sun provides energy for all weather and ocean currents. Without the Sun, life could not exist on Earth's surface.

Why It's Important

Understanding how matter and energy move through the Earth system makes it possible to

- predict how a temperature change in ocean water might affect the weather
- determine how clearing forests might affect rainfall
- explain where organisms on the ocean floor get energy to carry out life processes

Earth has changed over time and continues to change.

You see Earth changing all of the time. Rain turns dirt to mud, and a dry wind turns the mud to dust. Many changes are small and can take hundreds, thousands, or even millions of years to add up to much. Other changes are sudden and can destroy in minutes a house that had stood for many years.

What It Means

Events are always changing Earth's surface. Some events, such as the building or wearing away of mountains, occur over millions of years. Others, such as earthquakes, occur within seconds. A change can affect a small area or an entire continent, such as North America.

Records of Change

What was the distant past like? Think about how scientists learn about ancient people. They study what the people left behind and draw conclusions based on the evidence. In a similar way, scientists learn about Earth's past by examining the evidence they find in rock layers and by observing processes now occurring.

By observing that water breaks down rocks and carries the material away to other places, people learned that rivers can slowly carve deep valleys. Evidence from rocks and fossils along the edges of continents shows that all continents were once joined and then moved apart over time. A **fossil** is the trace of a once-living organism. Fossils also show that new types of plants and animals develop, and others, such as dinosaurs, die out.

Change Continues Today

Every year, earthquakes occur, volcanoes erupt, and rivers flood. Continents continue to move slowly. The Himalayan Mountains of Asia push a few millimeters higher. **Climate**—the long-term weather patterns of an area—may also change. Scientists are studying how changes in climates around the world might affect Earth even within this century.

Why It's Important

Understanding the changing Earth makes it possible to

- predict and prepare for events such as volcanic eruptions, landslides, floods, and climate changes
- design buildings to withstand shaking during earthquakes
- protect important environments for plants and animals

You may think of science as a body of knowledge or a collection of facts. More important, however, science is an active process that involves certain ways of looking at the world.

Scientific Habits of Mind

Scientists are curious. They ask questions. A scientist who finds an unusual rock by the side of a river would ask questions such as, "Did this rock form in this area?" or "Did this rock form elsewhere and get moved here?" Questions like these make a scientist want to investigate.

Scientists are observant. They look closely at the world around them. A scientist who studies rocks can learn a lot about a rock just by picking it up, looking at its color, and feeling how heavy it is.

Scientists are creative. They draw on what they know to form possible explanations for a pattern, an event, or an interesting phenomenon that they have observed. Then scientists put together a plan for testing their ideas.

Scientists are skeptical. Scientists don't accept an explanation or answer unless it is based on evidence and logical reasoning. They continually question their own conclusions as well as the conclusions suggested by other scientists. Scientists only trust evidence that can be confirmed by other people or other methods.

Scientists use seismographs to observe and measure vibrations that move through the ground.

This scientist is collecting a sample of melted rock from a hot lava flow in Hawaii.

Science Processes at Work

You can think of science as a continuous cycle of asking and seeking answers to questions about the world. Although there are many processes that scientists use, all scientists typically do the following:

- Ask a question
- Determine what is known
- Investigate
- Interpret results
- Share results

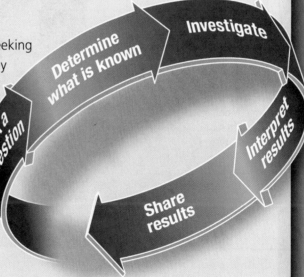

Ask a Question

It may surprise you that asking questions is an important skill. A scientific investigation may start when a scientist asks a question. Perhaps scientists observe an event or a process that they don't understand, or perhaps answering one question leads to another.

Determine What Is Known

When beginning an inquiry, scientists find out what is already known about a question. They study results from other scientific investigations, read journals, and talk with other scientists. The scientist who is trying to figure out where an unusual rock came from will study maps that show what types of rocks are already known to be in the area where the rock was found.

Investigate

Investigating is the process of collecting evidence. Two important ways of doing this are experimenting and observing.

An **experiment** is an organized procedure to study something under controlled conditions. For example, the scientist who found the rock by the river might notice that it is lighter in color where it is chipped. The scientist might design an experiment to determine why the rock is a different color on the inside. The scientist could break off a small piece of the inside of the rock and heat it up to see if it becomes the same color as the outside. The scientist would need to use a piece of the same rock that is being studied. A different rock might react differently to heat.

A scientist may use photography to study fast events, such as multiple flashes of lightning.

Rocks, such as this one from the Moon, can be subjected to different conditions in a laboratory.

Observing is the act of noting and recording an event, characteristic, or anything else detected with an instrument or with the senses. A scientist makes observations while performing an experiment. However, some things cannot be studied using experiments. For example, streaks of light called meteors occur when small rocks from outer space hit Earth's atmosphere. A scientist might study meteors by taking pictures of the sky at a time when meteors are likely to occur.

Forming hypotheses and making predictions are two other skills involved in scientific investigations. A **hypothesis** is a tentative explanation for an observation or a scientific problem that can be tested by further investigation. For example, the scientist might make the following hypothesis about the rock from the beach:

The rock is a meteorite, which is a rock that fell to the ground from outer space. The outside of the rock changed color because it was heated up from passing through Earth's atmosphere.

A **prediction** is an expectation of what will be observed or what will happen. To test the hypothesis that the rock's outside is black because it is a meteorite, the scientist might predict that a close examination of the rock will show that it has many characteristics in common with rocks that are already known to be meteorites.

Interpret Results

As scientists investigate, they analyze their evidence, or data, and begin to draw conclusions. **Analyzing data** involves looking at the evidence gathered through observations or experiments and trying to identify any patterns that might exist in the data. Scientists often need to make additional observations or perform more experiments before they are sure of their conclusions. Many times scientists make new predictions or revise their hypotheses.

Scientists use computers to gather and interpret data.

Scientists make images such as this computer drawing of a landscape to help share their results with others.

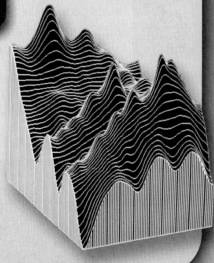

Share Results

An important part of scientific investigation is sharing results of experiments. Scientists read and publish in journals and attend conferences to communicate with other scientists around the world. Sharing data and procedures gives scientists a way to test each others' results. They also share results with the public through newspapers, television, and other media.

The Nature of Technology

When you think of technology, you may think of cars, computers, and cell phones. Imagine having no refrigerator or radio. It's difficult to think of a world without the products of what we call technology. Technology, however, is more than just devices that make our daily activities easier. Technology is the process of using scientific knowledge to design solutions to real-world problems.

Science and Technology

Science and technology go hand in hand. Each depends upon the other. Even a device as simple as a thermometer is designed using knowledge of the ways different materials respond to changes in temperature. In turn, thermometers have allowed scientists to learn more about the world. Greater knowledge of how materials respond to changes in temperature helped engineers to build items such as refrigerators. They have also built thermometers that could be read automatically by computers. New technologies lead to new scientific knowledge and new scientific knowledge leads to even better technologies.

The Process of Technological Design

The process of technological design involves many choices. What, for example, should be done to protect the residents of an area prone to severe storms such as tornadoes and hurricanes? Build stronger homes that can withstand the winds? Try to develop a way to detect the storms long before they occur? Or learn more about hurricanes in order to find new ways to protect people from the dangers? The steps people take to solve the problem depend a great deal on what they already know about the problem as well as what can reasonably be done. As you learn about the steps in the process of technological design, think about the different choices that could be made at each step.

Identify a Need

To study hurricanes, scientists needed to know what happens inside the most dangerous parts of the storm. However, it was not safe for scientists to go near the centers of hurricanes because the winds were too strong and changed direction too fast. Scientists needed a way to measure conditions deep inside the storm without putting themselves in danger.

Design and Develop

One approach was to design a robotic probe to make the measurements. The probe and instruments needed to be strong enough to withstand the fast winds near the center of a hurricane. The scientists also needed a way to send the probe into the storm and to get the data from the instruments quickly.

Scientists designed a device called a dropsonde, which could be dropped from an airplane flying over the hurricane. A dropsonde takes measurements from deep inside the storm and radios data back to the scientists.

Test and Improve

Even good technology can usually be improved. When scientists first used dropsondes, they learned about hurricanes. They also learned what things about the dropsondes worked well and what did not. For example, the scientists wanted better ways to keep track of where the probe moved. Newer dropsondes make use of the Global Positioning System, which is a way of pinpointing any position on Earth by using satellite signals.

Reading Text and Visuals

This book is organized to help you learn. Use these boxed pointers as a path to help you learn and remember the **Big Ideas** and **Key Concepts**.

Take notes.

Use the strategies on the **Getting Ready to Learn** page.

Read the Big Idea.

As you read **Key Concepts** for the chapter, relate them to **the Big Idea**.

CHAPTER

2 Weath

the BIG idea

Some features of weather have predictable patterns.

Key Concepts

SECTION
2.1 The atmosphere's air pressure changes.
Learn how air pressure changes and how it is measured.

SECTION
2.2 The atmosphere has wind patterns.
Learn how wind develops and about different types of wind.

SECTION
2.3 Most clouds form as air rises and cools.
Learn how water changes form in the atmosphere and about different types of clouds.

SECTION
2.4 Water falls to Earth's surface as precipitatio
Learn about the different types of precipitation and about acid rain.

Internet Preview

CLASSZONE.COM
Chapter 2 online resources: Content Review, two Visualizations, four Resource Centers, Math Tutorial, Test Practice

D 40 Unit: Earth's Atmosphere

CHAPTER 2

Getting Ready to Learn

CONCEPT REVIEW

- The Sun supplies the atmosphere's energy.
- Energy moves throughout the atmosphere.
- Matter can be solid, liquid, or gas.

VOCABULARY REVIEW

atmosphere p. 9
altitude p. 10
density p. 10
convection p. 19

CONTENT REVIEW
CLASSZONE.COM
Review concepts and vocabulary.

TAKING NOTES

COMBINATION NOTES

To take notes about a new concept, first make an informal outline of the information. Then make a sketch of the concept and label it so that you can study it later.

VOCABULARY STRATEGY

Place each vocabulary term at the center of a **description wheel**. Write some words describing it on the spokes.

See the Note-Taking Handbook on pages R45–R51.

SCIENCE NOTEBOOK

NOTES

Air pressure
- is the force of air molecules pushing on an area.
- pushes in all directions.

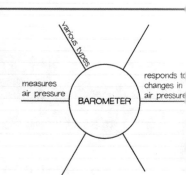

various types

measures air pressure

BAROMETER

responds to changes in air pressure

D 42 Unit: Earth's Atmosphere

KEY CONCEPT

2.1 The atmosphere's air pressure changes.

BEFORE, you learned

- Density is the amount of mass in a given volume of a substance
- Air becomes less dense as altitude increases
- Differences in density cause air to rise and sink

NOW, you will learn

- How the movement of air molecules causes air pressure
- How air pressure varies
- How differences in air pressure affect the atmosphere

VOCABULARY

air pressure p. 43
barometer p. 46

EXPLORE Air Pressure

What does air do to the egg?

PROCEDURE

1. Set a peeled hard-boiled egg in the mouth of a bottle. Make sure that the egg can't slip through.

2. Light the matches. Remove the egg, and drop the matches into the bottle. Quickly replace the egg.

3. Watch carefully, and record your observations.

WHAT DO YOU THINK?

- What happened when you placed the egg back on top of the bottle?
- What can your observations tell you about the air in the bottle?

MATERIALS

- peeled hard-boiled egg
- glass bottle
- 2 wooden matches

Air exerts pressure.

Air molecules move constantly. As they move, they bounce off each other like rubber balls. They also bounce off every surface they hit. As you read this book, billions of air molecules are bouncing off your body, the book, and everything else around you.

Each time an air molecule bounces off an object, it pushes, or exerts a force, on that object. When billions of air molecules bounce off a surface, the force is spread over the area of that surface. **Air pressure** is the force of air molecules pushing on an area. The greater the force, the higher the air pressure. Because air molecules move in all directions, air pressure pushes in all directions.

VOCABULARY
Add a description wheel for *air pressure* to your notebook.

CHECK YOUR READING How does the number of air molecules relate to air pressure?

Chapter 2: **Weather Patterns** 43 D

Reading Text and Visuals

COMBINATION NOTES
Record details about how air pressure varies.

Read one paragraph at a time.

Look for a topic sentence that explains the main idea of the paragraph. Figure out how the details relate to that idea. One paragraph might have several important ideas; you may have to reread to understand.

▼ **REMINDER**
Density is the amount of mass in a given volume of a substance.

Study the visuals.

- Read the title.
- Read all labels and captions.
- Figure out what the picture is showing. Notice colors, arrows, and lines.

Air pressure is related to altitude and density.

The air pressure at any area on Earth depends on the weight of the air above that area. If you hold out your hand, the force of air pushing down on your hand is greater than the weight of a bowling ball. So why don't you feel the air pushing down on your hand? Remember that air pushes in all directions. The pressure of air pushing down is balanced by the pressure of air pushing up from below.

Air pressure decreases as you move higher in the atmosphere. Think of a column of air directly over your body. If you stood at sea level, this column would stretch from where you stood to the top of the atmosphere. The air pressure on your body would be equal to the weight of all the air in the column. But if you stood on a mountain, the column of air would be shorter. With less air above you, the pressure would be lower. At an altitude of 5.5 kilometers (3.4 mi), air pressure is about half what it is at sea level.

Air pressure and density are related. Just as air pressure decreases with altitude, so does the density of air. Notice in the illustration that air molecules at sea level are closer together than air molecules over the mountain. Since the pressure is greater at sea level, the air molecules are pushed closer together. Therefore, the air at sea level is denser than air at high altitudes.

Air Pressure and Density

Above each location on Earth is a column of air that stretches to the top of the atmosphere.

Air pressure and density are lower at a high altitude because a shorter column of air pushes down.

Air pressure and density are higher at sea level because a taller column of air pushes down.

sea level

Doing Labs

To understand science, you have to see it in
action. Doing labs helps you understand
how things really work.

(1) Read the entire lab first.

(2) Form a hypothesis.

(3) Follow the procedure.

(4) Record the data.

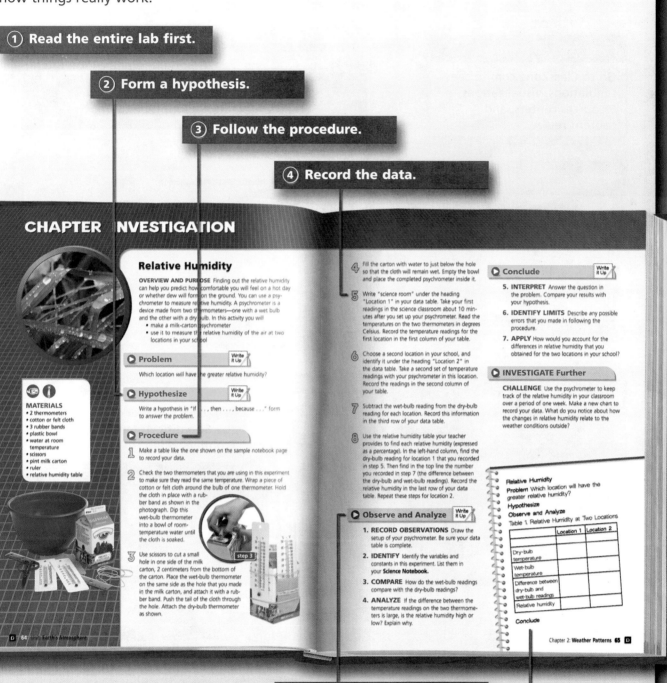

CHAPTER INVESTIGATION

Relative Humidity

OVERVIEW AND PURPOSE Finding out the relative humidity
can help you predict how comfortable you will feel on a hot day
or whether dew will form on the ground. You can use a psychrometer to measure relative humidity. A psychrometer is a
device made from two thermometers—one with a wet bulb
and the other with a dry bulb. In this activity you will
- make a milk-carton psychrometer
- use it to measure the relative humidity of the air at two
locations in your school

▶ Problem   [Write It Up]

Which location will have the greater relative humidity?

▶ Hypothesize   [Write It Up]

Write a hypothesis in "If . . . , then . . . , because . . ." form
to answer the problem.

MATERIALS
- 2 thermometers
- cotton or felt cloth
- 3 rubber bands
- plastic bowl
- water at room
  temperature
- scissors
- pint milk carton
- ruler
- relative humidity table

▶ Procedure

1. Make a table like the one shown on the sample notebook page
to record your data.

2. Check the two thermometers that you are using in this experiment
to make sure they read the same temperature. Wrap a piece of
cotton or felt cloth around the bulb of one thermometer. Hold
the cloth in place with a rub-
ber band as shown in the
photograph. Dip this
wet-bulb thermometer
into a bowl of room-
temperature water until
the cloth is soaked.

3. Use scissors to cut a small
hole in one side of the milk
carton, 2 centimeters from the bottom of
the carton. Place the wet-bulb thermometer
on the same side as the hole that you made
in the milk carton, and attach it with a rubber band. Push the tail of the cloth through
the hole. Attach the dry-bulb thermometer
as shown.

step 3

4. Fill the carton with water to just below the hole
so that the cloth will remain wet. Empty the bowl
and place the completed psychrometer inside it.

5. Write "science room" under the heading
"Location 1" in your data table. Take your first
readings in the science classroom about 10 minutes after you set up your psychrometer. Read the
temperatures on the two thermometers in degrees
Celsius. Record the temperature readings for the
first location in the first column of your table.

6. Choose a second location in your school, and
identify it under the heading "Location 2" in
the data table. Take a second set of temperature
readings with your psychrometer in this location.
Record the readings in the second column of
your table.

7. Subtract the wet-bulb reading from the dry-bulb
reading for each location. Record this information
in the third row of your data table.

8. Use the relative humidity table your teacher
provides to find each relative humidity (expressed
as a percentage). In the left-hand column, find the
dry-bulb reading for location 1 that you recorded
in step 5. Then find in the top line the number
you recorded in step 7 (the difference between
the dry-bulb and wet-bulb readings). Record the
relative humidity in the last row of your data
table. Repeat these steps for location 2.

▶ Observe and Analyze   [Write It Up]

1. **RECORD OBSERVATIONS** Draw the
setup of your psychrometer. Be sure your data
table is complete.

2. **IDENTIFY** Identify the variables and
constants in this experiment. List them in
your **Science Notebook.**

3. **COMPARE** How do the wet-bulb readings
compare with the dry-bulb readings?

4. **ANALYZE** If the difference between the
temperature readings on the two thermometers is large, is the relative humidity high or
low? Explain why.

▶ Conclude   [Write It Up]

5. **INTERPRET** Answer the question in
the problem. Compare your results with
your hypothesis.

6. **IDENTIFY LIMITS** Describe any possible
errors that you made in following the
procedure.

7. **APPLY** How would you account for the
differences in relative humidity that you
obtained for the two locations in your school?

▶ INVESTIGATE Further

CHALLENGE Use the psychrometer to keep
track of the relative humidity in your classroom
over a period of one week. Make a new chart to
record your data. What do you notice about how
the changes in relative humidity relate to the
weather conditions outside?

Relative Humidity
Problem Which location will have the
greater relative humidity?
Hypothesize
Observe and Analyze
Table 1. Relative Humidity at Two Locations

	Location 1	Location 2
Dry-bulb temperature		
Wet-bulb temperature		
Difference between dry-bulb and wet-bulb readings		
Relative humidity		

Conclude

Chapter 2: Weather Patterns **65**

(5) Analyze your results.

(6) Write your lab report.

Using Technology

The Internet is a great source of information about up-to-date science. The ClassZone Website and SciLinks have exciting sites for you to explore. Video clips and simulations can make science come alive.

Look for red banners.

Go to **ClassZone.com** to see simulations, visualizations, resources centers, and content review.

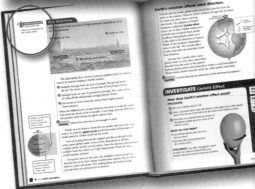

Watch the videos.

See science at work in the **Scientific American Frontiers video.**

Look up SciLinks.

Go to **scilinks.org** to explore the topic.

Atmospheric Pressure and Winds **Code: MDL010**

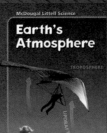

Earth's Atmosphere
Contents Overview

D

Unit Features

1 Earth's Changing Atmosphere   6

 the **BIG** idea

Earth's atmosphere is a blanket of
gases that supports and protects life.

2 Weather Patterns   40

the **BIG** idea

Some features of weather have predictable patterns.

3 Weather Fronts and Storms   76

the **BIG** idea

The interaction of air masses causes
changes in weather.

4 Climate and Climate Change   114

the **BIG** idea

Climates are long-term weather patterns
that may change over time.

FRONTIERS in Science

SCIENTIFIC AMERICAN FRONTIERS

"Dust Busting" is a 10-minute video that takes viewers underwater in the Caribbean Sea to observe a mysterious coral disease. Alan Alda introduces the work of three scientists who find evidence that the coral die-off links to dust storms in Northwest Africa.

The scientists collect evidence to support their hypothesis that African dust caused the coral disease. First, diseased coral samples from six islands reveal the same threadlike fungus. Second, the fungus is gene-mapped and found to match an African strain of the soil fungus *aspergillus*. Third, the scientists use space shuttle photography to view huge storm clouds that carried soil across the Atlantic. Fourth, the scientists filter the Caribbean air for dust, and again find the same *aspergillus*.

Finally, scientists drill core samples of boulder coral representing 30 years' worth of growth. In the lab, the core samples are dissolved, leaving a residue. They find high soil content trapped in the coral that lived during the peak years of the dust storms.

National Science Education Standards

A.1–7 Abilities Necessary to Do Scientific Inquiry

A.9.a–b, A.9.d–g Understandings about Scientific Inquiry

F.5.e Science and Technology in Society

G.1.a–b Science as a Human Endeavor

G.2.a, G.2.c Nature of Science

FRONTIERS in Science

DUST in the AIR

What happens around this beautiful island in the Caribbean when dust from an African storm travels thousands of kilometers across the ocean?

SCIENTIFIC AMERICAN FRONTIERS

Learn more about the scientists studying dust in the atmosphere. See the video "Dust Busters."

D 2 Unit: Earth's Atmosphere

ADDITIONAL RESOURCES

Technology Resources

 Scientific American Frontiers Video: *Dust Busting:* 11-minute video segment introduces the unit.

 ClassZone.com
CAREER LINK, careers in ecology

Guide student viewing and comprehension of the video:

 Video Teaching Guide, pp. 1–2; Video Viewing Guide, p. 3; Video Wrap-Up, p. 4

Scientific American Frontiers Video Guide, pp. 31–34

Unit projects procedures and rubrics:

 Unit Projects, pp. 5–10

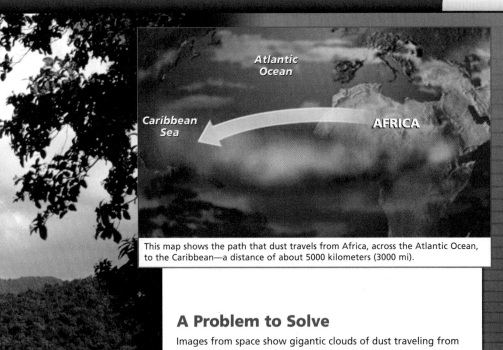

Atlantic
Ocean

Caribbean
Sea

AFRICA

This map shows the path that dust travels from Africa, across the Atlantic Ocean, to the Caribbean—a distance of about 5000 kilometers (3000 mi).

A Problem to Solve

Images from space show gigantic clouds of dust traveling from Africa thousands of kilometers across the Atlantic Ocean. Weather reports in the Caribbean warn listeners about African dust storms. Coral and manatees in Caribbean waters show signs of disease. Are these events connected?

A

Each year, natural events and human activities together send as much as 2 billion metric tons of material into the skies. Once dust enters the atmosphere, it moves with the other materials in the air.

But how do Earth's surface processes and the movement of air relate to diseased coral? Teams of scientists studied diseases in living things around the Caribbean. In addition, they examined satellite photographs and recorded when dust storms occurred. After analyzing these data, they hypothesized that materials in African dust were affecting living things in the Caribbean.

B

Satellite images show us how far dust can travel in the atmosphere. Experiments on air samples let scientists look at dust up close. Tests reveal that atmospheric dust includes many substances, including living material. As often happens in science, this new knowledge raises more questions. Could the living material in dust grow in a distant location? Could a fungus that lives in African soil end up in Caribbean waters?

Frontiers in Science 3   **D**

- Examine some effects of dust storms.
- Determine how dust particles in the air can be analyzed.
- Design an experiment to explore atmospheric changes.

Remind students that frontiers are undeveloped fields for discovery or research, and that the "Dust Busting" video shows real scientists gathering and analyzing data to ask questions and find answers. Have students look at the visuals and title on the first two pages and predict what questions the scientists are trying to answer.

INSTRUCT

Scientific Process

After students have read p. 3, ask: What problem did scientists attempt to solve? *Could dust from Africa cause disease in Caribbean coral?* What scientific processes or skills did scientists use to solve the problem? *ask a question, hypothesize*

Teach from Visuals

Ask students how the photographs of dust storms support the scientists' hypothesis. *They show that dust from the African storm did reach the Caribbean.*

DIFFERENTIATE INSTRUCTION

? More Reading Support

A What organisms are diseased in the Caribbean? *coral and manatees*

B What may have caused the diseases? *dust from Africa*

Below Level Have students use a globe or world map to locate the Caribbean Islands and the western coast of Africa. Have students trace the path of the dust across the Atlantic Ocean.

Scientific Process

Ask students to identify the parts of the scientific process described on this page. *investigate and interpret results*

Data Collection

Have students describe several ways the scientists collected data to support their hypothesis. *The scientists collected air samples during dust storms in the Caribbean, collected dust from the air, filtered air to trap dust, placed dust on nutrients, and looked for growth.*

Interpret Results

Make a table on the board using the following heads: "Helpful effects" and "Harmful effects." Have students fill in the effects of the African dust in the proper column. For guidance, tell them to use both the visuals and text. Point out that the cause is the dust from Africa; they are now evaluating its effects.

Helpful effects	Harmful effects
bits of metal: iron nourishes plants	fungi: cause disease in coral, sea fans
	bacteria: cause rapid growth of red algae, which hurts manatees, others

Integrate the Sciences

Aspergillus fungi belong to a group known as imperfect fungi. There are several species. *Aspergillus niger* is a fuzzy black type that grows on old jams or jellies. *Aspergillus flavus* grows on stale bread or stored grains. Some species of *aspergillus* are used to make antibiotics.

bromeliad plant

dust storm

Atlantic Ocean

AFRICA

sea fan

Wind-borne dust provides nutrients for this bromeliad plant growing on a tree trunk high in the rain forest of South America.

The huge dust storm shown in this satellite image carries both destructive fungus spores and life-sustaining nutrients across the Atlantic.

Fungus spores carried on dust particles have infected sea-fan corals growing on this reef near the island of St. John in the Caribbean Sea.

Answers Hidden in Dust

To explore these questions, scientists in the Caribbean gather air samples during dust storms. They collect dust from high in the air and from locations closer to Earth's surface. To collect the samples, scientists pull air through a paper filter, trapping the dust. Once they have caught the dust, the scientists are ready to perform tests to see what's really in the tiny particles.

? **C**

In the laboratory, researchers place dust samples on top of nutrients in petri dishes. Then they see if anything in the dust grows. Recent studies have shown that dust samples collected over the Caribbean contained African fungi and bacteria. More importantly, scientists saw that, even after their long voyage through the atmosphere, the living materials were able to grow.

? **D**

SCIENTIFIC AMERICAN FRONTIERS

View the "Dust Busters" segment of your *Scientific American Frontiers* video to learn about the detective work that went into solving the mystery of sea-fan disease.

IN THIS SCENE FROM THE VIDEO ▶ Biologist Ginger Garrison shows diseased coral to host Alan Alda.

MYSTERY SOLVED Sea fans are an important part of the Caribbean coral-reef community, but in the 1970s they began to die off. Recently marine biologist Garriet Smith was surprised to discover that a common soil fungus, called aspergillus, was

killing the sea fans. But how could a soil fungus reach an undersea reef?

The answer came from geologist Gene Shinn, who knew that global winds carry dust from Africa to the Caribbean. When Shinn read about Smith's research, he hypothesized that aspergillus might be arriving with African dust. Shinn teamed up with Smith and biologist Ginger Garrison to test the hypothesis. They collected Caribbean air samples during an African dust event and cultured dust from the samples. Aspergillus grew in their very first cultures.

DIFFERENTIATE INSTRUCTION

? **More Reading Support**

C How did scientists catch the African dust? *by pulling air through a paper filter*

D Why did scientists put the dust on top of nutrients? *to see what grew*

English Learners Use this opportunity to remind students of the meaning of scientific process words such as *hypothesize* and *analyze*. Also, review potentially unfamiliar terms or phrases such as *air samples, dust samples,* and *biologist*. In addition to reading these words and phrases in the text, students will hear them in the video.

Dust from Africa also contains tiny bits of metals, such as iron. The soil and atmosphere in the Caribbean are enriched by iron carried in African dust. Beautiful plants called bromeliads get the iron they need directly from the atmosphere.

Unfortunately, some of the materials found in the dust samples could be harmful to living things, such as manatees and corals. One of the fungi found in Caribbean dust samples is *Aspergillus sydowii,* which may cause diseases in sea fans and other corals. In addition, the dust contains bacteria that may speed the growth of toxic red algae, which can be harmful to manatees and other ocean animals.

Strong Connections

Dust storms affect the entire planet. On April 6–8, 2001, soils from the Gobi Desert in Mongolia and China blew into the air, creating a massive dust cloud. Satellite images showed the cloud traveling eastward. A few days later people in the western United States saw the sky turn a chalky white.

Such observations of atmospheric dust show us how events in one part of the planet can affect living and nonliving things thousands of kilometers away in ways we might not have imagined.

UNANSWERED Questions

Tiny particles of atmospheric dust may have huge effects. Yet the more we learn about the makeup and nature of dust, the more questions we have.

- How do dust storms affect human health?
- What can dust tell us about climate change?
- How can we use information about dust storms to predict climate change?
- How do materials in dust change ecosystems?

UNIT PROJECTS

As you study this unit, work alone or with a group on one of these projects.

TV News Report

Prepare a brief news report on recent dust storms, using visuals and a script.

- Research dust storms that have occurred recently. Find out how they were related to the weather.
- Copy or print visuals, and write and practice delivering your report. Then make your presentation.

Map the Dust

Make a map showing how dust arrives in your area or another location.

- Find out what the dust contains and how it moved there. Collect information from atlases, the Internet, newspapers, and magazines.
- Prepare your map, including all the areas you need to show. Include a key, a title, and a compass rose.

Design an Experiment

Design an experiment to explore how the atmosphere has changed in the past or how it is changing today. Research the forms of evidence scientists gather about the state of our atmosphere.

- Pick one question to investigate in an experiment. Write a hypothesis.
- List and assemble materials for your experiment. Create a data table and write up your procedure.
- Demonstrate or describe your experiment for the class.

 **CAREER CENTER**
CLASSZONE.COM
Learn about careers in meteorology.

Have students read the questions and think of some of their own. Remind them that scientists always end up with more questions—that inquiry is the driving force of science.

- With the class, generate on the board a list of new questions.
- Students can add to the list after they watch the Scientific American Frontiers Video.
- Students can use the list as a springboard for choosing their Unit Projects.

UNIT PROJECTS

Encourage students to pick the project that most appeals to them. Point out that each is long-term and will take several weeks to complete. You might group or pair students to work on projects, and in some cases guide student choice. Some of the projects have student choice built into them. Each project has two worksheet pages, including a rubric. Use the pages to guide students through criteria, process, and schedule.

R Unit Projects, pp. 5–10

REVISIT concepts introduced in this article:

Chapter 1
- the atmosphere and life, pp. 9–15
- air motion, pp. 16–21

Chapter 2
- global wind patterns, pp. 47–55

Chapter 3
- movement of air masses and storm systems, pp. 79–91

Chapter 4
- weather patterns, pp. 117–123

DIFFERENTIATE INSTRUCTION

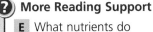 **More Reading Support**

E What nutrients do plants obtain from the African dust? *iron*

F The dust contains bacteria that can speed the growth of what? *toxic red algae*

Differentiate Unit Projects Projects are appropriate for varying abilities. Allow students to choose the ones that interest them most. Encourage them to vary the products they produce throughout the year.

Below Level Encourage students to try "TV News Report."

Advanced Encourage students to complete "Design an Experiment."

1 Earth's Changing Atmosphere

Earth Science
UNIFYING PRINCIPLES

PRINCIPLE 1
Heat energy inside Earth and radiation from the Sun provide energy for Earth's processes.

PRINCIPLE 2
Physical forces, such as gravity, affect the movement of all matter on Earth and throughout the universe.

PRINCIPLE 3
Matter and energy move among Earth's rocks and soil, atmosphere, waters, and living things.

PRINCIPLE 4
Earth has changed over time and continues to change.

Unit: Earth's Atmosphere
BIG IDEAS

CHAPTER 1
Earth's Changing Atmosphere
Earth's atmosphere is a blanket of gases that supports and protects life.

CHAPTER 2
Weather Patterns
Some features of weather have predictable patterns.

CHAPTER 3
Weather Fronts and Storms
The interaction of air masses causes changes in weather.

CHAPTER 4
Climate and Climate Change
Climates are long-term weather patterns that may change over time.

CHAPTER 1
KEY CONCEPTS

SECTION 1.1

Earth's atmosphere supports life.
1. The atmosphere makes life on Earth possible.
2. Natural processes modify the atmosphere.

SECTION 1.2

The Sun supplies the atmosphere's energy.
1. Energy from the Sun heats the atmosphere.
2. The atmosphere moves energy.
3. The atmosphere has temperature layers.

SECTION 1.3

Gases in the atmosphere absorb radiation.
1. Gases can absorb and give off radiation.
2. The ozone layer protects life from harmful radiation.
3. The greenhouse effect keeps Earth warm.

SECTION 1.4

Human activities affect the atmosphere.
1. Human activity can cause air pollution.
2. Human activities are increasing greenhouse gases.
3. Human activities produce chemicals that destroy the ozone layer.

The Big Idea Flow Chart is available on p. T1 in the **UNIT TRANSPARENCY BOOK.**

Previewing Content

1.1 Earth's atmosphere supports life. pp. 9–15

1. The atmosphere makes life on Earth possible.

The **atmosphere** is a whole layer of air that surrounds Earth. It supports and protects life in several ways, such as by

- absorbing harmful radiation
- maintaining Earth's temperature
- providing elements essential for life

The atmosphere has chemical and physical properties. For example, the density of the atmosphere decreases with altitude. **Density** is the amount of mass in a given volume of a substance. **Altitude** is the distance above sea level. The composition of the atmosphere is shown in the table below.

Composition of Lower Atmosphere	
Gas	**Percent**
Nitrogen	78.08
Oxygen	20.94
Argon	0.93
Carbon Dioxide	0.04
Other elements	0.01
Water Vapor	0–4*

*The amount of water vapor in the atmosphere at any given moment varies greatly, more so than other gases. As such, water vapor does not factor into the sum total of percentages in this table.

2. Natural processes modify the atmosphere.

Living things take part in **cycles,** or repeating processes, of gas exchange with the atmosphere. Three important cycles that affect the atmosphere are the **carbon cycle,** the **nitrogen cycle,** and the **water cycle.**

In the carbon cycle, plants take in carbon dioxide from the air and release oxygen during photosynthesis. During respiration, animals use oxygen and release carbon dioxide and water into the air. In the nitrogen cycle, nitrogen-fixing bacteria convert atmospheric nitrogen into solid forms and solutions. Living things use these forms of nitrogen, and when they decay, they release nitrogen into the soil. It eventually makes its way back into the air. In the water cycle, water is constantly circulated between Earth's surface and the atmosphere by evaporation, condensation, and precipitation.

1.2 The Sun supplies the atmosphere's energy. pp. 16–21

1. Energy from the Sun heats the atmosphere.

Most energy on Earth comes from the Sun. Some of this energy takes the form of visible light. Visible light is a type of radiation. **Radiation** is energy that moves across distances in the form of electromagnetic waves. On average, about 30% of incoming solar energy is reflected by clouds, the atmosphere, and Earth's surface. Therefore, about 70% of solar radiation is absorbed and becomes different forms of energy.

2. The atmosphere moves energy.

Energy moves by radiation, conduction, and convection. Earth's surface, heated by the Sun, radiates energy that is absorbed by certain atmospheric gases, which then warm the air. **Conduction** is the transfer of energy from one substance to another through direct contact. **Convection** is the transfer of energy from place to place by the motion of heated gas or liquid. Use the diagram below when discussing the transfer of energy.

Radiation, conduction, and convection move energy from place to place.

warm air
- Molecules move faster.
- Molecules are farther apart.
- Warm air is less dense.
- Warm air carries more energy than cool air.

cool air
- Molecules move slower.
- Molecules are closer together.
- Cool air is more dense.

1 Radiation Sunlight warms the ground.

2 Conduction The warm ground heats the air.

3 Convection Cool, dense air sinks downward and pushes warm air out of the way. Warm air carries energy upward.

3. The atmosphere has temperature layers.

The atmosphere's temperature changes with altitude. The pattern of these temperature changes defines atmospheric layers. Starting from Earth's surface, the layers are

- the troposphere, where temperatures decrease with altitude
- the stratosphere, where temperatures increase due to the presence of ozone, a gas that absorbs ultraviolet radiation
- the mesosphere, where temperatures again decrease with altitude
- the thermosphere, where temperatures rise

Common Misconceptions

MATTER IN CYCLES Students may focus on events in a cycle and not recognize the cycling of matter in an ecosystem. They may think matter is being created and destroyed rather than being moved and transformed. For example, students may not know

 MISCONCEPTION DATABASE
CLASSZONE.COM Background on student misconceptions

that a plant's mass increases mostly due to matter from carbon dioxide gas in the atmosphere.

T E This misconception is addressed on p. 12.

Previewing Content

1.3 Gases in the atmosphere absorb radiation. pp. 22–26

1. Gases can absorb and give off radiation.

Different gases in the atmosphere absorb and emit different types of radiation. In the stratosphere, ozone absorbs **ultraviolet radiation,** which has more energy per wave than visible light. In the troposphere, the following gases absorb and emit **infrared radiation,** which has less energy per wave than visible light:

- carbon dioxide
- methane
- water vapor
- nitrous oxide

2. The ozone layer protects life from harmful radiation.

Ozone (O_3) is a gas with molecules made of three oxygen atoms. In the stratosphere, ozone and atmospheric oxygen (O_2) break apart and form again in a complex, yet balanced, cycle. The ozone layer protects life on Earth by absorbing harmful ultraviolet (UV) rays. Exposure to UV radiation can cause sunburn, skin cancer, and damaged eyesight. The radiation can also harm crops and materials such as plastic or paint.

3. The greenhouse effect keeps Earth warm.

Water vapor, carbon dioxide, methane, nitrous oxide, and certain other gases keep Earth warm by absorbing and giving off infrared radiation. This process is known as the **greenhouse effect,** even though greenhouses are different because they mostly prevent convection. The gases themselves are collectively known as **greenhouse gases.** The greenhouse effect, which takes place mainly in the troposphere, involves the following steps:

- Solar radiation heats Earth's surface, which grows warm and emits infrared radiation.
- Greenhouse gases absorb some of this infrared radiation and allow the rest to pass into space.
- Greenhouse gases then emit infrared radiation. Some is absorbed by the ground, while some is lost to space.

1.4 Human activities affect the atmosphere. pp. 27–35

1. Human activity can cause air pollution.

Air pollution consists of smoke and other harmful materials that are added to the air. The two components of air pollution are gases and particulates. The gases include methane, ozone, carbon monoxide, sulfur oxides, and nitrogen oxides.
Particulates are tiny particles or droplets that are mixed in the air; they include dust, dirt, pollen, and sea salt. Air pollution can come from natural sources, such as volcanoes, or from human activities, such as the burning of fossil fuels. **Fossil fuels** are energy sources formed from the remains of ancient plants and animals. Air pollution can cause health problems and environmental damage.

2. Human activities are increasing greenhouse gases.

When levels of greenhouse gases increase, global temperatures increase. The burning of fossil fuels and other human activities have increased atmospheric carbon dioxide. Increased greenhouse gases may lead to global warming, which is an increase in Earth's temperatures.

3. Human activities produce chemicals that destroy the ozone layer.

Chlorofluorocarbons (CFCs) are chemicals that were once widely used in cooling systems, spray cans, and foam packing. CFCs react with sunlight and release chlorine, which destroys ozone. Substitute chemicals used today destroy ozone more slowly than chlorine.
The chemical reactions in the stratosphere that produce and destroy ozone depend on weather. Much of the ozone over the South Pole is destroyed in certain seasons, resulting in the so-called ozone hole. Ozone is also destroyed in other locations, though less dramatically.

Common Misconceptions

OZONE LAYER Students may hold the misconception that there are huge holes or gaps in the ozone layer. In fact, it is more correct to say that the ozone layer is thinning. Although not technically a "hole," this thinning still allows harmful ultraviolet rays to reach Earth's surface.

 This misconception is addressed on p. 32.

MISCONCEPTION DATABASE
CLASSZONE.COM Background on student misconceptions

EXPLORE (the BIG idea)

How Heavy Is Paper? p. 7 Students are introduced to the concept that air has substance.	**TIME** 10 minutes **MATERIALS** ruler, sheet of paper
How Does Heating Affect Air? p. 7 Students investigate the effects of changes in air temperature.	**TIME** 10 minutes **MATERIALS** balloon, small bottle, 2 bowls, water, ice
Internet Activity: Atmosphere, p. 7 Students compare the height of Earth's atmosphere to different features.	**TIME** 20 minutes **MATERIALS** computer with Internet access

labs and generate alternative labs.

SECTION		
1.1	**EXPLORE Air Resistance,** p. 9 Students observe a falling object in order to recognize the effect of air resistance.	**TIME** 10 minutes **MATERIALS** metal washer, coffee filter, tape
	INVESTIGATE Gas in the Air, p. 10 Students predict the effect exhaling will have on limewater.	**TIME** 10 minutes **MATERIALS** limewater, 2 jars, spoon

SECTION		
1.2	**INVESTIGATE Solar Radiation,** p. 17 Students measure the effect of reflection on temperature in order to understand solar radiation.	**TIME** 25 minutes **MATERIALS** 2 paper cups, clear plastic wrap, white paper, tape, 2 short thermometers, watch

SECTION		
1.3	**EXPLORE Radiation,** p. 22 Students investigate the energy of visible light and infrared radiation.	**TIME** 10 minutes **MATERIALS** lamp
	INVESTIGATE Greenhouse Gases, p. 24 Students graph the changing levels of carbon dioxide. **R** CO_2 Table Sheet, p. 42	**TIME** 30 minutes **MATERIALS** CO_2 Table Sheet, graph sheet, regular pencil, red pencil

SECTION		
1.4	**EXPLORE Air Pollution,** p. 27 Students will observe smoke from a burning candle to find out about air pollution.	**TIME** 10 minutes **MATERIALS** candle in holder, matches
	CHAPTER INVESTIGATION Observing Particulates, pp. 34–35 Students identify and measure air particulates at different locations and use the information to analyze air pollution trends.	**TIME** 40 minutes **MATERIALS** 2 index cards, ruler, scissors, transparent packing tape, magnifying glass, white paper, black paper, graph paper, calculator

R **Additional INVESTIGATION,** Oxygen in the Air, A, B, & C, pp. 71–79; Teacher Instructions, pp. 284–285

Previewing Chapter Resources

| | INTEGRATED TECHNOLOGY | | LABS AND ACTIVITIES |

CHAPTER 1
Earth's Changing Atmosphere

 CLASSZONE.COM
- eEdition Plus
- EasyPlanner Plus
- Misconception Database
- Content Review
- Test Practice
- Visualizations
- Resource Centers
- Internet Activity: Atmosphere
- Math Tutorial

 CD-ROMS
- eEdition
- EasyPlanner
- Power Presentations
- Content Review
- Lab Generator
- Test Generator

 AUDIO CDS
- Audio Readings
- Audio Readings in Spanish

 SCILINKS.ORG
SCI*LINKS*

 EXPLORE the Big Idea, p. 7
- How Heavy Is Paper?
- How Does Heating Affect Air?
- Internet Activity: Atmosphere

UNIT RESOURCE BOOK
- Family Letter, p. vii
- Spanish Family Letter, p. viii
- Unit Projects, pp. 5–10

Lab Generator CD-ROM
Generate customized labs.

SECTION
1.1 Earth's atmosphere supports life.
pp. 9–15

Time: 2 periods (1 block)

 Lesson Plan, pp. 11–12

 UNIT TRANSPARENCY BOOK
- Big Idea Flow Chart, p. T1
- Daily Vocabulary Scaffolding, p. T2
- Note-Taking Model, p. T3
- 3-Minute Warm-Up, p. T4
- "Cycles and the Atmosphere" Visual, p. T6

 • EXPLORE Air Resistance, p. 9
- INVESTIGATE Gas in the Air, p. 10
- Connecting Sciences, p. 15

UNIT RESOURCE BOOK
- Datasheet, Gas in the Air, p. 20
- Additional INVESTIGATION, Oxygen in the Air, A, B, & C, pp. 71–79

SECTION
1.2 The Sun supplies the atmosphere's energy.
pp. 16–21

Time: 2 periods (1 block)

 Lesson Plan, pp. 22–23

 VISUALIZATION, Radiation, Conduction, and Convection

 UNIT TRANSPARENCY BOOK
- Daily Vocabulary Scaffolding, p. T2
- 3-Minute Warm-Up, p. T4

 INVESTIGATE Solar Radiation, p. 17

UNIT RESOURCE BOOK
Datasheet, Solar Radiation, p. 31

SECTION
1.3 Gases in the atmosphere absorb radiation.
pp. 22–26

Time: 2 periods (1 block)

 Lesson Plan, pp. 33–34

 • **VISUALIZATION,** Greenhouse Effect
- **MATH TUTORIAL**

 UNIT TRANSPARENCY BOOK
- Daily Vocabulary Scaffolding, p. T2
- 3-Minute Warm-Up, p. T5

 • EXPLORE Radiation, p. 22
- INVESTIGATE Greenhouse Gases, p. 24
- Math in Science, p. 26

UNIT RESOURCE BOOK
- CO_2 Table Sheet, p. 42
- Datasheet, Greenhouse Gases, p. 43
- Math Support & Practice, pp. 60–61

SECTION
1.4 Human activities affect the atmosphere.
pp. 27–35

Time: 4 periods (2 blocks)

 Lesson Plan, pp. 45–46

 RESOURCE CENTER, Ozone Layer

 UNIT TRANSPARENCY BOOK
- Big Idea Flow Chart, p. T1
- Daily Vocabulary Scaffolding, p. T2
- 3-Minute Warm-Up, p. T5
- Chapter Outline, pp. T7–T8

 • EXPLORE Air Pollution, p. 27
- CHAPTER INVESTIGATION, Observing Particulates, pp. 34–35

UNIT RESOURCE BOOK
CHAPTER INVESTIGATION, Observing Particulates, A, B, & C, pp. 62–70

 5E Unit: Earth's Atmosphere

KEY TO ICONS

 CD/CD-ROM

 INTERNET

 Pupil Edition

 Teacher Edition

UNIT RESOURCE BOOK

UNIT TRANSPARENCY BOOK

UNIT ASSESSMENT BOOK

SPANISH ASSESSMENT BOOK

SCIENCE TOOLKIT

READING AND REINFORCEMENT

ASSESSMENT

STANDARDS

- Frame Game, B26–27
- Supporting Main Ideas, C42
- Daily Vocabulary Scaffolding, H1–8

 UNIT RESOURCE BOOK
- Vocabulary Practice, pp. 57–58
- Decoding Support, p. 59
- Summarizing the Chapter, pp. 80–81

 Audio Readings CD
Listen to Pupil Edition.

 Audio Readings in Spanish CD
Listen to Pupil Edition in Spanish.

 • Chapter Review, pp. 37–38
- Standardized Test Practice, p. 39

 UNIT ASSESSMENT BOOK
- Diagnostic Test, pp. 1–2
- Chapter Test, A, B, & C, pp. 7–18
- Alternative Assessment, pp. 19–20

 Spanish Chapter Test, pp. 173–176

 Test Generator CD-ROM
Generate customized tests.

 Lab Generator CD-ROM
Rubrics for Labs

National Standards
A.2–8, A.9.a–b, A.9.e–f, D.1.f, D.1.h, D.3.d, F.3.b, G.1.b

See p. 6 for the standards.

 UNIT RESOURCE BOOK
- Reading Study Guides, pp. 13–16
- Spanish Reading Study Guide, pp. 17–18
- Challenge and Extension, p. 19
- Reinforcing Key Concepts, p. 21

 Ongoing Assessment, pp. 9–14

 Section 1.1 Review, p. 14

 UNIT ASSESSMENT BOOK
Section 1.1 Quiz, p. 3

National Standards
A.2–7, A.9.a–b, A.9.e–f, D.1.f, D.1.h, G.1.b

 UNIT RESOURCE BOOK
- Reading Study Guides, pp. 24–27
- Spanish Reading Study Guide, pp. 28–29
- Challenge and Extension, p. 30
- Reinforcing Key Concepts, p. 32

 Ongoing Assessment, pp. 16, 18–21

 Section 1.2 Review, p. 21

 UNIT ASSESSMENT BOOK
Section 1.2 Quiz, p. 4

National Standards
A.2–7, A.9.a–b, A.9.e–f, D.1.h, D.3.d, G.1.b

 UNIT RESOURCE BOOK
- Reading Study Guides, pp. 35–38
- Spanish Reading Study Guide, pp. 39–40
- Challenge and Extension, p. 41
- Reinforcing Key Concepts, p. 44
- Challenge Reading, pp. 55–56

 Ongoing Assessment, pp. 22–23

 Section 1.3 Review, p. 25

 UNIT ASSESSMENT BOOK
Section 1.3 Quiz, p. 5

National Standards
A.2–8, A.9.a–c, A.9.e–f, D.1.h, G.1.b

 UNIT RESOURCE BOOK
- Reading Study Guides, pp. 47–50
- Spanish Reading Study Guide, pp. 51–52
- Challenge and Extension, p. 53
- Reinforcing Key Concepts, p. 54

 Ongoing Assessment, pp. 27–33

 Section 1.4 Review, p. 33

 UNIT ASSESSMENT BOOK
Section 1.4 Quiz, p. 6

National Standards
A.2–8, A.9.a–c, A.9.e–f, F.3.b, G.1.b

CHAPTER INVESTIGATION

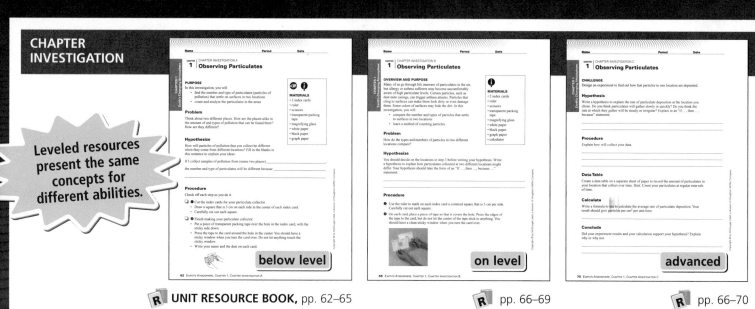

Leveled resources present the same concepts for different abilities.

UNIT RESOURCE BOOK, pp. 62–65

pp. 66–69

pp. 66–70

READING STUDY GUIDE

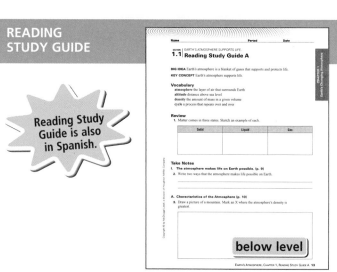
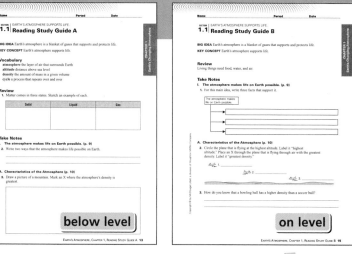
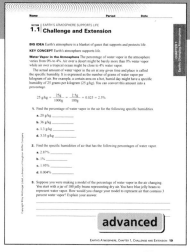

Reading Study Guide is also in Spanish.

UNIT RESOURCE BOOK, pp. 13–14

pp. 15–16

p. 19

CHAPTER TEST

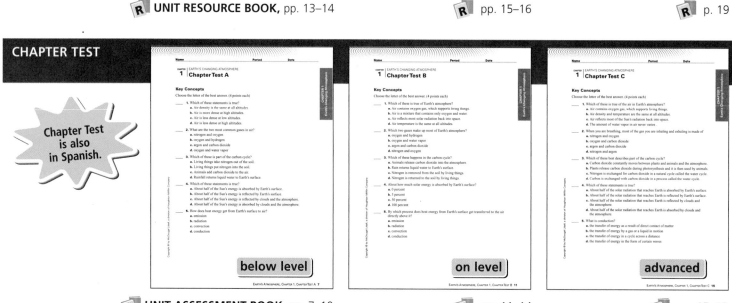

Chapter Test is also in Spanish.

UNIT ASSESSMENT BOOK, pp. 7–10

pp. 11–14

pp. 15–18

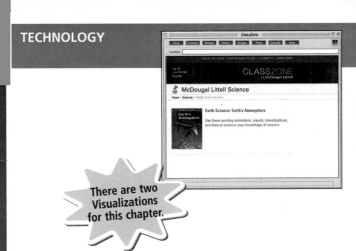

CLASSZONE.COM   CD/CD-ROMS   CLASSZONE.COM

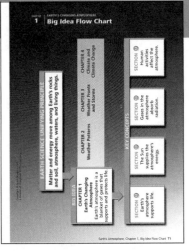

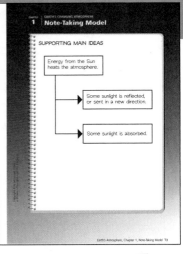

T UNIT TRANSPARENCY BOOK, p. T1   **T** p. T3   **T** p. T6

Reinforcing Key Concepts for each section

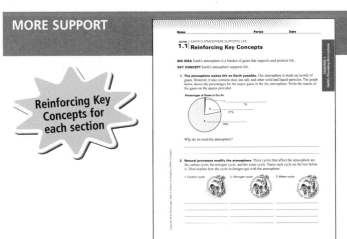

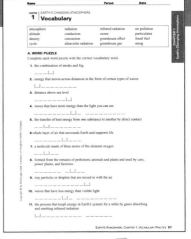

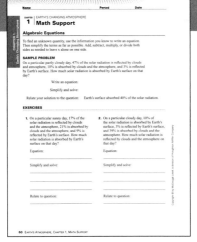

R UNIT RESOURCE BOOK, p. 21   **R** pp. 57–58   **R** p. 60

Chapter 1: **Earth's Changing Atmosphere 5H** **D**

INTRODUCE

the BIG idea

Have students look at the photograph of the girl flying a kite and discuss how the question in the box links to the Big Idea. For further discussion:

- What does air look like?
- What things in the sky depend on air?
- What things on the ground depend on air?

National Science Education Standards

Content

D.1.f Water, which covers the majority of Earth's surface, circulates through the crust, oceans, and atmosphere in what is known as the "water cycle."

D.1.h The atmosphere is a mixture of nitrogen, oxygen, and trace gases that include water vapor. The atmosphere has different properties at different elevations.

D.3.d The Sun is the major source of energy for phenomena on Earth's surface, such as growth of plants, winds, ocean currents, and the water cycle.

F.3.b Human activities can affect the speed of natural changes.

Process

A.2–8 Design and conduct an investigation; use tools to gather and interpret data; use evidence to describe, predict, explain, model; think critically to make relationships between evidence and explanation; recognize different explanations and predictions; communicate scientific procedures and explanations; use mathematics.

A.9.a–c, A.9.e–f Understand scientific inquiry by using different investigations, methods, mathematics, and explanations based on logic, evidence, and skepticism.

G.1.b Science requires different abilities.

CHAPTER

Earth's Changing Atmosphere

the BIG idea

Earth's atmosphere is a blanket of gases that supports and protects life.

What will make this kite soar?

Key Concepts

SECTION
1.1 **Earth's atmosphere supports life.**
Learn about the materials that make up the atmosphere.

SECTION
1.2 **The Sun supplies the atmosphere's energy.**
Learn how energy from the Sun affects the atmosphere.

SECTION
1.3 **Gases in the atmosphere absorb radiation.**
Learn about the ozone layer and the greenhouse effect.

SECTION
1.4 **Human activities affect the atmosphere.**
Learn about pollution, global warming, and changes in the ozone layer.

Internet Preview

CLASSZONE.COM
Chapter 1 online resources: Content Review, two Visualizations, two Resource Centers, Math Tutorial, Test Practice

 INTERNET PREVIEW

CLASSZONE.COM   For student use with the following pages:

Review and Practice
- Content Review, pp. 8, 36
- Math Tutorial: Equations, p. 26
- Test Practice, p. 39

Activities and Resources
- Internet Activity: Atmosphere, p. 7
- Visualizations: Radiation, Conduction, and Convection, p. 19; Greenhouse Effect, p. 24
- Resource Center: Ozone Layer, p. 32

Composition of the Atmosphere **Code: MDL009**

EXPLORE (the **BIG** idea)

How Heavy Is Paper?

Put a ruler on a table with one end off the edge. Tap on the ruler lightly and observe what happens. Then cover the ruler with a sheet of paper as shown. Tap again on the ruler and observe what happens.

Observe and Think
What happened to the ruler when you tapped lightly on it with and without the sheet of paper? Was the paper heavy enough by itself to hold the ruler down?

How Does Heating Affect Air?

Stretch the lip of a balloon over the neck of a small bottle. Next, fill a bowl with ice water and a second bowl with hot tap water. Place the bottle upright in the hot water. After 5 minutes, move the bottle to the cold water.

Observe and Think What changes did you observe in the balloon? What might have caused these changes?

Internet Activity: Atmosphere

Go to **ClassZone.com** to learn about Earth's atmosphere.

Observe and Think How does the thickness of the atmosphere compare with the height of a mountain or the altitude of the space shuttle in orbit?

NSTA _SCi_**LINKS**
scilinks.org

Composition of the Atmosphere **Code: MDL009**

Chapter 1: **Earth's Changing Atmosphere** 7 **D**

EXPLORE (the **BIG** idea)

These inquiry-based activities are appropriate for use at home or as a supplement to classroom instruction.

How Heavy Is Paper?

PURPOSE To introduce students to the concept that air has substance.

TIP _10 min._ Tell students to make sure that no person or breakable object is nearby.

Answer: Without the paper, the ruler popped up; with the paper, the ruler stayed on the table. The paper, along with air's mass, held the ruler down.

REVISIT after p. 10.

How Does Heating Affect Air?

PURPOSE To introduce students to the concept that temperature changes affect air, by having them observe how air in a bottle makes a balloon expand and contract.

TIP _10 min._ Hold the bottle while it is in the water so that it does not tip over.

Answer: In hot water, the balloon expands slightly; in cold water, it deflates. The air in the bottle expanded when heated and contracted when cooled.

REVISIT after p. 19.

Internet Activity: Atmosphere

PURPOSE To introduce students to the concept that the atmosphere extends into space. Students will develop a better idea of the height of the atmosphere.

TIP _10 min._ Have students make predictions about the height of the atmosphere before they conduct their research.

Answer: The troposphere extends above tall mountains. Planes fly in the troposphere or lower stratosphere. The space shuttle orbits in the upper thermosphere.

REVISIT after p. 21.

TEACHING WITH TECHNOLOGY

Computer Graphing Program Have students use a computer graphing program to construct a line graph of their data from "Investigate Solar Radiation," p. 17, and "Investigate Greenhouse Gases," p. 24.

CBL and Probeware If students have probeware, they can use a CO_2 gas sensor and an O_2 gas sensor on p. 11.

Chapter 1 **7** **D**

◀ CONCEPT REVIEW

Activate Prior Knowledge

- Ask students to identify the three states of matter.
- Have them describe the difference between atoms and molecules.
- Ask students to explain what happens to molecules when matter is heated. Do they move farther apart or closer together? Conversely, what happens to molecules when matter is cooled?

▶ TAKING NOTES

Supporting Main Ideas

Students may want to use different-colored pencils to organize the information in their charts. A blue pencil can be used for main ideas (blue headings). A red pencil can be used for supporting information.

Vocabulary Strategy

Ask students to think about how they learn best. Do visuals help them to understand concepts better than blocks of text? If so, they might want to use plenty of drawings in their frame game diagrams.

Vocabulary and Note-Taking Resources

- Vocabulary Practice, pp. 57–58
- Decoding Support, p. 59

- Daily Vocabulary Scaffolding, p. T2
- Note-Taking Model, p. T3

- Frame Game, B26–27
- Supporting Main Ideas, C42
- Daily Vocabulary Scaffolding, H1–8

◀ CONCEPT REVIEW

- Matter is made up of atoms.
- All things on or near Earth are pulled toward Earth by its gravity.
- Heating or cooling any material changes some of its properties.

◀ VOCABULARY REVIEW

See Glossary for definitions.

atom	mass
gas	molecule
gravity	

 CONTENT REVIEW
CLASSZONE.COM
Review concepts and vocabulary.

▶ TAKING NOTES

SUPPORTING MAIN IDEAS

Make a chart to show main ideas and the information that supports them. Write each blue heading from the chapter in a separate box. In boxes below it, add supporting information, such as reasons, explanations, and examples.

VOCABULARY STRATEGY

Write each new vocabulary term in the center of a **frame game** diagram. Decide what information to frame the term with. Use examples, descriptions, pictures, or sentences in which the term is used in context. You can change the frame to fit each term.

See the Note-Taking Handbook on pages R45–R51.

SCIENCE NOTEBOOK

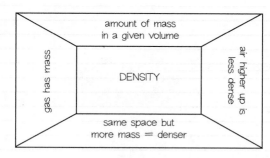

The atmosphere makes life on Earth possible.

- Living things use gases in the air.
- The atmosphere keeps Earth warm.
- The atmosphere protects life.

amount of mass in a given volume

gas has mass

DENSITY

air higher up is less dense

same space but more mass = denser

CHECK READINESS

Administer the Diagnostic Test to determine students' readiness for new science content and their mastery of requisite math skills.

 Diagnostic Test, pp. 1–2

Technology Resources

Students needing content and math skills should visit ClassZone.com.

- CONTENT REVIEW
- MATH TUTORIAL

 CONTENT REVIEW CD-ROM

1.1 Earth's atmosphere supports life.

◀ **BEFORE, you learned**
- Living things need food, water, and air
- Matter can be solid, liquid, or gas

▶ **NOW, you will learn**
- Why the atmosphere is important to living things
- What the atmosphere is made of
- How natural cycles affect the atmosphere

VOCABULARY

atmosphere p. 9
altitude p. 10
density p. 10
cycle p. 12

EXPLORE Air Resistance

How does air affect falling objects?

PROCEDURE

① Drop the washer from shoulder height.

② Tape the metal washer to the center of the coffee filter. The filter will act as a parachute.

③ Drop the washer with the parachute from shoulder height.

WHAT DO YOU THINK?
- What difference did the parachute make?
- What do your results tell you about air?

MATERIALS
- metal washer
- coffee filter
- tape

VOCABULARY
Remember to make a frame game diagram for the term *atmosphere*.

The atmosphere makes life on Earth possible.

Every time you breathe in, your lungs fill with air, which is a mixture of gases. Your body uses materials from the air to help you stay alive. The **atmosphere** is a whole layer of air that surrounds Earth. The atmosphere supports life and protects it. The gases of the atmosphere keep Earth warm and transport energy to different regions of the planet. Without the atmosphere, the oceans would not exist, life would not survive, and the planet would be a cold, lifeless rock.

Even though the atmosphere is very important to life, it is surprisingly thin. If the solid part of Earth were the size of a peach, most of the atmosphere would be no thicker than the peach fuzz surrounding the fruit. The atmosphere is a small but important part of the Earth system.

CHECK YOUR READING How does the atmosphere make life possible? Find three examples in the text above.

1.1 FOCUS

▶ **Set Learning Goals**

Students will
- Analyze how the atmosphere is important to living things.
- Explain what the atmosphere is made of.
- Describe how natural cycles affect the atmosphere.
- Predict how gases will be different in breath and air in an experiment.

◀ **3-Minute Warm-Up**

Display Transparency 4 or copy this exercise on the board:

Match each term in the first column with the correct word in the second column.

Column 1
1. water vapor *c*
2. ice *a*
3. water *d*

Column 2
a. solid
b. energy
c. gas
d. liquid

 3-Minute Warm-Up, p. T4

1.1 MOTIVATE

EXPLORE Air Resistance

PURPOSE To help students recognize the effect of air resistance on falling objects

TIP *10 min.* Have students vary the effect by crumpling the coffee filter.

WHAT DO YOU THINK? *It made the washer fall more slowly. Air has substance; it creates resistance.*

Ongoing Assessment

CHECK YOUR READING *The atmosphere supports and protects life. Sample answers: it supplies materials that your body uses; it transports energy to different regions of Earth; it keeps Earth warm.*

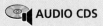

INVESTIGATE Gas in the Air

PURPOSE To predict the presence of different gases in the air

TIPS *10 min.* Bromthymol blue can be used as a substitute for limewater—it turns yellowish in the presence of carbon dioxide. Mix enough limewater for the class ahead of time, then suggest the following:

- Keep the limewater in a covered container until ready for use.
- Do not touch or drink the limewater.

WHAT DO YOU THINK? *The limewater in the first jar stayed clear. The limewater in the jar that contained exhaled breath turned cloudy. The exhaled breath reacted with the limewater in the second jar, indicating the presence of carbon dioxide. The limewater in the other jar did not react, indicating that the change was due to the exhaled breath and not just air.*

CHALLENGE *Sample answer: A burning candle could test the presence of oxygen.*

 Datasheet, Gas in the Air, p. 20

Technology Resources

Customize this student lab as needed or look for an alternative. Print rubrics to assess student lab reports.

 Lab Generator CD-ROM

EXPLORE (the **BIG** idea)

Revisit "How Heavy Is Paper?" on p. 7. Have students explain their results.

Ongoing Assessment

PHOTO CAPTION Answer: The air is less dense at that altitude, so there are fewer oxygen molecules to breathe.

Characteristics of the Atmosphere

In 1862 two British balloonists reached the highest **altitude,** or distance above sea level, any human had ever reached. As their balloon rose to 8.8 kilometers (5.5 mi), one balloonist fainted and the other barely managed to bring the balloon back down. They found that the air becomes thinner as altitude increases.

The thickness or thinness of air is measured by its density. **Density** is the amount of mass in a given volume of a substance. If two objects take up the same amount of space, then the object with more mass has a greater density than the one with less mass. For example, a bowling ball has a higher density than a soccer ball.

The atmosphere's density decreases as you travel upward. The air on top of a mountain is less dense than the air at sea level. A deep breath of mountain air fills your lungs but contains less mass—less gas—than a deep breath of air at sea level. Higher up, at altitudes where jets fly, a breath of air would contain only about one-tenth the mass of a breath of air at sea level. The air farther above Earth's surface contains even less mass. There is no definite top to the atmosphere. It just keeps getting less dense as you get farther from Earth's surface. However, altitudes 500 kilometers (300 mi) or more above Earth's surface can be called outer space.

The decrease of density with greater altitude means that most of the mass of the atmosphere is close to Earth's surface. In fact, more than 99 percent of the atmosphere's mass is in the lowest 30 kilometers (20 mi).

INFER This climber has reached the top of Mount Everest, 8850 m (29,000 ft) above sea level in Nepal. Why does he need an oxygen mask?

INVESTIGATE Gas in the Air

How do you know that air has different gases?
PROCEDURE

1. Put a spoonful of limewater into each jar. Limewater is clear, but turns milky in the presence of carbon dioxide.

2. Cover one jar. Add extra carbon dioxide to the second jar by exhaling gently into it before you cover it. Tighten the lids carefully to seal the jars.

3. Predict what will happen, then shake each jar.

WHAT DO YOU THINK?
- What happened to the limewater in each jar?
- How do you know that air is made of different gases?

CHALLENGE How would you test a different gas in the air?

SKILL FOCUS
Predicting

MATERIALS
- limewater
- 2 jars
- spoon

TIME
10 minutes

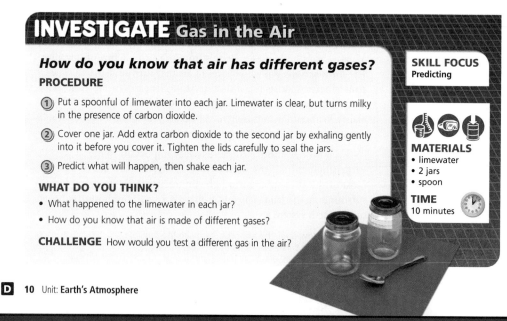

DIFFERENTIATE INSTRUCTION

⟨?⟩ More Reading Support

A What is density? *the amount of mass in a given volume*

B What happens to the atmosphere's density as you travel upward? *it decreases*

English Learners English learners may have difficulty using the words *affect* and *effect* correctly. Explain that *affect* is a verb and *effect* is a noun. A common trick for remembering the difference is that *affect* begins with the letter *a*. A verb is an action, which also begins with the letter *a*.

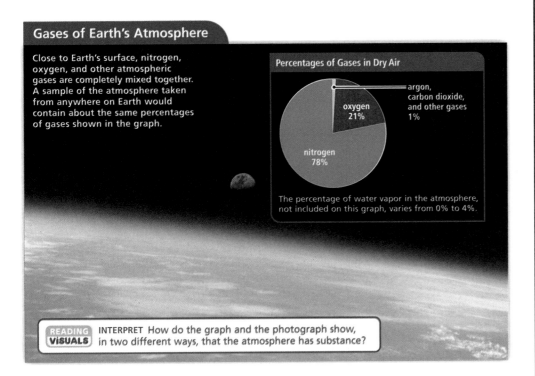

Gases of Earth's Atmosphere

Close to Earth's surface, nitrogen, oxygen, and other atmospheric gases are completely mixed together. A sample of the atmosphere taken from anywhere on Earth would contain about the same percentages of gases shown in the graph.

Percentages of Gases in Dry Air

oxygen 21%

argon, carbon dioxide, and other gases 1%

nitrogen 78%

The percentage of water vapor in the atmosphere, not included on this graph, varies from 0% to 4%.

READING VISUALS INTERPRET How do the graph and the photograph show, in two different ways, that the atmosphere has substance?

Materials in the Atmosphere

Most of the materials in the atmosphere are gases. However, the atmosphere also contains tiny particles of solid or liquid material such as dust, sea salt, and water droplets. Perhaps you have sat by an open window and noticed some of these particles on the window sill.

If you were to write a recipe for air, you would include nitrogen gas as the main ingredient. In dry air, about 78 percent of the gas is nitrogen. The next most common ingredient is oxygen gas, which makes up about 21 percent of the atmosphere. Argon, carbon dioxide, and other gases make up about 1 percent of the atmosphere. Unlike the amounts of nitrogen and other gases, the amount of water vapor varies a great deal. In some places at some times, water vapor can make up as much as 4 percent of the air.

READING TIP
As you read about the amounts of gases, find each gas on the graph above.

The atmosphere's gases provide materials essential for living things. Nitrogen promotes plant growth and is an important ingredient in the chemicals that make up living things. Oxygen is necessary for animals and plants to perform life processes. Plants use carbon dioxide and water to make food.

CHECK YOUR READING Which gas is the most common material in the air around you?

Teach from Visuals

To help students interpret the visual about gases of Earth's atmosphere, ask:

• Why isn't water vapor included in the graph? *because it varies from place to place and from time to time*

• What percentage of the atmosphere is made up of oxygen? *21 percent*

Real World Example

Air density decreases with altitude—a fact that can influence the outcome of a baseball game. In areas at high elevations, a baseball can travel about 10 percent farther than a ball hit with the same force in an area at sea level. This is because the air is less dense at higher elevations. Thus, a two-base hit in Atlanta might be a home run in Denver.

Teaching with Technology

Students can use an O_2 gas sensor or a CO_2 gas sensor to gather information on these gases.

Ongoing Assessment

Analyze how the atmosphere is important to living things.

Ask: What gases in the atmosphere are especially important to plants? *nitrogen, oxygen, carbon dioxide*

Explain what the atmosphere is made of.

Ask: What materials are found in the atmosphere? *Gases, such as nitrogen and oxygen, and tiny liquid and solid particles, such as dust and sea salt.*

READING VISUALS *Answer: The graph shows the composition of Earth's atmosphere. The photograph shows that there is something above the surface of Earth—the atmosphere.*

CHECK YOUR READING *Answer: nitrogen*

DIFFERENTIATE INSTRUCTION

More Reading Support

C Nitrogen makes up what percentage of air? *about 78 percent*

D What is the second most common gas in air? *oxygen*

Additional Investigation To reinforce Section 1.1 learning goals, use the following full-period investigation:

R **Additional INVESTIGATION,** Oxygen in the Air, A, B, & C, pp. 71–79, 284–285 (Advanced students should complete Levels B and C.)

Advanced Have students explain why the percentage of water vapor varies in the atmosphere. *Water evaporates from bodies of water, so wet regions have more water vapor.*

R Challenge and Extension, p. 19

Address Misconceptions

IDENTIFY Ask students where the matter that makes up plants comes from. If they do not include air or carbon dioxide in their answers, they may not be able to trace the cycling of matter, and they may hold the misconception that matter can be created.

CORRECT Use the diagrams on pp. 13, 15 to trace the path of carbon through a cycle. Have teams of students try the Challenge question on p. 15.

REASSESS Ask students to describe how matter moves through each of the three cycles. You may wish to use the Challenge question on p. 14. *Students should trace the motion of carbon, nitrogen, and water into and out of the atmosphere.*

Integrate the Sciences

Nitrogen is the most common gas in the atmosphere. However, in its stable form (N_2) it cannot be used by plants. Microscopic bacteria must first change the nitrogen into a usable form. One group of bacteria converts nitrogen into ammonia (NH_3). Another group combines the ammonia with oxygen to form nitrites. Still another group of bacteria changes the nitrites to nitrates, which can be absorbed by plants. Nitrogen-fixing bacteria live in the soil and roots of certain plants, such as legumes. For this reason, legumes are often planted with other crops to enrich the soil.

Ongoing Assessment

Describe how natural cycles affect the atmosphere.

Ask: How does the carbon cycle affect the atmosphere? *During photosynthesis, plants take in carbon dioxide from the air and release oxygen. Animals inhale mainly oxygen and release carbon dioxide and water. These processes create a continuous cycle in the atmosphere.*

Natural processes modify the atmosphere.

The exact amounts of some gases in the air change depending on location, time of day, season, and other factors. Water vapor, carbon dioxide, and other gases in the atmosphere are affected by both ongoing processes and sudden changes.

SUPPORTING MAIN IDEAS
Make a chart about processes that modify the atmosphere.

Ongoing Processes

You and all other living things participate in ongoing processes. For example, each day you breathe in and out about 13,000 liters (3,000 gal) of air—about as much air as would fill five school buses. When you breathe, your body exchanges gases with the atmosphere. The air you inhale is a slightly different mixture of gases than the air you exhale.

Living things take part in a repeated process of gas exchange with the atmosphere. In addition, living things continually exchange materials in solid and liquid form with the environment. Processes like these that repeat over and over are called **cycles.**

 E

 F

Three of the most important cycles that affect the atmosphere are the carbon cycle, the nitrogen cycle, and the water cycle.

① **The Carbon Cycle** Carbon dioxide (CO_2) and oxygen (O_2) gases constantly circulate, or cycle, among plants, animals, and the atmosphere. For example,

- Animals inhale air, use some of its oxygen, and exhale air that has less oxygen but more carbon dioxide and water
- Plants take in carbon dioxide and release oxygen as they make food in the process of photosynthesis

② **The Nitrogen Cycle** Different forms of nitrogen cycle among the atmosphere, the soil, and living organisms. For example,

- Tiny organisms remove nitrogen gas (N_2) from the air and transform it into other chemicals, which then enter the soil
- Plants and animals use solids and liquids that contain nitrogen, which returns to the soil when the organisms die and decay
- The soil slowly releases nitrogen back into the air as nitrogen gas

③ **The Water Cycle** Different forms of water (H_2O) cycle between Earth's surface and the atmosphere. For example,

- Liquid water from oceans and lakes changes into gas and enters the atmosphere
- Plants release water vapor from their leaves
- Liquid water falls from the atmosphere as rain

READING TiP

In the diagrams on page 13, color is used to show particular materials.

O_2 is red.

CO_2 is purple.

N_2 is aqua.

H_2O is blue.

DIFFERENTIATE INSTRUCTION

? **More Reading Support**

E How do living things affect the atmosphere? *they exchange gases*

F What important cycles affect the atmosphere? *carbon cycle, nitrogen cycle, water cycle*

Cycles and the Atmosphere

A tiger breathing, leaves decaying, trees growing—all are involved in cycles that affect our atmosphere. The diagrams to the right show how materials move in three important cycles.

1. Carbon Cycle

► The tiger exhales carbon dioxide (CO_2). Carbon dioxide is taken in by the tree.

► The tree releases oxygen (O_2). Oxygen is taken in by the tiger.

2. Nitrogen Cycle

► Tiny organisms convert nitrogen gas (N_2) to other forms used by the tree.

► Decaying leaves release nitrogen gas (N_2) back into the atmosphere.

3. Water Cycle

► Water vapor (H_2O gas) turns to liquid and rains down to Earth's surface.

► Water from the lake changes to gas and returns to the atmosphere.

READING VISUALS COMPARE AND CONTRAST How are the three cycles similar? How are they different?

Chapter 1: **Earth's Changing Atmosphere** 13 **D**

DIFFERENTIATE INSTRUCTION

Alternative Assessment Have students use different-colored markers to make their own versions of the cycles shown in the visual. Tell them to follow the color key for materials shown on p. 12. Students may want to create their diagrams using a computer graphics program. Students should label their drawings and include arrows showing the movement of materials in the cycles.

Teach from Visuals

To help students interpret the visual about cycles and the atmosphere:

• Ask: What do the arrows in all three diagrams represent? *the movement of oxygen, carbon dioxide, nitrogen, and water in cycles that affect the atmosphere*

• Have students compare the placement of the arrows in the diagrams. Ask: In each case, what are they pointing to? *diagram 1: the tree and the tiger; diagram 2: the decaying leaves and the tiny organisms in the soil; diagram 3: rain and the lake*

T The visual "Cycles and the Atmosphere" is available as T6 in the Unit Transparency Book.

Develop Critical Thinking

APPLY To reinforce students' analysis of the cycles, ask the following questions while they study the visual:

• When the tiger exhales carbon dioxide, does it go directly into the tree? Explain. *No, it goes into the air first, and then is taken in by the tree.*

• How did the decaying leaves get nitrogen? *They were once a part of the tree, which got nitrogen from the soil.*

• If water vapor stayed in the atmosphere and did not return to Earth's surface, how would it affect the tree? *All living things need water to survive, so the tree could not live unless water cycled back to Earth's surface, providing a source of nutrients.*

Ongoing Assessment

READING VISUALS *Answer: In all three cycles, a substance leaves the air and is returned to the air again and again. All three cycles are important to living things. The substances involved in the cycles are different, and they are removed and returned to the air in different ways.*

Ongoing Assessment

READING VISUALS *Sample answer: In the second image, a dust cloud covers the blue of the ocean, and the white clouds in the upper left of the first image are gone.*

Reinforce (the **BIG** idea)

Have students relate the section to the Big Idea.

 Reinforcing Key Concepts, p. 21

1.1 ASSESS & RETEACH

Assess

 Section 1.1 Quiz, p. 3

Reteach

Have students role-play the gases, materials, and living things involved in the carbon cycle. The room itself can represent the atmosphere. Two students can each represent an oxygen atom, one student can represent a carbon atom, one an animal, and one a plant. Station the plant and the animal ten feet apart. Have the two oxygen atoms and the carbon atom start together as a carbon dioxide molecule that the animal has just exhaled. All three should walk over to the plant. Remind students that in photosynthesis the plant takes in carbon dioxide and releases oxygen. See if students can guess what their next move should be. The carbon atom should remain with the plant, and the oxygen atoms should continue in a circular motion back to the animal. Other students can get involved in the cycle at any time as new oxygen or carbon atoms. Try modeling the water cycle and the nitrogen cycle in this manner.

Technology Resources

Have students visit **ClassZone.com** for reteaching of Key Concepts.

 CONTENT REVIEW

 CONTENT REVIEW CD-ROM

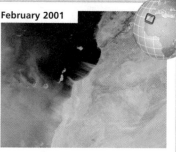
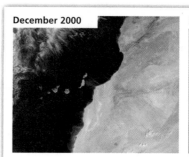

December 2000   February 2001

READING VISUALS COMPARE AND CONTRAST These satellite images show northwestern Africa before and during a dust storm. How does the second image differ from the first?

Sudden Changes

SUPPORTING MAIN IDEAS Record information about the events that cause sudden changes in the atmosphere.

In addition to ongoing processes, dramatic events may cause changes in the atmosphere. When sudden events occur, it takes time before the atmosphere is able to restore balance.

- **Volcanic Eruptions** Volcanoes shoot gases and huge amounts of ash into the atmosphere. Certain gases produce a haze that may affect the air for many months and lower temperatures worldwide.
- **Forest Fires** When forests burn, the carbon that makes up each tree combines with oxygen and enters the atmosphere as carbon dioxide. Wood ash also enters the atmosphere.
- **Dust Storms** Wind, water, or drought can loosen soil. Powerful windstorms may then raise clouds of this eroded soil, as in the second picture above. These storms add huge amounts of particles to the air for a time.

1.1 Review

KEY CONCEPTS

1. How is the atmosphere important to living things?
2. What substances make up air?
3. Draw a diagram to show how one natural cycle affects the atmosphere.

CRITICAL THINKING

4. **Apply** Give three examples from everyday life of how the atmosphere supports and protects life.
5. **Predict** How would the atmosphere in your area change if a disease killed all the plants?

CHALLENGE

6. **Compare** Carbon dioxide enters the oceans from the air. Some carbon becomes stored in shells, and then in rocks. Eventually, it can be released back into the air by volcanoes in the form of carbon dioxide. How are these slow processes similar to the cycles shown on page 13?

ANSWERS

1. It transports energy to different regions of Earth. It allows oceans to exist and life to survive.

2. nitrogen, oxygen, argon, carbon dioxide, water vapor, and other gases

3. Diagram should be similar to one of the diagrams on p. 13.

4. People need oxygen from the air to stay alive. Plants need air to make food. Birds need air to fly.

5. There would be more carbon dioxide and less oxygen in the air.

6. These processes also involve a constant and complete cycle involving the atmosphere.

Carbon Cycle Chemistry

The atmosphere is keeping you alive. Every time you breathe, you take in the oxygen that you need to live. But that's not the end of the story. The food you eat would not exist without the carbon dioxide in the air that you, and every other animal on Earth, breathe out.

A Closer Look at Oxygen and Carbon Dioxide

Gases in air are tiny molecules that are much too small to see, even if you look through a microscope. Chemists use diagrams to represent these molecules. Oxygen gas (O_2) is made of two atoms of oxygen, so a diagram of an oxygen gas molecule shows two red balls stuck together. A diagram of a carbon dioxide molecule (CO_2) looks similar, but it has one black carbon atom in addition to two red oxygen atoms.

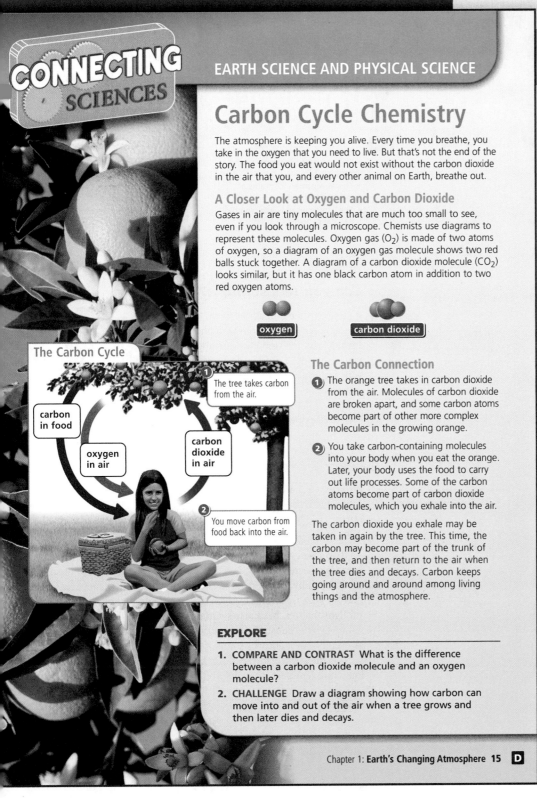

oxygen

carbon dioxide

The Carbon Cycle

The tree takes carbon from the air.

carbon in food

oxygen in air

carbon dioxide in air

You move carbon from food back into the air.

The Carbon Connection

1 The orange tree takes in carbon dioxide from the air. Molecules of carbon dioxide are broken apart, and some carbon atoms become part of other more complex molecules in the growing orange.

2 You take carbon-containing molecules into your body when you eat the orange. Later, your body uses the food to carry out life processes. Some of the carbon atoms become part of carbon dioxide molecules, which you exhale into the air.

The carbon dioxide you exhale may be taken in again by the tree. This time, the carbon may become part of the trunk of the tree, and then return to the air when the tree dies and decays. Carbon keeps going around and around among living things and the atmosphere.

EXPLORE

1. **COMPARE AND CONTRAST** What is the difference between a carbon dioxide molecule and an oxygen molecule?

2. **CHALLENGE** Draw a diagram showing how carbon can move into and out of the air when a tree grows and then later dies and decays.

Chapter 1: **Earth's Changing Atmosphere 15** **D**

Set Learning Goal

To understand the chemistry behind the carbon cycle

Present the Science

Share the following facts with students:

• Scientists use chemical formulas, such as O_2, to indicate the atoms in a molecule. The subscript 2 means that there are two atoms of the element oxygen in an oxygen gas molecule. In the same way, the formula CO_2 means that the molecule is made of one carbon atom and two oxygen atoms.

• Look at the illustration of "The Carbon Cycle." Notice that the atoms of carbon and oxygen take different paths. The carbon atoms go into and out of the air, while the oxygen atoms stay in the air.

Discussion Questions

Ask: If molecules of gas are too small to see, how do we know they're in the air? *Sample answer: Tests can be done that detect the presence of oxygen, carbon dioxide, and other gases in the air.*

Ask: What are some advantages of using a model? What are some disadvantages? *Sample answer: Models allow us to indirectly study things that are too big or too small to study directly. Since they are only representations of things or systems, often they cannot show exactly how something looks or works.*

Close

Ask: What could you use to model oxygen gas and carbon dioxide gas? *Sample answer: Two red foam balls joined by a toothpick could be used to model oxygen gas. A larger, black foam ball could be added to the red balls to model carbon dioxide.*

EXPLORE

1. *COMPARE AND CONTRAST The oxygen molecule is made up of two oxygen atoms. The carbon dioxide molecule is made up of two oxygen atoms and one carbon atom. The difference is one carbon atom.*

2. *CHALLENGE A diagram might show a carbon molecule from the air going into a leaf on the tree; then moving into the trunk; then coming out of the decaying trunk and going back into the air.*

Set Learning Goals

Students will

- Demonstrate how solar energy heats Earth's surface and atmosphere.
- Explain how the atmosphere moves heat energy around.
- Describe the layers of the atmosphere.
- Measure how reflection affects temperature in an experiment.

3-Minute Warm-Up

Display Transparency 4 or copy this exercise on the board:

Fill in the blank with the correct word.

1. The atmosphere transports _____ to different regions. *energy*

2. Air is a mixture of _____. *gases*

3. The _____ of the atmosphere changes with altitude. *density*

 3-Minute Warm-Up, p. T4

1.2 MOTIVATE

THINK ABOUT

PURPOSE To have students think about all the things affected by the Sun

DISCUSS Ask students where energy from sunlight goes. Generate a list of their answers on the board, and compare them to the answers below.

Answer: Some solar energy is used by plants during photosynthesis. Solar energy can make water evaporate, make the wind blow, cause colors to fade, and provide solar cells with the energy to produce electricity.

Ongoing Assessment

 Answer: Some is absorbed and some is reflected.

◀ **BEFORE, you learned**

- The atmosphere supports and protects life
- The atmosphere contains a mixture of gases
- The atmosphere is affected by natural processes

▶ **NOW, you will learn**

- How solar energy heats Earth's surface and atmosphere
- How the atmosphere moves heat energy around
- About the layers of the atmosphere

VOCABULARY

radiation p. 17
conduction p. 18
convection p. 19

THINK ABOUT

Can you feel sunlight?

If you have been on a hot beach, you have felt energy from sunlight. Perhaps you felt sunlight warming your skin or hot sand underneath your feet. It is easy to notice the energy of sunlight when it makes the ground or your skin warm. Where else does the energy from sunlight go?

 SUPPORTING MAIN IDEAS
Write the blue heading into your notes to begin a new chart. Add supporting details.

Energy from the Sun heats the atmosphere.

It may seem hard to believe, but almost all the energy around you comes from the Sun. That means that food energy, fires, and even the warmth of your own body can be traced back to energy from the Sun. A lot of this energy reaches Earth in a form you can see—visible light.

Two main things happen to the sunlight that reaches Earth. Some is reflected, or sent in a new direction. You see most of the objects around you by reflected light. The sand in the picture above looks light in color because it reflects much of the sunlight that hits it. Some of the sunlight that reaches Earth's surface is absorbed. The energy from this light heats the substance that absorbs it. The sand can become warm or even hot as it absorbs some of the sunlight that hits it. Some objects, such as the striped shirts above, have bright parts that reflect more light and dark parts that absorb more light.

CHECK YOUR READING What two things happen to the sunlight that reaches Earth?

RESOURCES FOR DIFFERENTIATED INSTRUCTION

Below Level
UNIT RESOURCE BOOK
- Reading Study Guide A, pp. 24–25
- Decoding Support, p. 59

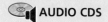 **AUDIO CDS**

Advanced
UNIT RESOURCE BOOK
Challenge and Extension, p. 30

English Learners
UNIT RESOURCE BOOK
Spanish Reading Study Guide, pp. 28–29

AUDIO CDS

- Audio Readings in Spanish
- Audio Readings (English)

The light that you can see is one type of radiation. **Radiation** (RAY-dee-AY-shuhn) is energy that travels across distances in the form of certain types of waves. Visible light and other types of radiation can be absorbed or reflected.

The diagram shows the average amounts of solar radiation, or radiation from the Sun, that are absorbed and reflected by Earth's atmosphere, clouds, and surface. Each arrow in the diagram represents 5 percent of the solar radiation that reaches Earth. As you can see, about 30 percent of the solar energy that reaches Earth is reflected. Clouds and snow-covered ground are white, so they reflect a lot of the radiation that hits them. Air also reflects some radiation. The energy of the reflected radiation goes back into outer space.

The other 70 percent of solar radiation that reaches Earth is absorbed. Most of this energy is absorbed by oceans, landforms, and living things. The absorbed energy heats Earth's surface. In the same way, energy that is absorbed by gas molecules, clouds, and dust particles heats the atmosphere.

Solar Radiation

Arrows show the average global reflection and absorption of solar radiation.

About 5% of solar energy is reflected by Earth's surface.

About 25% of solar energy is reflected by clouds and Earth's atmosphere.

About 20% of solar energy is absorbed by clouds and the atmosphere.

About 50% of solar energy is absorbed by Earth's surface.

The atmosphere is much smaller than shown.

INVESTIGATE Solar Radiation

How does reflection affect temperature?

PROCEDURE

1. Cover the top of one cup with plastic wrap. Cover the second cup with paper. Secure the plastic wrap and paper with tape.

2. Poke a small slit in each cup's cover. Insert a thermometer through each slit.

3. Place the cups in direct sunlight. Record their temperature every minute for 15 minutes.

WHAT DO YOU THINK?
- How did the temperature change inside each cup?
- How did the coverings contribute to these changes?

CHALLENGE What does the paper represent in this model?

SKILL FOCUS
Measuring

MATERIALS
- 2 cups
- plastic wrap
- white paper
- tape
- 2 short thermometers
- watch

TIME
25 minutes

Chapter 1: **Earth's Changing Atmosphere** 17 **D**

DIFFERENTIATE INSTRUCTION

More Reading Support

A What is radiation? *the transfer of energy across distances in the form of certain types of waves*

B What happens to most of the solar radiation that reaches Earth? *It is absorbed.*

English Learners English learners need constant reinforcement when learning new vocabulary. It is a good idea to use labels on classroom science materials. Also, having definitions for vocabulary terms available for quick reference will further support English learners. Have students make flash cards defining *radiation, conduction, convection,* and any other difficult terms or concepts.

INVESTIGATE Solar Radiation

PURPOSE To measure the effect of reflection on temperature to understand solar radiation

TIPS *25 min.* Suggest the following to students:

- Arrange the two cups in such a way that they receive equal amounts of light. A lamp may be used instead if care is taken to ensure equal amounts of light.

- To help recognize trends in the data, make graphs of the temperature changes for both cups.

WHAT DO YOU THINK? *The temperature inside both cups went up. The temperature in the paper-covered cup increased more slowly and did not get as high as the temperature in the cup covered with plastic wrap.*

CHALLENGE *It represents clouds in the atmosphere.*

Datasheet, Solar Radiation, p. 31

Technology Resources

Customize this student lab as needed or look for an alternative. Print rubrics to assess student lab reports.

Lab Generator CD-ROM

Metacognitive Strategy

Ask: What thoughts popped into your head as you completed this lab? Did the lab remind you of anything you have done before?

Teaching with Technology

Students can use a computer graphing program to make graphs of their data.

Teach Difficult Concepts

Students may have a hard time distinguishing between radiation, conduction, and convection. Give them an everyday example to help them visualize the concepts. For example, tell them to picture an electric stove with a pot of water on top. The burner of the stove radiates energy. Energy is also transferred by conduction to the bottom of the pot and to the water. The water begins to move, transferring energy by convection. The following demonstration will help reinforce these processes.

Teacher Demo

Obtain a lamp without a shade. Place the lamp on your desk and turn it on. Ask: What type of energy is the lamp giving off? *radiation* Lightly place a piece of metal against the light bulb for a second or two. Ask: What type of energy transfer is occurring now? *conduction* Hold your hand above the lamp. Ask: What type of energy transfer is occurring now? *convection*

Ongoing Assessment

Demonstrate how solar energy heats Earth's surface and atmosphere.

Ask: How is solar energy absorbed by Earth's surface and atmosphere? *on Earth's surface: by oceans, landforms, and living things; in the atmosphere: by gas molecules, clouds, and dust particles*

The atmosphere moves energy.

C

If you walk along a sunny beach, you may be comfortably warm except for the burning-hot soles of your feet. The sand may be much hotter than the air. The sand absorbs solar energy all day and stores it in one place. The air also absorbs solar energy but moves it around and spreads it out. Radiation, conduction, and convection are processes that move energy from place to place.

Radiation You have already read that solar radiation warms a sandy beach. You may be surprised to learn that radiation also transfers energy from the sand to the air. Earth's surface gives off a type of invisible radiation, called infrared radiation, that can be absorbed by certain gases. The energy from the radiation warms the air. The air also gives off infrared radiation. You will read more about this cycle of radiation in Section 1.3.

Conduction Another way that sand warms the air is through conduction. When you walk barefoot on a hot beach, rapidly moving molecules in the hot sand bump against molecules in your feet. This process transfers energy to your feet, which get hot. **Conduction** is the transfer of heat energy from one substance to another by direct contact. Earth's surface transfers energy to the atmosphere by conduction, such as when hot beach sand warms the air above it. Molecules of air can

VOCABULARY
Add new terms to your notebook.

D

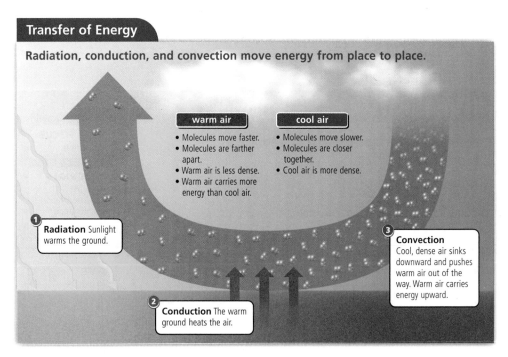

Transfer of Energy

Radiation, conduction, and convection move energy from place to place.

warm air
- Molecules move faster.
- Molecules are farther apart.
- Warm air is less dense.
- Warm air carries more energy than cool air.

cool air
- Molecules move slower.
- Molecules are closer together.
- Cool air is more dense.

1 Radiation Sunlight warms the ground.

2 Conduction The warm ground heats the air.

3 Convection Cool, dense air sinks downward and pushes warm air out of the way. Warm air carries energy upward.

DIFFERENTIATE INSTRUCTION

 More Reading Support

C What different things do sand and air do with solar energy? *Sand stores it; air moves and spreads it.*

D How is energy transferred in conduction? *through direct contact*

Advanced *Albedo* refers to how much radiation a surface reflects compared with how much it receives. A surface with a high albedo reflects most of the radiation it receives. Ask: Does snow have a high or low albedo? How do you know? *It has a high albedo because it is white and thus reflects most of the sunlight shining on it.*

 Challenge and Extension, p. 30

gain energy when they collide with molecules in grains of hot sand. The air just above the sand gets warm. Energy can also spread slowly through the air by conduction as air molecules bump into one another.

Moving hot air near the flames makes the mountain behind appear distorted.

Convection Heated air can move easily from place to place. When a heated liquid or gas moves, it carries energy along with it. **Convection** is the transfer of energy from place to place by the motion of gas or liquid. When scientists talk about convection in the atmosphere, they usually mean the motion of gases up and down rather than side to side. The heat energy comes from below and is moved upward. Think once more about the beach. First, radiation from the Sun warms the sand. Second, the hot sand conducts energy to the air. Third, the warm air carries energy upward in convection. Follow this cycle of radiation, conduction, and convection in the diagram on page 18.

 CHECK YOUR READING Compare conduction and convection. How are they similar?

Differences in density produce the motion of air convection. You have read that the atmosphere is less dense at higher altitudes. At any particular altitude, however, the density of air depends mostly on its temperature. Warm air has more energy, so the molecules move faster than they do in cool air. The motion makes the molecules collide more, so they stay farther apart. When there is more space between molecules, the air is less dense.

 REMINDER
Density is the amount of mass in a given volume of a substance.

Imagine a box full of warm air and another box of the same size full of cool air. If you could see air molecules, you would find more molecules—more mass—in the box of cool air. Cool, dense air is heavier, so it tends to sink and push warm, less dense air upward.

As it moves upward, warm air carries energy away from the ground. The air can cool as it rises. Eventually, the air can become cool enough—dense enough—to sink back to the ground, where it may heat up again.

 **VISUALIZATION**
CLASSZONE.COM
See radiation, conduction, and convection in action.

The atmosphere has temperature layers.

Density is not the only characteristic of the atmosphere that changes with altitude. Different parts of the atmosphere absorb and move energy in different ways. As a result, the air's temperature changes with altitude. Scientists use the patterns of these temperature changes to define four layers of the atmosphere. To explore these layers, turn the page and ride an imaginary elevator up through the atmosphere.

Chapter 1: **Earth's Changing Atmosphere** 19 **D**

History of Science

The upper layers of the atmosphere contain a layer called the ionosphere. This layer, which is within the thermosphere, contains ionized particles that can affect certain radio transmissions. AM radio signals bounce off the ionosphere and return to Earth. They can be reflected back and forth in this manner over long distances. This phenomenon was first observed in 1901, when an Italian physicist successfully received a radio signal sent from a distance of about 3000 km (approximately 2000 miles).

EXPLORE (the **BIG** idea)

Revisit "How Does Heating Affect Air?" on p. 7. Have students explain their results.

Ongoing Assessment

Explain how the atmosphere moves heat energy around.

Ask students to give an example of energy moving by conduction. *When you are walking on hot sand and your feet become hot, heat energy is moving by conduction.*

CHECK YOUR READING *Answer: Both are processes that move energy from place to place. Both involve the movement of molecules.*

Teach Difficult Concepts

In some sciences, the exosphere is important enough to consider it a fifth layer (beyond thermosphere). In some sciences, the thermosphere is subdivided.

Teach from Visuals

To help students interpret the "Temperature Layers" visual, ask:

• Does each layer have a set temperature or a range? *a range*

• Where in the troposphere would you find the warmest temperatures? *at the bottom*

Ongoing Assessment

Describe the layers of the atmosphere.

Ask: Where is the troposphere, and how is it heated? *It extends from 0 to 10 km above Earth's surface and is heated by the ground.*

READING VISUALS *Answer: Temperature decreases, then increases, then decreases, then increases.*

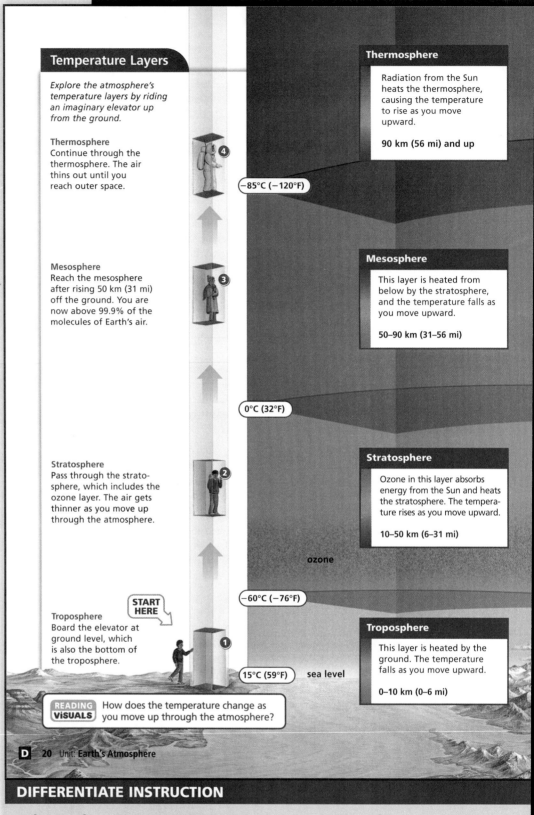

Temperature Layers

Explore the atmosphere's temperature layers by riding an imaginary elevator up from the ground.

Thermosphere
Continue through the thermosphere. The air thins out until you reach outer space.

④

−85°C (−120°F)

Mesosphere
Reach the mesosphere after rising 50 km (31 mi) off the ground. You are now above 99.9% of the molecules of Earth's air.

③

0°C (32°F)

Stratosphere
Pass through the stratosphere, which includes the ozone layer. The air gets thinner as you move up through the atmosphere.

②

ozone

START HERE

−60°C (−76°F)

Troposphere
Board the elevator at ground level, which is also the bottom of the troposphere.

①

15°C (59°F)   sea level

READING VISUALS How does the temperature change as you move up through the atmosphere?

Thermosphere
Radiation from the Sun heats the thermosphere, causing the temperature to rise as you move upward.

90 km (56 mi) and up

Mesosphere
This layer is heated from below by the stratosphere, and the temperature falls as you move upward.

50–90 km (31–56 mi)

Stratosphere
Ozone in this layer absorbs energy from the Sun and heats the stratosphere. The temperature rises as you move upward.

10–50 km (6–31 mi)

Troposphere
This layer is heated by the ground. The temperature falls as you move upward.

0–10 km (0–6 mi)

D   20   Unit: Earth's Atmosphere

DIFFERENTIATE INSTRUCTION

Advanced Have students use the visual to make a line graph that shows how temperature changes with altitude in the atmosphere. Students should label the *x*-axis "Temperature" and the *y*-axis "Altitude." Explain that atmospheric scientists plot altitude on the vertical axis—even though it is the independent variable—because it is easier for them to visualize. Tell students to connect their data points and to indicate where each atmospheric layer begins and ends. Afterwards, display students' graphs in the classroom so that students can better visualize patterns in the data.

1 **Troposphere** (TROH-puh-SFEER) The layer of the atmosphere nearest Earth's surface is called the troposphere because convection seems to turn the air over. This layer contains about 80 percent of the total mass of the atmosphere, including almost all of the water vapor present in the atmosphere. The troposphere is warmed from below by the ground. The temperature is highest at ground level and generally decreases about 6.5°C for each kilometer you rise.

2 **Stratosphere** (STRAT-uh-SFEER) Above the troposphere lies a clear, dry layer of the atmosphere called the stratosphere. Within the stratosphere are molecules of a gas called ozone. These molecules absorb a type of solar radiation that is harmful to life. The energy from the radiation raises the temperature of the air. The temperature increases as you rise high in the stratosphere.

3 **Mesosphere** (MEHZ-uh-SFEER) The air in the mesosphere is extremely thin. In fact, this layer contains less than 0.1 percent of the atmosphere's mass. Most meteors that enter the atmosphere burn up within the mesosphere. The mesosphere, like the troposphere, is heated from below, so the temperature in the mesosphere decreases as you rise.

4 **Thermosphere** (THUR-muh-SFEER) The thermosphere starts about 90 kilometers (56 mi) above Earth's surface. It grows less and less dense over hundreds of kilometers until it becomes outer space. The air high in this layer becomes very hot because the molecules absorb a certain type of solar radiation. However, even the hottest air in this layer would feel cold to you because the molecules are so spread out that they would not conduct much energy to your skin. The temperature in the thermosphere increases as you rise.

 CHECK YOUR READING How does the temperature change in each layer of the atmosphere?

> **READING TiP**
> You can use the word parts to help you recall the temperature layers.
> *tropo-*"turning"
> *strato-*"spreading out"
> *meso-*"middle"
> *thermo-*"heat"

1.2 Review

KEY CONCEPTS

1. What two things happen to solar radiation that reaches Earth?

2. Describe the three processes that transport energy.

3. What characteristic do scientists use to define four layers of Earth's atmosphere?

CRITICAL THINKING

4. **Draw Conclusions** How might a thick, puffy cloud reflect a different amount of the Sun's radiation than a thin, wispy one?

5. **Apply** Jet planes fly near the top of the troposphere. Is it more important to heat or to cool the passenger cabins? Explain your reasoning.

CHALLENGE

6. **Analyze** Earth loses about the same amount of energy as it absorbs from the Sun. If it did not, Earth's temperature would increase. Does the energy move from Earth's surface and atmosphere out to space through radiation, conduction, or convection? Give your reasons.

Chapter 1: **Earth's Changing Atmosphere** 21 **D**

ANSWERS

1. It is reflected or absorbed.

2. Radiation transfers energy in the form of waves; conduction transfers energy by direct contact; convection transfers energy by the motion of a gas or liquid.

3. patterns of temperature change (with altitude)

4. A thicker cloud has more substance to reflect light and other radiation.

5. It is more important to heat the cabins because the temperature at that height is approximately −60°C.

6. Energy moves out to space as radiation; there is no air in space that would allow energy to travel as conduction or convection.

Set Learning Goals
Students will

- Describe two ways that radiation and gases affect each other.
- Explain that the ozone layer absorbs ultraviolet radiation.
- Explain how Earth's surface and greenhouse gases affect infrared radiation.
- Graph experimental data that show changes in levels of greenhouse gases.

3-Minute Warm-Up

Display Transparency 5 or copy this exercise on the board:

1. Write 3 ways the atmosphere moves energy. *radiation, conduction, convection*
2. Which way involves waves? *radiation*
3. Which transfers energy by motion of a heated gas or a liquid? *convection*
4. Which involves direct contact? *conduction*

 3-Minute Warm-Up, p. T5

1.3 MOTIVATE

EXPLORE Radiation

PURPOSE To investigate the energy from visible light and infrared radiation

TIP *10 min.* A radiometer can be used to measure radiation.

WHAT DO YOU THINK? *When the lamp was on, the hand was bright and grew warm. When the lamp was off, the other hand was not bright, but it still grew somewhat warm. Visible light and infrared radiation combined made the hand warmer than infrared radiation alone.*

Ongoing Assessment

 Answer: Materials in the atmosphere can absorb light, reflect it, let it pass through, or emit radiation.

KEY CONCEPT

1.3 Gases in the atmosphere absorb radiation.

◀ **BEFORE, you learned**

- Solar radiation heats Earth's surface and atmosphere
- Earth's surface and atmosphere give off radiation
- The ozone layer is in the stratosphere

▶ **NOW, you will learn**

- More about how radiation and gases affect each other
- About the ozone layer and ultraviolet radiation
- About the greenhouse effect

VOCABULARY

ultraviolet radiation p. 23
infrared radiation p. 23
ozone p. 23
greenhouse effect p. 24
greenhouse gas p. 24

EXPLORE Radiation

Can you feel radiation?

PROCEDURE

1. Turn on the lamp and wait for it to become warm. It gives off visible and infrared radiation.
2. Hold one hand a short distance from the bulb. Record your observations.
3. Turn the lamp off. The bulb continues to give off infrared radiation. Hold your other hand a short distance from the bulb.

WHAT DO YOU THINK?

- What did you see and feel?
- How did radiation affect each hand?

MATERIALS
- lamp

Gases can absorb and give off radiation.

On a sunny day, objects around you look bright. Earth's atmosphere reflects or absorbs some sunlight, but allows most of the visible light to pass through to Earth's surface. A cloudy day is darker because clouds reflect and absorb much of the sunlight, so less light passes through to the ground.

The atmosphere can affect light in four ways. It can absorb light, reflect it, or let it pass through. Air can also emit, or give off, light. Although air does not emit much visible light, certain gases absorb and emit radiation that is similar to visible light.

> **SUPPORTING MAIN IDEAS**
> Remember to make a chart for each main idea.

 List four ways that the atmosphere can affect light.

RESOURCES FOR DIFFERENTIATED INSTRUCTION

Below Level
UNIT RESOURCE BOOK
- Reading Study Guide A, pp. 35–36
- Decoding Support, p. 59

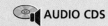 **AUDIO CDS**

Advanced
UNIT RESOURCE BOOK
- Challenge and Extension, p. 41
- Challenge Reading, pp. 55–56

English Learners
UNIT RESOURCE BOOK
Spanish Reading Study Guide, pp. 39–40

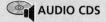 **AUDIO CDS**

- Audio Readings in Spanish
- Audio Readings (English)

Just as there are sounds humans cannot hear, there are forms of radiation that humans cannot see. Sounds can be too high to hear. In a similar way, waves of **ultraviolet radiation** (UHL-truh-VY-uh-liht) have more energy than the light you can see. Ultraviolet radiation can cause sunburn and other types of damage. Sounds can also be too low for humans to hear. In a similar way, waves of **infrared radiation** (IHN-fruh-REHD) have less energy than visible light. Infrared radiation usually warms the materials that absorb it. Different gases in the atmosphere absorb these two different types of radiation.

The ozone layer protects life from harmful radiation.

In Section 1.2, you read about a gas called ozone that forms in the stratosphere. An **ozone** molecule (O_3) is made of three atoms of the element oxygen. Your body uses regular oxygen gas (O_2), which has two atoms of oxygen. In the stratosphere, ozone and regular oxygen gases break apart and form again in a complex cycle. The reactions that destroy and form ozone normally balance each other, so the cycle can repeat endlessly. Even though ozone is mixed with nitrogen and other gases, the ozone in the stratosphere is called the ozone layer.

The ozone layer protects life on Earth by absorbing harmful ultraviolet radiation from the Sun. Too much ultraviolet radiation can cause sunburn, skin cancer, and damaged eyesight. Ultraviolet radiation can harm crops and materials such as plastic or paint. Ozone absorbs ultraviolet radiation but lets other types of radiation, such as visible light, pass through.

READING **TiP**

In this section, wavy arrows represent different types of radiation.

ultraviolet

visible

infrared

Ozone in the Stratosphere

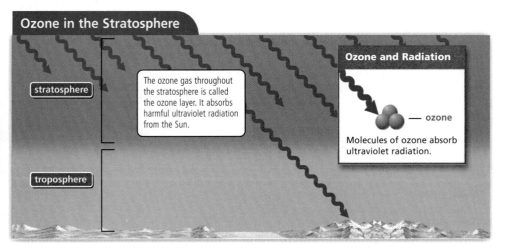

stratosphere

troposphere

The ozone gas throughout the stratosphere is called the ozone layer. It absorbs harmful ultraviolet radiation from the Sun.

Ozone and Radiation

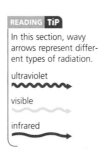

— ozone

Molecules of ozone absorb ultraviolet radiation.

Chapter 1: **Earth's Changing Atmosphere 23** **D**

INVESTIGATE Greenhouse Gases

PURPOSE Construct and interpret a graph to evaluate changes in levels of greenhouse gases

TIP *30 min.* Before beginning the activity, explain to students that temperature and levels of greenhouse gases are connected in a complex system of feedback—it is difficult to neatly label one as the cause and the other as the effect.

INTERPRET DATA *four times; Yes, during each period the CO_2 levels were also high.*

CHALLENGE *No, temperature and carbon dioxide levels changed together. It's not possible to determine from the graph if one was the cause. They may have affected one another or some other factor might have triggered the changes.*

- CO_2 Table Sheet, p. 42
- Datasheet, Greenhouse Gases, p. 43

Technology Resources

Customize this student lab as needed or look for an alternative. Print rubrics to assess student lab reports.

 Lab Generator CD-ROM

Metacognitive Strategy

Point out that it is difficult to determine cause and effect in this lab. Ask students to consider this and other problems they may have encountered. Have them write a short paragraph explaining how they overcame any problems.

Teaching with Technology

Students can also use a computer graphing program to create a graph of their data.

 **VISUALIZATION**
CLASSZONE.COM
See how the greenhouse effect works.

 C

REMINDER ▼

Ozone absorbs ultraviolet radiation in the stratosphere. Greenhouse gases absorb and emit infrared radiation in the troposphere.

? **D**

The greenhouse effect keeps Earth warm.

A jacket helps keep you warm on a cool day by slowing the movement of heat energy away from your body. In a similar way, certain gases in the atmosphere slow the movement of energy away from Earth's surface. The gases absorb and emit infrared radiation, which keeps energy in Earth's system for a while. This process was named the **greenhouse effect** because it reminded scientists of the way glass traps warmth inside a greenhouse.

Carbon dioxide, methane, water vapor, nitrous oxide, and other gases that absorb and give off infrared radiation are known as **greenhouse gases.** Unlike the glass roof and walls of a greenhouse, the greenhouse gases do not form a single layer. They are mixed together with nitrogen, oxygen, and other gases in the air. The atmosphere is densest in the troposphere—the lowest layer—so most of the greenhouse gas molecules are also in the troposphere.

Radiation from the Sun, including visible light, warms Earth's surface, which then emits infrared radiation. If the atmosphere had no greenhouse gases, the infrared radiation would go straight through the atmosphere into outer space. Earth's average surface temperature would be only about −18°C (0°F). Water would freeze, and it would be too cold for most forms of life on Earth to survive.

INVESTIGATE Greenhouse Gases

How have levels of greenhouse gases changed?

Scientists have used ice cores from Antarctica to calculate prehistoric carbon dioxide levels and temperatures. The CO_2 data table has the results for you to plot.

PROCEDURE

1. Plot the CO_2 levels on the graph sheet using a regular pencil. Draw line segments to connect the points.

2. Plot the temperatures on the same graph using a red pencil. Draw red line segments to connect the points.

INTERPRET DATA

- How many times during the past 400,000 years were average temperatures in Antarctica above −56°C?
- Do these changes seem to be connected to changes in carbon dioxide? Explain.

CHALLENGE Is it possible to tell from the graph whether temperature affected carbon dioxide levels or carbon dioxide levels affected temperature? Why or why not?

SKILL FOCUS
Graphing

MATERIALS
- CO_2 data table
- regular pencil
- red pencil

TIME
30 minutes

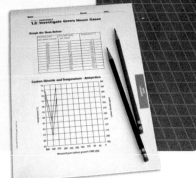

DIFFERENTIATE INSTRUCTION

? **More Reading Support**

C What process keeps Earth warm? *the greenhouse effect*

D What do greenhouse gases do? *absorb and give off infrared radiation*

Advanced Have students work together to make a large table displaying the differences between the ozone layer and the greenhouse effect. The table should have two rows labeled "ozone layer" and "greenhouse effect" and columns for gases involved, radiation involved, and layer of the atmosphere involved.

 Challenge and Extension, p. 41

The Greenhouse Effect

Greenhouse gas molecules absorb and emit infrared radiation.

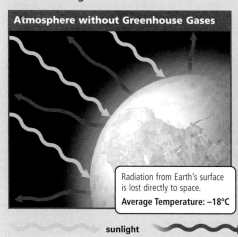

Atmosphere without Greenhouse Gases

Radiation from Earth's surface is lost directly to space.
Average Temperature: −18°C

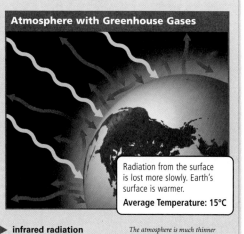

Atmosphere with Greenhouse Gases

Radiation from the surface is lost more slowly. Earth's surface is warmer.
Average Temperature: 15°C

sunlight → infrared radiation

The atmosphere is much thinner than shown here.

Earth's atmosphere does have greenhouse gases. These gases absorb some of the infrared radiation emitted by Earth's surface. The greenhouse gases can then give off this energy as infrared radiation. Some of the energy is absorbed again by the surface, while some of the energy goes out into space. The greenhouse effect keeps Earth's average surface temperature around 15°C (59°F). The energy stays in Earth's system longer with greenhouse gases than without them. In time, all the energy ends up back in outer space. If it did not, Earth would grow warmer and warmer as it absorbed more and more solar radiation.

1.3 Review

KEY CONCEPTS

1. Name and describe two of the ways gases can affect radiation.

2. What type of radiation does the ozone layer affect?

3. How do greenhouse gases keep Earth warm?

CRITICAL THINKING

4. **Infer** What would happen if gases in the atmosphere absorbed visible light?

5. **Compare and Contrast** How are ozone and greenhouse gases alike? How are they different?

⚫ CHALLENGE

6. **Predict** How would the temperature on Earth be affected if the amount of greenhouse gases in the atmosphere changed?

ANSWERS

1. Gases can absorb and give off radiation.

2. ultraviolet radiation

3. They absorb and emit infrared radiation, slowing the movement of energy away from Earth.

4. It would be more difficult to see; air would become warmer, especially in the troposphere; less solar radiation would reach Earth's surface.

5. Both absorb radiation. Ozone absorbs ultraviolet radiation and is found in the stratosphere. Greenhouse gases absorb and give off infrared radiation; their density is greatest in the troposphere.

6. More greenhouse gases: temperatures would go up; less greenhouse gases: temperatures would go down.

Ongoing Assessment

Explain the greenhouse effect.

Describe what the greenhouse gases are doing in the second image of the visual. *The greenhouse gases are absorbing some infrared radiation and giving off some. Earth's surface is warmer.*

Reinforce (the **BIG** idea)

Have students relate the section to the Big Idea.

 Reinforcing Key Concepts, p. 44

1.3 ASSESS & RETEACH

Assess

 Section 1.3 Quiz, p. 5

Reteach

Have students make an outline of Section 1.3 summarizing the main ideas and supporting details. Explain to them that the section's main ideas are the blue heads—the first one being "Gases can absorb and give off radiation." Make sure students support the three main ideas with supporting details. Tell students to look at topic sentences of paragraphs and titles of visuals to help identify supporting details, which may include vocabulary terms and other specific information.

Technology Resources

Have students visit **ClassZone.com** for reteaching of Key Concepts.

 CONTENT REVIEW

 CONTENT REVIEW CD-ROM

MATH IN SCIENCE
Math Skills Practice for Science

Set Learning Goal

To use algebraic equations to determine how much incoming solar radiation is absorbed by Earth's surface on certain days

Present the Science

Overall, Earth's surface absorbs much of the solar radiation that reaches it, mainly because the oceans that cover most of the planet are excellent absorbers of solar radiation. Clouds and snow look white because they reflect light well. Snow-covered ground reflects about 90% of light that hits it, while soil and pavement reflect only about 2%. The rest of the light is absorbed. The oceans that cover most of the planet are excellent absorbers of solar radiation.

Develop Algebra Skills

As students review the example, point out that when reading a verbal model, they should read the equation from left to right. In the last three lines, the calculations are stacked in a vertical manner and should be read like a typical addition or subtraction problem.

Ask: What does *x* represent? *an unknown quantity*

DIFFERENTIATION TIP To help students with cognitive disabilities, help them make a circle graph displaying radiation and absorption percentages.

Close

Ask: Why does Earth's surface reflect a different amount of solar radiation on cloudy days? *Less solar radiation gets through, so less is reflected.*

- Math Support, p. 60
- Math Practice, p. 61

Technology Resources

Students can visit **ClassZone.com** for practice with algebraic equations.

 MATH TUTORIAL

 MATH TUTORIAL
CLASSZONE.COM
Click on Math Tutorial for more help with equations.

Solar Radiation

The amount of sunlight that reaches Earth's surface varies from day to day. On a cloudy day, for example, clouds may absorb or reflect most of the sunlight before it reaches Earth's surface. You can use equations to determine how much incoming solar radiation is absorbed by Earth's surface on each day.

Example

On a particular cloudy day, 50% of the solar radiation coming into Earth is reflected by clouds and the atmosphere, 40% is absorbed by clouds and the atmosphere, and 1% is reflected by Earth's surface. How much is absorbed by Earth's surface?

Write a verbal model:

radiation reflected by clouds & atmosphere		radiation absorbed by clouds & atmosphere		radiation reflected by Earth's surface		radiation absorbed by Earth's surface		total incoming radiation
	+		+		+		=	

Substitute into the model: **50% + 40% + 1% + x = 100%**

Simplify the left side:		91% + x	=	100%
Subtract:		− 91%		− 91%
Simplify:		x	=	9%

ANSWER 9% of the incoming solar radiation is absorbed by Earth's surface.

Determine the amount of incoming solar radiation that is absorbed by Earth's surface on each day.

1. On a sunny day, 15% is reflected by clouds and the atmosphere, 20% is absorbed by clouds and the atmosphere, and 10% is reflected by Earth's surface.

2. On a partly cloudy day, 25% is reflected by clouds and the atmosphere, 20% is absorbed by clouds and the atmosphere, and 5% is reflected by Earth's surface.

CHALLENGE On a particular day, how much incoming solar radiation is absorbed by Earth's surface if 60% is reflected (either by clouds and the atmosphere or by Earth's surface), and half that amount is absorbed by the atmosphere?

sunny day

partly cloudy day

ANSWERS

1. 15% + 20% + 10% + x = 100%; 45% + x = 100%; x = 55%

2. 25% + 20% + 5% + x = 100%; 50% + x = 100%; x = 50%

CHALLENGE 60% + 30% + x = 100%; 90% + x = 100%; x = 10%

KEY CONCEPT

Human activities affect the atmosphere.

◀ **BEFORE, you learned**

- The atmosphere has gases that absorb and give off radiation
- The ozone layer absorbs ultraviolet radiation
- The greenhouse effect keeps Earth warm

▶ **NOW, you will learn**

- What the types and effects of pollution are
- About the effect of human activities on greenhouse gases
- How the ozone layer is changing

VOCABULARY

air pollution p. 27
particulate p. 28
fossil fuel p. 28
smog p. 28

EXPLORE Air Pollution

Where does smoke go?

PROCEDURE

1. Light the candle and let it burn for a minute or two. Observe the air around the candle.

2. Blow out the candle and observe the smoke until you cannot see it anymore.

MATERIALS
- candle in holder
- matches

WHAT DO YOU THINK?
- How far did the smoke from the candle travel?
- A burning candle produces invisible gases. Where do you think they went?

SUPPORTING MAIN IDEAS
Remember to start a new chart for each main idea.

Human activity can cause air pollution.

If someone in your kitchen burns a piece of toast, and if a fan is blowing in the hallway, everyone in your home will smell the smoke. That means that everyone will breathe some air containing smoke. Smoke and other harmful materials that are added to the air are called **air pollution.** Outdoors, wind can spread air pollution from place to place the way a fan does within your home.

When toast burns, you may be able to see smoke. If smoke drifts in from another room, it may be too thin to see, but you may be able to smell it. There are other types of air pollution that you cannot see or smell. Like smoke, they can be spread around by wind. Air pollution from one place can affect a wide area. However, most types of pollution leave the air or become thin enough to be harmless after a time.

CHECK YOUR READING How is air pollution moved around?

Chapter 1: **Earth's Changing Atmosphere** 27 **D**

RESOURCES FOR DIFFERENTIATED INSTRUCTION

Below Level

UNIT RESOURCE BOOK
- Reading Study Guide A, pp. 47–48
- Decoding Support, p. 59

🎧 **AUDIO CDS**

Advanced

UNIT RESOURCE BOOK
Challenge and Extension, p. 53

English Learners

UNIT RESOURCE BOOK
Spanish Reading Study Guide, pp. 51–52

🎧 **AUDIO CDS**

- Audio Readings in Spanish
- Audio Readings (English)

◐ **Set Learning Goals**

Students will

- Describe the types and effects of pollution.
- Describe global warming.
- Explain how the ozone layer is changing.

◐ **3-Minute Warm-Up**

Display Transparency 5 or copy this exercise on the board:

Are these statements true? If not, correct them.

1. Greenhouse gases absorb visible light. *Greenhouse gases absorb infrared radiation.*

2. The ozone layer is found in the troposphere. *The ozone layer is found in the stratosphere.*

3. Greenhouse gases include carbon dioxide and water vapor. *true*

T 3-Minute Warm-Up, p. T5

1.4 MOTIVATE

EXPLORE Air Pollution

PURPOSE To promote inquiry about what creates pollution and how fast and far it can travel

TIP *10 min.* For safety reasons, you may want to light one candle on your desk and have students gather round to observe the smoke. If students light their own candles, have them return any unused matches to you immediately upon completing the activity.

WHAT DO YOU THINK? *It traveled a few meters. They went in the same direction as the smoke.*

Ongoing Assessment

CHECK YOUR READING *Answer: by wind*

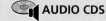

14 INSTRUCT

Teacher Demo

Tell students that plant roots hold soil together much like glue holds together pages in a book. Then use the following demonstration to show how dust and soil can enter the air. Place a book and a fan on your desk. Tell students that the fan represents the wind and the book represents grass-covered soil. Ask students to predict what will happen to the "soil" when the fan blows on it. *Nothing will happen; the pages are bound together.* Turn the fan on the book and allow students to see if their predictions were correct. Then place a sheet of paper on your desk. Ask: What will happen when the fan blows on the paper? *The paper will blow away.* Turn the fan on the paper so that students can see if their predictions were correct. Ask: What did the paper represent? *bare soil that entered the air*

Ongoing Assessment

CHECK YOUR READING *Answer: Gases and particles. An example of a gas is carbon monoxide; an example of a particle is dust.*

Types of Pollution

READING TiP
Pollution and *pollutant* have the same root, *pollute*—"to make unfit."

Scientists classify the separate types of air pollution, called pollutants, as either gases or particles. Gas pollutants include carbon monoxide, methane, ozone, sulfur oxides, and nitrogen oxides. Some of these gases occur naturally in the atmosphere. These gases are considered pollutants only when they are likely to cause harm. For example, ozone gas is good in the stratosphere but is harmful to breathe. When ozone is in the troposphere, it is a pollutant.

Particle pollutants can be easier to see than gas pollutants. **Particulates** are tiny particles or droplets that are mixed in with air. Smoke contains particulates. The wind can pick up other particulates, such as dust and dirt, pollen, and tiny bits of salt from the oceans. Some sources of pollutants are listed below.

CHECK YOUR READING What are the two types of pollutants? Give an example of each.

In cities and suburbs, most air pollution comes from the burning of fossil fuels such as oil, gasoline, and coal. **Fossil fuels** are fuels formed from the remains of prehistoric animals and plants. In London in the 1800s, burning coal provided much of the heat and energy for homes and factories. The resulting smoke and local weather conditions often produced a thick fog or cloud. The word **smog** describes this combination of smoke and fog. A newer type of air pollution is also called smog. Sunlight causes the fumes from gasoline, car exhaust, and other gases to react chemically. The reactions form new pollutants, such as ozone, which together are called smog. In cities, there can be enough smog to make a brownish haze.

Sources of Pollution

The burning of fossil fuels in power plants, cars, factories, and homes is a major source of pollution in the United States.

Human Activities

- fossil fuels: gases and particles
- unburned fuels: smog
- manufacturing: gases and particles
- tractors/construction equipment: dust and soil
- farming: fertilizers and pesticides

Natural Sources

- dust, pollen, soil, salt
- volcanoes and forest fires: gases and particles

D 28 Unit: **Earth's Atmosphere**

DIFFERENTIATE INSTRUCTION

(?) More Reading Support

A How do scientists classify types of air pollution? *as gases or particles*

B Where does most air pollution in cities come from? *from burning fossil fuels*

English Learners When two or more English learners share a native language, allow them to discuss vocabulary and concepts from the text in that language. The students may be able to help each other see the difference between similar words, such as *pollution* and *pollutant* from this section. You can also pair English learners with advanced students for help in practicing model English.

D 28 Unit: **Earth's Atmosphere**

Effects of Pollution

Air pollution can cause health problems. Polluted air may irritate your eyes, nose, throat, and lungs. It can smell bad or make it hard to breathe. Gases or chemicals from particulates can move from your lungs to other parts of your body. Exercising in polluted air can be dangerous because you take more air into your lungs when you exercise. Over time, people who breathe polluted air can develop lung disease and other health problems. Air pollution can cause extra problems for young children, older adults, and people who suffer from asthma.

CHECK YOUR READING Describe three of the ways in which pollution can affect people.

A man in Mexico City wears a gas mask while he sells newspapers. The green sign behind him warns people of a high ozone level.

Particulates can stick to surfaces and damage plants, buildings, and other objects outdoors. Dusty air or a dust storm can darken the day and make it difficult to see. Particulates can be carried high into the atmosphere, where they can reflect or absorb sunlight and even affect the weather. Rain clears the air by removing particles and some polluting gases from the air. However, some pollutants are still harmful when rain moves them from the air to the ground, lakes, and oceans.

Controlling Pollution

You may have experienced a smog or ozone alert. In some cities, smog becomes so bad that it is dangerous to exercise outdoors. Weather reports may include smog alerts so that people will know when to be careful. Cities may ask people not to drive cars when the weather conditions are likely to produce smog.

National, state, and local governments work together to reduce air pollution and protect people from its effects. Countries may come to agreements when the air pollution from one country affects another. Within the United States, Congress has passed laws to reduce air pollution. The Clean Air Act limits the amount of air pollution that factories and power plants are allowed to release. The act also sets rules for making car exhaust cleaner. The Environmental Protection Agency measures air pollution and works to enforce the laws passed by Congress.

Real World Example

Air pollution can be deadly. In 1880, a poisonous smog of sulfur dioxide gas formed over London; more than 2000 people died. In 1952, London experienced another toxic cloud of air pollution; this time, approximately 4000 people died. These and other incidents prompted many countries to adopt air pollution laws. Although pollution is still a problem in developed nations, people in developing countries are often hit hardest by health problems associated with low air quality. The World Health Organization estimates that 1400 deaths could be avoided annually in Jakarta, Indonesia, if air quality was improved.

Ongoing Assessment

Describe the types and effects of pollution.

Ask students to describe how one type of pollution can damage a person's health. *Chemicals from particulates, such as those released by factories, can be inhaled and, over time, cause someone to develop lung disease.*

CHECK YOUR READING *Answer: It can irritate eyes, nose, throat, and lungs. It can make it hard to breathe. It can cause lung disease.*

DIFFERENTIATE INSTRUCTION

? More Reading Support

C What can breathing polluted air do to people? *It can cause lung disease and other health problems.*

Alternative Assessment Have students draw a picture of a human figure and use captions, labels, and arrows to describe how pollution affects different parts of the body. For example, students might draw an arrow pointing to the nose or lungs with the caption, "pollution can irritate the nose and smell bad, or make it difficult to breathe."

Develop Critical Thinking

INFER Tell students that oceans are "carbon sinks"—that is, they absorb carbon dioxide from the air and store it. Cool water can absorb more carbon dioxide than warm water. Ask: What might happen to atmospheric levels of carbon dioxide if the oceans got warmer? *Carbon dioxide in the atmosphere would increase.* Tell students that water expands slightly when heated. Ask: What would happen to sea level if the oceans warmed up? *Sea level would rise.* Show students a map of the world. Have them locate major coastal cities. Ask: How might an increase in sea level affect these cities? *Sample answer: Some parts of the cities might be flooded.*

Teach Difficult Concepts

It is often difficult for students to grasp that a single human activity can affect the environment in multiple ways. For example, point out that tractors and construction equipment stir up particulates and burn fossil fuels. In this respect, they affect the environment by adding both particulates and gases to the air. Have students analyze the sources of air pollution listed in the text to deepen their understanding of the effects of pollution.

Teach from Visuals

After students examine the photographs and captions, have them make a table listing the sources of each greenhouse gas. CO_2: use of fossil fuels; CH_4: livestock, bacteria in rice fields, landfills; N_2O: fertilizers, chemical factories

Ongoing Assessment

 CHECK YOUR READING *Organisms such as trees may change the amount of greenhouse gases in the atmosphere. That change can affect temperatures on Earth, and can, in turn, affect organisms.*

Human activities are increasing greenhouse gases.

A source of air pollution usually affects areas close to it. In contrast, some natural processes and human activities change the amounts of gases throughout Earth's atmosphere.

Sources of Greenhouse Gases

 REMINDER Plants remove carbon dioxide from the air and store the carbon in solid forms.

You read in Section 1.1 how natural cycles move gases into and out of the atmosphere. Plant growth, forest fires, volcanoes, and other natural processes affect the amounts of carbon dioxide and other greenhouse gases in the atmosphere. The amounts of greenhouse gases then affect temperatures on Earth. In turn, the temperatures affect plant growth and other processes that produce or reduce greenhouse gases.

CHECK YOUR READING How do life and the atmosphere affect each other?

Most greenhouse gases occur naturally. They have helped keep temperatures within a range suitable for the plants and animals that live on Earth. However, human activities are producing greenhouse gases faster than natural processes can remove these gases from the

 **Greenhouse Gases from Human Activities**

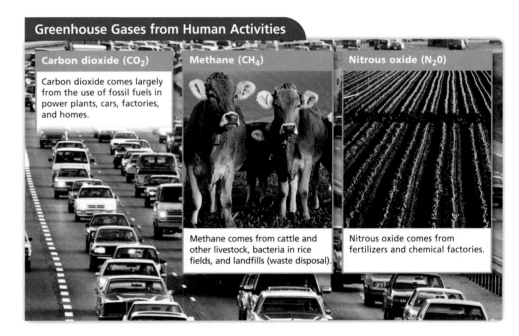

Carbon dioxide (CO₂)
Carbon dioxide comes largely from the use of fossil fuels in power plants, cars, factories, and homes.

Methane (CH₄)
Methane comes from cattle and other livestock, bacteria in rice fields, and landfills (waste disposal).

Nitrous oxide (N₂0)
Nitrous oxide comes from fertilizers and chemical factories.

DIFFERENTIATE INSTRUCTION

? More Reading Support

D Do greenhouse gases affect areas near their sources only? Explain.
No, they affect the atmosphere.

Advanced When determining the total effect of greenhouse gases, scientists must consider how well each gas absorbs and emits infrared radiation, and how long the gas stays in the atmosphere. Have students research these considerations for carbon dioxide and methane, and then debate which gas poses more of a problem. *Methane is about 20 times more effective than carbon dioxide at retaining energy, but it stays in the atmosphere for less time (only about 12 years).*

R Challenge and Extension, p. 53

atmosphere. Some activities that produce greenhouse gases are shown on page 30. Water vapor is also a greenhouse gas, but the amount of water vapor in the air depends more on weather than on human activity.

Global Warming

Many people are concerned about the amounts of greenhouse gases that humans are adding to the air. Carbon dioxide, for example, can stay in the atmosphere for more than 100 years, so the amounts keep adding up. The air contains about 30 percent more carbon dioxide than it did in the mid-1700s, and the level of carbon dioxide is now increasing about 0.4 percent per year.

CHECK YOUR READING How are carbon dioxide levels changing?

As the graph below shows, temperatures have risen in recent decades. Earth's atmosphere, water, and other systems work together in complex ways, so it is hard to know exactly how much greenhouse gases change the temperature. Scientists make computer models to understand the effects of greenhouse gases and explore what might happen in the future. The models predict that the average global temperature will continue to rise another 1.4–5.8°C (2.5–10.4°F) by the year 2100. This may not seem like a big change in temperature, but it can have big effects. Global warming can affect sources of food, the amount of water and other resources available, and even human health. You will read more about the possible effects of global warming in Chapter 4.

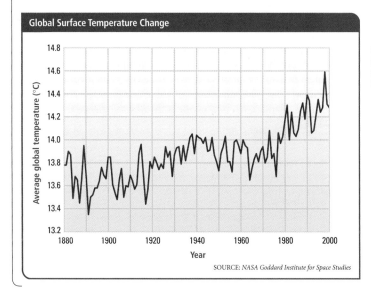

Global Surface Temperature Change

Earth's average temperature has risen over the last century.

SOURCE: *NASA Goddard Institute for Space Studies*

In the late 19th century, Swedish scientist Svante Arrhenius proposed that burning fossil fuels could affect global temperatures. It was not until the late 1950s, however, that scientists began to find concrete evidence of increasing levels of greenhouse gases. At that time, a study was set up in Hawaii to analyze air chemistry. The goal of the study was not to analyze air pollution—in fact, the researchers purposely chose an isolated location, far from factories and towns. The data showed a marked increase in CO_2 levels from 1958 to 1994 (from 315 parts per million to 360 parts per million).

Teach from Visuals

To help students interpret the "Global Surface Temperature Change" graph, ask:

• What does the *y*-axis show? *average global surface temperatures*

• What was the average temperature in 1880? *13.8°C*

• What trend do you see on the graph? *Within each decade, the temperature differences dip and rise but overall, the temperature has increased.*

• During which three decades did overall temperatures change the fastest? *1970–2000*

Ongoing Assessment

Describe global warming.

Ask: What is global warming? *an increase in average global temperature*

CHECK YOUR READING *They are increasing.*

More Reading Support

E Why do amounts of carbon dioxide in the air keep adding up? *Carbon dioxide can stay in the air for a long time.*

Inclusion Have a student volunteer take notes during lively class discussions. Use a different volunteer each day. Keep the notes in a folder on your desk so that students with hearing impairments can easily refer to them.

This commuter is traveling to work without burning fossil fuels.

 **RESOURCE CENTER**
CLASSZONE.COM

Examine the current state of the ozone layer.

F

Reducing Greenhouse Gases

Global warming is not a local issue. It affects the atmosphere around the entire planet. An international agreement to limit the amounts of greenhouse gases, called the Kyoto Protocol, would require developed nations to release no more greenhouse gases each year than they did in 1990. The Kyoto Protocol could take effect only if the nations releasing the most greenhouse gases accept the agreement. In 1990, more than one-third of the amount of greenhouse gases released came from the United States, which has not accepted the agreement.

New technologies may help fight the problem of global warming. Scientists are developing ways to heat and cool buildings, transport people and goods, and make products using less energy. Using less energy saves resources and money and it also reduces greenhouse gases. Scientists are also developing ways to produce energy without using any fossil fuels at all.

 How can technology help reduce global warming?

Human activities produce chemicals that destroy the ozone layer.

At ground level, ozone is a pollutant, but at higher altitudes it benefits life. The ozone layer in the stratosphere protects living things by absorbing harmful ultraviolet radiation. You read in Section 1.3 that ozone is constantly being formed and broken apart in a natural cycle.

In the 1970s, scientists found that certain chemicals were disrupting this cycle. An atom of chlorine (Cl), for example, can start a series of chemical reactions that break apart ozone (O_3) and form regular oxygen gas (O_2). The same atom of chlorine can repeat this process thousands of times. No new ozone is formed to balance the loss.

 What does chlorine do to the amount of ozone in the stratosphere?

Some natural processes put chlorine into the stratosphere, but about 85 percent of the chlorine there comes from human activity. Chemicals called chlorofluorocarbons (KLAWR-oh-FLUR-oh-KAHR-buhnz) have been manufactured for use in cooling systems, spray cans, and foam for packaging. These chemicals break down in the stratosphere and release chlorine and other ozone-destroying chemicals.

D 32 Unit: Earth's Atmosphere

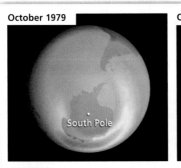
October 1979

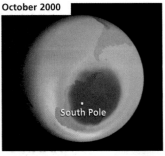
October 2000

South Pole

The size of the dark blue area of little ozone increased from 1979 to 2000.

less ozone — more ozone

SOURCE: *Goddard Space Flight Center/NASA*

READING VISUALS Compare the color at one location on both maps. How has the amount of ozone changed?

The amount of ozone in the stratosphere varies from place to place and changes with the seasons. Cold temperatures and sunshine make the ozone over Antarctica—the South Pole—especially sensitive to the chemicals that destroy ozone. The amount of ozone over Antarctica decreased by half from the 1970s to the mid-1990s. The maps above show the loss of ozone over Antarctica. Smaller but important changes were measured in other regions.

The ozone layer affects the whole world. Since 1987, more than 180 nations have signed an agreement called the Montreal Protocol. They have agreed on a plan to stop making and using chemicals that harm the ozone layer. Experts study the ozone layer and recommend changes to the agreement. The Montreal Protocol has been updated several times. Less harmful chemicals are now used instead of chlorofluorocarbons, but gases from past human activities are still in the ozone layer. If countries continue to follow the Montreal Protocol, ozone levels will return to normal in about 50 years.

1.4 Review

KEY CONCEPTS
1. Describe two of the sources of air pollution.
2. What are three human activities that increase the levels of greenhouse gases?
3. How do human activities affect the ozone layer?

CRITICAL THINKING
4. **Classify** List the following pollutants as either gases or particles: dust, ozone, pollen, carbon monoxide, methane.
5. **Predict** How might global warming affect the way you live in the future?

CHALLENGE
6. **Synthesize** In North America, winds typically blow from west to east. Where might pollution from your community end up? Use a map to help you answer the question.

ANSWERS

1. Volcanoes and the burning of fossil fuels add gases and particles to the air.

2. burning fossil fuels, farming practices, waste disposal, chemical production

3. Humans use products containing chemicals that destroy ozone in the stratosphere.

4. particles: pollen, dust; gases: ozone, carbon monoxide, methane

5. It might make the weather hotter and wetter, so it would be less comfortable to be outside. If crops are affected, you might have trouble buying the foods you like.

6. any place east of the student's location

Focus

PURPOSE To identify and measure air particulates at different locations and use the information to analyze air pollution trends

OVERVIEW Students will stick tape over square-shaped holes on two index cards and place the cards overnight at separate locations. The next day, they will inspect the particulates that accumulated on the cards. They will quantify and analyze the particulates. Students will find that:

- particulates vary in size, shape, and composition depending on location
- some locations have markedly more particulates

Lab Preparation

- Notify the custodian that students are doing this lab and that index cards should not be picked up or thrown away overnight.
- Use gooseneck lamps to help students see their particles more clearly; position the lamps so that the light shines in from the side.
- Prior to the investigation, have students read through the investigation and prepare their data tables. Or you may wish to copy and distribute datasheets and rubrics.

 UNIT RESOURCE BOOK, pp. 62–70

SCIENCE TOOLKIT, F14

Lab Management

Students should write their names and other information on the cards before they attach the tape—this way, particles on their hands won't accidentally stick to the exposed tape.

SAFETY Tell students not to touch the particulates that they collect.

INCLUSION Students with visual impairments can use microscopes rather than magnifying glasses so they can see the particles more clearly.

CHAPTER INVESTIGATION

Observing Particulates

OVERVIEW AND PURPOSE Many of us go through life unaware of particulates in the air, but allergy or asthma sufferers may become uncomfortably aware of high particulate levels. Certain particles, such as dust mite casings, can trigger asthma attacks. Particles that cling to surfaces can make them look dirty or even damage them. Some colors of surfaces may hide the dirt. In this investigation you will

- compare the number and types of particles that settle to surfaces in two different locations
- learn a method of counting particles

Problem

How do the types and numbers of particles in two different locations compare?

Hypothesize

You should decide on the locations in step 3 before writing your hypothesis. Write a hypothesis to explain how particulates collected at two different locations might differ. Your hypothesis should take the form of an "If . . . , then . . . , because . . ." statement.

Procedure

1. Use the ruler to mark on each index card a centered square that is 3 cm per side. Carefully cut out each square.

2. On each card, place a piece of tape so that it covers the hole. Press the edges of the tape to the card, but do not let the center of the tape stick to anything. You should have a clean sticky window when you turn the card over.

3. Choose two different collecting locations where you can safely leave your cards—sticky side up—undisturbed overnight. You might place them on outside and inside windowsills, on the ground and in a tree, or in different rooms.

4. Mark each card with your name, the date, and the location. Tape the cards in place or weigh them down so they will not blow away. Write your hypothesis. Collect your cards the next day.

MATERIALS
- 2 index cards
- ruler
- scissors
- transparent packing tape
- magnifying glass
- white paper
- black paper
- graph paper
- calculator

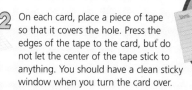

INVESTIGATION RESOURCES

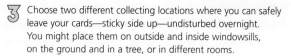

 CHAPTER INVESTIGATION, Observing Particulates
- Level A, pp. 62–65
- Level B, pp. 66–69
- Level C, p. 70

Advanced students should complete Levels B & C.

Writing a Lab Report, D12–13

Technology Resources

Customize this student lab as needed or look for an alternative. Print rubrics to assess student lab reports.

 Lab Generator CD-ROM

Observe and Analyze

1. **OBSERVE** Use the magnifying glass to inspect each card closely. Can you identify any of the particles? Try using white paper and black paper behind the card to help you see dark and light particles better. Describe and draw in your **Science Notebook** the types of particles from each card. How does the background affect the type or number of particles you see?

2. **RECORD** Make a data table like the one shown on the notebook page below. Then, place each card onto a piece of graph paper. Line up the top and left edges of each card's center square with the grid on the graph paper and tape the card down. Choose four graph-paper squares and count the number of visible particles in each square. Use the magnifying glass. Record your results on the data table.

3. **CALCULATE**

   AVERAGE Calculate the average number of particles per square for each card.

   $$\text{average} = \frac{\text{sum of particles in 4 squares}}{4}$$

   CONVERT Use the formula below to convert from particles per square to particles per square centimeter. If your squares were half a centimeter wide, then use 0.5 cm in the denominator below.

   $$\begin{array}{l}\text{particles} \\ \text{per cm}^2\end{array} = \begin{array}{l}\text{particles} \\ \text{per} \\ \text{square}\end{array} \times \left(\frac{1 \text{ square}}{\text{width of square (in cm)}}\right)^2$$

Conclude

1. **COMPARE** Compare the types of particles found on the cards. List similarities and differences. Compare the numbers of particles found on the cards.

2. **INTERPRET** Compare your results with your hypothesis. Do your data support your hypothesis?

3. **INFER** What can you infer about where the particles came from or how they reached each location? What evidence did you find to support these inferences?

4. **IDENTIFY LIMITS** What possible limitations or sources of error might have affected your results? Why was it necessary to average the number of particles from several squares?

5. **EVALUATE** Do you think the color of the graph paper affected the number of particles you were able to count?

6. **APPLY** What color would you choose for playground equipment in your area? Explain your choice.

INVESTIGATE Further

CHALLENGE Design an experiment to find out how fast particles in one location are deposited.

Observing Particulates

Problem How do the types and numbers of particles in two different locations compare?

Hypothesize

Observe and Analyze

Table 1. Number of Particles

	Number of Particles						Notes
	Sq. 1	Sq. 2	Sq. 3	Sq. 4	Ave./ sq.	Ave./ cm²	
Card 1							
Card 2							

Conclude

Chapter 1: **Earth's Changing Atmosphere** 35 **D**

Observe and Analyze

SAMPLE DATA location A—square 1: 10, square 2: 15, square 3: 12, square 4: 9, average/square: 11.5, average/cm²: 46. location B—square 1: 6, square 2: 9, square 3: 4, square 4: 7, average/square: 6.5, average/cm²: 26.

1. *Dust, ash, pollen, and soot could be identified. Soot was more easily seen against white. Dust was more easily seen against black.*

2. *Student results will vary.*

3. *Student answers will vary, but the average should be within the range of individual counts.*

Conclude

1. *The card placed outside had more particles than the card placed inside. The size and shape of the particles on the outside card varied more than did those on the inside card.*

2. *Answers will vary.*

3. *Soot on one card came from wood-burning stoves; two houses with wood-burning stoves were on either side of the tree where the card had been placed. On the other card, dust came from chalk used on the chalkboard; the card had been placed near the board.*

4. *Particles could have gotten on the tape when handling the cards. Some particles may not have stuck to the tape. Averaging was necessary because the particles did not fall evenly on the surface. Thus, the particles on one particular square may not have been representative of the whole.*

5. *Yes, light-colored particles were difficult to see.*

6. *Students might choose a color to hide the particles (light or dark), or else a color on which the particles would show up, indicating when the equipment needed cleaning.*

INVESTIGATE Further

CHALLENGE A card could be placed at a location each night over five days. Sample squares could be counted each day, and the average of these counts would show the rate of deposition per night.

Post-Lab Discussion

• Discuss whether it was easy to make inferences about the sources of the particles. Ask: How are air pollutants moved about? *by wind* Can you always expect the source of a pollutant to be close by? *no*

• Ask: What trends did you observe in the data? *Sample answer: Cards placed outside tended to have more particulates than cards placed indoors.*

BACK TO

the BIG idea

Ask students to compare how the atmosphere protects and supports life with the way humans should protect and support the atmosphere. *The atmosphere supports life by providing the gases that living things need for life processes, such as oxygen, carbon dioxide, nitrogen, and water. The atmosphere protects life by keeping Earth's temperature at a level that allows life to survive and by absorbing harmful radiation. Humans should protect and support the atmosphere by taking steps to limit air pollution, ozone depletion, and global warming.*

◑ KEY CONCEPTS SUMMARY

SECTION 1.1

Ask: Where is Earth's atmosphere most dense? *closest to Earth's surface*

SECTION 1.2

Ask: What things reflect the Sun's energy? What things absorb it? *The clouds, the atmosphere, and Earth's surface all reflect and absorb the Sun's energy.*

Ask: What happens when air is heated from below? *convection*

SECTION 1.3

Ask: What type of radiation does ozone absorb? *ultraviolet*

Ask: What type of radiation do greenhouse gases absorb? *infrared*

SECTION 1.4

Ask: What happens when the level of greenhouse gases increases? *Earth's temperature rises.*

Ask: How does riding a bike help reduce global warming? *No fossil fuels are burned when riding a bike; burning fossil fuels adds carbon dioxide to the air.*

Review Concepts

- Big Idea Flow Chart, p. T1
- Chapter Outline, pp. T7–T8

---

1 Chapter Review

the BIG idea

Earth's atmosphere is a blanket of gases that supports and protects life.

CONTENT REVIEW
CLASSZONE.COM

◑ KEY CONCEPTS SUMMARY

1.1 Earth's atmosphere supports life.

The **atmosphere** is a thin layer surrounding Earth. Gases in the atmosphere provide substances essential for living things. Natural **cycles** and sudden changes affect the atmosphere.

VOCABULARY
atmosphere p. 9
altitude p. 10
density p. 10
cycle p. 12

1.2 The Sun supplies the atmosphere's energy.

Energy from the Sun moves through Earth's atmosphere in three ways.

Density and temperature change with altitude. The layers, from top to bottom, are

- thermosphere
- mesosphere
- stratosphere
- troposphere

VOCABULARY
radiation p. 17
conduction p. 18
convection p. 19

1.3 Gases in the atmosphere absorb radiation.

Ozone molecules in the stratosphere absorb harmful ultraviolet radiation.

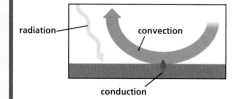

Greenhouse gases in the troposphere keep Earth warm by absorbing and emitting infrared radiation.

VOCABULARY
ultraviolet radiation p. 23
infrared radiation p. 23
ozone p. 23
greenhouse effect p. 24
greenhouse gas p. 24

1.4 Human activities affect the atmosphere.

Human activities have added pollutants and ozone-destroying chemicals to the atmosphere.

The amounts of greenhouse gases have been increasing and global temperatures are rising.

 ozone

 carbon dioxide

VOCABULARY
air pollution p. 27
particulate p. 28
fossil fuel p. 28
smog p. 28

Technology Resources

Have students visit **ClassZone.com** or use the CD-ROM for a cumulative review of concepts.

CONTENT REVIEW

CONTENT REVIEW CD-ROM

Engage students in a whole-class interactive review of Key Concepts. Edit content as you wish.

POWER PRESENTATIONS

Reviewing Vocabulary

Draw a word triangle for each of the vocabulary terms listed below. Define the term, use it in a sentence, and draw a picture to help you remember the term. A sample is shown below.

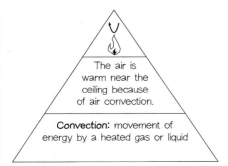

The air is warm near the ceiling because of air convection.

Convection: movement of energy by a heated gas or liquid

1. conduction
2. atmosphere
3. density
4. air pollution
5. altitude
6. radiation
7. cycle
8. particulate

Reviewing Key Concepts

Multiple Choice *Choose the letter of the best answer.*

9. Which of the following represents a sudden change in Earth's atmosphere?
   a. the carbon cycle
   b. the nitrogen cycle
   c. a rain shower
   d. a dust storm

10. The gas that makes up the largest percentage of the atmosphere's substance is
    a. nitrogen
    b. oxygen
    c. water vapor
    d. carbon dioxide

11. Which of the cycles below involves oxygen gas?
    a. the carbon cycle
    b. the water cycle
    c. the density cycle
    d. the argon cycle

12. What process moves energy from Earth's surface to high in the troposphere?
    a. solar energy
    b. conduction
    c. convection
    d. the nitrogen cycle

13. In which of the atmosphere's layers does temperature decrease as the altitude increases?
    a. the troposphere and the stratosphere
    b. the troposphere and the mesosphere
    c. the stratosphere and the mesosphere
    d. the stratosphere and the thermosphere

14. What keeps Earth's surface warm?
    a. conduction
    b. the ozone layer
    c. convection
    d. the greenhouse effect

15. Which gas absorbs ultraviolet radiation?
    a. carbon dioxide
    b. methane
    c. ozone
    d. water vapor

16. Which type of pollution includes harmful droplets?
    a. particulate
    b. gas
    c. dust
    d. smoke

Short Answer *Write a short answer to each question.*

17. Explain why ozone is helpful to life in the stratosphere but harmful in the troposphere.

18. Describe three of the ways human activities affect the atmosphere.

19. Write a brief paragraph describing how the photograph below provides evidence that Earth's atmosphere is in motion.

Reviewing Vocabulary

Check drawings for accuracy.

1. transfer of heat energy from one substance to another by direct contact; If you touch a hot stove, you may be burned through conduction.

2. layer of air that surrounds Earth; Earth's atmosphere is necessary for life.

3. amount of mass in a given volume of a substance; The density of air changes when it's heated.

4. harmful materials that are added to the air; Air pollution can smell bad.

5. distance above sea level; The air is less dense at a higher altitude.

6. transfer of energy across distances in the form of certain types of waves; Solar radiation provides energy to Earth.

7. process that repeats over and over; Rain is part of the water cycle.

8. tiny particles or droplets mixed in with air; Can spray paint add particulates to air?

Reviewing Key Concepts

9. d
10. a
11. a
12. c
13. b
14. d
15. c
16. a

17. Ozone absorbs harmful radiation in the stratosphere. But ozone itself is harmful to breathe when it is in the troposphere.

18. Humans burn fossil fuels, raise cattle, and add fertilizers to the soil. These activities add pollutants and greenhouse gases to the atmosphere.

19. The dandelion seeds are moving with the air. If the air was not moving, then the seeds would either stay on the stem or fall straight down.

ASSESSMENT RESOURCES

 UNIT ASSESSMENT BOOK
- Chapter Test A, pp. 7–10
- Chapter Test B, pp. 11–14
- Chapter Test C, pp. 15–18
- Alternative Assessment, pp. 19–20

 SPANISH ASSESSMENT BOOK
Spanish Chapter Test, pp. 173–176

Technology Resources

Edit test items and answer choices.

 Test Generator CD-ROM

Visit **ClassZone.com** to extend test practice.

 Test Practice

Thinking Critically

20. The blue water moved under the red water.

21. The blue water is more dense and thus sinks to the bottom.

22. the troposphere

23. It keeps Earth's temperature from getting too cold or too warm.

24. Light-colored dust would reflect more solar radiation, and dark-colored soot would absorb more solar radiation.

25. Smog forms when chemicals react with sunlight. At night, the Sun is not shining so less smog would form.

26. Radiation from the burner is like radiation from the Sun or the ground. Conduction from the pot to water is like conduction from the ground to air. Convection of water is like convection of air.

27. You can puff your cheeks with air.

28. If the power plant uses coal, then both choices involve burning fossil fuels—coal and natural gas—that add to global warming. If the power plant uses an alternative energy source, such as water, it would be a better environmental choice.

the BIG idea

29. <u>Solar radiation</u> heats the atmosphere. The atmosphere itself is made up of gases such as <u>carbon dioxide</u>, <u>water vapor</u>, and <u>oxygen</u>. Some of these are greenhouse gases, which keep Earth's temperature at a level that allows life to survive. Carbon, nitrogen, and <u>water</u> constantly circulate, or <u>cycle</u>, among plants, animals, and the atmosphere. In the <u>stratosphere</u>, <u>ozone</u> blocks ultraviolet rays.

30. The atmosphere that surrounds Earth is more dense close to the surface, in the layer called the troposphere. The air in the troposphere keeps the kite soaring.

UNIT PROJECTS

Give students the appropriate Unit Project worksheets from the URB for their projects. Both directions and rubrics can be used as a guide.

R Unit Projects, pp. 5–10

Thinking Critically

Use the photographs to answer the next two questions.

Ⓐ

cold water   hot water

Ⓑ

In the demonstration pictured above, hot water has been tinted red with food coloring, and cold water has been tinted blue. View B shows the results after the divider has been lifted and the motion of the water has stopped.

20. **OBSERVE** Describe how the hot water and the cold water moved when the divider was lifted.

21. **APPLY** Use your understanding of density to explain the motion of the water.

22. **CALCULATE** The top of Mount Everest is 8850 meters above sea level. Which layer of the atmosphere contains the top of this mountain? Use the information from page 20 and convert the units.

23. **APPLY** Why is radiation from Earth's surface and atmosphere important for living things?

24. **PREDICT** Dust is often light in color, while soot from fires is generally dark. What would happen to the amounts of solar radiation reflected and absorbed if a large amount of light-colored dust was added to the air? What if a large amount of dark soot was added?

25. **IDENTIFY EFFECT** When weather conditions and sunlight are likely to produce smog, cities may ask motorists to refuel their cars at night instead of early in the day. Why would this behavior make a difference?

26. **COMPARE** How are the processes in the diagram on page 19 similar to those in the illustration below?

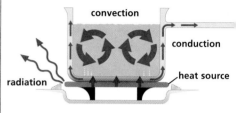
convection
conduction
radiation
heat source

27. **CONNECT** Give an example from everyday life that shows that the atmosphere has substance.

28. **EVALUATE** If you had a choice between burning natural gas to cook or using electricity from a power plant, which would you choose? Explain the issues involved. **Hint:** Where does the power plant get energy?

the BIG idea

29. **SYNTHESIZE** Write one or more paragraphs describing the specific ways that the atmosphere supports and protects life. In your description, use each of the terms below. Underline each term in your answer.

carbon dioxide	solar radiation
water	ozone
oxygen	stratosphere
cycle	

30. Look again at the photograph on pages 6–7. Now that you have finished the chapter, how would you change or add details to your answer to the question on the photograph?

UNIT PROJECTS

If you are doing a unit project, make a folder for your project. Include in your folder a list of the resources you will need, the date on which the project is due, and a schedule to track your progress. Begin gathering data.

MONITOR AND RETEACH

Pour some water into a glass beaker and heat it on a hot plate. Ask: The hot plate is radiating what? *energy* The beaker and the hot plate are touching—what kind of energy transfer involves direct contact? *conduction* If you hold your hand above the beaker, how does the energy get from the bottom of the pot to your hand once the water is boiling? *by convection*

Students may benefit from summarizing one or more sections of the chapter.

R Summarizing the Chapter, pp. 80–81

Standardized Test Practice

For practice on your state test, go to . . .

TEST PRACTICE
CLASSZONE.COM

Interpreting Graphs

The following three graphs show the amounts of three types of air pollutants released into the atmosphere in the United States each year from 1950 to 1990. Study the graphs closely and use the information to answer the first four questions.

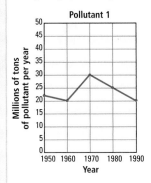
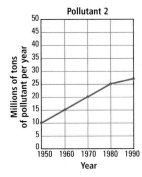
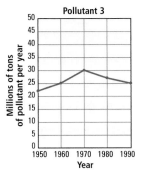

1. What conclusion can you make about pollutant 1?
  a. The release of pollutant 1 has steadily decreased since 1970.
  b. More pollutant 1 has been released since 1990.
  c. More pollutant 1 has been released since 1970.
  d. The release of pollutant 1 has not changed.

2. Based on the graph for pollutant 2, which of the following is true?
  a. The release of pollutant 2 declined after 1950.
  b. The release of pollutant 2 has increased since 1970.
  c. The release of pollutant 2 declined and then rose.
  d. About 15 million tons of pollutant 2 were released in 1990.

3. Compare the graphs for pollutants 1 and 2. Which of the following statements is supported by the graphs?
  a. In 1950, more pollutant 1 was released than pollutant 2.
  b. Since 1980, no pollutant 1 has been released.
  c. In 1990, twice as much pollutant 2 was released as pollutant 1.
  d. Since 1950, no pollutant 1 has been released.

4. About how many million tons of pollutant 3 entered the atmosphere in the United States in 1990?
  a. 10   **c.** 25
  b. 15   **d.** 30

Extended Response

Answer the next two questions in detail. Use in your answers some of the terms from the word box. In your answer, underline each term you use.

oxygen	nitrogen	energy
water	air density	carbon dioxide
altitude	absorption	

5. Luz builds a terrarium for her class science fair. She puts her pet slug in with the plants. She covers the terrarium with clear plastic that has vent holes. She places it in a sunlit window. How do the soil, plants, slug, sunlight, and plastic affect the air in Luz's terrarium?

6. Mile High Stadium in Denver, Colorado, makes bottled oxygen available to its players. Players at lower altitudes do not need extra oxygen. Explorers pack bottled oxygen when they climb tall mountains, such as Mount Everest. Explain why extra oxygen might be necessary for players in Mile High Stadium and climbers on tall mountains.

Chapter 1: **Earth's Changing Atmosphere** 39 **D**

Interpreting Graphs

1. a   3. a
2. b   4. c

Extended Response

5. RUBRIC
4 points for a response that correctly answers the question and uses the following terms accurately:
  • oxygen
  • water
  • nitrogen
  • absorption
  • energy
  • carbon dioxide

The plants take in <u>carbon dioxide</u> and release <u>oxygen</u> into the air. The slug takes in oxygen and releases carbon dioxide and <u>water</u>. The soil provides <u>nitrogen</u> and other nutrients for the plants and slug. The soil and plants <u>absorb energy</u> from sunlight and warm the terrarium. Gases move through the vent holes.

3 points uses four to five terms accurately
2 points uses two to three terms accurately
1 point uses one term accurately

6. RUBRIC
4 points for a response that correctly answers the question and uses the following terms accurately:
  • altitude
  • air density
  • oxygen

<u>Air density</u> decreases with <u>altitude</u>. There is less <u>oxygen</u> in each breath at Mile High Stadium and on tall mountains, so players and climbers need extra oxygen.

3 points correctly answers the question and uses two terms accurately
2 points correctly answers the question and uses one term accurately
1 point partially answers the question and uses one term accurately

METACOGNITIVE ACTIVITY

Have students answer the following questions in their **Science Notebook:**
1. Compare some of the note-taking strategies you have tried. Which ones work well for you?
2. What helped you determine the important things in this chapter?
3. Which topics in this chapter can help you begin your Unit Project?

Earth Science
UNIFYING PRINCIPLES

PRINCIPLE 1
Heat energy inside Earth and radiation from the Sun provide energy for Earth's processes.

PRINCIPLE 2
Physical forces, such as gravity, affect the movement of all matter on Earth and throughout the universe.

PRINCIPLE 3
Matter and energy move among Earth's rocks and soil, atmosphere, waters, and living things.

PRINCIPLE 4
Earth has changed over time and continues to change.

Unit: Earth's Atmosphere
BIG IDEAS

CHAPTER 1
Earth's Changing Atmosphere

Earth's atmosphere is a blanket of gases that supports and protects life.

CHAPTER 2
Weather Patterns

Some features of weather have predictable patterns.

CHAPTER 3
Weather Fronts and Storms

The interaction of air masses causes changes in weather.

CHAPTER 4
Climate and Climate Change

Climates are long-term weather patterns that may change over time.

CHAPTER 2
KEY CONCEPTS

SECTION 2.1

The atmosphere's air pressure changes.
1. Air exerts pressure.
2. Air pressure is related to altitude and density.

SECTION 2.2

The atmosphere has wind patterns.
1. Uneven heating causes air to move.
2. Earth's rotation affects wind direction.
3. Bands of calm air separate global wind belts.
4. Jet streams flow near the top of the troposphere.
5. Patterns of heating and cooling cause local winds and monsoons.

SECTION 2.3

Most clouds form as air rises and cools.
1. Temperature affects water in the air.
2. Water vapor condenses and forms clouds.

SECTION 2.4

Water falls to Earth's surface as precipitation.
1. Precipitation forms from water droplets or ice crystals.
2. Precipitation can carry pollution.

 The Big Idea Flow Chart is available on p. T9 in the **UNIT TRANSPARENCY BOOK.**

1. Air exerts pressure.

Gravity causes air molecules to be pulled toward Earth's surface. Air molecules bounce off objects and exert a force on these objects. **Air pressure** is defined as the force of molecules pushing on an area. Because air molecules move in all directions, air pressure pushes in all directions.

2. Air pressure is related to altitude and density.

Air pressure varies, depending upon the weight of the overlying atmosphere. Air pressure decreases with altitude because the higher an area is located, the less air there is pushing down on it. Density also decreases with altitude; the air molecules in air at sea level are denser than air molecules in air over a mountain because the higher air pressure at sea level pushes them closer together. Just as air pressure affects the density of air, density affects air pressure. Air pressure is usually higher in dense air than in thin air because dense air has more molecules bouncing around in it.

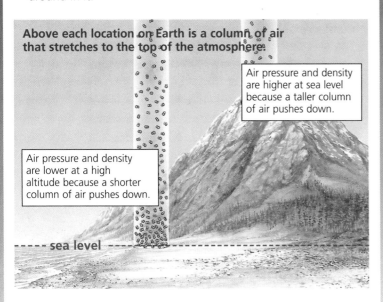

Above each location on Earth is a column of air that stretches to the top of the atmosphere.

Air pressure and density are higher at sea level because a taller column of air pushes down.

Air pressure and density are lower at a high altitude because a shorter column of air pushes down.

----- sea level -----

1. Uneven heating causes air to move.

The uneven heating of Earth's surface causes air pressure to differ from place to place at the same altitude. These pressure differences cause air to move horizontally as **wind.** Winds that travel for thousands of kilometers in steady patterns are called **global winds.**

2. Earth's rotation affects wind direction.

Earth rotates from west to east. This rotation changes the direction of objects moving over Earth's surface—a phenomenon known as the **Coriolis effect.** In the Northern Hemisphere, the Coriolis effect deflects winds to the right in the direction of motion. Winds in the Southern Hemisphere are deflected to the left.

3. Bands of calm air separate global wind belts.

Global winds are caused by the uneven heating of Earth's curved surface. Because of the Coriolis effect, winds do not flow directly from the high pressure over the poles to the low pressure at the equator. Instead, each hemisphere has three belts of global winds: the trade winds, the westerlies, and the easterlies. These wind belts are separated by calm regions of high or low pressure: the doldrums (sometimes called the intertropical convergence zone), the horse latitudes, the subpolar lows, and the polar highs.

4. Jet streams flow near the top of the troposphere.

The uneven heating of Earth's surface also causes jet streams. **Jet streams** travel for thousands of kilometers, usually in the upper troposphere. These long-distance winds move at great speeds, always from west to east, around the globe. Two main jet streams—a polar jet stream and a subtropical jet stream—are usually found in each hemisphere.

5. Patterns of heating and cooling cause local winds and monsoons.

Some winds change in regular patterns. For example, the different heating and cooling rates of land and water can cause winds to change direction daily (sea and land breezes) or seasonally (**monsoons**).

Common Misconceptions

AIR PRESSURE Students may think that air pressure pushes only downward. The air pressure at sea level is about 14.7 pounds per square inch. If air pressure were exerted only downward, you would feel 14.7 pounds of downward pressure on every square inch of your hand. You don't feel this pressure because air is pushing in all directions.

 This misconception is addressed on p. 44.

 MISCONCEPTION DATABASE
CLASSZONE.COM Background on student misconceptions

CORIOLIS EFFECT Students may think that the Coriolis effect causes water to swirl in a particular direction down a drain. In reality, the Coriolis effect influences movements only across large distances, such as the movements of global winds and ocean currents.

TE This misconception is addressed on p. 50.

2.3 Most clouds form as air rises and cools. pp. 56–65

1. Temperature affects water in the air.

Differences in temperature fuel the water cycle, wherein water is constantly recycled between Earth's surface and atmosphere. The water cycle is made up of three processes: evaporation, condensation, and precipitation.

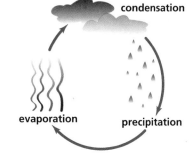

- **Evaporation** is the process by which liquid water changes into a gas.
- **Condensation** is the process by which a gas, such as water vapor, changes into a liquid.
- **Precipitation** is any type of liquid or solid water that falls to Earth's surface. You can copy the visual above to use when teaching the water cycle.

2. Water vapor condenses and forms clouds.

Clouds are made of condensed water vapor. They can form when warm air rises, expands, and cools. Water vapor in the air then condenses around tiny solid particles. Clouds are classified according to their altitudes, the ways they form, and their general characteristics. The main types of clouds are
- cirrus, or wispy clouds
- cumulus, or puffy clouds
- stratus, or layered clouds

There are many subtypes of clouds; their names are often combinations of Latin word parts that suggest their appearance.

Fog is another type of cloud. It rests on the ground or a body of water.

Common Misconceptions

WEIGHT OF HUMID AIR Students may think that on humid days the air feels heavy because of its water vapor content. However, water vapor weighs less than dry air—the molecular weight of water is 18, and the average molecular weight of dry air is 29. Therefore, the more humid a quantity of air is, the less it weighs.

 This misconception is addressed on p. 58.

2.4 Water falls to Earth's surface as precipitation. pp. 66–71

1. Precipitation forms from water droplets or ice crystals.

Precipitation of any kind originates from a cloud. About a million cloud droplets combine together to form a single raindrop. Precipitation can also form when below-freezing temperatures inside a cloud cause water vapor to change into ice crystals. Air temperature determines which type of precipitation falls to Earth's surface. Types of precipitation include: rain and drizzle, **freezing rain, sleet,** snow, and **hail.**

2. Precipitation can carry pollution.

Factories, power plants, and vehicles release sulfur dioxide and nitrogen oxides into the air. These gases combine with moisture in the air to produce sulfuric and nitric acids. The acids then mix with cloud droplets and fall to Earth as acid rain. **Acid rain** is precipitation that has become more acidic than normal because of pollution. Normal rain is made slightly acidic by the presence of dissolved CO_2. The table below compares the pH of acid rain in the United States with that of other substances. A neutral pH value is 7. The lower the pH value, the more acidic the substance is.

pH Values	
lemon	2.2–2.5
tomato	4.2
acid rain	5.5–4.2
rain	5.6
pure water	7.0
seawater	7.8–8.2

 MISCONCEPTION DATABASE

CLASSZONE.COM Background on student misconceptions

EXPLORE (the BIG idea)

labs and generate alternative labs.

Are You Stronger Than Air? p. 41
Students are introduced to the effects of air pressure.

TIME 10 minutes
MATERIALS wide-mouthed jar, plastic bag, rubber band

How Does Air Motion Affect Balloons? p. 41
Students observe air movement.

TIME 10 minutes
MATERIALS 2 balloons, string, pencil

Internet Activity: Wind, p. 41
Students are introduced to wind patterns.

TIME 20 minutes
MATERIALS computer with Internet access

SECTION 2.1

EXPLORE Air Pressure, p. 43
Students observe an effect of a change in air pressure.

TIME 10 minutes
MATERIALS peeled hard-boiled egg, glass bottle, 2 wooden matches

INVESTIGATE Air Pressure, p. 45
Students collect data to measure changes in air pressure.

TIME 15 minutes
MATERIALS round balloon, metal can, rubber band, tape, thin straw, ruler

---

SECTION 2.2

EXPLORE Solar Energy, p. 47
Students use a flashlight to see how light varies in intensity across a curved surface.

TIME 10 minutes
MATERIALS globe, flashlight, ruler

INVESTIGATE Coriolis Effect, p. 49
Students model how Earth's rotation affects winds.

TIME 10 minutes
MATERIALS round balloon, felt-tip pen

SECTION 2.3

EXPLORE Condensation, p. 56
Students observe condensation on a mirror.

TIME 5 minutes
MATERIALS hand mirror

INVESTIGATE Condensation, p. 59
Students observe cloud formation inside a plastic bottle.

TIME 10 minutes
MATERIALS clear 1-liter plastic bottle with cap, water at room temperature, tablespoon, matches

CHAPTER INVESTIGATION
Relative Humidity, pp. 64–65
Students construct a psychrometer and use it to measure relative humidity.

R Relative Humidity Table, p. 133

TIME 40 minutes
MATERIALS 2 thermometers, cotton or felt cloth, 3 rubber bands, plastic bowl, water at room temperature, scissors, pint milk carton, ruler, Relative Humidity Table

---

SECTION 2.4

INVESTIGATE Precipitation, p. 67
Students construct a rain gauge and use it to measure rainfall.

TIME 15 minutes
MATERIALS scissors, 1-liter plastic bottle, permanent marker, ruler, gravel

---

R **Additional INVESTIGATION,** Estimating Wind Speed, A, B, & C, pp. 143–151; Teacher Instructions, pp. 284–285

Previewing Chapter Resources

INTEGRATED TECHNOLOGY	LABS AND ACTIVITIES

CHAPTER 2
Weather Patterns

 CLASSZONE.COM
- eEdition Plus
- EasyPlanner Plus
- Misconception Database
- Content Review
- Test Practice
- Visualizations
- Resource Centers
- Internet Activity: Wind
- Math Tutorial

 CD-ROMS
- eEdition
- EasyPlanner
- Power Presentations
- Content Review
- Lab Generator
- Test Generator

AUDIO CDS
- Audio Readings
- Audio Readings in Spanish

SCILINKS.ORG
SCI LINKS

 EXPLORE the Big Idea, p. 41
- Are You Stronger Than Air?
- How Does Air Motion Affect Balloons?
- Internet Activity: Wind

UNIT RESOURCE BOOK
Unit Projects, pp. 5–10

 Lab Generator CD-ROM
Generate customized labs.

SECTION
2.1 The atmosphere's air pressure changes. pp. 43–46

Time: 2 periods (1 block)
Lesson Plan, pp. 82–83

 RESOURCE CENTER, Air Pressure

UNIT TRANSPARENCY BOOK
- Big Idea Flow Chart, p. T9
- Daily Vocabulary Scaffolding, p. T10
- Note-Taking Model, p. T11
- 3-Minute Warm-Up, p. T12

EXPLORE Air Pressure, p. 43
- INVESTIGATE Air Pressure, p. 45

UNIT RESOURCE BOOK
Datasheet, Air Pressure, p. 91

SECTION
2.2 The atmosphere has wind patterns. pp. 47–55

Time: 2 periods (1 block)
Lesson Plan, pp. 93–94

 • **RESOURCE CENTER,** Global Winds
- **VISUALIZATION,** Coriolis Effect
- **MATH TUTORIAL**

UNIT TRANSPARENCY BOOK
- Daily Vocabulary Scaffolding, p. T10
- 3-Minute Warm-Up, p. T12
- "Global Winds" Visual, p. T14

EXPLORE Solar Energy, p. 47
- INVESTIGATE Coriolis Effect, p. 49
- Math in Science, p. 55

UNIT RESOURCE BOOK
- Datasheet, Coriolis Effect, p. 102
- Additional INVESTIGATION, Estimating Wind Speed, A, B, & C, pp. 143–151
- Math Support and Practice, pp. 131–132

SECTION
2.3 Most clouds form as air rises and cools. pp. 56–65

Time: 3 periods (1.5 blocks)
Lesson Plan, pp. 104–105

 RESOURCE CENTER, Clouds

UNIT TRANSPARENCY BOOK
- Daily Vocabulary Scaffolding, p. T10
- 3-Minute Warm-Up, p. T13

EXPLORE Condensation, p. 56
- INVESTIGATE Condensation, p. 59
- CHAPTER INVESTIGATION, Relative Humidity, pp. 64–65

UNIT RESOURCE BOOK
- Datasheet, Condensation, p. 113
- CHAPTER INVESTIGATION, Relative Humidity, A, B, & C, pp. 134–142
- Relative Humidity Table, p. 133

SECTION
2.4 Water falls to Earth's surface as precipitation. pp. 66–71

Time: 3 periods (1.5 blocks)
Lesson Plan, pp. 115–116

 RESOURCE CENTER, Lightning

UNIT TRANSPARENCY BOOK
- Big Idea Flow Chart, p. T9
- Daily Vocabulary Scaffolding, p. T10
- 3-Minute Warm-Up, p. T13
- Chapter Outline, pp. T15–T16

INVESTIGATE Precipitation, p. 67
- Extreme Science, p. 71

UNIT RESOURCE BOOK
Datasheet, Precipitation, p. 124

READING AND REINFORCEMENT

- Description Wheel, B20–21
- Combination Notes, C36
- Daily Vocabulary Scaffolding, H1–8

 UNIT RESOURCE BOOK
- Vocabulary Practice, pp. 128–129
- Decoding Support, p. 130
- Summarizing the Chapter, pp. 152–153

Audio Readings CD
Listen to Pupil Edition.

Audio Readings in Spanish CD
Listen to Pupil Edition in Spanish.

 UNIT RESOURCE BOOK
- Reading Study Guides, A & B, pp. 84–87
- Spanish Reading Study Guide, pp. 88–89
- Challenge and Extension, p. 90
- Reinforcing Key Concepts, p. 92

 **UNIT RESOURCE BOOK**
- Reading Study Guides, A & B, pp. 95–98
- Spanish Reading Study Guide, pp. 99–100
- Challenge and Extension, p. 101
- Reinforcing Key Concepts, p. 103

 UNIT RESOURCE BOOK
- Reading Study Guides, A & B, pp. 106–109
- Spanish Reading Study Guide, pp. 110–111
- Challenge and Extension, p. 112
- Reinforcing Key Concepts, p. 114

 UNIT RESOURCE BOOK
- Reading Study Guides, A & B, pp. 117–120
- Spanish Reading Study Guide, pp. 121–122
- Challenge and Extension, p. 123
- Reinforcing Key Concepts, p. 125
- Challenge Reading, pp. 126–127

ASSESSMENT

- Chapter Review, pp. 73–74
- Standardized Test Practice, p. 75

 UNIT ASSESSMENT BOOK
- Diagnostic Test, pp. 21–22
- Chapter Test, A, B, & C, pp. 27–38
- Alternative Assessment, pp. 39–40

 Spanish Chapter Test, pp. 177–180

Test Generator CD-ROM
Generate customized tests.

Lab Generator CD-ROM
Rubrics for Labs

 Ongoing Assessment, pp. 43, 45–46

 Section 2.1 Review, p. 46

 UNIT ASSESSMENT BOOK
Section 2.1 Quiz, p. 23

 Ongoing Assessment, pp. 47–49, 51–54

 Section 2.2 Review, p. 54

UNIT ASSESSMENT BOOK
Section 2.2 Quiz, p. 24

 Ongoing Assessment, pp. 57, 59–63

 Section 2.3 Review, p. 63

UNIT ASSESSMENT BOOK
Section 2.3 Quiz, p. 25

 Ongoing Assessment, pp. 67–70

 Section 2.4 Review, p. 70

 UNIT ASSESSMENT BOOK
Section 2.4 Quiz, p. 26

STANDARDS

National Standards
A.2–8, A.9.a, A.9.c–e, D.1.f, D.1.i, D.1.j

See p. 40 for the standards.

National Standards
A.2–7, A.9.a–b, A.9.d–f

National Standards
A.2–8, A.9.a–f, D.1.j

National Standards
A.2–7, A.9.a–b, A.9.d–f, D.1.f, D.1.i

National Standards
A.2–7, A.9.a–b, A.9.d–f, D.1.f, D.1.i

CHAPTER INVESTIGATION

Leveled resources present the same concepts for different abilities.

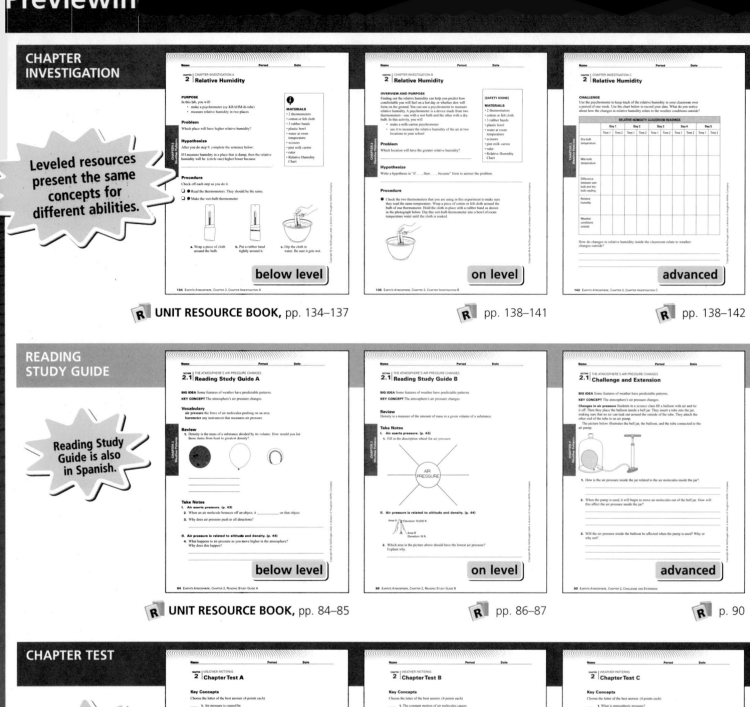

CHAPTER INVESTIGATION A
2 Relative Humidity

below level

UNIT RESOURCE BOOK, pp. 134–137

CHAPTER INVESTIGATION B
2 Relative Humidity

on level

pp. 138–141

CHAPTER INVESTIGATION C
2 Relative Humidity

advanced

pp. 138–142

READING STUDY GUIDE

Reading Study Guide is also in Spanish.

2.1 Reading Study Guide A

below level

UNIT RESOURCE BOOK, pp. 84–85

2.1 Reading Study Guide B

on level

pp. 86–87

2.1 Challenge and Extension

advanced

p. 90

CHAPTER TEST

Chapter Test is also in Spanish.

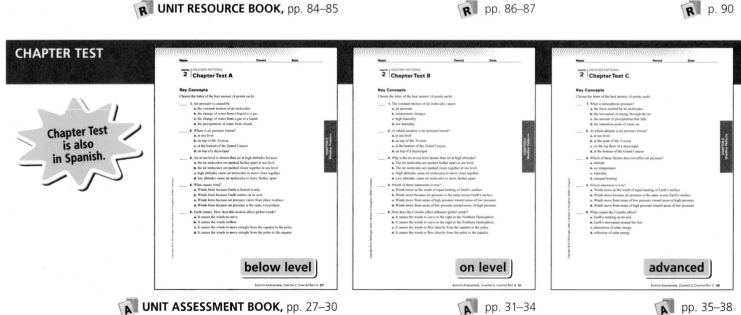

2 Chapter Test A

below level

UNIT ASSESSMENT BOOK, pp. 27–30

2 Chapter Test B

on level

pp. 31–34

2 Chapter Test C

advanced

pp. 35–38

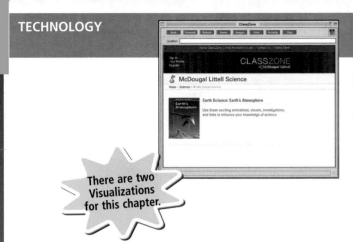

There are two Visualizations for this chapter.

 CLASSZONE.COM

 CD/CD-ROMS

CLASSZONE.COM

VISUAL CONTENT

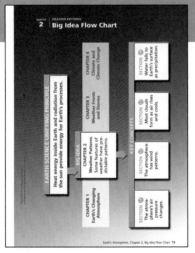

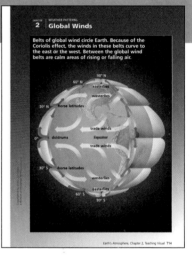

 **UNIT TRANSPARENCY BOOK,** p. T9

 p. T11

 p. T14

MORE SUPPORT

Reinforcing Key Concepts for each section

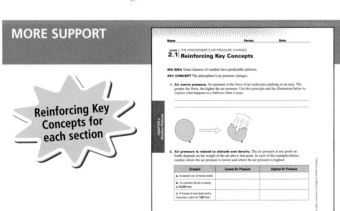

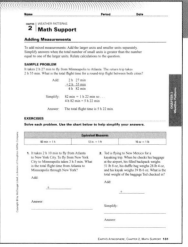

UNIT RESOURCE BOOK, p. 92

pp. 128–129

p. 131

INTRODUCE

the **BIG** idea

Have students look at the photograph of the girl watching storm clouds and discuss how the question in the box links to the Big Idea. For further discussion:

- Ask: How would you describe the weather today? Is it wet? dry? cold? warm?
- Describe any clouds in the sky.
- Ask: What relationships do you see between certain types of clouds and specific weather conditions, such as rain or warm temperatures?

National Science Education Standards

Content

D.1.f Water, which covers the majority of Earth's surface, circulates through the crust, oceans, and atmosphere in what is known as the water cycle. Water evaporates, rises and cools, condenses, and falls as rain or snow to the surface.

D.1.i Clouds formed by the condensation of water vapor affect weather, climate.

D.1.j Global patterns of atmospheric movements influence local weather.

Process

A.2–8 Design and conduct an investigation; use tools to gather and interpret data; use evidence to describe, predict, explain, model; think critically to make relationships between evidence and explanation; recognize different explanations and predictions; communicate scientific procedures and explanations; use mathematics.

A.9.a–e Understand scientific inquiry by using different investigations, methods, mathematics, technology, and explanations based on logic, evidence, and skepticism.

G.1.b Science requires different abilities.

CHAPTER

2 Weather Patterns

the **BIG** idea

Some features of weather have predictable patterns.

Key Concepts

SECTION

 2.1 The atmosphere's air pressure changes. Learn how air pressure changes and how it is measured.

SECTION

 2.2 The atmosphere has wind patterns. Learn how wind develops and about different types of wind.

SECTION

 2.3 Most clouds form as air rises and cools. Learn how water changes form in the atmosphere and about different types of clouds.

SECTION

 2.4 Water falls to Earth's surface as precipitation. Learn about the different types of precipitation and about acid rain.

Internet Preview

CLASSZONE.COM

Chapter 2 online resources: Content Review, two Visualizations, four Resource Centers, Math Tutorial, Test Practice

What weather conditions do you see in the distance?

INTERNET PREVIEW

CLASSZONE.COM For student use with the following pages:

Review and Practice
- Content Review, pp. 42, 72
- Math Tutorial: Adding Measures of Time, p. 55
- Test Practice, p. 75

Activities and Resources
- Internet Activity: Wind, p. 41
- Resource Centers: Air Pressure, p. 45; Global Winds, p. 50; Clouds, p. 60; Lightning, p. 71
- Visualization: Coriolis Effect, p. 48

Atmospheric Pressure and Winds **Code: MDL010**

EXPLORE (the BIG idea)

Are You Stronger Than Air?

Line a wide-mouthed jar with a plastic bag. Secure the bag tightly with a rubber band. Reach in and try to pull the bag out of the jar.

Observe and Think How easy was it to move the plastic bag? What was holding the bag in place?

How Does Air Motion Affect Balloons?

Tie two balloons to a pencil 5 centimeters apart as shown. Gently blow air between the balloons.

Observe and Think How did the balloons move? Why did the air make them move this way?

Internet Activity: Wind

Go to **ClassZone.com** to explore how breezes blowing over land and water change over the course of an entire day.

Observe and Think What patterns can you see in winds that occur near water?

NSTA scilinks.org **SCi LINKS**

Atmospheric Pressure and Winds **Code: MDL010**

TEACHING WITH TECHNOLOGY

CBL and Probeware If you have a graphing calculator and a barometer probe, take daily air pressure readings after teaching p. 46. If you have a relative humidity sensor, do the same after students perform the Chapter Investigation on pp. 64–65.

EXPLORE (the BIG idea)

These inquiry-based activities are appropriate for use at home or as a supplement to classroom instruction.

Are You Stronger Than Air?

PURPOSE To introduce students to the concept of air pressure. By observing how air "holds" a plastic bag in a jar, they will recognize that air exerts force.

TIP *10 min.* Make sure there are no holes in the plastic bag; otherwise, air might seep out.

Answer: It was somewhat hard to pull the plastic bag out of the jar. Air was holding the bag in place.

REVISIT after p. 46.

How Does Air Motion Affect Balloons?

PURPOSE To introduce students to the relationship between air pressure and air movement.

TIP *10 min.* Students should try to make balloons the same size and the same distance from the pencil.

Answer: The balloons moved closer together. The blowing caused the air between the balloons to be different from the air on the other sides of the balloons.

REVISIT after p. 45.

Internet Activity: Wind

PURPOSE To introduce students to local wind patterns.

TIP *20 min.* Students might try predicting whether sea breezes occur during the day or at night.

Sample answer: Winds near water blow inland during the day and out to sea at night.

REVISIT after p. 53.

PREPARE

◀ CONCEPT REVIEW

Activate Prior Knowledge

- Place an ice cube and a glass of water on your desk.
- Ask students to describe the states of matter of the ice and the water.
- Tell students that water exists as a gas, a liquid, and a solid in Earth's atmosphere. Have them infer how the Sun might affect water in the atmosphere.

▶ TAKING NOTES

Combination Notes

Combining a sketch with notes will help students to visualize a new concept and connect it with a concrete example. Using a two-column format, students can write their notes in one column and draw a sketch in the other.

Vocabulary Strategy

Description wheels can include as much information as students want to add. They become easy study devices when students look back through their notes.

Vocabulary and Note-Taking Resources

- Vocabulary Practice, pp. 128–129
- Decoding Support, p. 130

- Daily Vocabulary Scaffolding, p. T10
- Note-Taking Model, p. T11

- Description Wheel, B20–21
- Combination Notes, C36
- Daily Vocabulary Scaffolding, H1–8

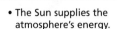

◀ CONCEPT REVIEW

- The Sun supplies the atmosphere's energy.
- Energy moves throughout the atmosphere.
- Matter can be solid, liquid, or gas.

◀ VOCABULARY REVIEW

atmosphere p. 9
altitude p. 10
density p. 10
convection p. 19

CONTENT REVIEW
CLASSZONE.COM
Review concepts and vocabulary.

▶ TAKING NOTES

COMBINATION NOTES

To take notes about a new concept, first make an informal outline of the information. Then make a sketch of the concept and label it so that you can study it later.

VOCABULARY STRATEGY

Place each vocabulary term at the center of a **description wheel.** Write some words describing it on the spokes.

See the Note-Taking Handbook on pages R45–R51.

D 42 Unit: Earth's Atmosphere

SCIENCE NOTEBOOK

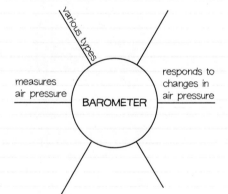

NOTES

Air pressure
- is the force of air molecules pushing on an area
- pushes in all directions

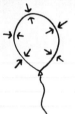

various types

measures air pressure

responds to changes in air pressure

BAROMETER

CHECK READINESS

Administer the Diagnostic Test to determine students' readiness for new science content and their mastery of requisite math skills.

  Diagnostic Test, pp. 21–22

Technology Resources

Students needing content and math skills should visit **ClassZone.com**.

- **CONTENT REVIEW**
- **MATH TUTORIAL**

  CONTENT REVIEW CD-ROM

KEY CONCEPT

2.1 The atmosphere's air pressure changes.

◀ **BEFORE, you learned**

- Density is the amount of mass in a given volume of a substance
- Air becomes less dense as altitude increases
- Differences in density cause air to rise and sink

▶ **NOW, you will learn**

- How the movement of air molecules causes air pressure
- How air pressure varies
- How differences in air pressure affect the atmosphere

VOCABULARY

air pressure p. 43
barometer p. 46

EXPLORE Air Pressure

What does air do to the egg?

PROCEDURE

1. Set a peeled hard-boiled egg in the mouth of a bottle. Make sure that the egg can't slip through.

2. Light the matches. Remove the egg, and drop the matches into the bottle. Quickly replace the egg.

3. Watch carefully, and record your observations.

WHAT DO YOU THINK?

- What happened when you placed the egg back on top of the bottle?
- What can your observations tell you about the air in the bottle?

MATERIALS
- peeled hard-boiled egg
- glass bottle
- 2 wooden matches

Air exerts pressure.

Air molecules move constantly. As they move, they bounce off each other like rubber balls. They also bounce off every surface they hit. As you read this book, billions of air molecules are bouncing off your body, the book, and everything else around you.

Each time an air molecule bounces off an object, it pushes, or exerts a force, on that object. When billions of air molecules bounce off a surface, the force is spread over the area of that surface. **Air pressure** is the force of air molecules pushing on an area. The greater the force, the higher the air pressure. Because air molecules move in all directions, air pressure pushes in all directions.

VOCABULARY
Add a description wheel for *air pressure* to your notebook.

CHECK YOUR READING How does the number of air molecules relate to air pressure?

2.1 FOCUS

▶ Set Learning Goals
Students will

- Recognize how the movement of air molecules causes air pressure.
- Describe how air pressure varies.
- Explain how differences in air pressure affect the atmosphere.
- Construct a barometer to measure changes in air pressure.

◀ 3-Minute Warm-Up

Display Transparency 12 or copy this exercise on the board:

Match the word with the definition.

density   atmosphere   altitude

1. the distance above sea level *altitude*
2. the amount of mass in a given volume of substance *density*
3. the whole layer of air that surrounds Earth *atmosphere*

T 3-Minute Warm-Up, p. T12

2.1 MOTIVATE

EXPLORE Air Pressure

PURPOSE To introduce the concept that air molecules exert force

TIP *10 min.* Ask students to return any remaining matches to your desk immediately after completing the activity.

WHAT DO YOU THINK? *The egg gets pushed into the bottle because the air pressure inside the bottle is lower than the air pressure outside. Students may conclude that the air inside the bottle is somehow different from the outside air.*

Ongoing Assessment

Recognize how the movement of air molecules causes air pressure.

Ask: What do air molecules do when they bounce off an object? *They exert a force on the object.*

CHECK YOUR READING *Answer: The greater the number of air molecules, the greater the air pressure.*

Chapter 2 **43** **D**

Address Misconceptions

IDENTIFY Ask: Does air press only in a downward direction? If students answer yes, they may hold the misconception that air pressure acts only in a downward direction.

CORRECT Hold your hand out in a horizontal position. Tell students that air molecules are bouncing off all sides of your hand, not just the top. These air molecules exert pressure in all directions.

REASSESS Ask: How would you describe the movement of air molecules? *They move in all directions.* In which direction does the force act on my hand? *The molecules push in all directions.*

Technology Resources

Visit **ClassZone.com** for background on common student misconceptions.

 MISCONCEPTION DATABASE

Teach from Visuals

To help students interpret the visual of air pressure and density at different locations, ask: How does the density of air molecules in the columns change from bottom to top? *Air molecules are more densely packed near the bottom of the columns. There are fewer and fewer air molecules toward the top.*

Air pressure is related to altitude and density.

COMBINATION NOTES
Record details about how air pressure varies.

A

The air pressure at any area on Earth depends on the weight of the air above that area. If you hold out your hand, the force of air pushing down on your hand is greater than the weight of a bowling ball. So why don't you feel the air pushing down on your hand? Remember that air pushes in all directions. The pressure of air pushing down is balanced by the pressure of air pushing up from below.

Air pressure decreases as you move higher in the atmosphere. Think of a column of air directly over your body. If you stood at sea level, this column would stretch from where you stood to the top of the atmosphere. The air pressure on your body would be equal to the weight of all the air in the column. But if you stood on a mountain, the column of air would be shorter. With less air above you, the pressure would be lower. At an altitude of 5.5 kilometers (3.4 mi), air pressure is about half what it is at sea level.

REMINDER
Density is the amount of mass in a given volume of a substance.

B

Air pressure and density are related. Just as air pressure decreases with altitude, so does the density of air. Notice in the illustration that air molecules at sea level are closer together than air molecules over the mountain. Since the pressure is greater at sea level, the air molecules are pushed closer together. Therefore, the air at sea level is denser than air at high altitudes.

Air Pressure and Density

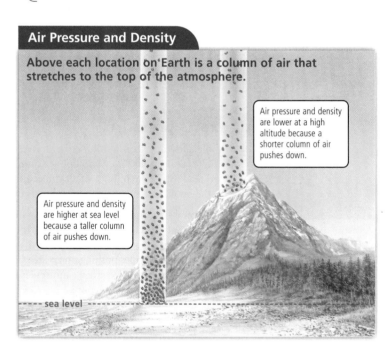

Above each location on Earth is a column of air that stretches to the top of the atmosphere.

Air pressure and density are lower at a high altitude because a shorter column of air pushes down.

Air pressure and density are higher at sea level because a taller column of air pushes down.

sea level

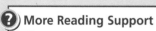

DIFFERENTIATE INSTRUCTION

More Reading Support

A As altitude increases, air pressure does what? *decreases*

B Air pressure is related to altitude and what else? *density*

English Learners English learners may need help with these terms and concepts: *sea level* on p. 44, *cutting the straw at an angle* on p. 45, and *chamber* on p. 46. They may not have prior knowledge of *riding an elevator* on p. 45, or *can of tennis balls* on p. 45.

Pressure and Air Motion

You've read that air pressure decreases as you move to higher altitudes. Air pressure also often varies in two locations at the same altitude. You can observe how such pressure differences affect air when you open a new can of tennis balls. You may hear a hiss as air rushes into the can. The air inside the sealed can of tennis balls is at a lower pressure than the air outside the can. When you break the seal, air moves from outside the can toward the lower pressure inside it.

RESOURCE CENTER
CLASSZONE.COM

Find out more about air pressure.

Air pressure differences in the atmosphere affect air in a similar way. If the air pressure were the same at all locations, air wouldn't move much. Because of differences in pressure, air starts to move from areas of higher pressure toward areas of lower pressure. The air may move only a short distance, or it may travel many kilometers. You will learn more about how air moves in response to pressure differences in Section 2.2.

CHECK YOUR READING How do differences in air pressure affect the movement of air?

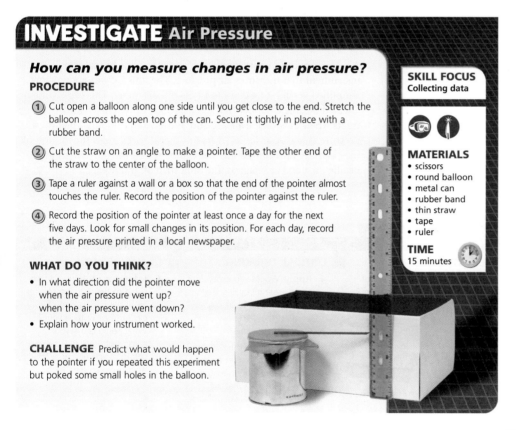

INVESTIGATE Air Pressure

How can you measure changes in air pressure?
PROCEDURE

1. Cut open a balloon along one side until you get close to the end. Stretch the balloon across the open top of the can. Secure it tightly in place with a rubber band.

2. Cut the straw on an angle to make a pointer. Tape the other end of the straw to the center of the balloon.

3. Tape a ruler against a wall or a box so that the end of the pointer almost touches the ruler. Record the position of the pointer against the ruler.

4. Record the position of the pointer at least once a day for the next five days. Look for small changes in its position. For each day, record the air pressure printed in a local newspaper.

WHAT DO YOU THINK?

- In what direction did the pointer move when the air pressure went up? when the air pressure went down?
- Explain how your instrument worked.

CHALLENGE Predict what would happen to the pointer if you repeated this experiment but poked some small holes in the balloon.

SKILL FOCUS
Collecting data

MATERIALS
- scissors
- round balloon
- metal can
- rubber band
- thin straw
- tape
- ruler

TIME
15 minutes

Chapter 2: **Weather Patterns 45** D

Ongoing Assessment

 READING VISUALS *Answer: the one on the right; because air pressure decreases with altitude*

EXPLORE (the BIG idea)

Revisit "Are You Stronger Than Air?" on p. 41. Have students explain their results.

Reinforce (the BIG idea)

Have students relate the section to the Big Idea.

 R Reinforcing Key Concepts, p. 92

2.1 ASSESS & RETEACH

Assess

A Section 2.1 Quiz, p. 23

Reteach

Help students review this section's concepts by writing the headings "Air Pressure" and "Air Molecules" on the board. Encourage students to state facts about each concept. Remind them that air pressure is the force of air molecules pushing on an area. *Air Pressure: pushes in all directions, decreases as altitude increases, causes air to move when there are pressure differences, can be measured with a barometer. Air Molecules: move constantly, exert pressure, are denser at low altitudes, move from areas of higher pressure toward areas of lower pressure*

Technology Resources

Have students visit **ClassZone.com** for reteaching of Key Concepts.

 CONTENT REVIEW

CONTENT REVIEW CD-ROM

How a Barometer Works

High Air Pressure

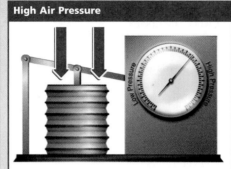

The flexible chamber on the barometer contracts when the air pressure increases.

Low Air Pressure

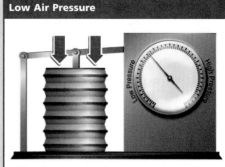

The chamber expands when the air pressure decreases.

READING VISUALS Which of these barometer readings would be the more likely one on a mountain? Explain why.

Barometers and Air Pressure

Air pressure can be measured in different ways. A **barometer** is any instrument that measures air pressure. The illustrations above show a simplified version of a common type of barometer. This type contains a sealed flexible chamber that has little air inside. The chamber contracts when the outside air pressure is high and expands when the air pressure is low. A series of levers or other devices turns the motion of the chamber into something that can be read—the movement of a needle on a dial or a jagged line on a strip of graph paper.

2.1 Review

KEY CONCEPTS

1. How does the movement of air molecules cause pressure?
2. How does altitude affect air pressure?
3. How is air density related to air pressure?

CRITICAL THINKING

4. **Apply** Would you expect the air pressure in a valley that's below sea level to be higher or lower than air pressure at sea level? Explain.
5. **Predict** Two barometers are placed one kilometer apart. One shows higher pressure than the other. What will happen to air between them?

CHALLENGE

6. **Infer** The eardrum is a thin sheet of tissue that separates air in the middle part of your ear from air outside your ear. What could cause your eardrum to make a popping sound as you ride up a tall building in an elevator?

ANSWERS

1. Air molecules move constantly and bounce off surfaces, exerting force or pressure on surfaces.

2. Air pressure decreases as altitude increases.

3. Higher air pressure indicates that air is denser.

4. Air pressure would be higher in the valley because air pressure decreases as altitude increases.

5. Air will start to move from the area of higher pressure toward the area of lower pressure.

6. The higher pressure inside the ear pushes the eardrum outward as the air pressure in the elevator decreases.

KEY CONCEPT

2.2 The atmosphere has wind patterns.

BEFORE, you learned

- Solar energy heats Earth's surface and atmosphere
- Differences in density cause air to move
- Air pressure differences set air in motion

NOW, you will learn

- About forces that affect wind
- About global winds
- About patterns of heating and cooling

VOCABULARY

weather p. 47
wind p. 47
global wind p. 48
Coriolis effect p. 49
jet stream p. 52
monsoon p. 54

EXPLORE Solar Energy

How does Earth's shape affect solar heating?

PROCEDURE

1. Place a globe on a desk in a darkened room.

2. Point a flashlight at the equator on the globe from a distance of about 15 centimeters. Keep the flashlight level. Observe the lighted area on the globe.

3. Keeping the flashlight level, raise it up and point it at the United States. Observe the lighted area.

WHAT DO YOU THINK?
- How were the two lighted areas different?
- What might have caused the difference?

MATERIALS
- globe
- flashlight
- ruler

Uneven heating causes air to move.

On local news broadcasts, weather forecasters often spend several minutes discussing what the weather will be like over the next few days. **Weather** is the condition of Earth's atmosphere at a particular time and place. Wind is an important part of weather. You will read about other weather factors later in this chapter.

Wind is air that moves horizontally, or parallel to the ground. Remember that air pressure can differ from place to place at the same altitude. Uneven heating of Earth's surface causes such pressure differences, which set air in motion. Over a short distance, wind moves directly from higher pressure toward lower pressure.

REMINDER
Remember that air pressure is the force that air molecules exert on an area.

CHECK YOUR READING What is the relationship between air pressure and wind?

RESOURCES FOR DIFFERENTIATED INSTRUCTION

Below Level
UNIT RESOURCE BOOK
- Reading Study Guide A, pp. 95–96
- Decoding Support, p. 130

 AUDIO CDS

R **Additional INVESTIGATION,**
Estimating Wind Speed, A, B, & C, pp. 143–151;
Teacher Instructions, pp. 284–285

Advanced
UNIT RESOURCE BOOK
Challenge and Extension, p. 101

English Learners
UNIT RESOURCE BOOK
Spanish Reading Study Guide, pp. 99–100

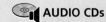 **AUDIO CDs**

- Audio Readings in Spanish
- Audio Readings (English)

2.2 FOCUS

▶ Set Learning Goals
Students will

- Describe the forces that affect wind.
- Describe global winds.
- Explain patterns of heating and cooling.
- Conduct an experiment to model the Coriolis effect.

◀ 3-Minute Warm-Up

Display Transparency 12 or copy this exercise on the board:

Are these statements true? If not, correct them.

1. Differences in pressure cause the horizontal movement of air. *true*

2. Air pressure and air density increase with altitude. *Air pressure and air density decrease with altitude.*

3. The Sun supplies most of Earth's energy. *true*

T 3-Minute Warm-Up, p. T12

2.2 MOTIVATE

EXPLORE Solar Energy

PURPOSE To introduce the concept that the intensity of sunlight varies on Earth

TIP *10 min.* Many globes are made of paper and cannot be labeled, but students might cover globes with paper and outline the lighted area on the paper.

WHAT DO YOU THINK? *The light was more concentrated at the equator and more spread out at the United States. The angle at which the light hit these locations was different.*

Ongoing Assessment

CHECK YOUR READING *Answer: Differences in air pressure cause winds.*

Teach from Visuals

To help students interpret the visual on wind formation:

- Ask: Is the wind moving toward high or low pressure? *low pressure*
- Tell students that in the lower atmosphere, temperature generally decreases as altitude increases. Then ask them to predict what will happen to the rising warm air. *It will cool, become more dense, and sink.*

Teach Difficult Concepts

Students may have a hard time understanding how differences in air pressure relate to wind strength. Remind them that air pressure is a force and that the effects of a force—in this case, wind—increase as the intensity of the force increases. To help students understand, you might try the demonstration below.

Teacher Demo

Obtain a bicycle pump. Slowly push down on the pump handle, allowing students to feel the resulting "breeze." Pull the handle back up, then push down forcibly, again allowing students to feel the air rush out. Ask: Which force was the strongest? *the second one* Which "wind" was the strongest? *the second one*

Ongoing Assessment

CHECK YOUR READING *Answer: The difference in air pressure between two areas determines the strength of wind.*

VISUALIZATION
CLASSZONE.COM
View an animation of the Coriolis effect.

How Wind Forms

Wind moves from an area of high pressure toward an area of low pressure.

① **Warmer air rises.**   ② **Cooler air sinks.**

low pressure   high pressure

③ **Wind moves across surface.**

? A

The illustration above shows a common pattern of air circulation caused by uneven heating of Earth's surface:

① Sunlight strongly heats an area of ground. The ground heats the air. The warm air rises, and an area of low pressure forms.

② Sunlight heats an area of ground less strongly. The cooler, dense air sinks slowly, and an area of high pressure forms.

③ Air moves as wind across the surface, from higher toward lower pressure.

When the difference in pressure between two areas is small, the wind may move too slowly to be noticeable. A very large pressure difference can produce wind strong enough to uproot trees.

CHECK YOUR READING What factor determines the strength of wind?

The distance winds travel varies. Some winds die out quickly after blowing a few meters. In contrast, **global winds** travel thousands of kilometers in steady patterns. Global winds last for weeks.

Uneven heating between the equator and the north and south poles causes global winds. Notice in the illustration at left how sunlight strikes Earth's curved surface. Near the equator, concentrated sunlight heats the surface to a high temperature. Warm air rises, producing low pressure.

In regions closer to the poles, the sunlight is more spread out. Because less of the Sun's energy reaches these regions, the air above them is cooler and denser. The sinking dense air produces high pressure that sets global winds in motion.

Sunlight is concentrated near the equator because it strikes the surface directly.

North Pole
Arctic Circle
Tropic of Cancer
Equator
Tropic of Capricorn

Sunlight is more spread out near the poles because it strikes at a lower angle.

DIFFERENTIATE INSTRUCTION

? More Reading Support

A The uneven heating of Earth causes what? *air circulation*

B What winds travel thousands of kilometers in steady patterns? *global winds*

English Learners English learners may have difficulty using the words *affect* and *effect* correctly. Explain that *affect* is a verb and *effect* is a noun. For example, on p. 49 the term *Coriolis effect* contains the noun *effect*. The Investigate on p. 49 contains an example of the verb *affect*: "How did the rotation affect the lines that you drew?"

Earth's rotation affects wind direction.

If Earth did not rotate, global winds would flow directly from the poles to the equator. However, Earth's rotation changes the direction of winds and other objects moving over Earth. The influence of Earth's rotation is called the **Coriolis effect** (KAWR-ee-OH-lihs). Global winds curve as Earth turns beneath them. In the Northern Hemisphere, winds curve to the right in the direction of motion. Winds in the Southern Hemisphere curve to the left. The Coriolis effect is noticeable only for winds that travel long distances.

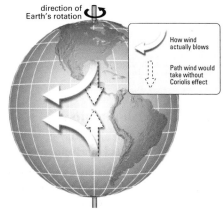

direction of Earth's rotation

How wind actually blows

Path wind would take without Coriolis effect

Because the Coriolis effect causes global winds to curve, they cannot flow directly from the poles to the equator. Instead, global winds travel along three routes in each hemisphere. These routes, which circle the world, are called global wind belts.

CHECK YOUR READING In which direction do winds curve in the Northern Hemisphere?

INVESTIGATE Coriolis Effect

How does Earth's rotation affect wind?

PROCEDURE

① Blow up a balloon and tie it off.

② Have a classmate slowly rotate the balloon to the right. Draw a line straight down from the top of the balloon to the center as the balloon rotates.

③ Now draw a line from the bottom of the balloon straight up to the center as the balloon rotates.

WHAT DO YOU THINK?

• How did the rotation affect the lines that you drew?

• How does this activity demonstrate the Coriolis effect?

CHALLENGE How might changing the speed at which the balloon is rotated affect your results? Repeat the activity to test your prediction.

SKILL FOCUS
Modeling

MATERIALS
• round balloon
• felt-tip pen

TIME
10 minutes

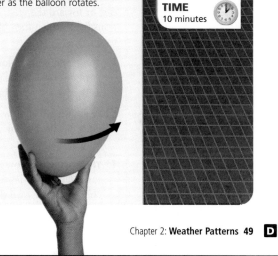

Chapter 2: **Weather Patterns** 49 **D**

Address Misconceptions

IDENTIFY Ask: Does water swirl down a drain one way in the Northern Hemisphere and the opposite way in the Southern Hemisphere? If students answer yes, they may hold the misconception that the Coriolis effect causes water to swirl in a particular direction down a drain. In reality, the Coriolis effect influences only movements across large distances, such as the movements of global winds and ocean currents.

CORRECT Refer students to the diagram on page 49. Ask: What do you see in the illustration, besides wind, that might be influenced by the Coriolis effect? *oceans*

REASSESS Ask: Does the Coriolis effect influence global winds or local breezes? Explain your answer. *It influences global winds, since it affects only things that move for long distances over Earth.* Would you expect the Coriolis effect to influence large oceans or something as small as a water basin? *large oceans*

Technology Resources

Visit **ClassZone.com** for background on common student misconceptions.

 MISCONCEPTION DATABASE

History of Science

One of the first models of air circulation was developed in 1735 by English scientist George Hadley. Hadley proposed that winds in each hemisphere circulated in one large cell. He contributed greatly to our understanding of the way air moves, but his model was far too simple to explain global wind patterns.

 **RESOURCE CENTER**
CLASSZONE.COM

Learn more about global winds.

READING TiP

As you read about each region or wind belt, locate it in the diagram on page 51.

Bands of calm air separate global wind belts.

Earth's rotation and the uneven heating of its surface cause a pattern of wind belts separated by calm regions. Each calm region is a zone of either high pressure or low pressure. The illustration on page 51 shows how each wind belt and the calm regions that border it form a giant loop of moving air. These loops are called circulation cells. The section of a cell that flows along Earth's surface is global wind. Notice that the direction of airflow changes from one circulation cell to the next.

Calm Regions

? **E**

The air usually stays calm in high-pressure and low-pressure zones. Winds are light, and they often change direction.

❶ **The doldrums** are a low-pressure zone near the equator. There, warm air rises to the top of the troposphere, which is the atmosphere's lowest layer. Then the air spreads out toward the poles. The rising, moist air produces clouds and heavy rain. During the hottest months, heavy evaporation from warm ocean water in the region fuels tropical storms.

❷ **The horse latitudes** are high-pressure zones located about 30° north and 30° south of the equator. Warm air traveling away from the equator cools and sinks in these regions. The weather tends to be clear and dry.

Wind Belts

As dense air sinks to Earth's surface in the horse latitudes and other high-pressure zones, it flows out toward regions of low pressure. This pattern of air movement produces three global wind belts in each hemisphere. Because of the Coriolis effect, the winds curve toward the east or toward the west. Some global winds are named for the directions from which they blow. The westerlies, for example, blow from west to east.

❸ **The trade winds** blow from the east, moving from the horse latitudes toward the equator. These strong, steady winds die out as they come near the equator.

? **F**

❹ **The westerlies** blow from the west, moving from the horse latitudes toward the poles. They bring storms across much of the United States.

❺ **The easterlies** blow from the east, moving from the polar regions toward the mid-latitudes. Stormy weather often occurs when the cold air of the easterlies meets the warmer air of the westerlies.

DIFFERENTIATE INSTRUCTION

? **More Reading Support**

E What low-pressure zone is found near the equator? *doldrums*

F What are the three wind belts? *trade winds, westerlies, and easterlies*

Additional Investigation To reinforce Section 2.2 learning goals, use the following full-period investigation:

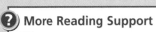 **Additional INVESTIGATION,** Estimating Wind Speed, A, B, & C, pp. 143–151, 284–285 (Advanced students should complete Levels B and C.)

Below Level For students struggling to understand where these zones are, explain that *latitude* refers to a distance in degrees north or south of the equator. Use a globe to show the latitudes of some global wind belts and calm regions.

Global Winds

Belts of global wind circle Earth. Because of the Coriolis effect, the winds in these belts curve to the east or the west. Between the global wind belts are calm areas of rising or falling air.

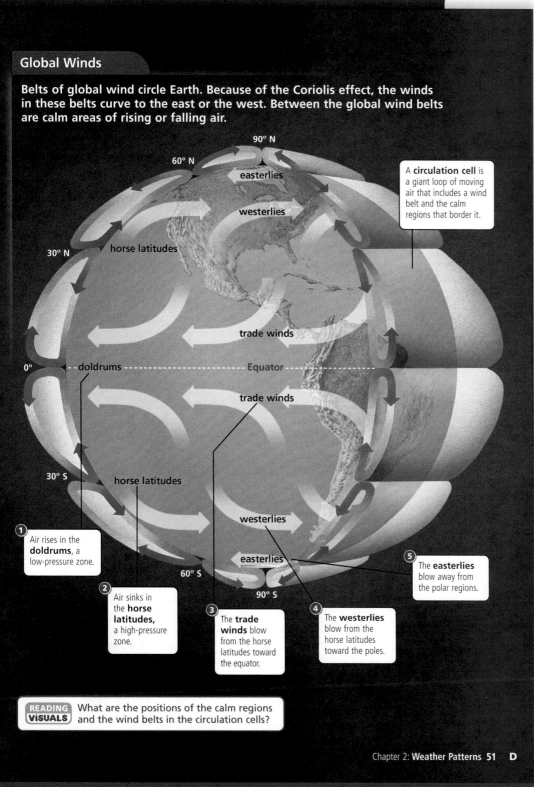

90° N
60° N
easterlies
westerlies
30° N
horse latitudes

A **circulation cell** is a giant loop of moving air that includes a wind belt and the calm regions that border it.

trade winds

0° --- **doldrums** ------------------------- **Equator** -----------

trade winds

30° S

horse latitudes

① Air rises in the **doldrums**, a low-pressure zone.

② Air sinks in the **horse latitudes**, a high-pressure zone.

westerlies

easterlies

60° S

90° S

③ The **trade winds** blow from the horse latitudes toward the equator.

④ The **westerlies** blow from the horse latitudes toward the poles.

⑤ The **easterlies** blow away from the polar regions.

> **READING VISUALS** What are the positions of the calm regions and the wind belts in the circulation cells?

Chapter 2: **Weather Patterns** 51 **D**

Teacher Demo

To help students understand how global winds affected early sailors, fashion a model ship from a piece of cork and cloth, or obtain a small plastic ship. Next, fill a long rectangular container with water and place the ship in the right, or east, end of the container. Place a fan near that end, taking care not to let the cord touch the water. Tell students that the fan represents the trade winds and the water represents the Atlantic Ocean—Europe is on the right side, and North America is on the left. Then turn the fan on and allow students to observe how the wind blows the ship across the Atlantic. Ask: What would happen if the people in the ship tried to recross the ocean along the same route? *The ship would be pushed back by the trade winds.*

Develop Critical Thinking

COMPARE AND CONTRAST Have students summarize what they have learned about wind belts. Ask: How do jet streams differ from global wind belts? How are they similar? *Jet streams flow faster and at higher altitudes than global winds. Also, jet streams loop north and south. Like the global wind belts, jet streams are caused by the uneven heating of Earth's surface and flow for thousands of kilometers.*

Ongoing Assessment

Describe global winds.

Ask: From which directions do the three global wind belts and the jet streams flow? *trade winds: east; westerlies: west; easterlies: east; jet streams: west*

Effects of Wind on Travel

Before the invention of steam engines, sailors used to dread traveling through the doldrums and the horse latitudes. There often wasn't enough wind to move their sailing ships. A ship might stall for days or even weeks, wasting precious supplies of food and fresh water.

 G

To avoid the calm regions, sailors sought out global wind belts. The trade winds got their name because traders used them to sail from east to west. For centuries, sailors relied on the trade winds to reach North America from Europe. They would return by sailing north to catch the westerlies and ride them across the Atlantic.

Jet streams flow near the top of the troposphere.

COMBINATION NOTES Record information about how jet streams flow and their effects on weather and travel.

H

Not all long-distance winds travel along Earth's surface. **Jet streams** usually flow in the upper troposphere from west to east for thousands of kilometers. Air often moves in jet streams at speeds greater than 200 kilometers per hour (124 mi/hr). Like global winds, jet streams form because Earth's surface is heated unevenly. Instead of following a straight line, jet streams loop north and south, as shown on the globe below.

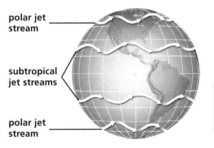

polar jet stream

subtropical jet streams

polar jet stream

Jet streams flow in a wavy pattern from west to east around the world. They change positions during the year.

Each hemisphere usually has two jet streams, a polar jet stream and a subtropical jet stream. The polar jet streams flow closer to the poles in summer than in winter.

The polar jet stream has a strong influence on weather in North America. It can pull cold air down from Canada into the United States and pull warm air up toward Canada. In addition, strong storms tend to form along its loops. Scientists must know where the jet stream is flowing to make accurate weather predictions.

Jet streams also affect air-travel times. They usually flow 10 to 15 kilometers (6–9 mi) above Earth's surface. Since airplanes often fly at these altitudes, their travel times can be lengthened or shortened by the strong wind of a jet stream.

DIFFERENTIATE INSTRUCTION

? **More Reading Support**

G What wind belt helped sailors reach North America from Europe? *trade winds*

H In what part of the atmosphere do jet streams flow? *upper troposphere*

Advanced Tell students that the polar jet stream flows faster in the winter than it does in the summer. Ask them to infer why. *Wind speed is related to differences in air pressure. Therefore, there must be greater differences in air pressure in the upper troposphere in the winter than in the summer.*

Patterns of heating and cooling cause local winds and monsoons.

Have you ever noticed how the wind can change in predictable ways? For example, at the beach on a hot day you will often feel a cool breeze coming off the water. At night a breeze will flow in the opposite direction. The change in the breeze occurs because water and land heat up and cool down at different rates.

Local Winds

Some winds change daily in a regular pattern. These local winds blow within small areas.

- Sea breezes and land breezes occur near shorelines. During the day, land heats up faster than water. The air over the land rises and expands. Denser ocean air moves into the area of low pressure, producing a sea breeze. As the illustration below shows, this pattern is reversed at night, when land cools faster than water. Warm air rises over the ocean, and cooler air flows in, producing a land breeze.

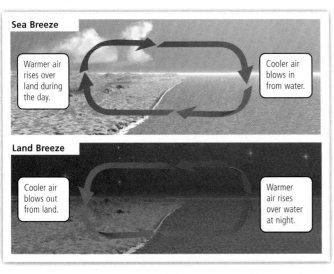

Sea Breeze

Warmer air rises over land during the day.

Cooler air blows in from water.

Land Breeze

Cooler air blows out from land.

Warmer air rises over water at night.

▼ **REMINDER**
Red arrows stand for warmer air. Blue arrows stand for cooler air.

- Valley breezes and mountain breezes are caused by a similar process. Mountain slopes heat up and cool faster than the valleys below them. During the day, valley breezes flow up mountains. At night mountain breezes flow down into valleys.

CHECK YOUR READING How do mountains and bodies of water affect patterns of heating and cooling?

Chapter 2: **Weather Patterns** 53 **D**

Teach from Visuals

To help students interpret the visuals of sea and land breezes, ask:

- Where is the area of low pressure that produces a sea breeze located? *over land*

- Where is the area of low pressure that produces a land breeze located? *over water*

- Why is air warmer over the land during the day and warmer over the water at night? *because land and water absorb and release heat at different rates*

EXPLORE the BIG idea

Revisit "Internet Activity: Wind" on p. 41. Have students describe their observations.

Ongoing Assessment

Explain patterns of heating and cooling.

Ask: If water heated up faster than land, in which direction would wind flow during the day near the coast? *out to sea*

CHECK YOUR READING *Answer: Mountain slopes heat up and cool down faster than the valleys below them, so that winds flow up the slopes during the day and down the slopes during the night. Bodies of water heat up and cool down slower than land, so that winds flow inland during the day and toward the water during the night.*

DIFFERENTIATE INSTRUCTION

? More Reading Support

I When do sea breezes occur? *during the day*

J When do mountain breezes occur? *at night*

Inclusion Visual learners have an easier time grasping concepts that are shown in a graphic. Pair verbal learners with visual learners and have them work together to diagram mountain and valley breezes. Students should label their diagrams and use arrows to indicate the directions of wind movement.

Ongoing Assessment

 CHECK YOUR READING *Answer: Winter monsoons originate over land and are cool and dry. Summer monsoons originate over water and are moist; they bring heavy rains.*

Reinforce (the **BIG** idea)

Have students relate the section to the Big Idea.

 Reinforcing Key Concepts, p. 103

ASSESS & RETEACH

Assess

 Section 2.2 Quiz, p. 24

Reteach

Make a transparency of a globe, using the diagram on p. 51 as a guide. Do not put any arrows or labels on the transparency. Place the transparency on an overhead projector. Then, with the help of the class, fill in the diagram with the wind belts, using a different-colored marker for each belt. Students should come up with the pertinent information. If they stall, ask leading questions, such as, In which direction do the trade winds blow? and What low-pressure zone is located near the equator? As an alternative activity, you can make copies of the diagram on p. 51, delete the labels and arrows, and let students fill in the information individually.

Technology Resources

Have students visit **ClassZone.com** for reteaching of Key Concepts.

 CONTENT REVIEW

CONTENT REVIEW CD-ROM

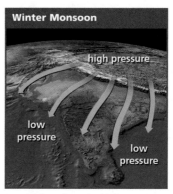
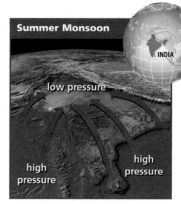

Dry air blows from the high-pressure area over the continent to the low-pressure areas over the ocean.

Moist air blows from the high-pressure areas over the ocean to the low-pressure area over the continent.

VOCABULARY
Add a description wheel for *monsoon* to your notebook.

Monsoons

Winds that change direction with the seasons are called **monsoons**. Like sea breezes and land breezes, monsoons are caused by the different heating and cooling rates of land and sea. However, monsoons flow longer distances and affect much larger areas.

Winter monsoons occur in regions where the land becomes much cooler than the sea during winter. High pressure builds over the land, and cool, dry wind blows out toward the sea. During summer this pattern reverses as the land becomes much warmer than the sea. Moist wind flows inland, often bringing heavy rains. The most extreme monsoons occur in South Asia and Southeast Asia. Farmers there depend on rain from the summer monsoon to grow crops.

CHECK YOUR READING How do monsoon winds affect rainfall?

2.2 Review

KEY CONCEPTS

1. How does the uneven heating of Earth's surface cause winds to flow?

2. How does Earth's rotation influence the movement of global winds?

3. Why do some winds change direction in areas where land is near water?

CRITICAL THINKING

4. **Compare and Contrast** How are global winds and local winds similar? How are they different?

5. **Analyze** Make a table that shows the causes and effects of local winds and monsoons.

CHALLENGE

6. **Predict** Suppose that a city is located in a valley between the sea and a mountain range. What kind of wind pattern would you predict for this area?

 54 Unit: Earth's Atmosphere

ANSWERS

1. It causes differences in air pressure, which causes air to move.

2. It causes global winds to curve.

3. Land and water heat up and cool down at different rates. These differences cause

daily or seasonal changes in air pressure, leading to changes in wind direction.

4. Both winds are caused by the uneven heating of Earth's surface. Global winds flow over longer distances and are affected by the Coriolis effect.

5. Check students' tables for accuracy.

6. During the day, air would blow from the sea into the city and out of the city up the mountain slopes. At night, the pattern would reverse.

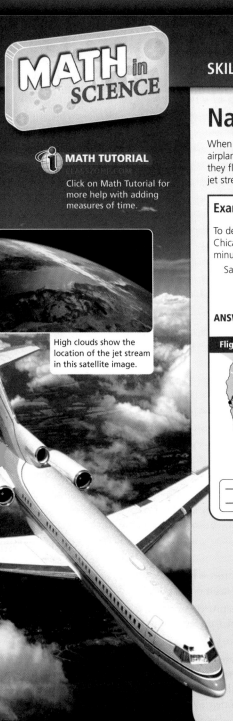

MATH TUTORIAL

Click on Math Tutorial for more help with adding measures of time.

High clouds show the location of the jet stream in this satellite image.

SKILL: ADDING MEASUREMENTS

Navigate the Jet Stream

When an airplane is flying in the same direction as a jet stream, the airplane gets a boost in its speed. Pilots can save an hour or more if they fly with the jet stream. On the other hand, flying against the jet stream can slow an airplane down.

Example

To determine the total flight time between San Francisco and Chicago, with a stop in Denver, you need to add the hours and minutes separately. Set up the problem like this:

San Francisco to Denver: 2 h   10 min
Denver to Chicago: <u>1 h   45 min</u>
Total flight time: 3 h   55 min

ANSWER The total flight time is 3 hours 55 minutes.

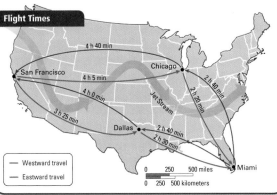

Flight Times

— Westward travel
— Eastward travel

4 h 40 min
4 h 5 min
4 h 0 min
3 h 25 min
2 h 40 min
2 h 20 min
2 h 40 min
2 h 30 min

San Francisco · Chicago · Jet Stream · Dallas · Miami

0   250   500 miles
0   250   500 kilometers

Use the map to answer the following questions.

1. What is the total flight time for an airliner flying from San Francisco to Miami through Chicago?

2. What is the total flight time for an airliner flying from San Francisco to Miami through Dallas?

3. How much time will the fastest possible trip from Miami to San Francisco take?

4. Compare the flight time from Chicago to San Francisco with the flight time from San Francisco to Chicago.

CHALLENGE What is the total flight time from Miami to San Francisco through Chicago? Convert minutes to hours if necessary.

Set Learning Goal

To add measurements to determine how flight times are affected by a jet stream

Present the Science

During World War II, U.S. pilots flew at high altitudes to avoid enemy fire. Their flight times were substantially reduced when they flew west to east in certain regions. The Swedish-American meteorologist Carl-Gustaf Rossby discovered belts of fast-moving, high-altitude winds, or jet streams.

Develop Computation Skills

- Remind students that they can divide a number of minutes by 60 to find the number of hours; the remainder is minutes. The number of minutes should never exceed 59.

- For the Challenge question, have students practice expressing numbers of minutes in terms of hours and minutes. Ask: How would you change 95 minutes to hours and minutes? *One hour is 60 minutes. Thus, 95 min = 60 min + 35 min = 1 h 35 min*

DIFFERENTIATION TIP For students with poor vision, list flight times in large writing on the board.

Close

Ask students to summarize how jet streams affect air travel. Tell them to refer to directions in their answer. *They decrease times for west-to-east flights and increase times for east-to-west flights.*

- Math Support, p. 131
- Math Practice, p. 132

Technology Resources

Students can visit **ClassZone.com** for practice in adding measurements.

 MATH TUTORIAL

ANSWERS

1. 4 h 5 min + 2 h 20 min = 6 h 25 min

2. 3 h 25 min + 2 h 30 min = 5 h 55 min

3. 2 h 40 min + 4 h 0 min = 6 h 40 min

4. The flight from San Francisco to Chicago is 35 minutes shorter (4 h 40 min − 4 h 5 min = 0 h 35 min).

CHALLENGE 2 h 40 min + 4 h 40 min = 6 h 80 min = 7 h 20 min

FOCUS

Set Learning Goals

Students will

- Explain how water in the atmosphere changes.
- Explain how clouds form.
- Describe types of clouds.
- Observe a model of how clouds form.

3-Minute Warm-Up

Display Transparency 13 or copy this exercise on the board:

Answer each question.

1. Does wind move horizontally or vertically? *horizontally*

2. Does warm air rise or sink? *rise*

3. Does air move from low- to high-pressure areas or from high to low? *high to low*

4. What does the Coriolis effect cause winds to do? *curve*

[T] 3-Minute Warm-Up, p. T13

2.3 MOTIVATE

EXPLORE Condensation

PURPOSE To introduce the concept of condensation

TIP *5 min.* Divide the class into small groups. A clear glass of cool water can serve as a substitute for the hand mirror.

WHAT DO YOU THINK? *Tiny water droplets condensed on the mirror. There was little temperature difference between the air in the room and the air the classmate breathed out. The mirror, however, was cooler than the classmate's breath, which caused water vapor in the breath to condense on the mirror.*

2.3 Most clouds form as air rises and cools.

 BEFORE, you learned
- Water vapor circulates from Earth to the atmosphere
- Warm air is less dense than cool air and tends to rise

NOW, you will learn
- How water in the atmosphere changes
- How clouds form
- About the types of clouds

VOCABULARY

evaporation p. 56
condensation p. 56
precipitation p. 57
humidity p. 58
saturation p. 58
relative humidity p. 58
dew point p. 58

EXPLORE Condensation

How does condensation occur?

PROCEDURE

① Observe the air as a classmate breathes out.

② Observe a mirror as a classmate breathes onto it.

WHAT DO YOU THINK?
- What changes did you observe on the mirror?
- Why could you see water on the mirror but not in the air when your classmate breathed out?

MATERIALS
hand mirror

Temperature affects water in the air.

Water is always in the atmosphere. You may see water in solid form, such as falling snow. Water may also be present as liquid water droplets. Even if you can't see any water, it is still part of the air as water vapor, an invisible gas. When temperatures change, water changes its form.

- **Evaporation** is the process by which a liquid changes into a gas. For water to evaporate, it needs extra energy.

- **Condensation** is the process by which a gas, such as water vapor, changes into a liquid. Condensation occurs when moist air cools.

The picture on the left shows the processes of evaporation and condensation at work. Water in a teakettle absorbs heat. It gets enough energy to evaporate into water vapor. The invisible water vapor rises and escapes from the kettle. When the vapor hits the cooler air outside the kettle, it cools and condenses into tiny but visible water droplets.

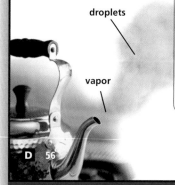

droplets

vapor

D 56

RESOURCES FOR DIFFERENTIATED INSTRUCTION

Below Level
UNIT RESOURCE BOOK
- Reading Study Guide A, pp. 106–107
- Decoding Support, p. 130

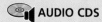 **AUDIO CDS**

Advanced
UNIT RESOURCE BOOK
Challenge and Extension, p. 112

English Learners
UNIT RESOURCE BOOK
Spanish Reading Study Guide, pp. 110–111

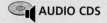 **AUDIO CDS**

- Audio Readings in Spanish
- Audio Readings (English)

Water in the Air

(?) A Vast amounts of Earth's water are recycled. The oceans hold most of the water. Water is also stored in lakes, rivers, and ice sheets; in plants; and underground. Energy from sunlight causes molecules to evaporate from the surface of a body of water. These molecules become part of the air in the form of water vapor.

(?) B As air rises in the atmosphere, it cools. The loss of heat causes water vapor to condense into tiny water droplets or ice crystals. If the droplets or crystals grow and become heavy enough, they fall as rain, snow, sleet, or hail. Any type of liquid or solid water that falls to Earth's surface is called **precipitation.** Earth's water goes through a never-ending cycle of evaporation, condensation, and precipitation.

Water vapor can also condense on solid surfaces. Have you ever gotten your shoes wet while walking on grass in the early morning? The grass was covered with dew, which is water that has condensed on cool surfaces at night. If the temperature is cold enough, water vapor can change directly into a covering of ice, called frost.

> **VOCABULARY**
> Add a description wheel for *precipitation* to your notebook.

CHECK YOUR READING Summarize the way water moves in the water cycle. For each part of the cycle, specify whether water exists as a gas, liquid, or solid.

Water Cycle

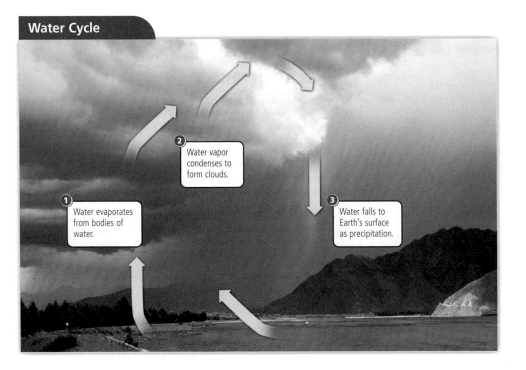

1. Water evaporates from bodies of water.
2. Water vapor condenses to form clouds.
3. Water falls to Earth's surface as precipitation.

Chapter 2: **Weather Patterns 57** **D**

IDENTIFY Ask: What weighs more: humid air or dry air? If students answer humid air, they may hold the misconception that on humid days the air feels heavy because of its water vapor content.

CORRECT Tell students that the molecular weight of water is 18. The molecular weight of dry air is, on average, 29. In fact, the more humid a quantity of air is, the less dense and heavy it is.

REASSESS Ask: Which is less dense, humid air or dry air? *humid air* Which would travel faster and farther, a baseball hit in humid air or a baseball hit in dry air? *a baseball hit in humid air*

Technology Resources

Visit **ClassZone.com** for background on common student misconceptions.

MISCONCEPTION DATABASE

Teach Difficult Concepts

Students may have a hard time understanding how temperature affects evaporation and condensation. Remind them that heat causes water molecules in air to move faster. It's difficult for these fast-moving molecules to join together and condense. In contrast, water molecules move slower and closer together as air cools, and the rate of condensation increases.

Humidity and Relative Humidity

On a warm summer day, evaporation of moisture from your skin can help you feel comfortable. However, a lot of water vapor in the air can cause less moisture to evaporate from your skin. With less evaporation, the air will seem hotter and damper. **Humidity** is the amount of water vapor in air. Humidity varies from place to place and from time to time.

The illustration shows how humidity increases in a sealed container. As water molecules evaporate into the air, some start to condense and return to the water. For a while the air gains water vapor because more water evaporates than condenses. But eventually the air reaches **saturation,** a condition in which the rates of evaporation and condensation are equal. Any additional water that evaporates is balanced by water that condenses.

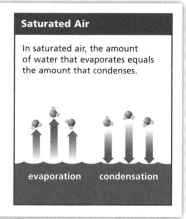

Unsaturated Air

In unsaturated air, more water evaporates into the air than condenses back into the water.

water molecule

evaporation   condensation

Saturated Air

In saturated air, the amount of water that evaporates equals the amount that condenses.

evaporation   condensation

READING TiP

Relative means "considered in comparison with something else."

The amount of water vapor in air at saturation depends on the temperature of the air. The warmer air is, the more water vapor it takes to saturate it. Scientists use this principle to describe the humidity of air in two different ways: relative humidity and dew point.

Relative humidity compares the amount of water vapor in air with the maximum amount of water vapor that can be present at that temperature. For example, air with 50 percent relative humidity has half the amount of water needed for saturation. If the amount of water vapor in air stays the same, relative humidity will decrease as the air heats up and increase as the air cools.

Dew point is the temperature at which air with a given amount of water vapor will reach saturation. For example, air with a dew point of 26°C (79°F) will become saturated if it cools to 26°C. The higher the dew point of air, the more water vapor the air contains.

DIFFERENTIATE INSTRUCTION

 More Reading Support

C What is humidity? *the amount of water vapor in the air*

D The temperature at which air will reach saturation is called what? *dew point*

Below Level To help students understand relative humidity, point out that it is always expressed as a percentage. Have students compare the numbers of water molecules shown evaporating and condensing in the two diagrams. Ask: Which diagram shows a balance between rates of evaporation and condensation? *the second, or right-hand, diagram* When rates of evaporation and condensation are balanced, what is the relative humidity of the air? *100 percent*

Water vapor condenses and forms clouds.

Clouds are made of condensed water vapor. As warm air rises in the atmosphere, it cools. When the air cools to its dew point—the temperature at which air reaches saturation—water vapor condenses into tiny droplets or ice crystals. These droplets and crystals are so light that they either float as clouds on rising air or fall very slowly.

level where condensation begins

Rising warm air can produce clouds. Water vapor begins to condense when the air cools to its dew point.

Recall how dew condenses on grass. Water must condense on something solid. There are no large solid surfaces in the air. However, the air is filled with tiny particles such as dust, smoke, and salt from the ocean. Water vapor condenses on these particles.

INVESTIGATE Condensation

How does a cloud form?

PROCEDURE

1. Add a spoonful of water to the bottle to increase the humidity inside it.
2. Lay the bottle on its side. Light a match, blow it out, and then stick the match into the bottle for a few seconds to let smoke flow in. Replace the cap.
3. Squeeze the bottle quickly and then release it. Observe what happens when the bottle is allowed to expand.

WHAT DO YOU THINK?

- What happened to the water vapor inside the bottle when you squeezed the bottle and then let it expand?
- How did the smoke affect what happened to the water vapor?

CHALLENGE How would the cloud change if you raised or lowered the temperature inside the bottle?

SKILL FOCUS
Observing

MATERIALS
- clear 1-liter plastic bottle with cap
- water at room temperature
- tablespoon
- matches

TIME
10 minutes

Chapter 2: Weather Patterns **59** **D**

? More Reading Support

E What are clouds made of? *condensed water vapor*

F What do cloud droplets condense on? *tiny solid particles*

Below Level In the Condensation lab above, some students may expect the cloud to look puffy and white—similar to a cumulus cloud. Stress that it takes billions upon billions of water droplets to form the fluffy white clouds we see in the sky.

INVESTIGATE
Condensation

PURPOSE To observe how clouds form

TIPS *10 min.* Suggest the following to students:

- To make it easier to observe changes in the bottle, place the bottle against a dark background.
- Test your prediction for the Challenge question.

WHAT DO YOU THINK? *The water vapor condensed and a cloud formed. Water must condense on something solid—without the smoke particles, the water could not have condensed.*

CHALLENGE *Sample answer: Lowering the temperature would increase the rate of condensation and cause a thicker cloud to form. Raising the temperature would decrease the rate of condensation.*

Datasheet, Condensation, p. 113

Technology Resources

Customize this student lab as needed or look for an alternative. Print rubrics to assess student lab reports.

Lab Generator CD-ROM

Metacognitive Strategy

Ask: What conclusion can you draw from "Investigate Condensation? *Water vapor, particulates, and a change in pressure are needed for a cloud to form.*

Ongoing Assessment

Explain how clouds form.

Ask: What is the first step in cloud formation? *Warm air rises and cools.*

Teacher Demo

Students may have a hard time understanding how clouds stay in the air. Use the following demonstration to show that it takes only the slightest updraft to keep cloud droplets aloft. Obtain a small, white downy feather. Place the feather in your hand, raise it to about eye level, then blow on it lightly, keeping the feather aloft. Afterwards, tell students that although clouds may appear huge when viewed from Earth's surface, the droplets that make up clouds are extremely small and light—it takes only a slight updraft to keep them, like the feather, aloft.

History of Science

In the early 1800s, two men worked separately to develop classification systems for clouds. The first man, Jean Baptiste Lamarck, published his system in his native language, French. He unwisely opted to have it printed in a journal that included astrological forecasts, and his work was therefore viewed as unscientific. The second man, Luke Howard of England, used Latin, the language of scholars during that time, to name the types of clouds. By using words that were understood in many countries, Howard ensured that his classification would stand the test of time—the cloud classification system used today stems from his original work.

Ongoing Assessment

CHECK YOUR READING *Answer: Clouds formed at high altitudes are made of ice crystals. Clouds formed at low altitudes are made of water droplets (or a mixture of ice crystals and water droplets).*

RESOURCE CENTER
CLASSZONE.COM
Observe different types of clouds.

COMBINATION NOTES
Record information about the three main cloud types.

? **G**

? **H**

Characteristics of Clouds

If you watch the sky over a period of time, you will probably observe clouds that do not look alike. Clouds have different characteristics because they form under different conditions. The shapes and sizes of clouds are mainly determined by air movement. For example, puffy clouds form in air that rises sharply or moves straight up and down. Flat, smooth clouds covering large areas form in air that rises gradually.

Location affects the composition of clouds. Since the troposphere gets colder with altitude, clouds that form at high altitudes are made of tiny ice crystals. Closer to Earth's surface, clouds are made of water droplets or a mixture of ice crystals and water droplets.

CHECK YOUR READING How are clouds that form at high altitudes different from clouds that form close to Earth's surface?

In the illustration on page 61, notice that some cloud names share word parts. That is because clouds are classified and named according to their altitudes, the ways they form, and their general characteristics. The three main types of clouds are cirrus, cumulus, and stratus. These names come from Latin words that suggest the clouds' appearances.

- **Cirrus** (SEER-uhs) means "curl of hair." Cirrus clouds appear feathery or wispy.
- **Cumulus** (KYOOM-yuh-luhs) means "heap" or "pile." Cumulus-type clouds can grow to be very tall.
- **Stratus** (STRAT-uhs) means "spread out." Stratus-type clouds form in flat layers.

Word parts are used to tell more about clouds. For example, names of clouds that produce precipitation contain the word part *nimbo-* or *nimbus.* Names of clouds that form at a medium altitude have the prefix *alto-.*

Cirrus Clouds

Cirrus clouds form in very cold air at high altitudes. Made of ice crystals, they have a wispy or feathery appearance. Strong winds often blow streamers or "tails" off cirrus clouds. These features show the direction of the wind in the upper troposphere. You will usually see cirrus clouds in fair weather. However, they can be a sign that a storm is approaching.

cirrus clouds

DIFFERENTIATE INSTRUCTION

? **More Reading Support**

G Clouds that form at high altitudes are made of what? *ice crystals*

H What does *cirrus* mean? *"curl of hair"*

Advanced Clouds can form when two air masses of different temperatures meet—as the warm air is forced upward, it expands and cools, and water vapor condenses. Clouds can also form when warm air reaches a mountain slope. Have students infer why. *Sample answer: When the warm air reaches the mountain, it is forced to rise. The air then expands and cools, and water vapor condenses.*

 Challenge and Extension, p. 112

Cloud Types

The three main cloud types are cirrus, cumulus, and stratus. These names can be combined with each other and with other word parts to identify more specific cloud types.

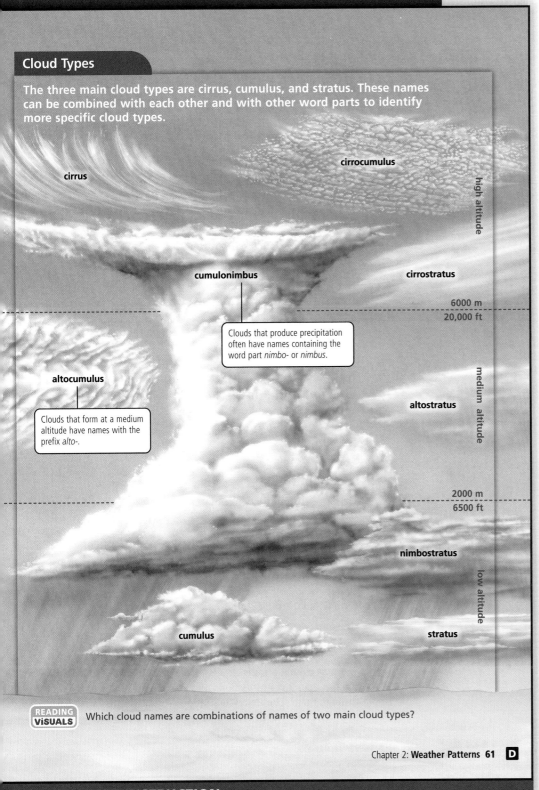

cirrus

cirrocumulus

high altitude

cirrostratus

cumulonimbus

6000 m
20,000 ft

Clouds that produce precipitation often have names containing the word part *nimbo-* or *nimbus.*

altocumulus

medium altitude

altostratus

Clouds that form at a medium altitude have names with the prefix *alto-.*

2000 m
6500 ft

nimbostratus

low altitude

cumulus

stratus

READING VISUALS Which cloud names are combinations of names of two main cloud types?

Chapter 2: **Weather Patterns** 61 **D**

Chapter 2 **61** **D**

Develop Critical Thinking

APPLY Ask the following questions to reinforce cloud characteristics:

- What keeps cumulus clouds separate from one another? *Warm air rises straight up and cooler air sinks along the sides of the clouds.*

- Why are stratus clouds generally smooth and spread out? *because they form without strong air movement*

- Scientists have many names for clouds, including *stratocumulus.* What can you infer about the location and shape of a stratocumulus cloud? *Sample answer: Its name contains the prefix strato- so it is a low-altitude cloud. It is puffy like a cumulus cloud, but spread out in a thick layer like a stratus cloud.*

Metacognitive Strategy

Help students to devise simple memory strategies, using descriptive terms that sound like cloud names. For example, *alto-* is related to *altitude,* stratus clouds have streamers, and cumulus clouds are like cotton balls.

Ongoing Assessment

CHECK YOUR READING *Answer: They are the tallest clouds, and they produce thunderstorms.*

READING TiP

As you read each description of a main cloud type, look back at the visual on page 61. Notice the different clouds that have the main cloud type as part of their names.

? **I**

Cumulus Clouds

Cumulus clouds are puffy white clouds with darker bases. They look like cotton balls floating in the sky. There are several varieties of cumulus clouds. Usually they appear in the daytime in fair weather, when warm air rises and its water vapor condenses. Cooler air sinks along the sides of the clouds, keeping cumulus clouds separate from one another.

cumulus clouds

If cumulus clouds keep growing taller, they can produce showers. The precipitation usually lasts less than half an hour because there are spaces between the clouds. The tallest clouds are cumulonimbus clouds, or thunderheads. These clouds produce thunderstorms that drop heavy rainfall. A cumulonimbus cloud can tower 18 kilometers (11 mi) above Earth's surface. By comparison, jet planes usually fly at about 10 kilometers (6 mi). Strong high-altitude winds often cause the top of the cloud to jut out sharply.

cumulonimbus clouds

CHECK YOUR READING How are cumulonimbus clouds different from other cumulus clouds?

Stratus Clouds

? **J**

Have you ever noticed on some days that the whole sky looks gray? You were looking at stratus clouds. They form in layers when air cools over a large area without rising or when the air is gently lifted. Stratus clouds are smooth because they form without strong air movement.

stratus clouds

Some low stratus clouds are so dark that they completely block out the sun. These clouds produce steady, light precipitation—unlike the brief showers that come from cumulus clouds. Stratus clouds that form at high altitudes are much thinner than low stratus clouds. You can see the Sun and the Moon through them. The ice crystals in high stratus clouds can make it seem as if there's a circle of colored light around the Sun or the Moon.

DIFFERENTIATE INSTRUCTION

? **More Reading Support**

I Cumulus clouds usually form in daytime in what kind of weather? *fair*

J What type of cloud forms in layers? *stratus*

Inclusion Physically challenged students may have difficulty drawing sketches or writing answers in their notebooks. Encourage these students to record their answers or observations on audiotape. For example, if an activity calls for students to draw different cloud types, allow physically challenged students to tape their descriptions of the types. If students do not have access to tape recorders, they can give oral descriptions.

This fog formed around Castleton Tower in Utah. The land cooled overnight, causing water vapor in the air above it to condense.

Fog

Fog is a cloud that rests on the ground or a body of water. Like stratus clouds, fog has a smooth appearance. It usually forms when a surface is colder than the air above it. Water vapor in the air condenses as it cools, forming a thick mist. Fog on land tends to be heaviest at dawn, after the ground has cooled overnight. It clears as the ground is heated up by sunlight.

Fog can look beautiful rolling over hills or partly covering structures such as bridges. However, it often makes transportation dangerous by limiting visibility. In the United States close to 700 people die each year in automobile accidents that occur in dense fog.

2.3 Review

KEY CONCEPTS

1. Describe the three forms in which water is present in the atmosphere.
2. How does altitude affect the composition of clouds?
3. How are clouds classified?

CRITICAL THINKING

4. **Summarize** Describe the main characteristics of cirrus, cumulus, and stratus clouds.
5. **Draw Conclusions** Why might cumulonimbus clouds be more likely to form on sunny days than on days with little sunlight?

CHALLENGE

6. **Apply** Imagine that the sky has turned very cloudy after a hot morning. You notice that the bread in your sandwich is soggy and the towels on the towel rack won't dry. Explain why these things are happening. Use the following terms in your answer: *condensation, evaporation, relative humidity.*

Chapter 2: **Weather Patterns 63**

ANSWERS

1. Sample answer: solid: snow; liquid: rain; gas: water vapor

2. At high altitudes, clouds are made of ice crystals. At lower altitudes, clouds are made of water droplets or a mixture of droplets and ice crystals.

3. according to altitude and appearance

4. cirrus: made of ice crystals, located at high altitudes; cumulus: puffy and white with darker bases; stratus: form in layers over a large area

5. Sunshine increases the air temperature, making air rise.

6. The clouds have lowered the air temperature, so that the rate of evaporation has decreased and the rate of condensation has increased. Relative humidity is high.

Ongoing Assessment

Describe types of clouds.

Ask: How does fog compare to cirrus, cumulus, and stratus clouds? *Fog is a smooth cloud that rests on the ground or a body of water. It is most like flat, layered stratus clouds, which can form close to Earth's surface. In contrast, wispy cirrus clouds form at high altitudes, and puffy cumulus clouds can grow quite tall.*

Reinforce (the **BIG** idea)

Have students relate the section to the Big Idea.

 Reinforcing Key Concepts, p. 114

2.3 ASSESS & RETEACH

Assess

 Section 2.3 Quiz, p. 25

Reteach

Have pairs of students work cooperatively to test each other on cloud types. Let students develop their own assessment procedures. For example, students may wish to sketch different clouds and have their partners identify them. Other pairs might focus on cloud prefixes and suffixes. Still other pairs might test each other on the weather conditions associated with various cloud types.

Technology Resources

Have students visit **ClassZone.com** for reteaching of Key Concepts.

 CONTENT REVIEW

 CONTENT REVIEW CD-ROM

CHAPTER INVESTIGATION

Focus

PURPOSE To construct a psychrometer in order to measure relative humidity

OVERVIEW Students will use thermometers and milk cartons to construct psychrometers. They will take wet-bulb and dry-bulb temperature readings at several locations around the school and use a chart to determine relative humidities. Students will find the following:

- Unless the relative humidity is 100 percent, wet-bulb readings are lower than dry-bulb readings.
- Relative humidity is related to changes in the weather.

Lab Preparation

- Review how to use the Relative Humidity Table before beginning the investigation. Tell students to use a ruler as a guide by placing it below the line for the dry-bulb reading.
- Prior to the investigation, have students read through the investigation and prepare their data tables. Or you may wish to copy and distribute datasheets and rubrics.

 UNIT RESOURCE BOOK, pp. 133–142

SCIENCE TOOLKIT, F14

Lab Management

Divide students into groups of three or four. Assign different groups to take two readings inside the school, two readings outside, and one reading inside and one reading outside. Then compare results and discuss patterns.

SAFETY Tell students to notify you immediately if a thermometer should break—they should not try to clean up the glass themselves.

INCLUSION Some students may have difficulty with the Relative Humidity Table. Review how to subtract measurements before beginning the investigation.

CHAPTER INVESTIGATION

Relative Humidity

OVERVIEW AND PURPOSE Finding out the relative humidity can help you predict how comfortable you will feel on a hot day or whether dew will form on the ground. You can use a psychrometer to measure relative humidity. A psychrometer is a device made from two thermometers—one with a wet bulb and the other with a dry bulb. In this activity you will

- make a milk-carton psychrometer
- use it to measure the relative humidity of the air at two locations in your school

▶ Problem
Write It Up

Which location will have the greater relative humidity?

▶ Hypothesize
Write It Up

Write a hypothesis in "If . . . , then . . . , because . . ." form to answer the problem.

▶ Procedure

MATERIALS
- 2 thermometers
- cotton or felt cloth
- 3 rubber bands
- plastic bowl
- water at room temperature
- scissors
- pint milk carton
- ruler
- Relative Humidity Chart

1. Make a table like the one shown on the sample notebook page to record your data.

2. Check the two thermometers that you are using in this experiment to make sure they read the same temperature. Wrap a piece of cotton or felt cloth around the bulb of one thermometer. Hold the cloth in place with a rubber band as shown in the photograph. Dip this wet-bulb thermometer into a bowl of room-temperature water until the cloth is soaked.

 step 3

3. Use scissors to cut a small hole in one side of the milk carton, 2 centimeters from the bottom of the carton. Place the wet-bulb thermometer on the same side as the hole that you made in the milk carton, and attach it with a rubber band. Push the tail of the cloth through the hole. Attach the dry-bulb thermometer as shown.

INVESTIGATION RESOURCES

 CHAPTER INVESTIGATION, Relative Humidity
- Relative Humidity Table, p. 133
- Level A, pp. 134–137
- Level B, pp. 138–141
- Level C, p. 142

Advanced students should complete Levels B & C.

 Writing a Lab Report, D12–13

Technology Resources

Customize this student lab as needed or look for an alternative. Print rubrics to assess student lab reports.

 Lab Generator CD-ROM

4 Fill the carton with water to just below the hole so that the cloth will remain wet. Empty the bowl and place the completed psychrometer inside it.

5 Write "science room" under the heading "Location 1" in your data table. Take your first readings in the science classroom about 10 minutes after you set up your psychrometer. Read the temperatures on the two thermometers in degrees Celsius. Record the temperature readings for the first location in the first column of your table.

6 Choose a second location in your school, and identify it under the heading "Location 2" in the data table. Take a second set of temperature readings with your psychrometer in this location. Record the readings in the second column of your table.

7 Subtract the wet-bulb reading from the dry-bulb reading for each location. Record this information in the third row of your data table.

8 Use the relative humidity table your teacher provides to find each relative humidity (expressed as a percentage). In the left-hand column, find the dry-bulb reading for location 1 that you recorded in step 5. Then find in the top line the number you recorded in step 7 (the difference between the dry-bulb and wet-bulb readings). Record the relative humidity in the last row of your data table. Repeat these steps for location 2.

▶ Observe and Analyze

1. **RECORD OBSERVATIONS** Draw the setup of your psychrometer. Be sure your data table is complete.

2. **IDENTIFY** Identify the variables and constants in this experiment. List them in your **Science Notebook.**

3. **COMPARE** How do the wet-bulb readings compare with the dry-bulb readings?

4. **ANALYZE** If the difference between the temperature readings on the two thermometers is large, is the relative humidity high or low? Explain why.

▶ Conclude [Write It Up]

1. **INTERPRET** Answer the question in the problem. Compare your results with your hypothesis.

2. **IDENTIFY LIMITS** Describe any possible errors that you made in following the procedure.

3. **APPLY** How would you account for the differences in relative humidity that you obtained for the two locations in your school?

▶ INVESTIGATE Further

CHALLENGE Use the psychrometer to keep track of the relative humidity in your classroom over a period of one week. Make a new chart to record your data. What do you notice about how the changes in relative humidity relate to the weather conditions outside?

Relative Humidity

Problem Which location will have the greater relative humidity?

Hypothesize

Observe and Analyze

Table 1. Relative Humidity at Two Locations

	Location 1	Location 2
Dry-bulb temperature		
Wet-bulb temperature		
Difference between dry-bulb and wet-bulb readings		
Relative humidity		

Conclude

▶ Observe and Analyze

SAMPLE DATA location 1: dry-bulb temperature 24°C, wet-bulb temperature 21°C, relative humidity 76%; location 2: dry-bulb temperature 22°C, wet-bulb temperature 18°C, relative humidity 68%

1. Students should provide accurate drawings and complete tables.

2. independent variable: location of reading; dependent variable: humidity; constant: psychrometer setup

3. Answers will vary, but in general wet-bulb readings should be lower than dry-bulb readings unless the relative humidity is 100 percent.

4. It is low, because the difference shows that water is evaporating quickly from the wet bulb.

▶ Conclude

5. Answers will vary, depending on observations and results in the investigation.

6. Sample answer: Temperature readings may have been inaccurate.

7. Sample answer: Trees, windows, the heating system, and other factors may affect the humidity recorded at a particular location.

▶ INVESTIGATE Further

CHALLENGE Sample answer: Relative humidity increases as temperature decreases, and vice versa.

Post-Lab Discussion

Ask: Which groups tended to record the greatest differences in relative humidity readings? *Answer: groups that took one measurement inside and one measurement outside*

Teaching with Technology

Have students use CBL and a relative humidity sensor to take relative humidity readings outside and inside. Make a data table of their findings on the board, and calculate an average for indoor and outdoor readings.

Set Learning Goals

Students will

- Explain how precipitation forms.
- Describe how precipitation is measured.
- Define acid rain.
- Construct a rain gauge to measure rainfall in an experiment.

3-Minute Warm-Up

Display Transparency 13 or copy this exercise on the board:

Match each definition with the correct term.

Definitions

1. liquid or solid water that falls to Earth's surface *b*

2. the amount of water vapor in air compared with the maximum amount that can be present at that temperature *d*

3. the condition of Earth's atmosphere at a particular time and place *a*

4. the process by which a gas changes into a liquid *c*

Terms

a. weather   c. condensation

b. precipitation   d. relative humidity

 3-Minute Warm-Up, p. T13

2.4 MOTIVATE

THINK ABOUT

PURPOSE To introduce the concept of how water droplets combine to form larger droplets

DEMONSTRATE Sprinkle water droplets on a tilted cookie sheet and have students observe how the droplets combine and eventually flow down the cookie sheet.

Sample answer: Some drops are heavier than others. When they become too heavy to remain suspended, they fall.

KEY CONCEPT

2.4 Water falls to Earth's surface as precipitation.

◀ **BEFORE, you learned**

- Water moves between Earth's surface and the atmosphere
- Water vapor condenses into clouds

▶ **NOW, you will learn**

- How precipitation forms
- How precipitation is measured
- About acid rain

VOCABULARY

freezing rain p. 68
sleet p. 68
hail p. 68
acid rain p. 70

THINK ABOUT

Why does steam from a shower form large drops?

When you run a hot shower, the bathroom fills up with water vapor. The vapor condenses into tiny droplets that make it seem as if you are standing in fog. You may also see larger drops running down cool surfaces, such as a mirror. Why do some drops fall while others remain suspended?

Precipitation forms from water droplets or ice crystals.

All precipitation comes from clouds. For example, rain occurs when water droplets in a cloud fall to the ground. Then why doesn't every cloud produce precipitation? Cloud droplets are much smaller than a typical raindrop. They weigh so little that it takes only a slight upward movement of air to hold them up. In order for rain to fall from a cloud and reach Earth's surface, the cloud droplets must become larger and heavier.

One way that precipitation can form is through the combining of cloud droplets. The tiny droplets of water move up and down in clouds. Some collide with each other and combine, forming slightly bigger droplets. As the droplets continue to combine, they grow larger and larger. Eventually they become heavy enough to fall. It takes about a million droplets to make a single raindrop.

Water droplets combining to form a raindrop

RESOURCES FOR DIFFERENTIATED INSTRUCTION

Below Level
UNIT RESOURCE BOOK
- Reading Study Guide A, pp. 117–118
- Decoding Support, p. 130

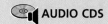 **AUDIO CDS**

Advanced
UNIT RESOURCE BOOK
- Challenge and Extension, p. 123
- Challenge Reading, pp. 126–127

English Learners
UNIT RESOURCE BOOK
Spanish Reading Study Guide, pp. 121–122

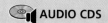 **AUDIO CDS**

- Audio Readings in Spanish
- Audio Readings (English)

Another way that precipitation can form is through the growth of ice crystals. When the temperature inside a cloud is below freezing, water vapor changes into tiny ice crystals. The crystals grow by collecting more water vapor or by colliding and merging with one another. When the crystals become heavy enough, they fall from the cloud. Snow isn't the only type of precipitation that forms this way. Most rain in the United States actually starts out as falling ice crystals. Before the crystals reach the ground, they melt in a layer of warm air.

 CHECK YOUR READING How do cloud droplets become large enough to fall as precipitation?

Measuring Precipitation

Scientists use a rain gauge to measure rainfall. A funnel or opening at the top of the gauge allows rain to flow into a cylinder. By measuring the water collected, you can find out how much rain fell in a storm or over a period of time.

> **READING TIP**
>
> A gauge (gayj) is an instrument used for measuring or testing.

Snow depth can be measured with a long ruler. Because the amount of water in snow varies, scientists use a special gauge to find out how much water the snow contains. A built-in heater melts the snow so that it can be measured just like rain.

INVESTIGATE Precipitation

How much rain falls during a storm?

PROCEDURE

① Cut off the top third of the bottle. Set this part aside.

② Put some gravel at the bottom of the bottle to keep it from tipping over. Add water to cover the gravel. Draw a horizontal line on the bottle at the top of the water. Use a ruler to mark off centimeters on the bottle above the line that you drew. Now take the part of the bottle that you set aside and turn it upside down. Fit it inside the bottle to create a funnel.

③ Place the bottle outside when a rainstorm is expected. Make sure that nothing will block rain from entering it. Check your rain gauge after 24 hours. Observe and record the rainfall.

WHAT DO YOU THINK?
- How much rain fell during the time period?
- How do the measurements compare with your observations?

CHALLENGE Do you think you would measure the same amount of rain if you used a wider rain gauge? Explain.

SKILL FOCUS
Measuring

MATERIALS
- scissors
- 1-liter plastic bottle
- gravel
- water
- permanent marker
- ruler

TIME
15 minutes

Chapter 2: **Weather Patterns** 67 **D**

DIFFERENTIATE INSTRUCTION

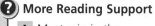

More Reading Support

A Most rain in the United States starts out as what? *ice crystals*

B How do scientists measure rainfall? *with rain gauges*

English Learners Have students write the definitions for *freezing rain, sleet, hail,* and *acid rain* in their Science Word Dictionaries. English learners may be unfamiliar with the concept of steam in a shower (p. 66) and Mount Everest (p. 71). Also, be sure that students do not confuse the words *lightning* and *lighting* (p. 71).

2.4 INSTRUCT

INVESTIGATE Precipitation

PURPOSE To measure rainfall to find the amount that fell during a storm

TIPS *15 min.* Suggest the following to students:

- Place the rain gauge in a secure place where it will not be tipped over.
- If there is little rainfall in your area, use a spray bottle or a faucet to model rainfall.

WHAT DO YOU THINK? *Answers will vary, depending on student observations and measurements.*

CHALLENGE *Sample answer: The results will be the same if the top of the funnel and the bottom of the gauge have the same diameter.*

 Datasheet, Precipitation, p. 124

Technology Resources

Customize this student lab as needed or look for an alternative. Print rubrics to assess student lab reports.

 Lab Generator CD-ROM

Ongoing Assessment

Explain how precipitation forms.

Ask: How does precipitation form from ice crystals? *Water vapor in clouds changes into ice crystals, which grow until they become heavy enough to fall.*

 CHECK YOUR READING *Answer: by combining with one another*

Real World Example

Weather forecasters were not always the professionals we see on television today. During the 1940s and 1950s, weather was not considered real news and was presented more like entertainment. One of the first weather announcers was an animated sheep called Wooly Lamb. Later, cartoonists, musicians, and beauty contestants presented the weather, sometimes singing and dancing their way through the forecasts.

Integrate the Sciences

Raindrops can join together and grow in size as long as the surface tension—the force that holds them together—is greater than the frictional drag of the air they fall through. When a raindrop reaches a size of about 5 mm, however, frictional drag becomes greater than surface tension, and the raindrop breaks up into smaller drops.

Ongoing Assessment

Describe how precipitation is measured.

Ask: How is snow measured? *with rulers and with gauges that have built-in heaters*

 CHECK YOUR READING *Answer: freezing rain, sleet, and snow*

When you watch weather reports on television, you often see storm systems passing across a weather map. Some of these images are made with Doppler radar. The radar shows which areas are getting precipitation and how fast it is falling. Forecasters use this information to estimate the total amount of precipitation an area will receive.

COMBINATION NOTES Record information on precipitation in your combination notes.

Types of Precipitation

Precipitation reaches Earth's surface in various forms. Some precipitation freezes or melts as it falls through the atmosphere.

1 **Rain and Drizzle** Rain is the most common type of precipitation. Raindrops form from liquid cloud droplets or from ice crystals that melt as they fall. A light rain with very small drops is called drizzle. Drizzle usually comes from stratus clouds, which don't have enough air movement to build up larger raindrops.

2 **Freezing Rain** Raindrops may freeze when they hit the ground or other surfaces in cold weather. **Freezing rain** covers surfaces with a coating of ice. During an ice storm, roads become slippery and dangerous. The weight of ice can also bring down trees and power lines.

3 **Sleet** When rain passes through a layer of cold air, it can freeze before hitting the ground. The small pellets of ice that form are called **sleet.**

4 **Snow** As ice crystals grow and merge in clouds, they become snowflakes. Snowflakes come in many different shapes and sizes. Usually they have six sides or branches. When snow falls through moist air that is near freezing, the flakes tend to join together in clumps. When snow falls through colder and drier air, snowflakes don't join together, and the snow is powdery.

Most snowflakes have six branches or sides.

5 **Hail** Surprisingly, the largest type of frozen precipitation often arrives in warm weather. Lumps or balls of ice that fall from cumulonimbus clouds are called **hail.** During a thunderstorm, violent air currents hurl ice pellets around the cloud. These pellets grow as water droplets freeze onto them at high elevations. Some start to fall and then are pushed back up again. They may repeat this process several times, adding a layer of ice each time. Eventually they fall to the ground.

Large hailstones can damage property and injure people and animals. The biggest hailstone ever found in the United States weighed 1.7 pounds and was about as wide as a compact disc.

 CHECK YOUR READING Which forms of precipitation undergo a change after they leave a cloud?

DIFFERENTIATE INSTRUCTION

? **More Reading Support**

C What is a light rain with very small drops called? *drizzle*

D Hail falls from what type of clouds? *cumulonimbus*

Below Level Use simple demonstrations to help students visualize different types of precipitation. For example, a spray bottle with an adjustable nozzle can be used to model the difference between rain and drizzle. Use the same bottle to spray water on an ice pack to model freezing rain.

Advanced Have students who are interested in learning about the smell caused by rain read the following article:

R Challenge Reading, pp. 126–127

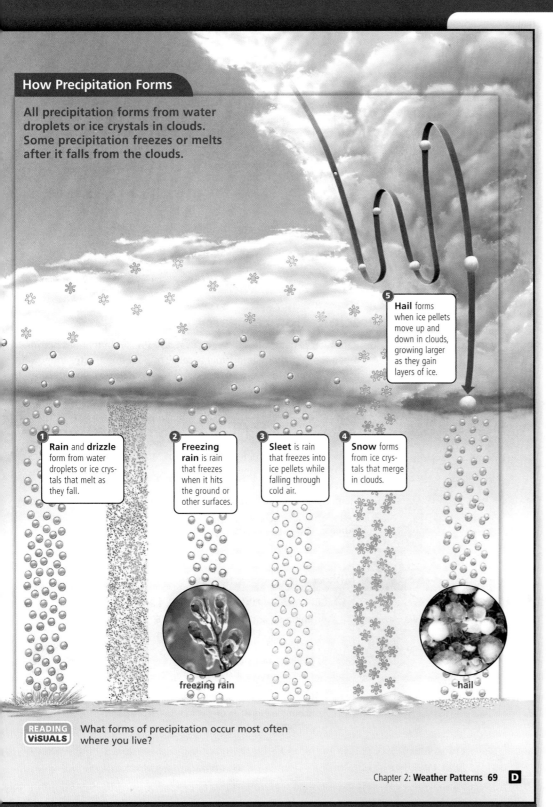

How Precipitation Forms

All precipitation forms from water droplets or ice crystals in clouds. Some precipitation freezes or melts after it falls from the clouds.

5 **Hail** forms when ice pellets move up and down in clouds, growing larger as they gain layers of ice.

1 **Rain** and **drizzle** form from water droplets or ice crystals that melt as they fall.

2 **Freezing rain** is rain that freezes when it hits the ground or other surfaces.

3 **Sleet** is rain that freezes into ice pellets while falling through cold air.

4 **Snow** forms from ice crystals that merge in clouds.

freezing rain

hail

READING VISUALS What forms of precipitation occur most often where you live?

Chapter 2: **Weather Patterns** 69 **D**

Teach from Visuals

To help students interpret the visual on precipitation formation:

- Have them compare and contrast freezing rain and sleet. *Both fall from clouds as raindrops. Freezing rain freezes once it hits the ground or cold surfaces. Sleet freezes as it falls through cold air.*

- Ask: Which type of precipitation always forms from ice crystals? *Snow is the only type that always forms from ice crystals.*

- Ask: Which types of precipitation are the most similar? Explain your answer. *Sample answer: Rain and drizzle are the most similar because they both form from water droplets or from ice crystals that melt as they fall. The only real difference is in the size of the drops—in a drizzle, the drops are generally smaller than raindrops.*

Develop Critical Thinking

INFER To help students better understand precipitation, ask the following questions:

- What is the major factor in determining which type of precipitation falls to Earth's surface? *air temperature*

- What does the fact that most rain starts out as falling ice crystals tell you about temperatures in clouds? *Sample answer: Temperatures in clouds are generally colder than temperatures closer to Earth's surface.*

Ongoing Assessment

READING VISUALS *Answers will vary, depending on the climate of the area.*

DIFFERENTIATE INSTRUCTION

Alternative Assessment Have students make booklets showing the different types of precipitation. Students can cut out photographs from magazines, download images from the Internet, or draw pictures themselves. Encourage interested students to take their own photographs for the booklets. Students should label all pictures and include captions explaining how the precipitation forms and any changes it may undergo as it falls to Earth's surface.

Advanced

R Challenge and Extension, p. 123

Ongoing Assessment

Define acid rain.

Ask: What is acid rain? *rain that is more acidic than normal because of pollution*

 Answer: Sulfur dioxide and nitrogen oxides enter the air as pollution and combine with water vapor to form acids. The acids mix with cloud droplets or ice crystals that fall as precipitation.

Reinforce (the **BIG** idea)

Have students relate the section to the Big Idea.

 Reinforcing Key Concepts, p. 125

ASSESS & RETEACH

Assess

A Section 2.4 Quiz, p. 26

Reteach

To be sure students understand the relationship between cloud types and precipitation, give them the following scenario: You're watching a weather forecast on television. The forecaster says that hail is falling to the north of your area and a light drizzle is falling to the south. Infer which types of clouds are to the north and south of your area. *Hail falls from cumulonimbus clouds, so these types of clouds are to the north. Drizzle usually falls from stratus clouds, so these types of clouds are to the south.*

Technology Resources

Have students visit **ClassZone.com** for reteaching of Key Concepts.

 CONTENT REVIEW

 CONTENT REVIEW CD-ROM

These trees have few needles because acid rain has damaged the trees.

Precipitation can carry pollution.

Rainwater is naturally a little acidic. **Acid rain** is rain that has become much more acidic than normal because of pollution. Factories, power plants, automobiles, and some natural sources release sulfur dioxide and nitrogen oxides into the air. These gases can combine with water vapor to form sulfuric acid and nitric acid. The acids mix with cloud droplets or ice crystals that eventually fall to Earth's surface as precipitation.

Because wind can blow air pollution hundreds of kilometers, acid rain may fall far from the source of the pollution. Acid rain harms trees and raises the acidity of lakes, making it difficult for fish to live in them. Acid rain also damages the surfaces of buildings and sculptures.

VOCABULARY
Add a description wheel for *acid rain* to your notebook.

 CHECK YOUR READING How does acid rain form? Your answer should mention water vapor.

2.4 Review

KEY CONCEPTS

1. What are the two ways that rain can form?
2. How are rain and snow measured?
3. What human activities cause acid rain?

CRITICAL THINKING

4. **Compare and Contrast** How are sleet and freezing rain similar? How are they different?
5. **Draw Conclusions** When a large hailstone is cut open, four layers can be seen. What conclusions can you draw about the formation of the hailstone?

CHALLENGE

6. **Predict** Temperatures in a cloud and on the ground are below freezing. A warmer layer of air lies between the cloud and the ground. What type of precipitation do you predict will occur? Explain.

ANSWERS

1. from water droplets that fall from clouds or from ice crystals that melt as they fall through warm air

2. Rain is measured with a rain gauge. Snow depth can be measured with a ruler, and snow's water content is

measured with a heated rain gauge.

3. transportation, manufacturing, and power generation

4. Both are types of frozen precipitation. Sleet freezes as it falls through the air. Freezing rain remains liquid until it falls on a cold surface.

5. The hailstone moved up and down within a cloud at least four times, gaining new layers.

6. freezing rain; ice crystals from the cold cloud will melt as they fall through the layer of warm air and will refreeze upon contact with the cold ground.

EXTREME SCIENCE

Caught Inside a Thunderhead

In 1959, engine failure forced Lieutenant Colonel William Rankin to eject from his plane at a high altitude. When his parachute opened, he thought he was out of danger. However, he soon realized that he was caught inside a cumulonimbus cloud during a fierce thunderstorm.

As Rankin hung by his parachute, violent air movement inside the cloud tossed him "up, down, sideways, clockwise." The rain was so heavy that he feared he would drown in midair. Lightning flashed all around him. Rankin finally landed 40 minutes after his adventure began. He had many injuries, including bruises from hailstones. Fortunately, none of the storm's lightning had struck him.

Where Lightning Strikes

Ground flashes/km²/year

	0.1
	0.5
	1.0
	2.0
	3.0
	4.0
	6.0
	8.0
	10.0
	12.0
	14.0
	16.0

SOURCE: Global Atmospherics, Inc., Tucson, AZ

Water, Wind, Hail, and Lightning

- A cumulonimbus cloud, or thunderhead, can rise to over 18 kilometers above Earth's surface. That's about twice the elevation of Mount Everest.
- A cumulonimbus cloud may contain 500,000 tons of water.
- Thunderstorm clouds cause 8 million lightning flashes each day.

EXPLORE

1. **ANALYZE** Find where you live on the map. Use the color key to figure out how often lightning strikes each square kilometer in your area.

2. **CHALLENGE** Use information from the Resource Center to propose an explanation for the pattern of lightning frequencies shown on the map.

 **RESOURCE CENTER**
CLASSZONE.COM
Learn more about lightning.

Lightning flashes to the ground from a thunderhead, or cumulonimbus cloud.

Set Learning Goal

To recognize patterns of lightning frequency

Present the Science

On average, lightning strikes about 100 times per second. In the United States it occurs most frequently in the Southeast, where the weather is dominated by maritime tropical air masses. Lightning is one of the most devastating natural hazards—the National Weather Service estimates that 7500 forest fires are caused by lightning each year. In addition, lightning accounts for 200 deaths annually in the United States alone. Property damage adds up to hundreds of millions of dollars yearly.

Discussion Questions

Discuss some of the hazards associated with thunderstorms, such as high winds, hail, fires, and floods. Help students to see that they can reduce their risk of injury by following certain safety guidelines.

Ask: What should you do if you see a thunderstorm approaching? *seek shelter immediately*

Ask: What should you do if you are caught outdoors in a thunderstorm and no shelter is available? *stay away from trees, fences, and other objects that lightning is likely to strike*

Close

Ask: Which area gets the most lightning? *Florida* Which area gets the least? *West Coast*

Technology Resources

Students can visit **ClassZone.com** to find out more about lightning strikes in their area.

 RESOURCE CENTER

EXPLORE

1. *ANALYZE Answers will vary, depending on students' location.*

2. *CHALLENGE It takes the right combination of weather conditions for thunderstorms to develop. For example, some areas are too cold or too dry.*

BACK TO

the BIG idea

Have students look back at the photograph on pp. 40–41. Ask them to use the photograph to summarize what they've learned about clouds and to predict what weather conditions will result. *Answer: The clouds in the distance appear tall and dark. They are probably cumulonimbus clouds, which are a type of cumulus cloud. They usually form during the day in fair weather, when warm air rises and condenses. Cumulonimbus clouds can be 18 km high and produce thunderstorms with heavy rainfall.*

KEY CONCEPTS SUMMARY

SECTION 2.1

Ask: Do the air molecules at the bottom of the column represent denser or thinner air? *denser*

SECTION 2.2

Ask: What has caused the area on the left to have higher pressure than the area on the right? *uneven heating of Earth's surface*

Ask: What is probably happening to the air in the area of low pressure? *It is rising and expanding.*

SECTION 2.3

Ask: What must be present in the air for cloud droplets to form? *tiny particles of solids, such as dust or smoke*

Ask: What type of cloud is shown in the illustration? *cumulus*

SECTION 2.4

Ask: What happens to a water droplet when it becomes too heavy for air to hold up? *It falls as precipitation.*

Ask: What other types of precipitation form from ice crystals? *drizzle, freezing rain, sleet, hail*

Review Concepts

- Big Idea Flow Chart, p. T9
- Chapter Outline, pp. T15–T16

2 Chapter Review

the BIG idea

Some features of weather have predictable patterns.

CONTENT REVIEW
CLASSZONE.COM

KEY CONCEPTS SUMMARY

2.1 The atmosphere's air pressure changes.

Air pressure is the force of air molecules pushing on an area. Air pressure decreases as you move higher in the atmosphere. Air pressure can also differ in two locations at the same altitude.

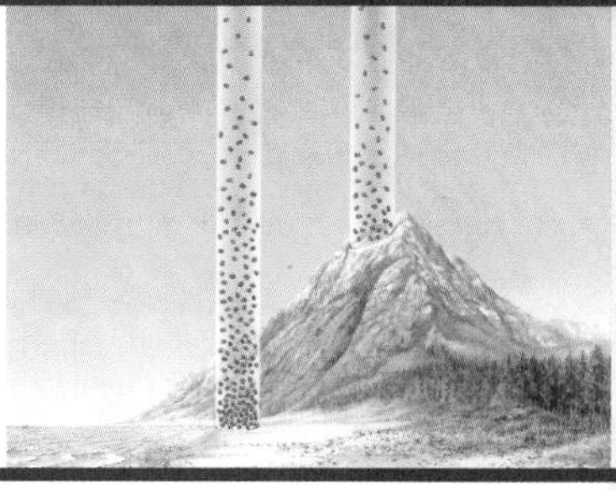

VOCABULARY
air pressure p. 43
barometer p. 46

2.2 The atmosphere has wind patterns.

Wind blows from areas of high pressure toward areas of low pressure. Earth's rotation causes long-distance winds to curve.

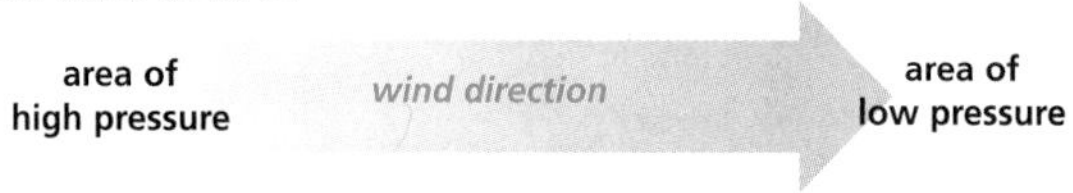

VOCABULARY
weather p. 47
wind p. 47
global wind p. 48
Coriolis effect p. 49
jet stream p. 52
monsoon p. 54

2.3 Most clouds form as air rises and cools.

Clouds are made of tiny water droplets or ice crystals that condense from water vapor in rising air.

VOCABULARY
evaporation p. 56
condensation p. 56
precipitation p. 57
humidity p. 58
saturation p. 58
relative humidity p. 58
dew point p. 58

2.4 Water falls to Earth's surface as precipitation.

Water droplets in clouds merge to form raindrops.

Ice crystals in clouds can form snow, rain, and other types of precipitation.

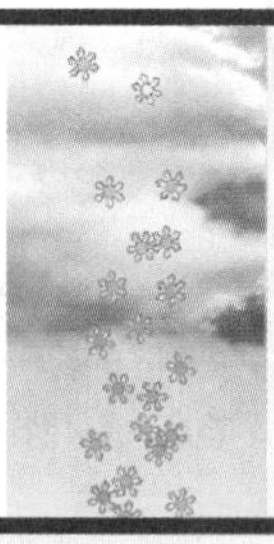

VOCABULARY
freezing rain p. 68
sleet p. 68
hail p. 68
acid rain p. 70

Technology Resources

Have students visit **ClassZone.com** or use the CD-ROM for a cumulative review of concepts.

CONTENT REVIEW

CONTENT REVIEW CD-ROM

Engage students in a whole-class interactive review of Key Concepts. Edit content as you wish.

POWER PRESENTATIONS

Reviewing Vocabulary

Write a definition of each term. Use the meaning of the underlined root to help you.

Word	Root Meaning	Definition
EXAMPLE air <u>pressure</u>	to apply force	the force of air molecules pushing on an area
1. <u>barometer</u>	weight	
2. <u>saturation</u>	to fill	
3. <u>global</u> wind	sphere	
4. <u>monsoon</u>	season	
5. <u>evaporation</u>	steam	
6. <u>condensation</u>	thick	
7. <u>humidity</u>	moist	
8. <u>precipitation</u>	thrown down	

Reviewing Key Concepts

Multiple Choice *Choose the letter of the best answer.*

9. The movement of air molecules causes
   a. air density   c. humidity
   b. air pressure   d. relative humidity

10. Winds curve as they move across Earth's surface because of
    a. the Coriolis effect   c. humidity
    b. air pressure   d. relative humidity

11. Jet streams generally flow toward the
    a. north   c. east
    b. south   d. west

12. Condensation increases with greater
    a. relative humidity   c. air pressure
    b. air temperature   d. wind speed

13. Any type of liquid or solid water that falls to Earth's surface is called
    a. precipitation   c. a monsoon
    b. dew   d. humidity

14. What are low-altitude clouds composed of?
    a. snowflakes   c. water droplets
    b. raindrops   d. water vapor

15. Clouds made of ice crystals form under conditions of
    a. strong winds   c. low humidity
    b. high altitude d. high pressure

16. Which type of cloud is most likely to bring thunderstorms?
    a. stratus   c. cumulonimbus
    b. altostratus d. cirrus

17. Over short distances wind blows toward areas of
    a. high pressure   c. low temperature
    b. high density   d. low pressure

18. The doldrums and the horse latitudes are both regions of
    a. high air pressure   c. heavy rains
    b. light winds   d. low temperatures

19. As altitude increases, air pressure usually
    a. decreases   c. varies more
    b. increases   d. varies less

Short Answer *Write a short answer to each question.*

20. What causes land breezes to flow at night?

21. Why does hair take longer to dry after a shower on days with high relative humidity?

22. How does air pressure affect air density?

23. Why are dust and other particles necessary for precipitation?

24. How did global wind belts and calm regions affect transportation in the past?

Reviewing Vocabulary

1. an instrument that measures air pressure

2. a condition in which the evaporation of water into the air is balanced by the condensation of water

3. winds that travel thousands of kilometers in steady patterns

4. winds that change direction with the seasons

5. the process by which a liquid changes to a gas

6. the process by which a gas changes into a liquid

7. the amount of water vapor in the air

8. liquid or solid water that falls to Earth's surface

Reviewing Key Concepts

9. b

10. a

11. c

12. a

13. a

14. c

15. b

16. c

17. d

18. b

19. a

20. Land cools off faster than the sea, and air flows toward the resulting low-pressure area over the water.

21. The humid air is close to saturation, so evaporation is slow.

22. Density increases as air pressure increases, because higher pressure pushes air molecules closer together.

23. Such particles are solids but are light enough to stay in the atmosphere for long periods. Water vapor will only condense on something solid.

24. Sailors used to seek out global wind belts to speed their sailing ships. They also avoided zones of high and low pressure because the winds there were often too light to move ships.

ASSESSMENT RESOURCES

 UNIT ASSESSMENT BOOK
- Chapter Test A, pp. 27–30
- Chapter Test B, pp. 31–34
- Chapter Test C, pp. 35–38
- Alternative Assessment, pp. 39–40

 SPANISH ASSESSMENT BOOK
Spanish Chapter Test, pp. 177–180

Technology Resources

Edit test items and answer choices.

 Test Generator CD-ROM

Visit **ClassZone.com** to extend test practice.

 Test Practice

Thinking Critically

25. The sunlight warms the air and the soil in the terrarium and gives energy to plants.

26. The diagram should indicate water evaporating from the soil, condensing on the glass, and sliding or falling down.

27. Air is warmer inside the terrarium than outside it.

28. Sample answer: a week or two

29. Ice would cool the bottom of the terrarium, so water would condense on the ground. This might cause fog to form.

30. The terrarium would probably dry out as water vapor escaped through the hole.

31. Both are caused by the different heating and cooling rates of land and water. Monsoons are seasonal, whereas sea breezes occur daily.

32. The air will become less dense because air expands as it rises.

33. First, sulfur dioxide and nitrogen oxides could have been released into the air. Winds flowing eastward could have moved the gases over the forest. The gases could have combined with water vapor in clouds to form acids that eventually fell as acid rain.

34. sleet

35. freezing rain

36. rain

37. snow

38. hail

the **BIG** idea

39. Answers should reflect information learned in the chapter.

40. Responses should indicate how energy from the Sun produces the basic elements of weather.

UNIT PROJECTS

Check to make sure students are working on their projects. Check schedules and work in progress.

 Unit Projects, pp. 5–10

Thinking Critically

The soil in this terrarium was soaked with water two weeks ago. Then the box was sealed so that no moisture could escape. Use the diagram to answer the next six questions.

25. **IDENTIFY EFFECTS** How does sunlight affect conditions inside the terrarium?

26. **ANALYZE** Draw a diagram of the water cycle inside the terrarium.

27. **INFER** What do the water drops on the glass indicate about the temperatures inside and outside the terrarium?

28. **PREDICT** Explain how long you think the plants will live without being watered.

29. **PREDICT** What would happen if you placed the terrarium on top of a block of ice?

30. **HYPOTHESIZE** How would conditions inside the terrarium change if there were a hole in one side of it?

31. **COMPARE AND CONTRAST** How are sea breezes and monsoon winds alike, and how are they different?

32. **PREDICT** A cumulus cloud is growing taller. What will happen to the density of the air beneath it? Explain.

33. **INFER** Imagine that a group of factories and power plants lies 200 kilometers to the west of a forest where trees are dying. Describe three steps in a process that could be causing the trees to die.

IDENTIFY EFFECTS Write the type of precipitation that would form under each set of conditions.

Conditions	Precipitation
34. above-freezing air inside a cloud and freezing air beneath it	
35. above-freezing air beneath a cloud and freezing temperatures on the ground	
36. below-freezing air inside a cloud and above-freezing temperatures in the air beneath it and on the ground	
37. below-freezing air inside a cloud and beneath it	
38. ice pellets hurled around by air currents inside a cloud	

the **BIG** idea

39. Look again at the photograph on pages 40–41. Now that you have finished the chapter, how would you change your response to the question on the photograph?

40. **WRITE** Write one or more paragraphs explaining how energy from the Sun influences the weather. In your discussion, include at least three of the following topics:
    - global wind belts
    - high- and low-pressure areas
    - local winds
    - monsoons
    - the water cycle
    - cloud formation

UNIT PROJECTS

If you need to do an experiment for your unit project, gather the materials. Be sure to allow enough time to observe results before the project is due.

MONITOR AND RETEACH

If students have trouble applying the concepts in items 25–33, review each step of the water cycle. Students should refer to the diagram on p. 57, then make a three-part sketch of the water cycle.

Part 1 should show how water evaporates from bodies of water.
Part 2 should show how water vapor condenses to form clouds.
Part 3 should show water falling to Earth as precipitation.
Students may benefit from summarizing one or more sections of the chapter.

 Summarizing the Chapter, pp. 152–153

Standardized Test Practice

For practice on your state test, go to . . .

TEST PRACTICE
CLASSZONE.COM

Analyzing a Diagram

This diagram shows the water cycle. Use it to answer the questions below.

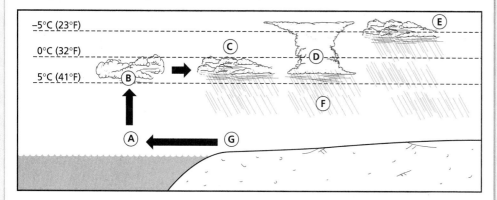

1. Where is evaporation occurring?
a. A   **c.** F
b. D   **d.** G

2. Where is condensation occurring?
a. A   **c.** F
b. B   **d.** G

3. Where is precipitation shown?
a. A   **c.** E
b. C   **d.** F

4. Where is hail most likely to form?
a. C   **c.** E
b. D   **d.** F

5. From which cloud will precipitation fall as snow and then turn to rain?
a. B   **c.** D
b. C   **d.** E

6. Which is the best estimate for the temperature in B?
a. 8°C (46°F)   **c.** −3°C (27°F)
b. 3°C (37°F)   **d.** −8°C (17°F)

7. What does the arrow pointing up between A and B indicate?
a. the movement of moisture
b. the direction of the wind
c. a low pressure area
d. a reflection off the water

Extended Response

Answer the two questions below in detail. Include some of the terms shown in the word box. In your answers underline each term you use.

low air pressure	cool air	west
high air pressure	warm air	east
Coriolis effect		

8. Whenever Richard rides in an elevator to the top of a skyscraper, he feels a pop inside his ears. Explain what is happening in the air to produce the pop in Richard's ears.

9. Winds tend to blow from west to east across the United States. If Earth spun in the other direction, how might the winds across the United States be different? Use the terms *east*, *west*, and *Coriolis effect* in your answer.

Chapter 2: **Weather Patterns** 75 **D**

Analyzing a Diagram

1. a   3. d   5. d   7. a
2. b   4. b   6. b

Extended Response

8. RUBRIC

4 points for a response that correctly answers the question and uses the following terms accurately:

- low air pressure
- high air pressure

Sample: As Richard rides up in the elevator, the air pressure decreases as his altitude increases. The air inside his ear is still at a <u>high air pressure</u>, so it tries to move toward the area of <u>low air pressure</u> outside his ear.

3 points correctly answers the question and uses one term accurately
2 points correctly answers the question, but does not use the terms

9. RUBRIC

4 points for a response that correctly answers the question and uses the following terms accurately:

- east
- west
- Coriolis effect

Sample: The <u>Coriolis effect</u> would still cause the global winds to curve, but the wind belt over the United States would probably move from <u>east</u> to <u>west</u> instead.

3 points correctly answers the question and uses the term *Coriolis effect* accurately
2 points correctly uses the term *Coriolis effect*
1 point indicates that the global winds curve

METACOGNITIVE ACTIVITY

Have students answer the following questions in their **Science Notebook:**

1. Which topics in this chapter would you like to learn more about?

2. How do the concepts in this chapter relate to your life?

3. How should you revise your plan for experimenting if your Unit Project is not working to your expectations?

3 Weather Fronts and Storms

Earth Science
UNIFYING PRINCIPLES

PRINCIPLE 1

Heat energy inside Earth and radiation from the Sun provide energy for Earth's processes.

PRINCIPLE 2

Physical forces, such as gravity, affect the movement of all matter on Earth and throughout the universe.

PRINCIPLE 3

Matter and energy move among Earth's rocks and soil, atmosphere, waters, and living things.

PRINCIPLE 4

Earth has changed over time and continues to change.

Unit: Earth's Atmosphere
BIG IDEAS

CHAPTER 1
Earth's Changing Atmosphere

Earth's atmosphere is a blanket of gases that supports and protects life.

Chapter 2
Weather Patterns

Some features of weather have predictable patterns.

CHAPTER 3
Weather Fronts and Storms

The interaction of air masses causes changes in weather.

CHAPTER 4
Climate and Climate Change

Climates are long-term weather patterns that may change over time.

CHAPTER 3
KEY CONCEPTS

SECTION 3.1

Weather changes as air masses move.

1. Air masses are large bodies of air.

2. Weather changes where air masses meet.

SECTION 3.2

Low-pressure systems can become storms.

1. Hurricanes form over warm ocean water.

2. Winter storms produce snow and ice.

SECTION 3.3

Vertical air motion can cause severe storms.

1. Thunderstorms form from rising moist air.

2. Tornadoes form in severe thunderstorms.

SECTION 3.4

Weather forecasters use advanced technologies.

1. Weather data come from many sources.

2. Weather data can be displayed on maps.

3. Forecasters use computer models to predict weather.

The Big Idea Flow Chart is available on p. T17 in the **UNIT TRANSPARENCY BOOK.**

Previewing Content

 Weather changes as air masses move. pp. 79–86

1. Air masses are large bodies of air.

An **air mass** is a large volume of air in which temperature and humidity are nearly the same at different locations at the same altitude. (Air gets colder as you move up.)

Air masses are named for two characteristics of the regions where they form:

• continental (dry) or maritime (moist)
• polar (cold) or tropical (warm)

As global winds move air masses, they may change air masses' characteristics slowly. Thus, a maritime polar air mass that moves over land may become less moist.

2. Weather changes where air masses meet.

A **front** is the boundary between air masses. Three types of fronts are: cold fronts, warm fronts, and stationary fronts. Each front can produce a different type of weather. In cold fronts, warm air is pushed steeply up by cold air. Brief, heavy storms may form. In warm fronts, warm air rises gently over cold air. Prolonged periods of steady rain or snow may occur. In a stationary front, neither air mass advances. Clouds may form along the front. A fourth type of front, an occluded front, occurs when one front overtakes another. An example is shown below. Occluded fronts are common in low-pressure systems.

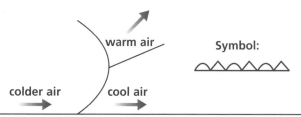

An occluded front occurs when one front overtakes another. The air in between is pushed upward.

Regions of high and low air pressure give rise to systems of weather. A **high-pressure system** is shown by isobars (lines on a map that connect places that have the same air pressure) that form closed loops around a local high, or center of high pressure. High-pressure systems often bring fair weather. A **low-pressure system** is shown by isobars that form closed loops around a local low. Such a low often forms where air masses meet, and it may develop into a stormy system that includes several fronts.

 Low-pressure systems can become storms. pp. 87–91

1. Hurricanes form over warm ocean water.

A **hurricane** begins as a tropical depression, or low-pressure system over warm tropical water. The depression is called a **tropical storm** when wind speeds reach 65 km/h and a hurricane when wind speeds reach 120 km/h. Warm ocean water provides the energy needed for hurricane formation. When hurricanes reach land or cooler water, they lose energy and eventually die out. The effects of hurricanes include:

• **storm surges,** or huge masses of water pushed inland by a hurricane
• heavy rains and floods
• wind damage
• tornadoes

2. Winter storms produce snow and ice.

Winter storms form when two air masses collide, producing a strong low-pressure system. Different types of winter storms include blizzards, lake-effect snow, and ice storms. **Blizzards** are blinding snowstorms with winds of at least 56 km/h and low temperatures. Lake-effect snow forms when cold air gains moisture and warmth as it passes over large bodies of water; when the air reaches land, it cools again and releases its moisture as snow. Ice storms develop when the air is warmer than the surface. When cold rain reaches the colder ground, it freezes.

Common Misconceptions

PRESSURE SYSTEMS Students may hold the misconception that high-pressure centers are associated with warm temperatures and low-pressure centers are associated with cold temperatures. In fact, both types of centers may cause warm and cold temperatures. For

 MISCONCEPTION DATABASE
CLASSZONE.COM Background on student misconceptions

example, cold waves are long periods of below-normal temperatures caused by strong high-pressure systems.

 This misconception is addressed on p. 84.

Vertical air motion can cause severe storms. pp. 92–97

1. Thunderstorms form from rising moist air.

Lightning is the spark of electricity that causes a bright flash of light during a storm. The air around the lightning is heated and cooled quickly, producing a sound wave known as thunder. A **thunderstorm** is a storm with lightning and thunder. Thunderstorms form in the following way:

Step 1 Warm, humid air is forced upward. As condensation occurs and energy is released, a cumulonimbus cloud forms.

Step 2 Ice particles near the top of the cloud begin to fall, producing strong downdrafts next to the updrafts. Winds and heavy rain or hail accompany this severe stage of the storm.

Step 3 The downdrafts spread out and block the updrafts. The storm dies out.

The effects of thunderstorms include flash floods, strong winds, hail, and lightning. Use the visual below when discussing lightning.

Lightning occurs when opposite electrically-charged particles between a cloud and the ground meet.

2. Tornadoes form in severe thunderstorms.

Under some conditions, the up-and-down air motion of a thunderstorm may produce a **tornado.** A tornado is a violently rotating column of air between a cloud and the ground. Most tornadoes occur in North America in the spring, when wind conditions are just right to form these violent storms. Tornadoes can tear off roofs and damage trees. The strongest tornadoes can lift cars or demolish buildings.

Common Misconceptions

LIGHTNING Students may hold the misconception that lightning never strikes twice in the same place. In reality, lightning tends to strike the highest features in a given location. Sometimes these features are repeatedly hit.

TE This misconception is addressed on p. 93.

Weather forecasters use advanced technologies. pp. 98–105

1. Weather data comes from many sources.

A **meteorologist** is a scientist who studies the weather. Meteorologists may develop weather forecasts by using data from radar stations, satellites, and instrument packages in ground stations, weather buoys, airplanes, and ships.

2. Weather data can be displayed on maps.

The gathered weather data are combined, summarized, and displayed on maps for ease of use. Surface weather maps usually show highs, lows, fronts, and other current or predicted features. Air pressure is often depicted by **isobars,** lines that connect places that have the same air pressure. Satellite images include both visible-light and infrared images. Visible-light images show clouds in sunlight; infrared images show clouds by day or night and also show cloud heights. Maps can also show patterns of temperature and other information.

3. Forecasters use computer models to predict weather.

Anyone can make simple forecasts based on observations and a knowledge of weather patterns. Meteorologists rely on data gathered from other sources and computer models to analyze weather data and make forecasts. Computers can create maps of weather data. Meteorologists analyze the various forecasts and use their own expertise to make a weather prediction. Short-term forecasts—up to three days in advance—are more reliable than long-term forecasts, especially near stormy systems, where atmospheric conditions change quickly.

MISCONCEPTION DATABASE
CLASSZONE.COM Background on student misconceptions

EXPLORE (the BIG idea)

How Does Cold Air Move? p. 77 Students are introduced to the movement of air masses.	**TIME** 10 minutes **MATERIALS** refrigerator
How Does Weather Move? p. 77 Students are introduced to the effect fronts have on weather.	**TIME** 15 minutes **MATERIALS** newspaper weather maps (spanning three consecutive days)
Internet Activity: Weather Safety, p. 77 Students investigate weather safety measures.	**TIME** 15 minutes **MATERIALS** computer with Internet access

SECTION 3.1

EXPLORE Air Masses, p. 79 To help students recognize the effect of a surface on temperature and humidity.	**TIME** 15 minutes **MATERIALS** 3 bowls, ice, warm water, 3 shoe boxes, plastic wrap
INVESTIGATE Air Masses, p. 81 Students infer how differences in density affect colliding air masses.	**TIME** 25 minutes **MATERIALS** 500-mL beaker, stiff cardboard, scissors, 2 cups, small beaker, salt, water, food coloring

SECTION 3.2

EXPLORE Hurricanes, p. 87 Students observe how friction affects a spinning top and relate the information to hurricane strength.	**TIME** 10 minutes **MATERIALS** sheet of paper, top
INVESTIGATE Ice, p. 90 Students observe how salt affects ice to infer why it is put on icy roads.	**TIME** 10 minutes **MATERIALS** 2 ice cubes, 2 cups, table salt

SECTION 3.3

EXPLORE Lightning, p. 92 Students use static electricity to model lightning and thunder.	**TIME** 10 minutes **MATERIALS** thumbtack, eraser, aluminum foil, plastic foam tray, wool fabric
INVESTIGATE Updrafts, p. 94 Students observe the motion of heated water to infer how updrafts form.	**TIME** 20 minutes **MATERIALS** 4 cardboard squares, 5 foam cups, clear container, cool tap water, food coloring, eye dropper, hot tap water

SECTION 3.4

EXPLORE Weather Maps, p. 98 Students interpret symbols on a weather map and relate a weather forecast to actual weather conditions.	**TIME** 10 minutes **MATERIALS** newspaper weather map
CHAPTER INVESTIGATION **Design a Weather Center,** pp. 104–105 Students observe, measure, and record weather conditions, then analyze the data.	**TIME** 40 minutes **MATERIALS** thermometer, magnetic compass, other weather instruments such as wind vane and psychrometer, graph paper

R **Additional INVESTIGATION,** Hurricane Hugo, A, B, & C, pp. 213–221; Teacher Instructions, pp. 284–285

Previewing Chapter Resources

| | INTEGRATED TECHNOLOGY | LABS AND ACTIVITIES |

CHAPTER 3
Weather Fronts and Storms

 CLASSZONE.COM
- eEdition Plus
- EasyPlanner Plus
- Misconception Database
- Content Review
- Test Practice
- Visualizations
- Resource Centers
- Internet Activity: Weather Safety
- Math Tutorial

 SCILINKS.ORG

 SCI LINKS

 CD-ROMS
- eEdition
- EasyPlanner
- Power Presentations
- Content Review
- Lab Generator
- Test Generator

AUDIO CDS
- Audio Readings
- Audio Readings in Spanish

 EXPLORE the Big Idea, p. 77
- How Does Cold Air Move?
- How Does Weather Move?
- Internet Activity: Weather Safety

UNIT RESOURCE BOOK
Unit Projects, pp. 5–10

 Lab Generator CD-ROM
Generate customized labs.

SECTION
3.1 Weather changes as air masses move.
pp. 79–86

Time: 2 periods (1 block)

 Lesson Plan, pp. 154–155

 • **VISUALIZATION,** Warm and Cold Fronts
• **MATH TUTORIAL**

 UNIT TRANSPARENCY BOOK
- Big Idea Flow Chart, p. T17
- Daily Vocabulary Scaffolding, p. T18
- Note-Taking Model, p. T19
- 3-Minute Warm-Up, p. T20
- "Fronts and Weather" Visual, p. T22

 • EXPLORE Air Masses, p. 79
• INVESTIGATE Air Masses, p. 81
• Math in Science, p. 86

 UNIT RESOURCE BOOK
- Datasheet, Air Masses, p. 163
- Math Support, p. 202
- Math Practice, p. 203

SECTION
3.2 Low-pressure systems can become storms.
pp. 87–91

Time: 2 periods (1 block)

 Lesson Plan, pp. 165–166

 VISUALIZATION, Progress of a Hurricane

 UNIT TRANSPARENCY BOOK
- Daily Vocabulary Scaffolding, p. T18
- 3-Minute Warm-Up, p. T20

 • EXPLORE Hurricanes, p. 87
• INVESTIGATE Ice, p. 90

 UNIT RESOURCE BOOK
- Datasheet, Ice, p. 174
- Additional INVESTIGATION, Hurricane Hugo, A, B, & C, pp. 213–221

SECTION
3.3 Vertical air motion can cause severe storms.
pp. 92–97

Time: 2 periods (1 block)

 Lesson Plan, pp. 176–177

 UNIT TRANSPARENCY BOOK
- Daily Vocabulary Scaffolding, p. T18
- 3-Minute Warm-Up, p. T21

 • EXPLORE Lightning, p. 92
• INVESTIGATE Updrafts, p. 94
• Think Science, p. 97

 UNIT RESOURCE BOOK
Datasheet, Updrafts, p. 185

SECTION
3.4 Weather forecasters use advanced technologies.
pp. 98–105

Time: 4 periods (2 blocks)

 Lesson Plan, pp. 187–188

 RESOURCE CENTER, Weather Forecasting

UNIT TRANSPARENCY BOOK
- Big Idea Flow Chart, p. T17
- Daily Vocabulary Scaffolding, p. T18
- 3-Minute Warm-Up, p. T21
- Chapter Outline, pp. T23–T24

 • EXPLORE Weather Maps, p. 98
• CHAPTER INVESTIGATION, Design a Weather Center, pp. 104–105

UNIT RESOURCE BOOK
CHAPTER INVESTIGATION, Design a Weather Center, A, B, & C, pp. 204–212

READING AND REINFORCEMENT

- Word Triangle, B18–19
- Main Idea Web, C38–39
- Daily Vocabulary Scaffolding, H1–8

 UNIT RESOURCE BOOK
- Vocabulary Practice, pp. 199–200
- Decoding Support, p. 201
- Summarizing the Chapter, pp. 222–223

 Audio Readings CD
Listen to Pupil Edition.

Audio Readings in Spanish CD
Listen to Pupil Edition in Spanish.

 UNIT RESOURCE BOOK
- Reading Study Guide, A & B, pp. 156–159
- Spanish Reading Study Guide, pp. 160–161
- Challenge and Extension, p. 162
- Reinforcing Key Concepts, p. 164

 UNIT RESOURCE BOOK
- Reading Study Guide, A & B, pp. 167–170
- Spanish Reading Study Guide, pp. 171–172
- Challenge and Extension, p. 173
- Reinforcing Key Concepts, p. 175
- Challenge Reading, pp. 197–198

 UNIT RESOURCE BOOK
- Reading Study Guide, A & B, pp. 178–181
- Spanish Reading Study Guide, pp. 182–183
- Challenge and Extension, p. 184
- Reinforcing Key Concepts, p. 186

UNIT RESOURCE BOOK
- Reading Study Guide, A & B, pp. 189–192
- Spanish Reading Study Guide, pp. 193–194
- Challenge and Extension, p. 195
- Reinforcing Key Concepts, p. 196

ASSESSMENT

- Chapter Review, pp. 107–108
- Standardized Test Practice, p. 109

 UNIT ASSESSMENT BOOK
- Diagnostic Test, pp. 41–42
- Chapter Test, Levels A, B, & C, pp. 47–58
- Alternative Assessment, pp. 59–60

 Spanish Chapter Test, pp. 181–184

 Test Generator CD-ROM
Generate customized tests.

Lab Generator CD-ROM
Rubrics for Labs

 Ongoing Assessment, pp. 79–85

 Section 3.1 Review, p. 85

 UNIT ASSESSMENT BOOK
Section 3.1 Quiz, p. 43

 Ongoing Assessment, pp. 88–91

 Section 3.2 Review, p. 91

 UNIT ASSESSMENT BOOK
Section 3.2 Quiz, p. 44

 Ongoing Assessment, pp. 92–96

 Section 3.3 Review, p. 96

UNIT ASSESSMENT BOOK
Section 3.3 Quiz, p. 45

 Ongoing Assessment, pp. 98–103

 Section 3.4 Review, p. 103

 UNIT ASSESSMENT BOOK
Section 3.4 Quiz, p. 46

STANDARDS

National Standards
A.1–8, A.9.a–g, D.1.i, D.1.j, E.2–3, E.5, F.3.a, F.4.b

See p. 76 for the standards.

National Standards
A.2–8, A.9.a–f, D.1.i, F.4.b

National Standards
A.2–7, A.9.a–b, A.9.d–f, D.1.j, F.4.b

National Standards
A.2–8, A.9.a–c, A.9.e–f, D.1.i, F.4.b

National Standards
A.1–8, A.9.a–g, E.2–5

CHAPTER INVESTIGATION

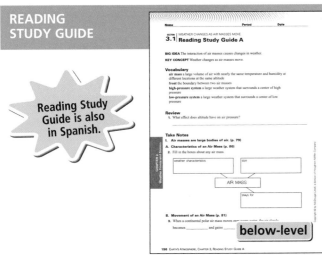

Leveled resources present the same concepts for different abilities.

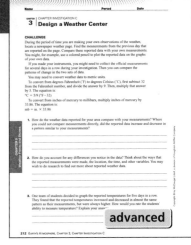

R UNIT RESOURCE BOOK, pp. 204–207   **R** pp. 208–211   **R** pp. 208–212

READING STUDY GUIDE

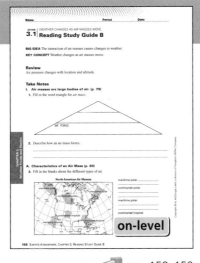

Reading Study Guide is also in Spanish.

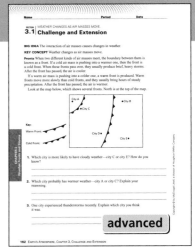

R UNIT RESOURCE BOOK, pp. 156–157   **R** pp. 158–159   **R** p. 162

CHAPTER TEST

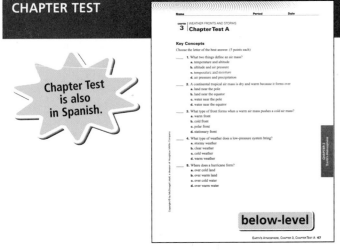

Chapter Test is also in Spanish.

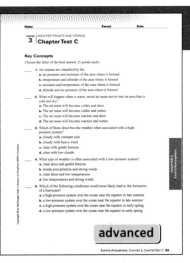

A UNIT ASSESSMENT BOOK, pp. 47–50   **A** pp. 51–54   **A** pp. 55–58

There are two Visualizations for this chapter.

 CLASSZONE.COM

 CD/CD-ROMS

 CLASSZONE.COM

VISUAL CONTENT

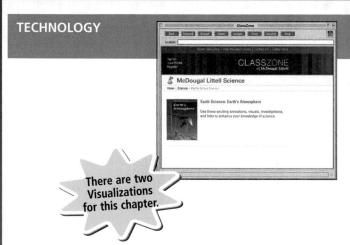

CHAPTER 3 WEATHER FRONTS AND STORMS
Big Idea Flow Chart

T UNIT TRANSPARENCY BOOK, p. T17

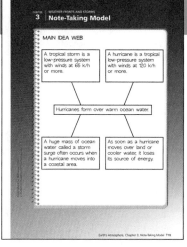

CHAPTER 3 WEATHER FRONTS AND STORMS
Note-Taking Model

MAIN IDEA WEB

A tropical storm is a low-pressure system with winds at 65 k/h or more.

A hurricane is a tropical low-pressure system with winds at 120 k/h or more.

Hurricanes form over warm ocean water.

A huge mass of ocean water called a storm surge often occurs when a hurricane moves into a coastal area.

As soon as a hurricane moves over land or cooler water, it loses its source of energy.

T p. T19

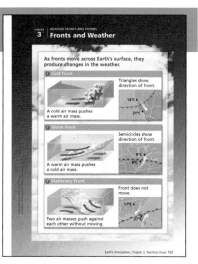

CHAPTER 3 WEATHER FRONTS AND STORMS
Fronts and Weather

As fronts move across Earth's surface, they produce changes in the weather.

Cold Front — Triangles show direction of front.
A cold air mass pushes a warm air mass.

Warm Front — Semicircles show direction of front.
A warm air mass pushes a cold air mass.

Stationary Front — Front does not move.
Two air masses push against each other without moving.

T p. T22

MORE SUPPORT

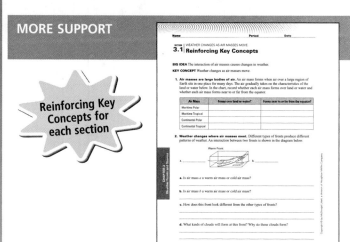

SECTION WEATHER CHANGES AS AIR MASSES MOVE
3.1 Reinforcing Key Concepts

Reinforcing Key Concepts for each section

R UNIT RESOURCE BOOK, p. 164

CHAPTER 3 WEATHER FRONTS AND STORMS
3 Vocabulary

R pp. 199–200

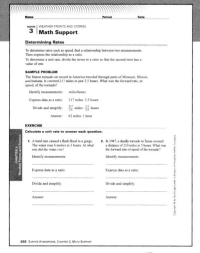

CHAPTER 3 WEATHER FRONTS AND STORMS
3 Math Support

R p. 202

3 Weather Fronts and Storms

INTRODUCE

the **BIG** idea

Have students look at the photograph of the storm and discuss how the question in the box links to the Big Idea:

- What happens during a storm?
- How can weather move a house?
- How do you think weather forecasters know when a storm is coming?

National Science Education Standards

Content

D.1.i Clouds form by condensation of water vapor; affect weather, climate.

D.1.j Global patterns of atmospheric movement influence local weather. Oceans have a major effect on climate, because water in the oceans holds a large amount of heat.

F.3.a Processes of the Earth system, such as storms, can cause hazards.

Process

A.1–8 Identify questions that can be answered through scientific investigations; design and conduct an investigation; use tools to gather and interpret data; use evidence to describe, predict, explain, model; think critically to make relationships between evidence and explanation; recognize different explanations and predictions; communicate scientific procedures and explanations; use mathematics.

A.9.a–f Understand scientific inquiry by using different investigations, methods, mathematics, technology, and explanations based on logic, evidence, and skepticism.

E.2–5 Design, evaluate, and implement a solution or product; communicate technological design.

F.4.b Understand the risks associated with natural hazards.

the **BIG** idea

The interaction of air masses causes changes in weather.

What types of weather can move a house?

Key Concepts

SECTION
3.1 **Weather changes as air masses move.** Learn about air masses, fronts, and high- and low-pressure systems.

SECTION
3.2 **Low-pressure systems can become storms.** Learn about hurricanes and winter storms.

SECTION
3.3 **Vertical air motion can cause severe storms.** Learn about thunderstorms, lightning, and tornadoes.

SECTION
3.4 **Weather forecasters use advanced technologies.** Learn about different types of weather data and how forecasters predict weather.

Internet Preview

CLASSZONE.COM
Chapter 3 online resources: Content Review, two Visualizations, two Resource Centers, Math Tutorial, Test Practice

INTERNET PREVIEW

CLASSZONE.COM For student use with the following pages:

Review and Practice
- Content Review, pp. 78, 106
- Math Tutorial: Rates as Ratios, p. 86
- Test Practice, p. 109

Activities and Resources
- Internet Activity: Weather Safety, p. 77
- Visualizations: Warm and Cold Fronts, p. 82; Hurricanes, p. 88
- Resource Center: Weather Forecasting, p. 99

Severe Weather
Code: MDL011

How Does Cold Air Move?

Hold one hand near the top of a refrigerator door and the other hand near the bottom. Open the refrigerator door just a little bit.

Observe and Think How did each hand feel before and after you opened the door? How did the air move?

How Does Weather Move?

Collect newspaper weather maps for three consecutive days. Identify at least one flagged line on a map (identifying a weather front) and track the line's movement over the three days.

Observe and Think What type of weather did you find each day where the line passed? Why did this line move the way it did?

Internet Activity: Weather Safety

Go to **ClassZone.com** to find information about weather safety. Find out the types of dangerous weather that may affect your region.

Observe and Think What can you do ahead of time to be ready for severe weather?

NSTA
scilinks.org
SCI*LINKS*

Severe Weather Code: MDL011

Chapter 3: **Weather Fronts and Storms** 77 **D**

TEACHING WITH TECHNOLOGY

Animated Maps Have students access online weather maps that show weather patterns through animations.

CBL and Probeware If students have probeware, they can use a temperature probe for the Chapter Investigation on pp. 104–105. Depending on what other weather instrument they choose, they may be able to use additional probeware as well.

EXPLORE (the **BIG** idea)

These inquiry-based activities are appropriate for use at home or as a supplement to classroom instruction.

How Does Cold Air Move?

PURPOSE To introduce students to the concept of air masses. Students will feel cold air move downward after the refrigerator door is opened.

TIP *10 min.* Tell students to pay attention to temperature differences and air movement.

Answer: top: little change; bottom: cold; cold air moved down and out

REVISIT after p. 81.

How Does Weather Move?

PURPOSE To introduce students to the concept of weather fronts. Students will track the movement of a front over three days.

TIP *10 min.* Have students choose a front near a city that has its temperature listed.

Answer: Fronts tend to move eastward. Fronts moving north will bring warm weather, and fronts moving south will bring cold weather.

REVISIT after p. 83.

Internet Activity: Weather Safety

PURPOSE To introduce students to weather safety issues. Students will identify the types of severe weather likely in their region and research safety measures.

TIP *15 min.* Have students discuss any severe weather they have experienced. Have them describe the storm and its effects. What is the most common type of severe weather in your area?

Sample answer: Plan an evacuation route or select a place in your house where you'll be safe if a storm strikes. Stock up on clean water and cans of food. Have a first-aid kit in the house and car.

REVISIT after p. 96.

Chapter 3 **77** **D**

PREPARE

CONCEPT REVIEW

Activate Prior Knowledge

- Ask students to describe cloud formation in terms of air density and temperature—that is, clouds form as warm, less dense air rises, expands, and cools.

- Ask students to explain what would happen to sinking air. Would the water vapor in the air condense or evaporate? Would clouds form?

TAKING NOTES

Main Idea Web

Tell students to write the blue heading in the center and draw a box around it. As they read, they should look for topic sentences that convey important details related to the main idea. Highlighted words and red headings are also important terms and details. Students should write the related details around the main idea, draw boxes around them, and then connect them to the main idea.

Vocabulary Strategy

Drawings in word triangles are especially useful because they present information visually. Tell students to make drawings that help them remember what the terms mean. Often, the drawings will not look like physical objects. They may wish to use symbols in their drawings, such as arrows to represent motion.

Vocabulary and Note-Taking Resources

- Vocabulary Practice, pp. 199–200
- Decoding Support, p. 201

- Daily Vocabulary Scaffolding, p. T18
- Note-Taking Model, p. T19

- Word Triangle, B18–19
- Main Idea Web, C38–39
- Daily Vocabulary Scaffolding, H1–8

CHAPTER 3
Getting Ready to Learn

CONCEPT REVIEW

- Air temperature decreases as you rise in the troposphere.
- Temperature affects air density.
- Pressure differences make air move.
- Uneven heating of Earth's surface produces winds.
- Clouds form as air rises, expands, and cools.

VOCABULARY REVIEW

altitude p. 10
convection p. 19
evaporation p. 56
condensation p. 56
relative humidity p. 58

 CONTENT REVIEW
CLASSZONE.COM
Review concepts and vocabulary.

TAKING NOTES

MAIN IDEA WEB

Write each new blue heading—a main idea—in a box. Then put notes with important terms and details into boxes around the main idea.

VOCABULARY STRATEGY

Draw a **word triangle** diagram for each new vocabulary term. In the bottom row write and define the term. In the middle row, use the term correctly in a sentence. At the top, draw a small picture to help you remember the term.

See the Note-Taking Handbook on pages R45–R51.

SCIENCE NOTEBOOK

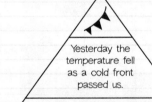

Marine air masses form over water.

Continental air masses form over land.

Air masses are large bodies of air.

Tropical air masses are warm.

Polar air masses are cold.

Yesterday the temperature fell as a cold front passed us.

front: the boundary between two air masses

CHECK READINESS

Administer the Diagnostic Test to determine students' readiness for new science content and their mastery of requisite math skills.

 Diagnostic Test, pp. 41–42

Technology Resources

Students needing content and math skills should visit **ClassZone.com**.

- **CONTENT REVIEW**
- **MATH TUTORIAL**

 CONTENT REVIEW CD-ROM

KEY CONCEPT

3.1 Weather changes as air masses move.

◀ **BEFORE, you learned**
- Air pressure changes with location and altitude
- Water vapor in the atmosphere condenses when air rises

▶ **NOW, you will learn**
- What air masses are
- What happens when air masses meet
- How pressure systems affect the weather

VOCABULARY

air mass p. 79
front p. 82
high-pressure system p. 84
low-pressure system p. 85

EXPLORE Air Masses

How does an air mass form?

PROCEDURE

① Put ice into one bowl and warm water into a second bowl. Leave the third bowl empty.

② Place each bowl in a different box and cover the box with plastic wrap. Wait a few minutes.

③ Put your hand into each box in turn.

MATERIALS
- 3 bowls
- ice
- warm water
- 3 shoe boxes
- plastic wrap

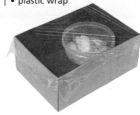

WHAT DO YOU THINK?
- How would you describe the air in each box?
- Which box's air feels the most humid? Why?

MAIN IDEA WEB
Organize important terms and details about air masses.

Air masses are large bodies of air.

You have probably experienced the effects of air masses—one day is hot and humid, and the next day is cool and pleasant. The weather changes when a new air mass moves into your area. An **air mass** is a large volume of air in which temperature and humidity are nearly the same in different locations at the same altitude. An air mass can cover many thousands of square kilometers.

An air mass forms when the air over a large region of Earth sits in one place for many days. The air gradually takes on the characteristics of the land or water below it. Where Earth's surface is cold, the air becomes cold. Where Earth's surface is wet, the air becomes moist. As an air mass moves, it brings its temperature and moisture to new locations.

CHECK YOUR READING Explain how the weather can change with the arrival of a new air mass. Your answer should include two ways that weather changes.

RESOURCES FOR DIFFERENTIATED INSTRUCTION

Below Level
UNIT RESOURCE BOOK
- Reading Study Guide A, pp. 156–157
- Decoding Support, p. 201

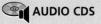 **AUDIO CDS**

Advanced
UNIT RESOURCE BOOK
Challenge and Extension, p. 162

English Learners
UNIT RESOURCE BOOK
Spanish Reading Study Guide, pp. 160–161

AUDIO CDS
- Audio Readings in Spanish
- Audio Readings (English)

3.1 FOCUS

▶ Set Learning Goals
Students will
- Describe air masses.
- Explain what happens when air masses meet.
- Determine how two types of pressure systems affect the weather.
- Infer from an experiment how density affects colliding air masses.

◀ 3-Minute Warm-Up

Display Transparency 20 or copy this exercise on the board:

Are these statements true? If not, correct them.

1. The gas that varies from 0% to 4% in Earth's atmosphere is nitrogen. *The gas that varies from 0% to 4% is water vapor.*

2. The Coriolis effect influences air motion across Earth's surface. *True*

3. The changing of a gas to a liquid is evaporation. *The changing of a gas to a liquid is condensation.*

 3-Minute Warm-Up, p. T20

3.1 MOTIVATE

EXPLORE Air Masses

PURPOSE To help students recognize the effect of a surface on temperature and humidity

TIP *15 min.* Leave the plastic wrap loose at a corner so it can be easily lifted.

WHAT DO YOU THINK? *box with ice: cool; box with warm water: warm and moist; box with empty bowl: dry and at room temperature. The box with warm water was most humid because the air was likely saturated*

Ongoing Assessment

CHECK YOUR READING *Sample answer: It could become cooler and drier over cold land.*

Teach from Visuals

To help students interpret the "North American Land Masses" visual, ask:

- What do the arrows show? *the place where an air mass forms and the direction in which it might move*

- Dry, warm air is typical of which air mass? *continental tropical*

- What type of air mass would likely bring wet, cold weather? *maritime polar*

- What types of air masses affect your location most often? *Sample answer for a student in Florida: maritime tropical*

Real World Example

For convenience's sake, meteorologists often use letters or symbols to designate weather phenomena. For example, the lowercase letters *c* and *m* represent continental and maritime air masses, respectively. Capital letters, such as *T* (tropical) and *P* (polar), indicate the source of an air mass. Thus, a maritime tropical air mass would be abbreviated to mT.

Ongoing Assessment

Describe air masses.

Ask: How does a maritime tropical air mass compare with a continental tropical air mass? *The maritime tropical air mass is moist and warm. The continental tropical air mass is dry and warm.*

Answer: over land

North American Air Masses

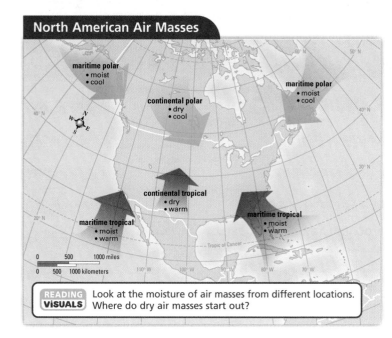

maritime polar
• moist
• cool

maritime polar
• moist
• cool

continental polar
• dry
• cool

continental tropical
• dry
• warm

maritime tropical
• moist
• warm

maritime tropical
• moist
• warm

— Tropic of Cancer —

0   500   1000 miles
0   500   1000 kilometers

READING VISUALS Look at the moisture of air masses from different locations. Where do dry air masses start out?

Characteristics of an Air Mass

Some regions of Earth's surface, such as those shown in the map above, produce air masses again and again. The characteristics of an air mass depend on the region where it forms. A hot desert produces dry, hot air masses, while cool ocean waters produce moist, cool air masses. Scientists classify air masses into categories according to the characteristics of regions. Each category name is made of two words—one for moisture, one for temperature.

The first word of an air mass's category name tells whether the air mass formed over water or dry land. It describes the moisture of the air mass.

- **Continental** air masses form over land. Air becomes dry as it loses its moisture to the dry land below it.

- **Maritime** (MAR-ih-TYM) air masses form over water. Air becomes moist as it gains water vapor from the water below it.

The second word of a category name tells whether an air mass formed close to the equator. It describes the air mass's temperature.

- **Tropical** air masses form near the equator. Air becomes warm as it gains energy from the warm land or water.

- **Polar** air masses form far from the equator. Air becomes cool as it loses energy to the cold land or water.

READING TIP

The word *maritime* has the same root as the word *marine*. Both come from the Latin word *mare*, which means "sea."

 A

B

DIFFERENTIATE INSTRUCTION

 More Reading Support

A Where do maritime air masses form? *over water*

B What two words identify the temperature of air masses? *tropical and polar*

English Learners English learners may need help with the concepts of *continental, maritime, tropical,* and *polar.* Explain that *continental* refers to land, as in the word *continent,* and that *maritime* refers to the ocean, as in the word *marine.* Use a globe to show students tropical and polar regions.

The combination of words gives the characteristics of the air mass. A maritime tropical air mass is moist and warm, while a continental polar air mass is dry and cold.

 CHECK YOUR READING What can you tell from each word of an air mass's name?

Movement of an Air Mass

Air masses can travel away from the regions where they form. They move with the global pattern of winds. In most of the United States, air masses generally move from west to east. They may move along with the jet stream in more complex and changing patterns.

When an air mass moves to a new region, it carries along its characteristic moisture and temperature. As the air moves over Earth's surface, the characteristics of the surface begin to change the air mass. For example, if a continental polar air mass moves over warm water, the air near the surface will become warmer and gain moisture. These changes begin where the air touches the surface. It may take days or weeks for the changes to spread upward through the entire air mass. An air mass that moves quickly may not change much. If it moves quickly enough, a continental polar air mass can move cold air from northern Canada all the way to the southern United States.

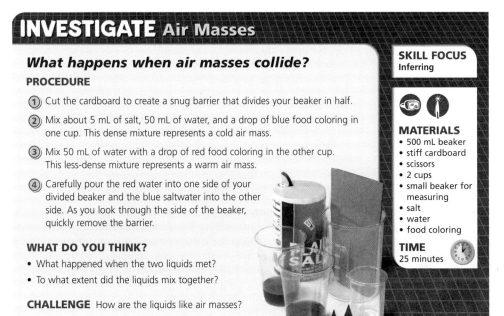

INVESTIGATE Air Masses

What happens when air masses collide?

PROCEDURE

1. Cut the cardboard to create a snug barrier that divides your beaker in half.

2. Mix about 5 mL of salt, 50 mL of water, and a drop of blue food coloring in one cup. This dense mixture represents a cold air mass.

3. Mix 50 mL of water with a drop of red food coloring in the other cup. This less-dense mixture represents a warm air mass.

4. Carefully pour the red water into one side of your divided beaker and the blue saltwater into the other side. As you look through the side of the beaker, quickly remove the barrier.

WHAT DO YOU THINK?

- What happened when the two liquids met?
- To what extent did the liquids mix together?

CHALLENGE How are the liquids like air masses?

SKILL FOCUS
Inferring

MATERIALS
- 500 mL beaker
- stiff cardboard
- scissors
- 2 cups
- small beaker for measuring
- salt
- water
- food coloring

TIME
25 minutes

Chapter 3: **Weather Fronts and Storms** 81 **D**

INVESTIGATE Air Masses

PURPOSE Infer how density affects colliding air masses

TIPS *25 min.* Mix the water ahead of time. Then suggest the following:

- Cut the cardboard slightly larger than the container; gently mash the edges as you push it into the container.

- Make sure the bottom of the card-board is snug against the container. If the container has a curved bottom, dampen the bottom of the cardboard so that it will mold to the container's shape.

- Repeat the experiment several times to be sure of your results.

WHAT DO YOU THINK? *The dense, blue liquid moved under the less dense, red liquid. They didn't mix very much.*

CHALLENGE *Air masses also move without mixing much.*

 Datasheet, Air Masses, p. 163

Technology Resources

Customize this student lab as needed or look for an alternative. Print rubrics to assess student lab reports.

Lab Generator CD-ROM

Metacognitive Strategy

Ask: What questions came to mind as you watched the water move? How did you find answers to your questions?

EXPLORE the **BIG** idea

Revisit "How Does Cold Air Move?" on p. 77. Have students explain the reasons for their observations.

Ongoing Assessment

CHECK YOUR READING *Answer: first word indicates moisture, second word indicates temperature*

Chapter 3 **81** **D**

Teach Difficult Concepts

Students may have difficulty understanding how water in the atmosphere and temperature affect one another. If dry air loses energy, the temperature drops. If humid air loses energy, water vapor condenses and releases energy, so the temperature drops less. Energy that might cause a change in temperature instead causes a change in the state of water, so the temperature change is more moderate. As a result, moist air masses tend to have more moderate temperatures than dry air masses. A continental air mass might be hot or cold, whereas a maritime air mass that originated at a similar latitude will be merely warm or cool.

History of Science

The term "front" was first used by Norwegian scientists during World War I. At that time, many meteorologists were conducting research on the interactions of air masses. The clash of opposing air masses was considered analogous to clashing armies on the battlefront.

Ongoing Assessment

Explain what happens when air masses meet.

Ask: What happens when cold, dense air pushes warmer air? *A cold front forms as the cold, dense air moves forward, pushing the warmer air up.* What kind of weather would you expect? *Clouds and brief, heavy storms are likely.*

 Answer: The temperature would decrease.

Weather changes where air masses meet.

D

When a new air mass moves over your area, you can expect the weather to change. Perhaps you have heard a weather forecaster talk about fronts. A **front** is a boundary between air masses. The weather near a front can differ from the weather inside the rest of an air mass. As one air mass pushes another, some of the air at the boundary will be pushed upward. Clouds can form in this rising air. The weather often becomes cloudy or stormy as a front passes. Afterward, you experience the temperature and humidity of the air mass that has moved in.

Fronts and Weather

Different types of fronts produce different patterns of weather. When a cold, dense air mass pushes warmer air, it produces a cold front. When a warm air mass pushes colder air, it produces a warm front. These names tell you which way the temperature will change but not how much it will change. A cold front can turn a heat wave into normal summer weather or turn cold winter air into very cold weather.

CHECK YOUR READING How would the weather change if a cold front moved into your area?

E

1 Cold fronts can move into regions quickly. As you can see on page 83, a cold front is steeper than the other types of fronts. As a mass of cold, dense air moves forward, warmer air ahead of it is pushed upward. Water vapor in the warm air condenses as the air rises. Cold fronts often produce tall cumulonimbus clouds and precipitation. Brief, heavy storms are likely. After the storms, the air is cooler and often very clear.

2 Warm fronts move more slowly than cold fronts. Warm air moves gradually up and over a mass of denser and colder air. Moisture in the warm air condenses all along the sloping front, producing cloud-covered skies. As a warm front approaches, you may first see high cirrus clouds, then high stratus clouds, then lower and lower stratus clouds. Often, a warm front brings many hours of steady rain or snow. After the front passes, the air is warmer.

3 Stationary fronts occur when air masses first meet or when a cold or warm front stops moving. For a while, the boundary between the air masses stays in the same location—it stays stationary. The air in each air mass can still move sideways along the front or upward. The upward air motion may produce clouds that cover the sky, sometimes for days at a time. When the front starts moving, it becomes a warm front if the warm air advances and pushes the cold air. If the cold air moves forward instead, the front becomes a cold front.

MAIN IDEA WEB
Organize the notes you take about fronts.

VISUALIZATION
CLASSZONE.COM

See how the air moves in warm fronts and cold fronts.

DIFFERENTIATE INSTRUCTION

 More Reading Support

D A boundary between air masses is called what? *front*

E What are three types of fronts? *cold, warm, and stationary*

Advanced Have students look at a weather Web site to determine what the fourth type of front is (occluded front). Occluded fronts often form when a rapidly moving cold front overtakes the slower-moving cool air mass in a warm front. The warm air is then "wedged" between two cooler air masses and is forced upward. Have students explain the symbol for an occluded front. *The symbol is a cold and warm front merged, with both fronts pointing in the same direction.*

Fronts and Weather

As fronts move across Earth's surface, they produce changes in the weather.

① Cold Front

A **cold front** forms when a cold air mass pushes a warm air mass and forces the warm air to rise. As the warm air rises, its moisture condenses and forms tall clouds.

Triangles show the direction that a cold front moves.

San Francisco
14°C (58°F)

Los Angeles
21°C (69°F)

② Warm Front

A **warm front** forms when a warm air mass pushes a cold air mass. The warm air rises slowly over the cold air and its moisture condenses into flat clouds.

Semicircles show the direction that a warm front moves.

Detroit
6°C (42°F)

Indianapolis
8°C (47°F)

③ Stationary Front

A **stationary front** occurs when two air masses push against each other without moving. A stationary front becomes a warm or cold front when one air mass advances.

Alternating triangles and semicircles show a stationary front.

Atlanta
17°C (62°F)

Orlando
27°C (80°F)

READING VISUALS PREDICT Which city will the cold front affect next?

DIFFERENTIATE INSTRUCTION

Below Level Use analogies to help students distinguish between the three types of fronts. For example, tell students to think of the triangles that represent a cold front as icicles. They can visualize the semicircles that represent a warm front as water droplets. A stationary front is the boundary between two different air masses, so its symbol is a combination of "icicles" and "water droplets." Encourage students to think of other ways to distinguish between the front symbols. For example, blue is often associated with cold temperatures and red is often associated with warm temperatures.

Teach from Visuals

Make sure students understand that the front symbols (triangles, semicircles) point outward in the direction in which the front is moving.

To help students interpret the "Fronts and Weather" visual, ask:

- How do the symbols for cold fronts and warm fronts differ? *They differ by shape—a cold front symbol is a line with triangles; a warm front symbol is a line with with semicircles.*

- Which city will soon experience a cold front? *Los Angeles* Which will experience a warm front? *Detroit*

- Compare the "slope" of rising air in a cold front and a warm front. *In a cold front, warm air rises steeply over cold air. In a warm front, warm air rises in a gentle slope over cold air.*

T The visual "Fronts and Weather" is available as T22 in the Unit Transparency Book.

Develop Critical Thinking

INFER Ask: Why do you think the symbol for a stationary front is a combination of triangles and semicircles? *A stationary front is the boundary between two different air masses. It may become either a warm or a cold front once it starts moving. The symbol for a stationary front is a combination of the symbols for cold and warm fronts.*

EXPLORE (the **BIG** idea)

Revisit "How Does Weather Move?" on p. 77. Have students explain the reasons for their observations.

Ongoing Assessment

READING VISUALS Answer: Los Angeles

Teach Difficult Concepts

Students may be confused by the terms *center* and *system*. Explain that *center* refers to the highest or lowest pressure in a region. *System* refers to both the center and the air surrounding the center. In a well-organized pressure system, air moves all the way around the high or low center.

Address Misconceptions

IDENTIFY Ask: If a high-pressure system moved over us, what would happen to the weather? If students say that it would be warmer or colder, ask if all high-pressure systems bring warmer (or colder) weather. If students think they do, they may hold the misconception that high pressure involves a particular temperature.

CORRECT If students think that high pressure means warm temperatures, describe or give examples of the clear, cold weather of a cold wave. If students think that high pressure means cold temperatures, describe or give examples of the cloudless, rainless days that can occur during a heat wave. Both can be caused by high-pressure systems.

REASSESS Ask students to describe the weather at the high in the visual. *The sky is clear; the temperature is not known.*

Technology Resources

Visit **ClassZone.com** for background on common student misconceptions.

 MISCONCEPTION DATABASE

Ongoing Assessment

Explain what happens when air masses meet.

Ask how two air masses can produce a low-pressure system. *A low-pressure center forms between the air masses and the fronts become part of the system.*

CHECK YOUR READING *Answer: fair (clear) and calm*

READING VISUALS *Answer: It looks similar to convection (p. 48), or global wind cells (p. 51), and local winds (p. 53).*

High-Pressure Systems

You may have seen the letters H and L on a weather map. These letters mark high-pressure centers and low-pressure centers, often simply called highs and lows. Each center is the location of the highest or lowest pressure in a region. The pressure differences cause air to move in ways that may make a high or low become the center of a whole system of weather.

At a high-pressure center, air sinks slowly down. As the air nears the ground, it spreads out toward areas of lower pressure. In the Northern Hemisphere, the Coriolis effect makes the air turn clockwise as it moves outward. A **high-pressure system** is formed when air moves all the way around a high-pressure center. Most high-pressure systems are large and change slowly. When a high-pressure system stays in one location for a long time, an air mass may form. The air—and resulting air mass—can be warm or cold, moist or dry.

A high-pressure system generally brings clear skies and calm air or gentle breezes. This is because as air sinks to lower altitudes, it warms up a little bit. Water droplets evaporate, so clouds often disappear.

 READING TiP
A *system* includes different parts that work together.

CHECK YOUR READING What type of weather do you expect in a high-pressure system?

Weather Systems in the Northern Hemisphere

High-pressure systems and low-pressure systems produce patterns of weather across Earth's surface.

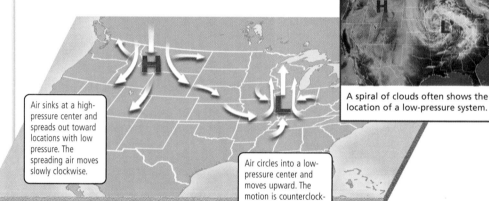

A spiral of clouds often shows the location of a low-pressure system.

Air sinks at a high-pressure center and spreads out toward locations with low pressure. The spreading air moves slowly clockwise.

Air circles into a low-pressure center and moves upward. The motion is counterclockwise and can be quick.

READING VISUALS With your finger, trace the motion of air, starting above the high. Where have you seen similar patterns in earlier chapters?

DIFFERENTIATE INSTRUCTION

? More Reading Support

F What do the letters H and L stand for on a weather map? *high- and low-pressure centers*

Advanced Ask students what they have learned about the Coriolis effect in relation to the movement of air in high-pressure systems. Ask them to infer how air moves around a high-pressure system in the Southern Hemisphere. *in a counterclockwise direction*

Low-Pressure Systems

A small area of low pressure can also develop into a larger system. A **low-pressure system** is a large weather system that surrounds a center of low pressure. It begins as air moves around and inward toward the lowest pressure and then up to higher altitudes. The upward motion of the air lowers the air pressure further, and so the air moves faster. The pattern of motion strengthens into a low-pressure weather system. The rising air produces stormy weather. In the Northern Hemisphere, the air in a low-pressure system circles in a counterclockwise direction.

A low-pressure system can develop wherever there is a center of low pressure. One place this often happens is along a boundary between a warm air mass and a cold air mass. The diagram shows an example of this process.

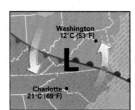

Washington
12°C (53°F)

L

Charlotte
21°C (69°F)

- Part of the boundary between the air masses moves south and becomes a cold front.
- Part of the boundary moves north and becomes a warm front.
- A center of low pressure forms where the ends of the two fronts meet.

The low-pressure center and fronts become parts of a whole system of weather. Rising air at the fronts and at the low can cause very stormy weather.

The diagram on page 84 shows how air moves between pressure centers. Air moves down, out, and around a high-pressure center. Then it swirls around and into a low-pressure center and moves upward. Highs and lows affect each other as they move across the surface. Large weather systems generally move with the pattern of global winds—west to east over most of North America. But, within a weather system, winds can blow in different directions.

3.1 Review

KEY CONCEPTS

1. What are the two characteristics of an air mass that you need to know in order to classify it?
2. What happens when a warmer air mass pushes a cooler air mass?
3. What type of weather system brings calm, clear weather?

CRITICAL THINKING

4. **Compare and Contrast** Explain how air moves differently in low- and high-pressure systems.
5. **Apply** If the weather becomes stormy for a short time and then becomes colder, which type of front has passed?

🌀 CHALLENGE

6. **Synthesize** You check a barometer and observe that the air pressure has been dropping all day. Is tonight's weather more likely to be calm or stormy?

ANSWERS

1. temperature and moisture

2. A warm front forms. The warm air rises slowly over the cold air and its moisture condenses into clouds.

3. a high-pressure system

4. Air sinks into a high-pressure center and spreads out in a clockwise direction. Air spirals around a low-pressure center and moves in a counterclockwise direction.

5. a cold front

6. It is likely to be stormy because decreasing pressure indicates that a low-pressure system or front is approaching; both are associated with clouds and possibly storms.

Ongoing Assessment

Determine how pressure systems affect the weather.

Ask: What type of weather is often associated with low-pressure systems? *stormy weather*

Teach from Visuals

To help students interpret the weather system maps on p. 84, ask:

- What do the arrows show? *They show how air moves around and between high- and low-pressure centers.*
- Locate the *H* and *L* on the inset map. What is different about these areas? *L is surrounded by a spiral of clouds; H is clear.*

Reinforce (the BIG idea)

Have students relate the section to the Big Idea.

 Reinforcing Key Concepts, p. 164

3.1 ASSESS & RETEACH

Assess

 Section 3.1 Quiz, p. 43

Reteach

Display a map of the United States that has all states labeled. Then place students in pairs and provide each pair with a newspaper weather map. Choose states that have fronts going through them and assign a different state to each pair. Have students identify the type of front, and the high- or low-pressure system, that are influencing the weather in their assigned state.

Technology Resources

Have students visit **ClassZone.com** for reteaching of Key Concepts.

 CONTENT REVIEW

 CONTENT REVIEW CD-ROM

MATH IN SCIENCE
Math Skills Practice for Science

Set Learning Goal
To determine rates to measure the speed of a moving cold front

Present the Science
Fronts move and change as air masses move. Cold fronts tend to move faster than warm fronts.

Develop Algebra Skills
Tell students that a ratio is a way of comparing numbers. A ratio can also be written as *500 km : one day* or as *500 km to one day.* Also, remind students that the mean is simply the average of the rates. To calculate the mean, add the rates together, then divide by the total number of rates.

DIFFERENTIATION TIP Students with learning disabilities may have an easier time estimating the front's movement if they use a pencil and the edge of a sheet of paper to mark off the distances traveled. They can compare the marked-off distances to the scale.

Close
Ask: Does the front appear to be speeding up or slowing down? Explain. *It appears to be slowing down because the movement of the front between Friday and Saturday is less than the front's movement on previous days.*

• Math Support, p. 202
• Math Practice, p. 203

MATH in SCIENCE

SKILL: DETERMINING RATES

Movement of a Front

Scientists measure the speeds of weather fronts to forecast weather conditions. The speed at which a front moves is an example of a rate. A rate can be written as a ratio. For example, the rate of a front that moves a distance of 500 kilometers in 1 day can be written as follows:

500 kilometers : 1 day

The map below shows the movement of a cold front over four consecutive days. Use the map scale to determine the distance that the front moves on each day.

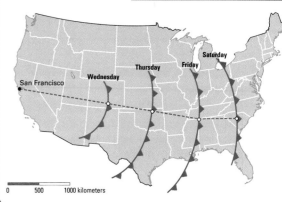

Cold Front Movement

Answer the following questions.

1. What was the front's rate of movement between Wednesday and Thursday? Express your answer as a ratio.

? : 1 day

2. What was the front's rate of movement between Friday and Saturday? Express your answer as a ratio.

3. What was the mean rate of the front's movement from Wednesday to Saturday? Remember, *mean* means "average." Express your answer as a ratio.

CHALLENGE Use the rate from Wednesday to Saturday to estimate the day on which the front must have moved through San Francisco.

ANSWERS

1. 750 km : 1 day
2. 600 km : 1 day
3. 700 km : 1 day

$$\begin{array}{r} 750 \\ 750 \\ +600 \\ \hline 2100 \end{array}$$

$$\frac{2100}{3} = 700$$

Students' measurements may vary by 50 km or so.

CHALLENGE *On Wednesday, the front was about 1400 km from San Francisco. It is moving at a rate of roughly 700 km per day. It would have passed San Francisco on Monday.*

KEY CONCEPT

3.2 Low-pressure systems can become storms.

◀ **BEFORE**, you learned

- Moving air masses cause changes in weather
- A low-pressure system brings stormy weather

▶ **NOW**, you will learn

- How hurricanes develop
- About the dangers of hurricanes
- About different types of winter storms

VOCABULARY

tropical storm p. 87
hurricane p. 87
storm surge p. 89
blizzard p. 90

EXPLORE Hurricanes

What things make hurricanes lose strength?

PROCEDURE

① Crumple a piece of paper, then flatten it out. Crumple and flatten it out again.

② Spin the top on the flattened paper. Count the seconds until it stops spinning.

③ Spin the top on a smooth surface. Count the seconds until it stops spinning.

MATERIALS
- sheet of paper
- top

WHAT DO YOU THINK?
How does the texture of the surface affect the rate at which the top loses energy?

MAIN IDEA WEB
Remember to make notes about hurricanes.

Hurricanes form over warm ocean water.

Near the equator, warm ocean water provides the energy that can turn a low-pressure center into a violent storm. As water evaporates from the ocean, energy moves from the ocean water into the air. This energy makes warm air rise faster. Tall clouds and strong winds develop. As winds blow across the water from different directions into the low, the Coriolis effect bends their paths into a spiral. The winds blow faster and faster around the low, which becomes the center of a storm system.

A **tropical storm** is a low-pressure system that starts near the equator and has winds that blow at 65 kilometers per hour (40 mi/h) or more. A **hurricane** (HUR-ih-KAYN) is a tropical low-pressure system with winds blowing at speeds of 120 kilometers per hour (74 mi/h) or more—strong enough to uproot trees. Hurricanes are called typhoons or cyclones when they form over the Indian Ocean or the western Pacific Ocean.

Chapter 3: **Weather Fronts and Storms** 87 **D**

RESOURCES FOR DIFFERENTIATED INSTRUCTION

Below Level

UNIT RESOURCE BOOK
- Reading Study Guide A, pp. 167–168
- Decoding Support, p. 201

 AUDIO CDS

R **Additional INVESTIGATION,**
Hurricane Hugo, A, B, & C, pp. 213–221;
Teacher Instructions, pp. 284–285

Advanced

UNIT RESOURCE BOOK
- Challenge and Extension, p. 173
- Challenge Reading, pp. 197–198

English Learners

UNIT RESOURCE BOOK
Spanish Reading Study Guide, pp. 171–172

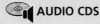 **AUDIO CDS**

- Audio Readings in Spanish
- Audio Readings (English)

3.2 FOCUS

▶ **Set Learning Goals**

Students will

- Explain how hurricanes develop.
- Recognize the dangers from hurricanes.
- Compare the different types of winter storms.
- Infer through experimentation why salt is put on icy roads.

◀ **3-Minute Warm-Up**

Display Transparency 20 or copy this exercise on the board:

Draw a diagram to show how air moves around a low-pressure system. Label the low-pressure center and use arrows to show the direction of air movement.

T 3-Minute Warm-Up, p. T20

3.2 MOTIVATE

EXPLORE Hurricanes

PURPOSE To help students understand one factor that affects hurricane strength

TIP *10 min.* Have students work in pairs. While one student observes the spinning top, his or her partner can keep track of the time using a stopwatch or clock, or by counting seconds.

WHAT DO YOU THINK? *The top loses energy faster on a rough surface. It spins longer on a smooth surface.*

Teach Difficult Concepts

Ask students if they have heard the term *cyclone.* This term has several meanings. Students may have heard it used informally to mean "tornado." Meteorologists use the term to refer to a low-pressure system, whether or not that system has hurricane-force winds. It is also used to refer to a hurricane in the western Pacific Ocean.

3.2 INSTRUCT

Teach from Visuals

To help students interpret the visual "Structure of a Hurricane," ask:

- How does the size of the hurricane compare to the size of Florida? *It is about the same length, but wider.*

- How would you describe the path of the center of the storm? *began in the Atlantic, moved northwest toward Florida, then headed north, following the eastern coast of the United States*

History of Science

In 1971, engineer Herbert Saffir and meteorologist Dr. Robert Simpson jointly developed a classification system for hurricanes. The Saffir-Simpson hurricane scale ranks hurricanes from 1 to 5, with 5 being the most powerful. Factors such as wind speed, lowest pressure reading, and damage potential contribute to the rankings. A category 1 hurricane causes minimal damage. A category 3 hurricane causes floods and structural damage to small buildings and mobile homes. A category 5 hurricane is considered cata-strophic. Only two category 5 hurricanes have struck the United States, the last being Hurricane Camille in 1969.

Ongoing Assessment

Explain how hurricanes develop.

Ask: How does a low-pressure system develop into a hurricane? *Sample answer: Water evaporates over a warm ocean, moving energy from the ocean to the air. The warm, moist air rises quickly. Tall clouds and strong winds form. The winds blow faster and faster in a spiral around the low-pressure center.*

 CHECK YOUR READING *Answer: warm ocean water*

 READING VISUALS *Answer: land*

 VISUALIZATION CLASSZONE.COM
Watch the progress of a hurricane.

Formation of Hurricanes

In the eastern United States, hurricanes most often strike between August and October. Energy from warm water is necessary for a low-pressure center to build into a tropical storm and then into a hurricane. The ocean water where these storms develop only gets warm enough—26°C (80°F) or more—near the end of summer.

Tropical storms and hurricanes generally move westward with the trade winds. Near land, however, they will often move north, south, or even back eastward. As long as a storm stays above warm water, it can grow bigger and more powerful. As soon as a hurricane moves over land or over cooler water, it loses its source of energy. The winds lose strength and the storm dies out. If a hurricane moves over land, the rough surface of the land reduces the winds even more.

The map below shows the progress of a storm. The tropical storm gained energy and became a hurricane as it moved westward. When the hurricane moved north, the storm lost energy and was called a tropical storm again as its winds slowed.

CHECK YOUR READING What is the source of a hurricane's energy?

Structure of a Hurricane

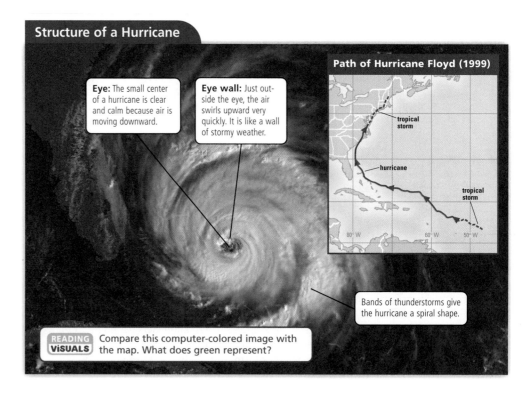

Eye: The small center of a hurricane is clear and calm because air is moving downward.

Eye wall: Just outside the eye, the air swirls upward very quickly. It is like a wall of stormy weather.

Bands of thunderstorms give the hurricane a spiral shape.

Path of Hurricane Floyd (1999)

tropical storm

hurricane

tropical storm

80° W   60° W   50° W

READING VISUALS Compare this computer-colored image with the map. What does green represent?

DIFFERENTIATE INSTRUCTION

? More Reading Support

A When do most hurricanes strike in the United States? *August–October*

B A hurricane begins to lose energy when it moves over what? *land or cooler water*

Additional Investigation To reinforce Section 3.2 learning goals, use the following full-period investigation:

R **Additional INVESTIGATION,** Hurricane Hugo, A, B, & C, pp. 213–221, 284–285
(Advanced students should complete Levels B and C.)

English Learners English learners may need help with the use of *lake effect* on p. 90 as both a noun and an adjective (in *lake-effect snow*). Also, identifying the Great Lakes (p. 90) on a map or globe may supply needed background knowledge.

At the center of a hurricane is a small area of clear weather, 20–50 kilometers (10–30 mi) in diameter, called the eye. The storm's center is calm because air moves downward there. Just around the eye, the air moves very quickly around and upward, forming a tall ring of cumulonimbus clouds called the eye wall. This ring produces very heavy rains and tremendous winds. Farther from the center, bands of heavy clouds and rain spiral inward toward the eye.

Effects of Hurricanes

A hurricane can pound a coast with huge waves and sweep the land with strong winds and heavy rains. The storms cause damage and dangerous conditions in several ways. Hurricane winds can lift cars, uproot trees, and tear the roofs off buildings. Hurricanes may also produce tornadoes that cause even more damage. Heavy rains from hurricanes may make rivers overflow their banks and flood nearby areas. When a hurricane moves into a coastal area, it often pushes a huge mass of ocean water known as a **storm surge.** In a storm surge, the sea level rises several meters, backing up rivers and flooding the shore. A storm surge can be destructive and deadly. Large waves add to the destruction. A hurricane may affect an area for a few hours or a few days, but the damage may take weeks or even months to clean up.

CHECK YOUR READING What are the effects of hurricanes? Make a list for your answer.

The National Hurricane Center helps people know when to prepare for a hurricane. The center puts out a tropical-storm or hurricane watch when a storm is likely to strike within 36 hours. People may be evacuated, or moved away for safety, from areas where they may be in danger. As the danger gets closer—24 hours or less—the center issues a tropical-storm or hurricane warning. The warning stays in effect until the danger has passed.

> ### ⚠ SAFETY TIPS
> #### HURRICANES
> - Before a storm, prepare a plan to leave the area. Gather emergency supplies.
> - Listen to weather reports for storm updates.
> - Secure loose objects outside, and cover windows.
> - If ordered to evacuate, leave immediately.
> - During a storm, stay indoors and away from windows.
> - After a storm, be aware of power lines, hanging branches, and flooded areas.

NORTH CAROLINA

Topsail Island

COMPARE AND CONTRAST These pictures show a shoreline in North Carolina before and after Hurricane Fran in 1996. Compare the houses, road, and water in the two pictures.

Chapter 3: **Weather Fronts and Storms** 89 **D**

DIFFERENTIATE INSTRUCTION

❓ More Reading Support

C What is the calm center of a hurricane called? *the eye*

D A huge mass of ocean water, pushed inland by a hurricane, is called what? *storm surge*

Advanced Students can plot the paths of current or past tropical storms and hurricanes on a map of the Atlantic or Pacific Ocean. They can use symbols or colors to represent different stages of the storms. Ask students to consider the sizes of the storms as well as the locations of their centers.

R
- Challenge and Extension, p. 173
- Challenge Reading, pp. 197–198

Real World Example

Real World Example

The 1983 hurricane that devastated Long Island and southern New England made a 12-day journey across the Atlantic before slamming into the coast. Neither the U.S. Weather Bureau nor the general public knew the storm was coming. Today almost nobody is surprised by a hurricane. In 2003, the National Weather Service began providing hurricane forecasts five days in advance of a storm's arrival. This allows time for people and resources to be moved to safety.

Teacher Demo

Do the following demonstration to help students visualize the relationship between storm surges and floods. Lay a piece of plastic on the floor near a wall. Cut off one short end of a shoebox and place the shoebox on the plastic so that its uncut end is flush against the wall. Put packing peanuts in the box. Tell students that the filled shoebox represents a flowing river. Then pour some more packing peanuts on the plastic in front of the shoebox and, using the cut-off piece of cardboard or your hands, shove the packing peanuts toward the shoebox so that the first pile of packing peanuts is forced back and spill out. Ask: What did the second pile of packing peanuts represent? *a storm surge* What happened to the "river" in this model? *It overflowed its banks.*

Ongoing Assessment

Recognize the dangers from hurricanes.

Ask: What should you do if a hurricane is approaching your area? *Prepare, listen to weather reports, and evacuate if advised. If you remain in your town, stay indoors and away from windows.*

CHECK YOUR READING *Answer: storm surge, strong winds, heavy rains, tornadoes, floods, huge waves*

INVESTIGATE Ice

PURPOSE Observe how salt affects ice to infer why it is put on icy roads.

TIPS *10 min.* Place students in small groups, then suggest the following:

- Use about a teaspoon of salt on one ice cube.
- Place a thin, but complete, layer of salt on the ice.

WHAT DO YOU THINK? *The salted ice melted faster. People put salt on roads to help the ice melt faster so that it will be safer to drive.*

CHALLENGE *Sample answer: Sand and cinders increase traction. In addition, cinders are dark and thus absorb sunlight, which in turn makes the ice melt faster. Students can repeat this experiment using sand or cinders on an ice cube rather than salt. Be sure students test only one variable at a time.*

 Datasheet, Ice, p. 174

Teaching with Technology

Have students check the National Weather Service's Web site for current storm watches and storm warnings for the United States.

Ongoing Assessment

Understand the differences between a winter storm watch and a winter storm warning.

Ask: How does a winter storm watch differ from a winter storm warning? *A watch is further in advance. A warning is more immediate and definite.*

Winter storms produce snow and ice.

Most severe winter storms in the United States are part of low-pressure systems. Unlike hurricanes, the systems that cause winter storms form when two air masses collide. A continental polar air mass that forms over snow-covered ground is especially cold, dry, and dense. It can force moist air to rise very quickly, producing a stormy low-pressure system.

The National Weather Service (NWS) alerts people to dangerous weather. The NWS issues a winter storm watch up to 48 hours before a storm is expected. A winter storm warning means that dangerous conditions are already present or will affect an area shortly.

Blizzards Strong winds can blow so much snow into the air at once that it becomes difficult to see and dangerous to travel. **Blizzards** are blinding snowstorms with winds of at least 56 kilometers per hour (35 mi/h) and low temperatures—usually below –7°C (20°F). Blizzards occur in many parts of the northern and central United States. Wind and snow can knock down trees and power lines. Without heat, buildings can become very cold, and water in pipes may freeze. Schools, hospitals, and businesses may have to close. Deep, heavy snow on top of a building may cause the roof to cave in.

Lake-Effect Snowstorms Some of the heaviest snows fall in the areas just east and south of the Great Lakes. Cold air from the northwest gains moisture and warmth as it passes over the Great Lakes. Over cold land, the air cools again and releases the moisture as snow. The lake effect can cover areas downwind of the Great Lakes with clouds and snow even when the rest of the region has clear weather.

VOCABULARY
Remember to add a word triangle diagram for *blizzard*.

INVESTIGATE Ice

Why put salt on icy roads?

PROCEDURE

1. Place one ice cube in each cup.
2. Sprinkle salt onto the top of one of the ice cubes and observe the cubes for several minutes.

WHAT DO YOU THINK?
- Which ice cube melted more?
- Why do people put salt on roads in winter?

CHALLENGE Why do people put sand or cinders on icy roads? Design an experiment to test your ideas.

SKILL FOCUS
Observing

MATERIALS
- 2 ice cubes
- 2 cups
- table salt

TIME
10 minutes

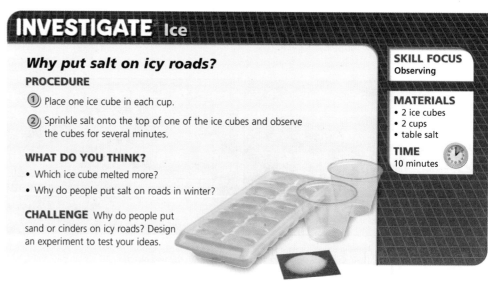

DIFFERENTIATE INSTRUCTION

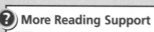

More Reading Support

E What type of weather system may include severe winter storms? *a low-pressure system*

F Where do lake-effect snowstorms occur? *near the Great Lakes*

Below Level When discussing lake-effect snow, display a large map of the Great Lakes area. Read the student text aloud, using the map to point out how cold air from the northwest sweeps over the lakes. Show where the heaviest snows can be expected. *just east and south of the lakes*

Ice Storms When rain falls onto freezing-cold ground, conditions can become dangerous. The cold rain freezes as it touches the ground and other surfaces. This freezing rain covers everything with heavy, smooth ice. The ice-covered roads become slippery and dangerous. Drivers may find it hard to steer and to stop their cars. Branches or even whole trees may break from the weight of ice. Falling branches can block roads, tear down power and telephone lines, and cause other damage. Damage from ice storms can sometimes shut down entire cities.

 CHECK YOUR READING What type of precipitation occurs in each type of winter storm?

3.2 Review

KEY CONCEPTS

1. Where and when do hurricanes form?

2. In what two ways can hurricanes cause floods?

3. List three of the possible dangers from winter storms.

CRITICAL THINKING

4. **Compare and Contrast** What are the differences between the eye and the eye wall of a hurricane?

5. **Compare** What do hurricanes and winter storms have in common?

❶ CHALLENGE

6. **Apply** If the wind is blowing from the west and the conditions are right for lake-effect snow, will the snow fall to the north, south, east, or west of a lake? Drawing a diagram may help you work out an answer.

ANSWERS

1. Hurricanes form over warm ocean water near the equator. They typically form in late summer from August to October.

2. Heavy rains can cause rivers to overflow their banks. Storm surges can flood coastal areas.

3. Sample answer: slippery roads, fallen power lines, caved-in buildings

4. Air in the eye is moving downward and is calm. Air in the stormy eye wall is swirling rapidly upward.

5. Both are low-pressure systems associated with stormy weather.

6. The snow will fall to the east of the lake.

Ongoing Assessment

Compare the different types of winter storms.

Ask: What causes most winter storms? *weather systems that form when two air masses collide*

 CHECK YOUR READING *Answer: blizzards: heavy snow; lake-effect snow: snow; ice storms: freezing rain*

Reinforce (the **BIG** idea)

Have students relate the section to the Big Idea.

 R Reinforcing Key Concepts, p. 175

3.2 ASSESS & RETEACH

Assess

A Section 3.2 Quiz, p. 44

Reteach

Place students in small groups and have them develop an emergency plan for their town in the event of severe weather. Students can play the role of local officials. They should consider the effects of a type of storm likely to affect their area and should decide how to protect and assist residents, protect public property, and restore services after the storm. Encourage students to be creative. They can write press releases or conduct a press conference, describing the storm and what actions will be taken when a powerful storm strikes.

Technology Resources

Have students visit **ClassZone.com** for reteaching of Key Concepts.

 CONTENT REVIEW

 CONTENT REVIEW CD-ROM

Set Learning Goals

Students will

• Explain how thunderstorms develop.
• Describe the effects of thunderstorms.
• Describe tornadoes and their effects.
• Infer through experimentation why updrafts form.

3-Minute Warm-Up

Display Transparency 21 or copy this exercise on the board.

What type of clouds often form at a cold front? Draw a diagram to show how this happens. *Cumulonimbus clouds form along cold fronts. Diagrams should resemble the first visual on p. 83 and depict a cross-section view of a cold front pushing warm, humid air upward into a cumulonimbus cloud.*

 3-Minute Warm-Up, p. T21

3.3 MOTIVATE

EXPLORE Lightning

PURPOSE To introduce the link between lightning and thunder

TIP *10 min.* A sticky note or a small piece of the tray, glued or taped to the foil, can be used as a substitute for the eraser.

WHAT DO YOU THINK? *There was a small flash and a faint snap. The snap modeled miniature thunder.*

Ongoing Assessment

 Answer: Thunder is an effect of lightning.

KEY CONCEPT

3.3 Vertical air motion can cause severe storms.

 BEFORE, you learned

• Fronts produce changes in weather
• Rising moist air can produce clouds and precipitation

 NOW, you will learn

• How thunderstorms develop
• About the effects of thunderstorms
• About tornadoes and their effects

VOCABULARY

thunderstorm p. 92
tornado p. 95

EXPLORE Lightning

Does miniature lightning cause thunder?

PROCEDURE

1. Use a thumbtack to attach the eraser to the center of a piece of foil.
2. Rub the foam tray quickly back and forth several times on the wool. Set the tray down.
3. Using the eraser as a handle, pick up the foil and set it onto the tray. Slowly move your finger close to the foil.

WHAT DO YOU THINK?
What happened when you touched the foil?

MATERIALS

• thumbtack
• eraser
• aluminum foil
• plastic foam tray
• wool fabric

Thunderstorms form from rising moist air.

If you have ever shuffled your shoes on a carpet, you may have felt a small shock when you touched a doorknob. Electrical charges collected on your body and then jumped to the doorknob in a spark of electricity.

In a similar way, electrical charges build up near the tops and bottoms of clouds as pellets of ice move up and down through the clouds. Suddenly, a charge sparks from one part of a cloud to another or between a cloud and the ground. The spark of electricity, called lightning, causes a bright flash of light. The air around the lightning is briefly heated to a temperature hotter than the surface of the Sun. This fast heating produces a sharp wave of air that travels away from the lightning. When the wave reaches you, you hear it as a crack of thunder. A **thunderstorm** is a storm with lightning and thunder.

 Is thunder a cause or an effect of lightning?

 VOCABULARY
Put new terms into a word triangle diagram.

RESOURCES FOR DIFFERENTIATED INSTRUCTION

Below Level
UNIT RESOURCE BOOK
• Reading Study Guide A, pp. 178–181
• Decoding Support, p. 201

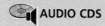 **AUDIO CDS**

Advanced
UNIT RESOURCE BOOK
Challenge and Extension, p. 184

English Learners
UNIT RESOURCE BOOK
Spanish Reading Study Guide, pp. 182–183

 **AUDIO CDS**

• Audio Readings in Spanish
• Audio Readings (English)

Formation of Thunderstorms

A

Thunderstorms get their energy from humid air. When warm, humid air near the ground moves vertically into cooler air above, the rising air, or updraft, can build a thunderstorm quickly.

B

❶ Rising humid air forms a cumulus cloud. The water vapor releases energy when it condenses into cloud droplets. This energy increases the air motion. The cloud continues building up into the tall cumulonimbus cloud of a thunderstorm.

❷ Ice particles form in the low temperatures near the top of the cloud. As the ice particles grow large, they begin to fall and pull cold air down with them. This strong downdraft brings heavy rain or hail—the most severe stage of a thunderstorm.

❸ The downdraft can spread out and block more warm air from moving upward into the cloud. The storm slows down and ends.

Thunderstorms can form at a cold front or within an air mass. At a cold front, air can be forced upward quickly. Within an air mass, uneven heating can produce convection and thunderstorms. In some regions, the conditions that produce thunderstorms occur almost daily during part of the year. In Florida, for example, the wet land and air warm up during a long summer day. Then, as you see in the diagram, cool sea breezes blow in from both coasts of the peninsula at once. The two sea breezes together push the warm, humid air over the land upward quickly. Thunderstorms form in the rising air.

In contrast, the summer air along the coast of California is usually too dry to produce thunderstorms. The air over the land heats up, and a sea breeze forms, but there is not enough moisture in the rising warm air to form clouds and precipitation.

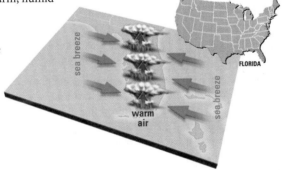

sea breeze | sea breeze | warm air | FLORIDA

Teach from Visuals

To help students interpret the visual on thunderstorm formation, ask:

- Which diagram shows the most severe stage of a thunderstorm? *diagram 2*
- Compare the first two stages. Why does the cloud become tall? *air moves upward*

Address Misconceptions

IDENTIFY Ask: If a building is struck by lightning, is it safe from lightning in the future? If students answer "yes," they may hold the misconception that lightning never strikes the same place twice.

CORRECT Tell students that lightning tends to strike the highest features in a given location, such as lone trees or flagpoles.

REASSESS Ask: If these tall features aren't destroyed by lightning, will they be struck again? Why? *They will be struck again because if they aren't destroyed, they'll still be the highest features in a given location.*

Technology Resources

Visit **ClassZone.com** for background on common student misconceptions.

 MISCONCEPTION DATABASE

Ongoing Assessment

Explain how thunderstorms develop.

Ask students to describe the three stages of thunderstorm development. *Stage 1: rising air forms a cumulonimbus cloud; stage 2: falling ice particles form downdrafts and heavy precipitation; stage 3: downdrafts spread out, updrafts stop, and the storm dies out.*

DIFFERENTIATE INSTRUCTION

? More Reading Support

A Where do thunderstorms get their energy from? *humid air*

B What air motion produces thunderstorms? *rising air*

English Learners English learners may need help with the following uses of terms: "*crack* of thunder" on p. 92 (not like a *crack in a wall*); "winds *once* knocked down" on p. 94 (as in "at a time in the past," not to be confused with something that happens "one time"); the use of *may* and *might* on p. 96 to indicate examples or typical results.

INVESTIGATE Updrafts

PURPOSE Observe the motion of heated water to infer how updrafts form.

TIP *20 min.* Use the 5th cup to hold 2 drops of food coloring. Make sure students are careful adding the coloring.

WHAT DO YOU THINK? *The water above the cup of hot water was heated, became less dense, and moved upward. Just as the heated water rose, heated air in a thunderstorm rises.*

CHALLENGE *Sample answer: Observe the motion of leaves, dust, or smoke in the air.*

 Datasheet, Updrafts, p. 185

Technology Resources

Customize this student lab as needed or look for an alternative. Print rubrics to assess student lab reports.

 Lab Generator CD-ROM

Ongoing Assessment

Describe the effects of thunderstorms.

Ask: How can rain from thunderstorms be dangerous and cause damage?
Heavy rain can cause floods, which can wash away people and objects.

CHECK YOUR READING *Answer: The effects of thunderstorms include flash floods, winds, hail, and lightning. Students will vary on which effects they find surprising.*

INVESTIGATE Updrafts

How do updrafts form?

PROCEDURE

1. Set up the cardboard, the cups, the container, and the cool water as shown in the photograph. Wait for the water to become still.

2. Use the eyedropper to place 2–3 drops of coloring at the bottom of the water.

3. Slide a cup of hot water (about 70°C) beneath the food coloring.

WHAT DO YOU THINK?

In what ways was the motion of the water like the air in a thunderstorm?

CHALLENGE How could you observe updrafts in air?

SKILL FOCUS
Inferring

MATERIALS
• 4 cardboard squares
• 5 foam cups
• clear container
• cool water
• food coloring
• eyedropper
• hot tap water

TIME
20 minutes

Effects of Thunderstorms

A thunderstorm may provide cool rain at the end of a hot, dry spell. The rain can provide water for crops and restore lakes and streams. However, thunderstorms are often dangerous.

Flash floods can be strong enough to wash away people, cars, and even houses. One thunderstorm can produce millions of liters of rain. If a thunderstorm dumps all its rain in one place, or if a series of thunderstorms dump rain onto the same area, the water can cover the ground or make rivers overflow their banks.

Winds from a thunderstorm can be very strong. They can blow in bursts that exceed 270 kilometers per hour (170 mi/hr). Thunderstorm winds once knocked down a stretch of forest in Canada that was about 16 kilometers (10 mi) wide and 80 kilometers (50 mi) long. Thunderstorms can also produce sudden, dangerous bursts of air that move downward and spread out.

Hail causes nearly $1 billion in damage to property and crops in the United States every year. Hail can wipe out entire fields of a valuable crop in a few minutes. Large hailstones can damage roofs and kill livestock.

Lightning can kill or seriously injure any person it hits. It can damage power lines and other equipment. Lightning can also spark dangerous forest fires.

CHECK YOUR READING In what ways are thunderstorms dangerous? Did any surprise you?

SAFETY TIPS
THUNDERSTORMS

• Stay alert when storms are predicted or dark, tall clouds are visible.

• If you hear thunder, seek shelter immediately and stay there for 30 minutes after the last thunder ends.

• Avoid bodies of water, lone trees, flagpoles, and metal objects.

• Stay away from the telephone, electrical appliances, and pipes.

• If flash floods are expected, move away from low ground.

• Do not try to cross flowing water, even if it looks shallow.

DIFFERENTIATE INSTRUCTION

? **More Reading Support**

C Does a flash flood happen quickly or slowly?
quickly

D What should you do when you hear thunder?
seek shelter immediately

Tornadoes form in severe thunderstorms.

E

Under some conditions, the up-and-down air motion that produces tall clouds, lightning, and hail may produce a tornado. A **tornado** is a violently rotating column of air stretching from a cloud to the ground. A tornado moves along the ground in a winding path underneath the cloud. The column may even rise off the ground and then come down in a different place.

READING TiP

A spinning column of air is not called a tornado unless it touches the ground. If it touches water instead, it is called a waterspout.

You cannot see air moving. A tornado may become visible when water droplets appear below the cloud in the center of the rotating column. A tornado may lift dust and debris from the ground, so the bottom of the column becomes visible, as you see in the photographs below. Water droplets and debris may make a tornado look like an upright column or a twisted rope.

CHECK YOUR READING What makes a tornado become visible?

F

More tornadoes occur in North America than anywhere else in the world. Warm, humid air masses move north from the Gulf of Mexico to the central plains of the United States. There, the warm air masses often meet cold, dense air and form thunderstorms. In the spring, the winds in this region often produce the conditions that form tornadoes. A thunderstorm may form a series of tornadoes or even a group of tornadoes all at once.

Tornado Formation

As a tornado forms, a funnel cloud seems to stretch down from the cloud above.

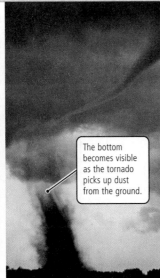

The bottom becomes visible as the tornado picks up dust from the ground.

The tornado moves along the ground before it dies out.

Chapter 3: **Weather Fronts and Storms** 95 **D**

DIFFERENTIATE INSTRUCTION

More Reading Support

E What type of storm may produce a tornado? *a thunderstorm*

F Where do a lot of tornadoes occur? *in North America*

Advanced Have interested students develop a storm-safety plan for the class. They might examine existing procedures, review safety advice from the Federal Emergency Management Agency, and look at tips and survivor stories on the National Weather Service's Web site.

R Challenge and Extension, p. 184

Real World Example

The National Skywarn Program is a network of trained severe storm spotters. Organized by the National Weather Service (NWS), the network is made up of amateur weather enthusiasts, who keep a watch on the sky and immediately report dangerous conditions to their nearest NWS office. The network is particularly useful for tornadoes, which can develop so quickly that even the most advanced technology can't predict when and where they'll strike. In such cases, a reliable eyewitness report may save the lives of hundreds of people in the path of the twister.

Teach from Visuals

Help students notice the less visible parts of the tornado by having them trace the tornado's column in each photograph with their finger. The column curves slightly to the left as the funnel extends down to the slight disturbance on the ground in the first photograph, to the left and then down to the dark bottom in the second photograph; and almost straight down the center in the third photograph.

Ongoing Assessment

CHECK YOUR READING *Answer: water droplets in the center of the rotating column and dust and debris from ground*

Describe tornadoes and their effects.

Ask: One percent of tornadoes are very violent—what kind of damage can they do? *Answer: They can lift or completely demolish sturdy buildings.*

EXPLORE (the BIG idea)

Revisit "Internet Activity: Weather Safety" on p. 77. Have students explain their observations.

Reinforce (the BIG idea)

Have students relate the section to the Big Idea.

 Reinforcing Key Concepts, p. 186

3.3 ASSESS & RETEACH

Assess

 Section 3.3 Quiz, p. 45

Reteach

Tell students to imagine they work for the National Skywarn Program. It is their job to notify the National Weather Service when dangerous conditions develop. Tell them you will describe several weather conditions, and they can choose one of three options in response: Continue normal activities, closely monitor the weather, notify the NWS immediately.

Then give students the following scenarios:

• A cold front is approaching. *Monitor the weather closely.*

• A funnel cloud is spotted. *Notify the NWS immediately.*

• A high-pressure system has developed. *Continue normal activities.*

Technology Resources

Have students visit **ClassZone.com** for reteaching of Key Concepts.

 CONTENT REVIEW

 CONTENT REVIEW CD-ROM

Effects of Tornadoes

The powerful winds of a tornado can cause damage as the bottom of the tornado moves along the ground. Tornado winds can also pick up and slam dirt and small objects into buildings or anything else in the tornado's path.

The most common tornadoes are small and last only a few minutes. Their winds may be strong enough to break branches off trees, damage chimneys, and tear highway billboards. A typical path along the ground may be 100 meters (300 ft) wide and 1.5 kilometers (1 mi) long.

Larger tornadoes are less common but have stronger winds and last longer. About 20 percent of tornadoes are strong enough to knock over large trees, lift cars off the ground, and tear the roofs off houses. Very few—about 1 percent of all tornadoes—are violent enough to lift or completely demolish sturdy buildings. These huge tornadoes may last more than two hours. You can find more details about tornadoes in the Appendix at the back of this book.

A tornado moves along with its thunderstorm. It travels at the same pace and weaves a path that is impossible to predict. A tornado may appear suddenly and then disappear before anyone has time to report it. However, the conditions that form tornadoes may persist, so citizens' reports are still useful. The National Weather Service issues a tornado watch when the weather conditions might produce tornadoes. A tornado warning is issued when a tornado has been detected.

⚠ SAFETY TIPS

TORNADOES

• Listen for tornado warnings when severe weather is predicted.

• If you are in a car or mobile home, get out and go into a sturdy building or a ditch or depression.

• Go to the basement if possible.

• Avoid windows and open areas.

• Protect your head and neck.

3.3 Review

KEY CONCEPTS

1. What conditions produce thunderstorms?

2. How can rain from thunderstorms become dangerous?

3. How do tornadoes cause damage?

CRITICAL THINKING

4. **Compare** What do hail and tornadoes have in common? Hint: Think about how each forms.

5. **Synthesize** Which type of front is most likely to produce thunderstorms and tornadoes? Explain why.

⊘ CHALLENGE

6. **Compare and Contrast** If you saw the photograph above in a newspaper, what details would tell you that the damage was due to a tornado and not a hurricane?

ANSWERS

1. Warm, humid air near the ground moves into cooler air above and rises quickly.

2. If one thunderstorm dumps all of its rain in one place or if a series of thunderstorms dump rain over one area, floods can develop.

3. Winds can break branches off trees, damage chimneys, and tear roofs off houses.

4. Both start from the up-and-down motion in a storm.

5. The warm air at a cold front rises quickly, so it is likely to produce thunderstorms and tornadoes.

6. Some of the houses in the photograph are untouched. There's a small path of destruction, which is indicative of a tornado.

Think SCIENCE

SKILL: EVALUATING HYPOTHESES

What Type of Weather Buried This Truck?

This picture was taken soon after a weather event partly buried this truck in Britannia Beach, British Columbia.

◗ Observations and Inferences

One observer made this analysis.

a. The truck, the tree, and two fences in the background were partly buried by sand and stones.

b. No stones are visible inside the truck.

c. The rounded stones must have come from an ocean or river.

d. The tree near the truck has green leaves. The wind must have been too weak to tear off the leaves.

e. The area is near the Pacific Ocean. It is far from the equator. There is a very large island between the location and the ocean.

◗ Hypotheses

The observer made the following hypotheses.

a. A storm surge carried sand and stones from the Pacific Ocean. The material covered a large area. The truck floated, so it was not filled with material.

b. A tornado picked up the truck with other material. It dumped everything together, and the material partly buried the truck, fences, and tree.

c. Thunderstorms produced a flash flood that carried sand and stones from a riverbed to this area. The flood receded and left material that covered the area.

d. The truck was parked on a pile of snow during a blizzard. When the snow melted, the area under the truck collapsed and the truck sank into the ground.

◗ Evaluate Each Hypothesis

Review each hypothesis and think about whether the observations support it. Some facts may rule out some hypotheses. Some facts may neither support nor weaken some hypotheses.

CHALLENGE How could you model one or more of the hypotheses with a toy truck, sand, and a basin of water?

BRITISH COLUMBIA

Britannia Beach

A waterway leads south and west from Britannia Beach to a bay, around an island, to the Pacific Ocean.

ANSWERS

HYPOTHESIS a Not reasonable. The large island would have likely lessened the surge.

HYPOTHESIS b Not reasonable. The truck would have stones on top as well as inside if all the debris was dumped together.

HYPOTHESIS c Reasonable. No observations contradict this hypothesis.

HYPOTHESIS d Not reasonable. The leaves on the trees indicate that it is not winter. Plus, a truck is not heavy enough to sink into stone-covered ground.

CHALLENGE Sample answer: To model a flash flood you could observe how the sand settles around the truck to see if your hypothesis is supported.

Set Learning Goal

To evaluate hypotheses by checking them against observations and inferences

Present the Science

The Canadian city of Britannia Beach, British Columbia, is located by Howe Sound, a wide channel of water on the west coast that connects to the Pacific Ocean. Britannia Beach is close to the city of Vancouver.

The flash flood that buried this truck is the type that strikes low lying areas near a water channel, stream, or river. This flood of water can uproot trees, tear down buildings, and pull down bridges and dams.

Guide the Activity

- Remind students that an inference is a conclusion based on observations. Ask them to give an example of an inference on the part of the observer. *Example: The wind must have been too weak to tear off the leaves.*

- Encourage students to use the visuals to make their own observations and inferences.

- Suggest that students review the different types of weather to see what information applies to this event. For example, a hurricane would probably lose energy as it moved over the cool water far from the equator.

- Students might make a table to compare each observation and inference to each hypothesis.

COOPERATIVE LEARNING STRATEGY
Have students work in groups of four to analyze the hypotheses. Afterwards, each student in the group should provide a brief explanation of why the group either accepted or rejected a particular hypothesis.

Close

Ask: Which hypothesis did you find least convincing? Why? *The first, because the island would block a storm surge.*

Set Learning Goals

Students will

- Explain the different ways weather data is collected.
- Explain how different types of weather data are displayed.
- Describe how meteorologists forecast the weather.

3-Minute Warm-Up

Display Transparency 21 or copy this exercise on the board:

Fill in the blank with the correct word.

1. The boundary between two air masses is called a _____. *front*

2. Stormy weather is often associated with _____ pressure systems. *low-*

3. Calm, clear weather is usually associated with _____ pressure systems. *high-*

 3-Minute Warm-Up, p. T21

 MOTIVATE

EXPLORE Weather Maps

PURPOSE To interpret symbols on a weather map and relate a weather forecast to actual weather conditions

TIP *10 min.* Large-circulation newspapers generally have the most detailed weather maps. You can also print out weather maps from the Internet, using the Web sites of local television stations or the National Weather Service.

WHAT DO YOU THINK? *Warm fronts, cold fronts, high- and low-pressure systems. Short-term weather forecasts should be comparable to actual weather conditions.*

Ongoing Assessment

 *Answer: weather conditions in the region around you and forecasts*

KEY CONCEPT

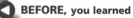

3.4 Weather forecasters use advanced technologies.

◀ BEFORE, you learned

- Weather changes when air masses move
- High-pressure systems bring fair weather
- Fronts and low-pressure systems bring stormy weather

▶ NOW, you will learn

- How weather data are collected
- How weather data are displayed
- How meteorologists forecast the weather

VOCABULARY

meteorologist p. 98
isobar p. 101

EXPLORE Weather Maps

What does a weather map show?

PROCEDURE

1. Look at the weather outside. Write down the conditions you observe.

2. Use the map to check the weather conditions for your region.

MATERIALS

newspaper
weather map

WHAT DO YOU THINK?

- What symbols on the map do you recognize?
- How does the information on the weather map compare with the weather you observed outside?

VOCABULARY
Make a word triangle for *meteorologist*.

Weather data come from many sources.

Looking at the weather outside in the morning can help you decide what to wear. Different things give you clues to the current weather. If you see plants swaying from side to side, you might infer that it is windy. If you see a gray sky and wet, shiny streets, you might decide to wear a raincoat.

You might also check a weather report to get more information. A weather report can show conditions in your area and also in the region around you. You can look for weather nearby that might move into your area during the day. More detailed predictions of how the weather will move and change may be included in a weather report by a meteorologist. A **meteorologist** (MEE-tee-uh-RAHL-uh-jihst) is a scientist who studies weather.

 CHECK YOUR READING What information can a weather report show?

RESOURCES FOR DIFFERENTIATED INSTRUCTION

Below Level

UNIT RESOURCE BOOK
- Reading Study Guide A, pp. 189–190
- Decoding Support, p. 201

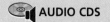 AUDIO CDS

Advanced

UNIT RESOURCE BOOK
Challenge and Extension, p. 195

English Learners

UNIT RESOURCE BOOK
Spanish Reading Study Guide, pp. 193–194

AUDIO CDS

- Audio Readings in Spanish
- Audio Readings (English)

In order to predict the weather, meteorologists look at past and current conditions. They use many forms of technology to gather data. The illustration below shows how weather information is gathered. For example, radar stations and satellites use advanced technologies to gather data for large areas at a time.

Instruments within the atmosphere can make measurements of local weather conditions. Newer instruments can make measurements frequently and automatically and then report the results almost instantly. Instruments are placed in many ground stations on land and weather buoys at sea. Instruments can also be carried by balloons, ships, and planes. These instruments report a series of measurements along a path within the atmosphere.

RESOURCE CENTER
CLASSZONE.COM

Learn more about weather forecasting and your local weather.

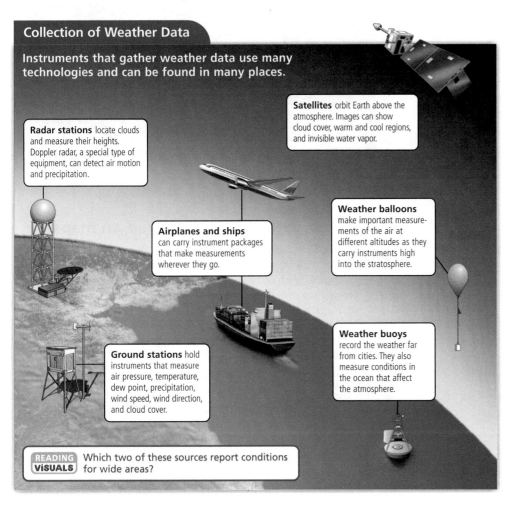

Collection of Weather Data

Instruments that gather weather data use many technologies and can be found in many places.

Radar stations locate clouds and measure their heights. Doppler radar, a special type of equipment, can detect air motion and precipitation.

Satellites orbit Earth above the atmosphere. Images can show cloud cover, warm and cool regions, and invisible water vapor.

Airplanes and ships can carry instrument packages that make measurements wherever they go.

Weather balloons make important measurements of the air at different altitudes as they carry instruments high into the stratosphere.

Ground stations hold instruments that measure air pressure, temperature, dew point, precipitation, wind speed, wind direction, and cloud cover.

Weather buoys record the weather far from cities. They also measure conditions in the ocean that affect the atmosphere.

READING VISUALS Which two of these sources report conditions for wide areas?

Chapter 3: **Weather Fronts and Storms** 99 **D**

DIFFERENTIATE INSTRUCTION

More Reading Support

A Meteorologists look at past conditions to do what? *predict weather*

B Which instruments get data for large areas? *radar stations, satellites*

English Learners English learners may not have prior knowledge of *Doppler Radar,* p. 100, and *scale and interval* on p. 105. On this page, students may need further explanation of weather balloons and weather buoys. Invite students to look for the devices on the Internet or in other reference sources to find definitions and pictures.

Develop Critical Thinking

APPLY Have students apply what they read about weather instruments in earlier chapters. Ask them to describe which type of instruments might be found in a ground station, and what these instruments measure. *Sample answer: thermometers to measure temperature, barometers to measure air pressure, rain gauges to measure precipitation, and wind vanes to determine wind direction*

Integrate the Sciences

Doppler radar is based on the Doppler effect, which is a change in the frequency of sound or electromagnetic waves. In meteorology, radio waves are "bounced off" rain drops; the scattered waves are picked up by receivers, and computers then calculate the distance and speed of the approaching storm. In astronomy the Doppler effect is used to analyze the motion of galaxies moving away from each other. This is evidence that the universe is expanding.

Teach from Visuals

To help students interpret the visual of weather data instruments, ask:

• Which instrument would you use to find the height of clouds? *radar*

• Which instrument could give you information on ocean conditions? *weather buoys*

• What type of information do ground stations gather? *air pressure, temperature, dew point, precipitation, wind speed, wind direction, cloud cover*

Ongoing Assessment

Explain the different ways weather data is collected.

Ask: What types of weather data are collected by satellites? *information about cloud cover, warm and cool regions, and water vapor*

READING VISUALS *Answer: radar stations, satellites*

Teach from Visuals

To help students interpret the "Information on a Weather Map" visual, ask:

- What type of pressure system is located off the east coast? *low-pressure system*
- Notice the front associated with this system—is it the same throughout? *No; the very northern part of the front is stationary while the remainder is a cold front.*
- Study the Station Symbol. How much of the circle is filled to show cloud cover? *all of it* If cloud cover were 50%, what fraction of the circle would be filled? *one-half*

Mathematics Connection

Tell students that the cloud-cover part of a station symbol is a modified circle graph. Fractions of 0, 1/4, 1/2, and 3/4 are shown in the usual way. A fraction that is 1/8 more than one of these has a small bar added to the appropriate symbol. The bar makes the symbol easier to read when it is small. Provide students with some symbols that have different amounts of cloud cover. Then have students calculate the decimal fraction that corresponds to each symbol. Have them provide the exact fraction (such as 0.375 for a cloud cover of 3/8) and then round to one decimal place to approximate the cloud cover (0.4 in this case).

Symbols and decimal equivalents are in the Appendix.

Ongoing Assessment

Explain how different types of weather data are displayed.

Ask students to explain how precipitation is displayed on a weather map. *Different colors indicate amounts of precipitation.*

CHECK YOUR READING *Answer: Information is shown by symbols and colored areas on maps.*

Information on a Weather Map

Meteorologists use maps to display a lot of weather information at once.

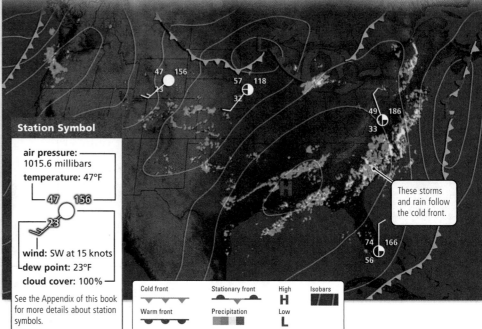

These storms and rain follow the cold front.

Station Symbol

air pressure: 1015.6 millibars
temperature: 47°F

wind: SW at 15 knots
dew point: 23°F
cloud cover: 100%

See the Appendix of this book for more details about station symbols.

| Cold front | Stationary front | High **H** | Isobars |
| Warm front | Precipitation | Low **L** | |

Weather data can be displayed on maps.

MAIN IDEA WEB
Add to your notebook information about weather data.

Automatic measurements from many sources constantly pour in to the National Oceanic and Atmospheric Administration. Scientists use computers to record and use the enormous amount of data gathered. One way to make the information easier to understand is to show it on maps. A single map can show many different types of data together to give a more complete picture of the weather. The map above combines information from ground stations with Doppler radar measurements of precipitation.

- Precipitation is shown as patches of blue, green, yellow, and red. The colors indicate the amounts of rain or other precipitation.
- Station symbols on the map show data from ground stations. Only a few stations are shown.
- Symbols showing fronts and pressure patterns are added to the map to make the overall weather patterns easier to see.

CHECK YOUR READING How is information from Doppler radar shown?

DIFFERENTIATE INSTRUCTION

? More Reading Support

C What organization gathers weather data from many sources? *National Oceanic and Atmospheric Administration*

Below Level Have students search the National Weather Service Web site or newspapers for examples of different weather maps and images. Have them orally describe the data on the maps.

Computer programs are used to combine information from many ground stations. The resulting calculations give the highs, lows, and fronts that are marked on the map. The cold front near the East Coast has triangles to show that the front is moving eastward. This cold front produced the heavy rain that is visible in the Doppler radar data.

Air Pressure on Weather Maps

The map below shows conditions from the same date as the map on page 100. Thin lines represent air pressure. An **isobar** (EYE-suh-BAHR) is a line that connects places that have the same air pressure. Each isobar represents a different air pressure value. All the isobars together, combined with the symbols for highs and lows, show the patterns of air pressure that produce weather systems.

Each isobar is labeled with the air pressure for that whole line in units called millibars (MIHL-uh-BAHRZ). A lower number means a lower air pressure. As you read earlier, differences in pressure cause air to move. Meteorologists use isobars to understand air motion.

Sometimes air-pressure measurements are listed in inches of mercury. This unit comes from an old type of barometer that measures how high the air pressure pushes a column of mercury, a liquid metal. Computer-controlled instruments are used more often today, but the measurements may be converted to inches of mercury.

> **READING TiP**
> Iso- means "equal," and bar means "pressure."

Understanding Isobars

Isobars show pressure patterns, which determine winds.

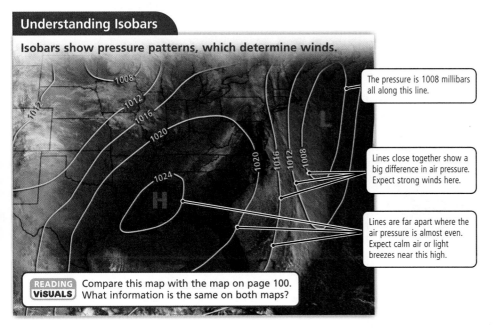

The pressure is 1008 millibars all along this line.

Lines close together show a big difference in air pressure. Expect strong winds here.

Lines are far apart where the air pressure is almost even. Expect calm air or light breezes near this high.

> **READING VISUALS** Compare this map with the map on page 100. What information is the same on both maps?

To help students better understand isobars, tell them that the prefix *iso-* comes from the Greek word *isos*, which means equal. Explain that scientists often use lines that connect points of equal values on maps. Isotherms, for example, are lines that connect points of equal temperature. Use the following demonstration to help students relate the information to similar maps.

Teacher Demo

Show students a topographic map. Ask: What do contour lines show? *points of equal elevation* Next, draw three closed contour lines on the board to make a topographic map of a hill. Label the largest, outside circle 240 km. Label the middle circle 260 km. Label the innermost circle 280 km. Inside the innermost circle, write the elevation 300 km. Ask: If this were a map that showed isobars, would it represent a high- or low-pressure system? Explain. *It would represent a high-pressure system because the numbers get progressively larger.*

Teach from Visuals

To help students interpret the visual, point out that isobars are closed. Closed isobars generally are found in well-developed pressure systems. Ask: Which center appears to be developing into a well-organized system? *the low center*

Teaching with Technology

Have students view annotated maps to see weather changes.

Ongoing Assessment

> **READING VISUALS** *Answer: H, L, isobars*

DIFFERENTIATE INSTRUCTION

More Reading Support

D Which type of weather measurement is shown by isobars on a map? *air pressure*

Advanced Have students compile information to make a station symbol that demonstrates local weather at a particular time. Once outside, they can approximate cloud cover and use a barometer and thermometer to find air pressure and temperature. Help them use a compass to determine wind direction. You can supplement this activity and fill in the holes (such as wind speed and dew point) by checking a weather map from a local newspaper, or by having students look for local weather information on the Internet.

R Challenge and Extension, p. 195

Satellite Images

Visible Light

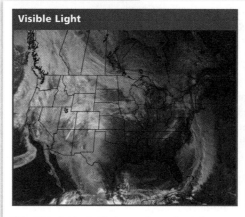

This visible-light satellite image shows clouds from above. The patches of white are clouds.

Infrared Radiation

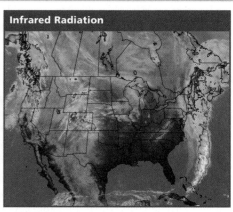

This infrared satellite image also shows clouds, but uses colors to show where there are tall clouds.

READING VISUALS Find a location on these maps and the map on page 100. What were the weather conditions?

Satellite Images and Special Maps

Satellites take different types of images from space. Some images record the visible light that reflects off clouds and Earth's surface. Clouds and snow-covered land look white in sunlight. Unfortunately, visible-light images do not show much at night.

Another type of image shows infrared radiation given off by the warm surface and cooler clouds. These infrared images can show cloud patterns even at night because objects with different temperatures show up differently. Air temperatures change with altitude, so infrared images also show which clouds are low and which are high or tall. You can see in the maps above how visible and infrared satellite images show similar clouds but different details. Outlines of the states have been added to make the images easier to understand.

Data from ground stations and other sources can be used to make other types of maps. The map at left shows the pattern of temperatures on the same date as the images above and the map on page 100. Other maps may show winds or amounts of pollution. A map can be made to show any type of measurement or weather prediction. Different types of maps are often used together to give a more complete picture of the current weather.

CHECK YOUR READING Why would a weather report show more than one map?

The colors on this map represent different ranges of temperature (°F).

? E

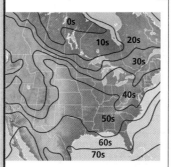

DIFFERENTIATE INSTRUCTION

? More Reading Support

E Which type of image shows cloud patterns at night? *infrared image*

Alternative Assessment Have students find different types of maps, using newspapers, television, or the Internet as resources. Then have them make charts listing all the maps found and what each one demonstrates. Have students write a brief paragraph comparing and contrasting the different maps. What are the benefits and limitations of each? Which one displays the most information?

Forecasters use computer models to predict weather.

Instruments can only measure the current weather conditions. Most people want to know what the weather will be like in the future.

Forecasters can make some predictions from their own observations. If they see cirrus clouds above and high stratus clouds to the west, they might infer that a warm front is approaching. They would predict weather typical for a warm front—more clouds, then rain, and eventually warmer weather. If they also have information from other places, the forecasters might be able to tell where the warm front is already and how fast it is moving. They might be able to predict how soon it will arrive and even how warm the weather will be after the front passes.

Computers have become an important tool for forecasting weather. When weather stations send in data, computers can create maps right away. Computer models combine many types of data to forecast what might happen next. Different computer models give different types of forecasts. Scientists study the computer forecasts, then apply their knowledge and experience to make weather predictions.

Forecasting the weather is complicated. As a result, some forecasts are more dependable than others. The farther in advance a forecast is made, the more time there is for small differences between the predicted and the actual weather to add up. For this reason, short-range forecasts—up to three days in advance—are the most accurate. Forecasts of fast-changing weather, such as severe storms, are less accurate far in advance. It is best to watch for new predictions close to the time the storm is forecast.

Forecasters use maps and satellite images to communicate weather conditions and predictions.

3.4 Review

KEY CONCEPTS

1. List three of the sources of weather data.
2. What does a map with isobars show?
3. How do meteorologists use computers?

CRITICAL THINKING

4. **Draw Conclusions** Why do meteorologists not combine all their weather information into one map?
5. **Analyze** How is the information from radar and satellites different from the information from ground stations?

CHALLENGE

6. **Apply** Suppose you are planning an afternoon picnic a week in advance. Fair weather is forecast for that day, but a storm is expected that night. What will you do? Explain your reasoning.

ANSWERS

1. Accept any three of the following: satellites, radar stations, instruments on weather balloons and ships, ground stations.

2. patterns of pressure

3. to collect, organize, and display data, and to predict weather

4. There is too much information to display on one map—it would be very difficult to read and interpret the map.

5. Radar and satellites gather data for large areas at a time; ground stations report conditions for one specific place.

6. Have a rain date or sheltered space. Stormy weather can change quickly.

Ongoing Assessment

Describe how meteorologists forecast the weather.

Ask: How do observations help meteorologists forecast the weather? *Meteorologists might observe clouds or weather conditions to infer that a front is approaching or use observations that have been collected and displayed on maps.*

Reinforce (the **BIG** idea)

Have students relate the section to the Big Idea.

 Reinforcing Key Concepts, p. 196

3.4 ASSESS & RETEACH

Assess

 Section 3.4 Quiz, p. 46

Reteach

Divide students into pairs. Photocopy a weather map from a national news source and distribute a copy to each group. Try to use a map that has a lot of information on it. If possible, use one with station symbols. Ask students what information the map tells them. Make a list of their responses on the board. Call their attention to features they may have missed or misinterpreted.

Technology Resources

Have students visit **ClassZone.com** for reteaching of Key Concepts.

 CONTENT REVIEW

 CONTENT REVIEW CD-ROM

Focus

PURPOSE Students observe, measure, and record weather conditions, then analyze the data.

OVERVIEW Students will use their senses and homemade or commercial instruments to observe and measure weather conditions over a period of time. They will graph numerical data and search for trends. Students will find that:

- weather is complicated
- some types of data, such as cloud cover and precipitation, are strongly related
- some observations, such as the types of clouds or the changes in air pressure, may be used to make reasonable one-day forecasts

Lab Preparation

- You may want to set up a weather station outside.
- Discuss the characteristics of a good observation chart.
- Prior to the investigation, have students read through the investigation and prepare their data tables. Or you may wish to copy and distribute datasheets and rubrics.

 UNIT RESOURCE BOOK, pp. 204–212

 SCIENCE TOOLKIT, F13

Lab Management

- Have students work together in small groups. Each group might construct a different instrument. The class as a whole can then share data.
- Tell students to choose their observation sites carefully. For example, wind vanes should be used in open areas.

SAFETY Tell students to notify you immediately if a thermometer should break.

INCLUSION Mount a thermometer with large numbers outside the window so that students with visual and physical impairments can easily read it.

Design a Weather Center

 DESIGN —YOUR OWN—

OVERVIEW AND PURPOSE The accuracy of a weather forecast depends largely on the type and quality of the data that it is based on. In this lab, you will use what you have learned about weather to

- observe and measure weather conditions
- record and analyze the weather-related data

▶ Procedure

MATERIALS
- thermometer
- magnetic compass
- other weather instruments
- graph paper

1. Survey the possible sources of weather data in and around your classroom. You can use a thermometer to record the outside air temperature. You can observe cloud types and the amount of cloud cover from a window or doorway. You can also observe precipitation and notice if it is heavy or light. If there is a flag in view, use it to find the wind direction and to estimate wind speed.

2. Assemble or make tools for your observations. You may want to make a reference chart with pictures of different cloud types or other information. Decide if you wish to use homemade weather instruments. You may have made a barometer, a psychrometer, and a rain gauge already. If not, see the instructions on pages 45, 64, and 67. You may also wish to do research to learn how to make or use other weather instruments.

3. Make an initial set of observations. Write down the date and time in your **Science Notebook.** Record the readings from the thermometer and other instruments.

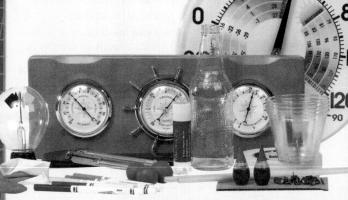

INVESTIGATION RESOURCES

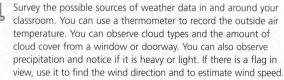 CHAPTER INVESTIGATION, Design a Weather Center
- Level A, pp. 204–207
- Level B, pp. 208–211
- Level C, p. 212

Advanced students should complete Levels B & C.

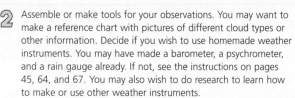 Writing a Lab Report, D12–13

Technology Resources

Customize this student lab as needed or look for an alternative. Print rubrics to assess student lab reports.

 Lab Generator CD-ROM

4. Decide how to record your observations of the clouds, the wind, and any precipitation. Organize your notes to make it easy for you to record later observations in a consistent way.

5. Create a chart with a row for each type of observation you are making. You might darken fractions of circles to record amounts of cloud cover, as in the station symbols on page 100. Make sure each row has a heading and enough room for numbers, words, or sketches. Include a row for notes that do not belong in the data rows.

6. Record your observations every day at the same time. Try to make the observations exactly the same way each time. If you have to redraw your chart, copy the information carefully.

▶ Observe and Analyze Write It Up

1. **GRAPH** Graph the data you collected that represent measurable quantities. Use graphs that are appropriate to your data. Often a simple line graph will work. Choose an appropriate scale and interval based on the range of your data. Make the *x*-axis of each graph the same so that you can compare the different types of data easily.

2. **COMPARE AND CONTRAST** Look at your graphs for patterns in your data. Some aspects of weather change at the same time because they are related to each other. Did one type of change occur before a different type of change? If so, this pattern may help you predict weather.

▶ Conclude Write It Up

1. **INTERPRET** Did a front pass through your area during the period you observed? What observations helped you answer this question?

2. **EVALUATE** Why was it necessary to observe at the same time each day?

3. **APPLY** If you predicted that each day's weather would be repeated the next day, how often would you be right?

▶ INVESTIGATE Further

CHALLENGE Locate a newspaper weather page for the period during which you were making your weather observations. How do the weather data reported for your area compare with your measurements? How do you account for any differences you notice in the data?

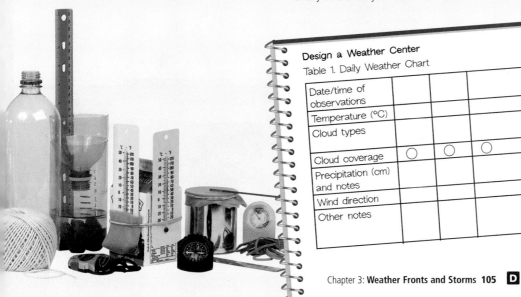

Design a Weather Center
Table 1. Daily Weather Chart

Date/time of observations			
Temperature (°C)			
Cloud types			
Cloud coverage	○	○	○
Precipitation (cm) and notes			
Wind direction			
Other notes			

Chapter 3: **Weather Fronts and Storms** 105 **D**

▶ Observe and Analyze Write It Up

SAMPLE DATA Day 1: temperature: 18°C, cloud type: stratus, cloud coverage: 100%, precipitation: 3.6 cm, wind direction: northwest

1. *Graphs should generally not be bar graphs. They should accurately reflect gathered data. Students may want to make at least three graphs, plotting the days on the x-axes. A variable such as temperature, air pressure, and amount of precipitation should be plotted on each y-axis.*

2. *Sample answer: Decreases in air pressure and cloud formation occurred together.*

▶ Conclude Write It Up

1. *Sample answer: A cold front passed through the area. Clouds formed, rain fell, and temperatures dropped following the passage of the front.*

2. *Sample answer: The data would not be comparable if some readings were taken at night and others were taken during the day.*

3. *Answers will depend on students' location. Some areas have variable weather; others have fairly consistent weather over long periods of time.*

▶ INVESTIGATE Further

CHALLENGE Weather data should be comparable to student measurements. Differences may be due to local variations in weather conditions or differences in instruments and measurement techniques.

Post-Lab Discussion

• Have several volunteers share their graphs with the class. Discuss the similarities and differences among the observations. Ask students to hypothesize why these similarities and/or differences exist.

• Ask: After observing your results, what would you want to study further? If you could do a follow-up experiment, what would it be? What different weather instruments would you use?

BACK TO

Refer students back to the visual on p. 80. Help them to relate the interactions of air masses to weather changes. Ask: How might these types of air masses produce a cold front in Maine? *A polar air mass from the north might push into a tropical air mass.* How might a winter storm system be produced? *The meeting of a continental polar air mass and one of the warm air masses might produce a low and fronts, as shown on p. 85.*

◀ KEY CONCEPTS SUMMARY

SECTION 3.1

Ask: What type of front is shown in the visual? *cold front* What other types of fronts did you learn about? *warm fronts and stationary fronts*

Ask: In which direction does air move around a low-pressure system? *counterclockwise*

SECTION 3.2

Ask: Would you expect a hurricane to develop during winter? Why or why not? *No; in winter, ocean water is not warm enough to provide the energy to form a hurricane.*

SECTION 3.3

Ask: What are some dangers of thunderstorms and tornadoes? *thunderstorms: flash floods, strong winds, hail, lightning; tornadoes: damaging winds, flying objects*

SECTION 3.4

Ask: What are some sources of weather data? *ground and radar stations, satellite*

Ask: How are these sources related to the map? *They provide the data used to produce maps.*

Review Concepts

• Big Idea Flow Chart, p. T17
• Chapter Outline, pp. T23–24

 Chapter Review

The interaction of air masses causes changes in weather.

 **CONTENT REVIEW**
CLASSZONE.COM

◀ KEY CONCEPTS SUMMARY

3.1 **Weather changes as air masses move.**

Air masses meet and produce **fronts,** which can bring lowered pressure and stormy weather. Fronts can be cold, warm, or stationary.

VOCABULARY
air mass p. 79
front p. 82
high-pressure system p. 84
low-pressure system p. 85

3.2 **Low-pressure systems can become storms.**

Hurricanes and winter storms develop from low-pressure systems.

Hurricanes form over warm ocean water.

VOCABULARY
tropical storm p. 87
hurricane p. 87
storm surge p. 89
blizzard p. 90

3.3 **Vertical air motion can cause severe storms.**

Rising moist air can produce **thunderstorms.** The up-and-down motion of air in a thunderstorm can produce a **tornado.**

VOCABULARY
thunderstorm p. 92
tornado p. 95

3.4 **Weather forecasters use advanced technologies.**

Weather information comes from many sources.

Meteorologists use weather data and computer models to forecast weather.

VOCABULARY
meteorologist p. 98
isobar p. 101

Technology Resources

Have students visit **ClassZone.com** or use the CD-ROM for a cumulative review of concepts.

 CONTENT REVIEW

 CONTENT REVIEW CD-ROM

Engage students in a whole-class interactive review of Key Concepts. Edit content as you wish.

 POWER PRESENTATIONS

Reviewing Vocabulary

Describe each term below, using the related term as part of the description.

Term	Related Term	Description
EXAMPLE hurricane	low-pressure system	a low-pressure system in the tropics with winds at least 120 km/h
1. front	air mass	
2. low-pressure system	low-pressure center	
3. storm surge	hurricane	
4. tropical storm	low-pressure system	
5. air mass	humidity	
6. thunderstorm	convection	
7. tornado	thunderstorm	
8. blizzard	low-pressure system	

Reviewing Key Concepts

Multiple Choice *Choose the letter of the best answer.*

9. What qualities are nearly the same at different locations in a single air mass?
   a. temperature and pressure
   b. temperature and humidity
   c. air pressure and wind speed
   d. air pressure and humidity

10. Which is the name for an air mass that forms over the ocean near the equator?
   a. maritime tropical
   c. continental tropical
   b. maritime polar
   d. continental polar

11. A meteorologist is a scientist who
   a. predicts meteor showers
   b. studies maps
   c. studies the weather
   d. changes the weather

12. An isobar shows locations with the same
   a. temperature
   c. air pressure
   b. rainfall
   d. wind speed

13. Which is produced when a warm air mass pushes a colder air mass?
   a. a stationary front
   c. a warm front
   b. a cold front
   d. a thunderstorm

14. Which can be measured in inches of mercury?
   a. air pressure
   c. hail
   b. temperature
   d. lightning

15. Which source provides measurements for just one location?
   a. ground station
   c. weather balloon
   b. radar station
   d. satellite

16. Compared with warm fronts, cold fronts are
   a. faster moving
   c. more cloudy
   b. less dense
   d. less steep

17. Which statement is usually true of high-pressure systems in North America?
   a. They bring fair weather.
   b. They change quickly.
   c. The air in them is cold and dense.
   d. The air in them moves counterclockwise.

18. Thunderstorms often begin with the rising of
   a. cool, dry air
   c. warm, dry air
   b. cool, humid air
   d. warm, humid air

19. What is the relationship between lightning and thunder?
   a. They have separate causes.
   b. They have the same cause.
   c. Lightning causes thunder.
   d. Thunder causes lightning.

Short Answer *Write a short answer to each question.*

20. Why are hurricanes in the eastern United States more likely in autumn than in spring?

21. What causes lake-effect snow?

22. In what four ways can thunderstorms be dangerous?

Reviewing Vocabulary

1. a boundary between air masses

2. a weather system that surrounds a low-pressure center

3. a huge mass of water pushed by a hurricane

4. a low-pressure system in the tropics with winds of at least 65 km/h

5. a large volume of air characterized by a particular humidity and temperature

6. a storm with lightning and thunder (often produced by convection)

7. a rotating column of air between a thunderstorm cloud and the ground

8. a blinding snowstorm associated with a low-pressure system

Reviewing Key Concepts

9. b

10. a

11. c

12. c

13. c

14. a

15. a

16. a

17. a

18. d

19. c

20. Ocean water is too cold in the spring to provide the energy needed for hurricane formation.

21. Cold air gains warmth and moisture as it passes over the Great Lakes. When it reaches land, it cools again and releases the moisture as snow.

22. They can cause flash floods that wash away houses. The winds of thunderstorms can damage trees and roofs. The hail from thunderstorms can damage crops. Lightning can cause fires and loss of life.

ASSESSMENT RESOURCES

UNIT ASSESSMENT BOOK
- Chapter Test A, pp. 47–50
- Chapter Test B, pp. 51–54
- Chapter Test C, pp. 55–58
- Alternative Assessment, pp. 59–60

SPANISH ASSESSMENT BOOK
Spanish Chapter Test, pp. 181–184

Technology Resources

Edit test items and answer choices.

 Test Generator CD-ROM

Visit **ClassZone.com** to extend test practice.

 Test Practice

Thinking Critically

23. continental polar—dry (no clouds or rain at fronts) and cold (from north)

24. They make it stormy.

25. Washington D.C.; It is in the path of a front.

26. Oklahoma City is behind the front, in the colder air mass. Little Rock is in the warmer air mass.

27. It will get colder as the front passes.

28. No, winter weather in the north and moderate temperatures in the south suggest winter.

29. Answers depend on local conditions.

30. Diagrams should indicate that both visible light images and infrared images show cloud cover. Visible light works in daytime only. Infrared works at night and also shows cloud height.

31. brief, heavy precipitation

32. cloudy, followed by rain or snow

33. clouds and thunderstorms

34. cloudy and rain

35. fair weather

36. possible tornado

37. possible tropical storm or hurricane

38. freezing rain or ice storm

39. The air moves down; weather is usually fair.

40. A hurricane is most dangerous because its effects include storm surges, floods, high winds, tornadoes, and thunderstorms.

the BIG idea

41. It looks as though a storm surge is occurring. Storm surges are caused by hurricanes.

42. Diagrams might show: high-pressure system replaced by a low-pressure system; collision of warm and cold air; rising of warm, humid air; raindrop formation

UNIT PROJECTS

Collect schedules, materials lists, and questions. Be sure dates and materials are obtainable, and questions are focused.

 Unit Projects, pp. 5–10

Thinking Critically

Use this weather map to answer the next six questions. The numbers under each city name are the highest and the lowest temperature for the day in degrees Fahrenheit.

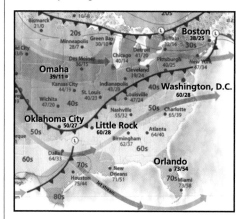

23. **INFER** Name and describe the air mass that has moved south to Omaha from Canada.

24. **IDENTIFY EFFECTS** How are two low-pressure systems affecting the weather near Boston?

25. **PREDICT** Explain whether Washington, D.C., or Orlando is more likely to have a big change in weather in the next two days.

26. **COMPARE AND CONTRAST** Explain the difference in temperature between Oklahoma City and Little Rock.

27. **PREDICT** How will the weather in Little Rock change in the next day or two?

28. **APPLY** Does this map indicate that it is hurricane season? Explain your reasoning.

29. **CONNECT** Describe today's weather and explain what fronts and pressure systems might be influencing it.

30. **COMPARE AND CONTRAST** Use a Venn diagram to compare images from visible light and infrared radiation.

PREDICT *For each set of conditions listed in the chart, write a weather prediction.*

Conditions	Prediction
31. A cold front is moving into an area that has warm, moist air.	
32. A warm front is moving into an area that has cold, dense air.	
33. A cool sea breeze is blowing inland, causing warm, humid air to rise.	
34. Air pressure is falling and the temperature is rising.	
35. Air pressure is increasing and the temperature is steady.	
36. A thunderstorm is developing spinning winds at its center.	
37. A low-pressure center is over the Atlantic Ocean where the water temperature is above 27°C (81°F).	
38. Cold air is pushing warm air where the air is 2°C (36°F) and the ground is -3°C (27°F).	

39. **COMPARE** How is the air motion in the eye of a hurricane similar to the air motion at a high-pressure center?

40. **EVALUATE** Which type of storm is most dangerous? Explain your reasoning.

the BIG idea

41. Look again at the photograph on pages 76–77. Now that you have finished the chapter, how would you change your response to the question on the photograph?

42. **SEQUENCE** Draw a storyboard with at least four sketches to show how cool, sunny weather might change into warm, rainy weather.

UNIT PROJECTS

Check your schedule for your unit project. How are you doing? Be sure that you have placed data or notes from your research in your project folder.

MONITOR AND RETEACH

If students have trouble applying the concepts in items 23–28, draw the symbols for highs, lows, and fronts on the board. Have students identify each symbol and describe associated weather conditions. Break down the formation of a cold front into three steps. **Step 1** should show how cold air pushes warm air steeply upward. **Step 2** should show that as the warm air rises, its moisture condenses and forms tall clouds. **Step 3** should show heavy raindrops falling.
Students may benefit from summarizing sections of the chapter.

 Summarizing the Chapter, pp. 222–223

Standardized Test Practice

For practice on your state test, go to . . . **TEST PRACTICE** CLASSZONE.COM

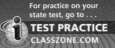

Analyzing a Map

Use this weather map to answer the questions below.

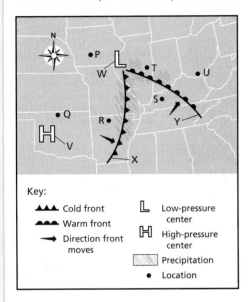

Key:

▲▲▲ Cold front	Ⅼ Low-pressure center
▀▀▀ Warm front	Ⅱ High-pressure center
→ Direction front moves	▨ Precipitation
	• Location

1. Which letter labels a cold front?

  a. Q   **c.** X

  b. U   **d.** Y

2. Which word best describes the general movement of the fronts?

  a. to the north   **c.** clockwise

  b. to the east   **d.** counterclockwise

3. A warm front occurs where warm air moves into colder air. Which of these locations is probably warmest?

  a. R   **c.** T

  b. S   **d.** U

4. Temperatures usually change quickly near a front and more slowly away from a front. The temperature at Q is 10°C (50°F). The temperature at S is 20°C (68°F). Which is the best estimate for the temperature at R?

  a. 6°C (43°F)   **c.** 20°C (68°F)

  b. 11°C (52°F)   **d.** 24°C (75°F)

5. If the fronts continue to move as shown, which location will get warmer soon?

  a. Q   **c.** S

  b. R   **d.** T

6. Low pressure often brings stormy weather, and high pressure often brings fair weather. Which of these locations is most likely to have clear skies?

  a. Q   **c.** S

  b. R   **d.** U

Extended Response

Use the map above to answer the two questions below in detail. Include some of the terms shown in the word box. Underline each term you use in your answers.

cold front	humid	west
warm front	east	prevailing winds

7. Along which front on the weather map above would you expect to find cumulonimbus clouds? Explain why.

8. The weather system shown on the map above is in the continental United States. In which direction do you expect it to move? Explain why.

Analyzing a Map

1. c   3. b   5. d

2. d   4. b   6. a

Extended Response

7. RUBRIC

4 points for a response that correctly answers the question and uses the following terms accurately:

- cold front
- humid

Sample: the cold front; Cold fronts push warm air up. Water vapor in the warm, humid air condenses as the air rises. This produces cumulonimbus clouds and then storms.

3 points for a response that correctly answers the question and uses one term accurately

2 points for a response that correctly answers the question, but doesn't use the terms

8. RUBRIC

4 points for a response that correctly answers the question and uses the following terms accurately:

- prevailing winds
- west
- east

Sample: west to east; Weather systems are moved by the global pattern of prevailing winds, which move west to east. Sometimes the jet stream interferes with these wind patterns and causes systems to change directions.

3 points for a response that uses two terms accurately

2 points for a response that correctly answers the question and uses one term accurately

1 point for a response that correctly answers the question, but doesn't use the terms

---

METACOGNITIVE ACTIVITY

Have students answer the following questions in their **Science Notebook:**

1. Would you like to be a meteorologist? Why or why not?

2. Do you think scientists should work to control the weather, or is it better to let nature take its course? Please give reasons for your response.

3. What new things have you learned about weather while working on your Unit Project?

TIMELINES in Science

OBSERVING THE ATMOSPHERE

The atmosphere is always changing, and scientists are developing better ways to observe these changes. Accurate weather forecasts help people make everyday decisions, such as what kind of clothing to wear. Forecasts also allow us to plan for dangerous storms and other natural disasters. Scientists are now warning of long-term changes to the atmosphere that can affect the entire world. These predictions are possible because of the work of scientists and observers over hundreds of years.

The timeline shows some historical events in the study of Earth's air and weather. The boxes below the timeline show how technology has led to new knowledge about the atmosphere and show how that knowledge has been applied.

1686

Trade Winds Are Linked to Sun's Energy

Sailors have used trade winds for centuries to sail from Europe to the Americas. Now, Edmund Halley, a British astronomer, explains global winds in a new theory. He argues that trade winds blowing toward the equator replace air that rises due to solar heating.

EVENTS

1640   1660   1680

APPLICATIONS AND TECHNOLOGY

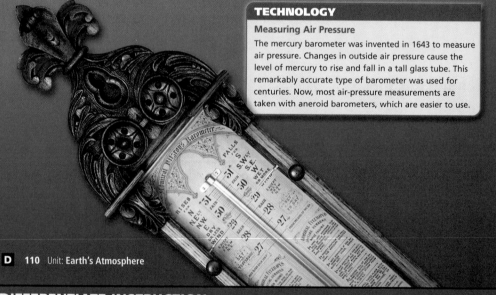

TECHNOLOGY

Measuring Air Pressure

The mercury barometer was invented in 1643 to measure air pressure. Changes in outside air pressure cause the level of mercury to rise and fall in a tall glass tube. This remarkably accurate type of barometer was used for centuries. Now, most air-pressure measurements are taken with aneroid barometers, which are easier to use.

DIFFERENTIATE INSTRUCTION

Below Level To assist students in reading the timeline, suggest they write the dates and headlines in proper sequence on a sheet of paper. They can use this sheet as an overall guide as they study different parts of the timeline.

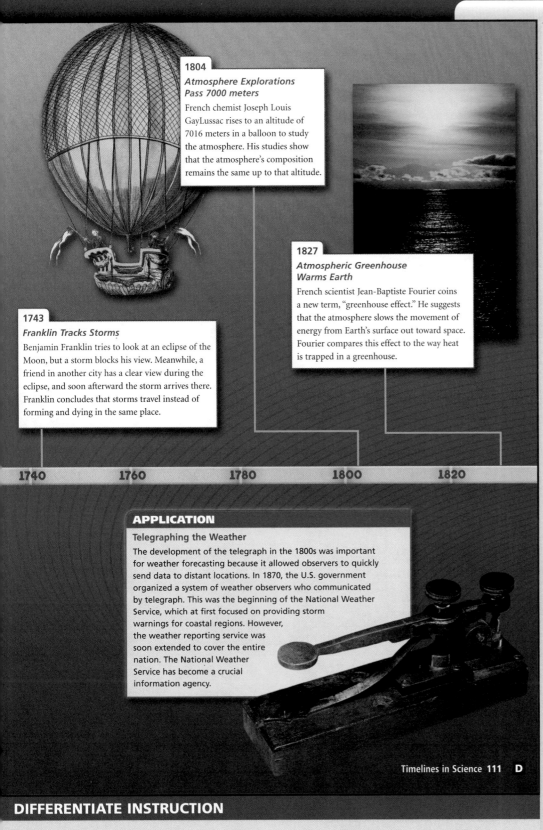

1804

Atmosphere Explorations Pass 7000 meters

French chemist Joseph Louis GayLussac rises to an altitude of 7016 meters in a balloon to study the atmosphere. His studies show that the atmosphere's composition remains the same up to that altitude.

1827

Atmospheric Greenhouse Warms Earth

French scientist Jean-Baptiste Fourier coins a new term, "greenhouse effect." He suggests that the atmosphere slows the movement of energy from Earth's surface out toward space. Fourier compares this effect to the way heat is trapped in a greenhouse.

1743

Franklin Tracks Storms

Benjamin Franklin tries to look at an eclipse of the Moon, but a storm blocks his view. Meanwhile, a friend in another city has a clear view during the eclipse, and soon afterward the storm arrives there. Franklin concludes that storms travel instead of forming and dying in the same place.

1740   1760   1780   1800   1820

APPLICATION

Telegraphing the Weather

The development of the telegraph in the 1800s was important for weather forecasting because it allowed observers to quickly send data to distant locations. In 1870, the U.S. government organized a system of weather observers who communicated by telegraph. This was the beginning of the National Weather Service, which at first focused on providing storm warnings for coastal regions. However, the weather reporting service was soon extended to cover the entire nation. The National Weather Service has become a crucial information agency.

Timelines in Science **111   D**

Scientific Process

Unlike chemistry, where data are often gathered through experimental techniques, atmospheric research is largely observational. Scientists must observe complex weather and climate phenomena over extended periods of time. Only then can they attempt to draw conclusions about weather patterns. As they read the timeline, tell students to think about why knowledge of the atmosphere and weather could not be gained quickly.

Social Studies Connection

1740 TO 1800 The latter half of the 1700s was a time of great conflict. The Seven Years' War, fought in Europe, North America, and India, began in 1756. The American Revolution started in 1775. The French Revolution began in 1787 and continued until 1799. Ask students why turbulent times in history often spark widespread changes in science. *Sample answer: When society undergoes vast changes, people are often more willing to question widely held beliefs and to change their ideas about how the world works.*

Application

WEATHER DATA The Chinese kept the first known weather records during the Shang dynasty around 13th century B.C. Aristotle's Meteorologica, written in 340 B.C., is often credited as the first scientific work of meteorology. Stress to students that it is only natural that people would want to know more about the weather—weather affects our lives greatly. For example, weather determines how crops grow, what types of homes to build, and where people live. Ask students how weather affects their daily lives. *Sample answer: Weather determines what people wear and what outside activities they can do.*

DIFFERENTIATE INSTRUCTION

Advanced Over a two-week period, have students record the daily weather predictions made by their local television station or newspaper. Students can then compare the predictions to actual weather conditions. Tell students to determine beforehand the criteria they will use to rate the predictions. For example, they should decide if it is more important to accurately predict the time of a storm or its severity.

Teach from Visuals

After students have examined the photo of a storm front, ask them to describe the clouds on either side of the front. *On one side of the front, the clouds form a thick, continuous layer. On the other side of the front, there are blue skies with only a few scattered clouds.*

Technology

PICTURING THE WEATHER Orbiting weather satellites and radar stations on land allow the measuring of weather data over large areas rather than just at isolated points. The National Weather Service has organized Doppler radar sites into a global network known as Nexrad. These radar systems can measure precipitation, warn of possible flooding, and identify rotating weather patterns such as tornadoes. Satellites gather global views of cloud and moisture distribution, surface properties, and temperature. This information helps formulate weather forecasts 5 to 7 days in advance and can help warn residents about a coming weather disaster.

Integrate the Sciences

Doppler radar is based on the Doppler effect, which describes how the frequencies of waves change as the source of the waves moves toward or away from the observer. The Doppler effect is used by astronomers to determine how fast other galaxies are moving away from our own galaxy, the Milky Way. This, in turn, indicates how the universe is expanding. Current studies indicate that this expansion may be accelerating over time.

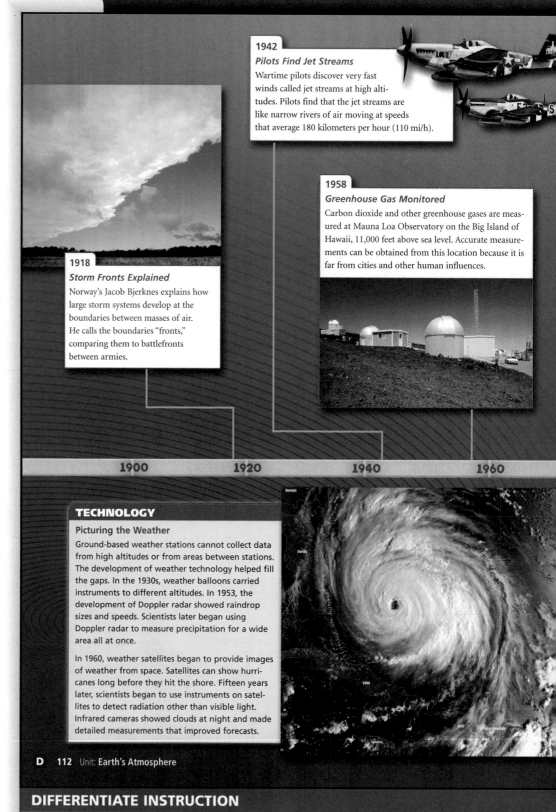

1942
Pilots Find Jet Streams
Wartime pilots discover very fast winds called jet streams at high altitudes. Pilots find that the jet streams are like narrow rivers of air moving at speeds that average 180 kilometers per hour (110 mi/h).

1958
Greenhouse Gas Monitored
Carbon dioxide and other greenhouse gases are measured at Mauna Loa Observatory on the Big Island of Hawaii, 11,000 feet above sea level. Accurate measurements can be obtained from this location because it is far from cities and other human influences.

1918
Storm Fronts Explained
Norway's Jacob Bjerknes explains how large storm systems develop at the boundaries between masses of air. He calls the boundaries "fronts," comparing them to battlefronts between armies.

1900   1920   1940   1960

TECHNOLOGY

Picturing the Weather
Ground-based weather stations cannot collect data from high altitudes or from areas between stations. The development of weather technology helped fill the gaps. In the 1930s, weather balloons carried instruments to different altitudes. In 1953, the development of Doppler radar showed raindrop sizes and speeds. Scientists later began using Doppler radar to measure precipitation for a wide area all at once.

In 1960, weather satellites began to provide images of weather from space. Satellites can show hurricanes long before they hit the shore. Fifteen years later, scientists began to use instruments on satellites to detect radiation other than visible light. Infrared cameras showed clouds at night and made detailed measurements that improved forecasts.

DIFFERENTIATE INSTRUCTION

English Learners Take the opportunity to note that some events or objects get their names because they are similar, or analogous, to other events or objects. For example, certain weather patterns are called fronts because they are analogous to battlefronts between armies. Tell students that the "greenhouse effect" was named that because the phenomenon reminded scientists of a greenhouse that traps heat within its walls. Scientists later determined that the two processes were different, but the name remained.

1985

Hole Found in Ozone Layer

Using data from a ground-based instrument in Antarctica, scientists discover a large area where the protective layer of ozone is very thin. They call it the ozone hole. The discovery confirms earlier predictions that certain industrial chemicals can result in ozone destruction.

 RESOURCE CENTER
CLASSZONE.COM

Learn more about current research on the atmosphere.

1980   2000

APPLICATION

Computer Modeling

Scientists use computers not only to collect data but also to make models of the atmosphere. Models show how the atmosphere changed in the past and how it may change in the future. As computers become faster and better, the models can be made more detailed and therefore more reliable.

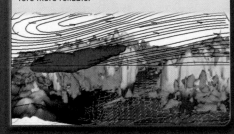

INTO THE **FUTURE**

With frequent measurements of much of Earth's atmosphere, scientists can now understand a lot more about weather. Supercomputers let scientists make models of ordinary weather and complicated storms.

In the future, scientists will better understand the way the oceans and the atmosphere affect one another. They will make models of complex patterns that involve long-term changes in the oceans and the atmosphere.

Researchers will use models of Earth's past weather to understand the changes happening today. They will make more detailed predictions about future changes. People will be able to make better decisions about human activities that affect Earth's atmosphere. Researchers will continue to improve and use their understanding of the atmospheres of other worlds to understand Earth.

ACTIVITIES

Reliving History

Ancient peoples made simple weather instruments, such as wind vanes. You can make a wind vane and then map the wind directions in your neighborhood.

Push a straight pin through the middle of a drinking straw and then into an eraser at the end of a pencil. Tape a square of cardboard vertically to one end of the straw. Put a small piece of clay on the other end so that the wind vane is balanced. The straw will turn so that the clay end of the straw points into the wind.

Use your wind vane and a magnetic compass to find the wind direction in several places in your neighborhood. Record the results on a copy of a map. Do you notice any patterns?

Writing About Science

Suppose scientists learn to control the weather. What factors have to be considered in choosing the weather? Write a conversation in which opposing viewpoints are debated.

DIFFERENTIATE INSTRUCTION

Climate and Climate Change

Earth Science
UNIFYING PRINCIPLES

PRINCIPLE 1

Heat energy inside Earth and radiation from the Sun provide energy for Earth's processes.

PRINCIPLE 2

Physical forces, such as gravity, affect the movement of all matter on Earth and throughout the universe.

PRINCIPLE 3

Matter and energy move among Earth's rocks and soil, atmosphere, waters, and living things.

PRINCIPLE 4

Earth has changed over time and continues to change.

Unit: Earth's Atmosphere
BIG IDEAS

CHAPTER 1
Earth's Changing Atmosphere
Earth's atmosphere is a blanket of gases that supports and protects life.

CHAPTER 2
Weather Patterns
Some features of weather have predictable patterns.

CHAPTER 3
Weather Fronts and Storms
The interaction of air masses causes changes in weather.

CHAPTER 4
Climate and Climate Change
Climates are long-term weather patterns that may change over time.

CHAPTER 4
KEY CONCEPTS

SECTION **4.1**

Climate is a long-term weather pattern.

1. Geography affects climate.

2. Seasonal changes are part of climate.

SECTION **4.2**

Earth has a variety of climates.

1. Scientists have identified six major climate zones.

2. Natural features and human activity can affect local climates.

SECTION **4.3**

Climates can change suddenly or slowly.

1. Climates cool when particles block sunlight.

2. Climates change as continents move.

3. Some climate changes repeat over time.

4. Human activities are changing climate.

T The Big Idea Flow Chart is available on p. T25 in the **UNIT TRANSPARENCY BOOK.**

4.1 Climate is a long-term weather pattern. pp. 117–124

1. Geography affects climate.

Climate is distinct from weather. Weather denotes conditions from moment to moment, and **climate** denotes characteristic weather patterns occurring over time.

Some of the geographical factors that affect climate include

- **latitude**—the distance north or south of the equator
- altitude—the height above sea level
- presence or absence of large bodies of water
- **ocean currents,** which transfer energy between global regions

2. Seasonal changes are part of climate.

Seasons occur because Earth's Northern Hemisphere and Southern Hemisphere receive different amounts of the Sun's energy over the course of a year.

Chapter 2, "Earth, Moon, and Sun," in the unit "Space Science," presents the full astronomical explanation for Earth's seasons.

Seasons are associated with specific patterns of temperature and precipitation (rain, snow, sleet, freezing rain, or hail). For a climate of a specific place, temperature and precipitation patterns over time can be plotted on a single graph. The line plot shows temperature, labeled "Degrees Celsius" on the left vertical axis. The bar plot shows precipitation and is labeled "Centimeters precipitation" on the right vertical axis. The horizontal axis shows months of the year, abbreviated as capital letters.

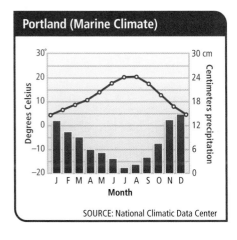

Portland (Marine Climate)

SOURCE: National Climatic Data Center

4.2 Earth has a variety of climates. pp. 125–131

1. Scientists have identified six major climate zones.

A **climate zone** is a zone encompassing places that have similar patterns of temperature and precipitation. Scientists have classified six major climate zones on Earth.

- humid tropical
- dry
- moist mid-latitude with mild winters
- moist mid-latitude with severe winters
- polar
- highland

Using the criteria of patterns of temperature and precipitation, scientists further subdivide climate zones into distinct subclimates. The single exception is the highland climate zone, which can have many variable subclimates depending upon steepness of slope.

2. Natural features and human activity can affect local climates.

In addition to climates and subclimates, Earth has microclimates. The prefix *micro-* means "very small." So a **microclimate** is literally a "very small climate." More broadly, it is a distinct climate of a relatively small area within a subclimate.

Two particularly important microclimates are

- the **urban heat island,** a warm body of air over a city
- a **rain shadow,** the dry area on the downwind side of a mountain. The visual below illustrates a rain shadow.

Air cools as it flows up. Water vapor condenses into clouds that release precipitation.

After blowing over, the air is much drier.

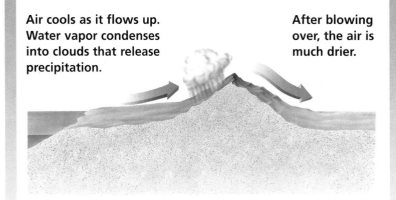

 MISCONCEPTION DATABASE
CLASSZONE.COM Background on student misconceptions

Common Misconceptions

LENGTH OF DAYS Students may assume that the number of hours of daylight is the same throughout a hemisphere on any particular day. However, the length of daylight within either the Northern or Southern Hemisphere on a particular day varies by latitude of locale.

 This misconception is addressed on p. 122.

4.3 Climates can change suddenly or slowly. pp. 132–139

1. Climates cool when particles block sunlight.

Particulates—tiny solid and liquid particles mixed in the air—can block sunlight and prevent the Sun's energy from reaching Earth's surface. Some natural events fill the atmosphere with clouds of dust or other particles on a huge, even global scale.

- Volcanoes send clouds of gas and dust into the stratosphere. When this gas combines with water, sulfuric acid droplets form and block sunlight.
- On rare occasions, very large space rocks, or asteroids, enter Earth's atmosphere and strike the surface, raising immense clouds of dust. Many scientists believe that such an event 65 million years ago contributed to the extinction of dinosaurs.

2. Climates change as continents move.

- Scientists believe that Earth's continents were once joined together in a supercontinent called Pangaea.
- Pangaea began to break apart about 200 million years ago. The continents have been moving apart slowly ever since due to the movement of Earth's tectonic plates. The maps below show how the supercontinent broke up into separate continents.
- As continents move to different latitudes, their climates change. Such changes occur over many millions of years.

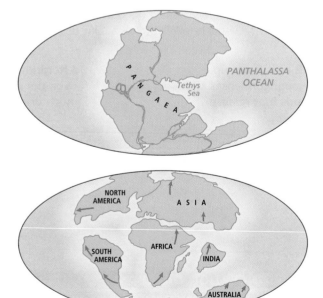

3. Some climate changes repeat over time.

- **Ice ages** are climate changes that repeat in cycles of tens of thousands of years. During an ice age, Earth undergoes global cooling, and ice sheets spread out from the polar regions to the middle latitudes. Continental glaciers may cover large parts of continents.
- **El Niño** is a a type of climate change that occurs every three to seven years. During El Niño, the trade winds that blow east to west across the Pacific Ocean weaken, which causes a warm water current to flow in the eastern Pacific. This disturbance of wind patterns and ocean currents affects climates throughout much of North and South America and in other parts of the world. El Niño is part of a larger pattern of climate change that includes La Niña. During La Niña, the water in the eastern Pacific is colder than usual.

4. Human activities are changing climate.

Scientists predict a rise in global temperature of 1.4°C to 5.8° C (2.5°F to 10.4°F) over the next 100 years. No one knows exactly what effects global warming will have on Earth, its climate, and life on the planet, but most climate scientists predict the following changes:

- The average sea level will rise.
- Some plant and animal species will experience changes in their habitat.
- Humans and plants may benefit or suffer from warmer temperatures and precipitation changes.

EXPLORE the BIG idea

labs and generate alternative labs.

Why Are Climates Different? p. 115
Students are introduced to climate variations.

TIME 10 minutes
MATERIALS newspaper weather map

How Do Microclimates Form? p. 115
Students are introduced to varying temperature readings.

TIME 10 minutes
MATERIALS thermometer

Internet Activity: El Niño, p. 115
Students view precipitation and temperature data for their locale.

TIME 20 minutes
MATERIALS computer with Internet access

SECTION 4.1

EXPLORE Solar Energy, p. 117
Students discover how the angle of light affects the heating of an object.

TIME 15 minutes
MATERIALS 2 thermometers, 2 black paper squares, 1 cardboard tube from a paper towel roll, sunny windowsill or lamp

INVESTIGATE Heating and Cooling Rates, p. 119
Students compare rates of heating and cooling in soil and water.

TIME 25 minutes
MATERIALS 2 cups, ruler, soil, water at room temperature, 2 thermometers, sunlight or lamp

---

SECTION 4.2

CHAPTER INVESTIGATION
Microclimates, pp. 130–131
Students take weather measurements at two outdoor sites and compare the data to find out how natural and artificial features affect microclimate, or local climate.

TIME 40 minutes
MATERIALS 2 thermometers, 2 other weather instruments of the same kind

---

SECTION 4.3

INVESTIGATE Climate Change, p. 133
Students measure temperatures to understand how blocking sunlight can affect temperature.

TIME 20 minutes
MATERIALS white tissue paper, tape, 2 thermometers

 Additional INVESTIGATION, Modeling El Niño, A, B, & C, pp. 272–281; Teacher Instructions, pp. 284–285

Previewing Chapter Resources

	INTEGRATED TECHNOLOGY	LABS AND ACTIVITIES

CHAPTER 4
Climate and Climate Change

 CLASSZONE.COM
- eEdition Plus
- EasyPlanner Plus
- Misconception Database
- Content Review
- Test Practice
- Simulation
- Resource Centers
- Internet Activity: El Niño
- Math Tutorial

 SCILINKS.ORG
 SCI LINKS

 CD-ROMS
- eEdition
- EasyPlanner
- Power Presentations
- Content Review
- Lab Generator
- Test Generator

 AUDIO CDS
- Audio Readings
- Audio Readings in Spanish

 EXPLORE the Big Idea, p. 115
- Why Are Climates Different?
- How Do Microclimates Form?
- Internet Activity: El Niño

 UNIT RESOURCE BOOK
Unit Projects, pp. 5–10

 Lab Generator CD-ROM
Generate customized labs.

SECTION
 4.1

Climate is a long-term weather pattern.
pp. 117–124

Time: 2 periods (1 block)
 Lesson Plan, pp. 224–225

 SIMULATION, Latitude and Altitude

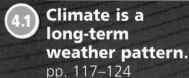 **UNIT TRANSPARENCY BOOK**
- Big Idea Flow Chart, p. T25
- Daily Vocabulary Scaffolding, p. T26
- Note-Taking Model, p. T27
- 3-Minute Warm-Up, p. T28
- "Latitude and Temperature" Visual, p. T30

 • EXPLORE Solar Energy, p. 117
• INVESTIGATE Heating and Cooling Rates, p. 119
• Science on the Job, p. 124

 UNIT RESOURCE BOOK
Datasheet, Heating and Cooling Rates, p. 233

SECTION
 4.2

Earth has a variety of climates.
pp. 125–131

Time: 3 periods (1.5 blocks)
 Lesson Plan, pp. 235–236

 RESOURCE CENTER, Climate Zones

 UNIT TRANSPARENCY BOOK
- Daily Vocabulary Scaffolding, p. T26
- 3-Minute Warm-Up, p. T28

 CHAPTER INVESTIGATION, Microclimates, pp. 130–131

 UNIT RESOURCE BOOK
CHAPTER INVESTIGATION, Microclimates, A, B, & C, pp. 263–271

SECTION
 4.3

Climates can change suddenly or slowly.
pp. 132–139

Time: 3 periods (1.5 blocks)
 Lesson Plan, pp. 245–246

 • **RESOURCE CENTERS,** Climate Change; Global Warming
• **MATH TUTORIAL**

 UNIT TRANSPARENCY BOOK
- Big Idea Flow Chart, p. T25
- Daily Vocabulary Scaffolding, p. T26
- 3-Minute Warm-Up, p. T29
- Chapter Outline, pp. T31–T32

 • INVESTIGATE Climate Change, p. 133
• Math in Science, p. 139

 UNIT RESOURCE BOOK
- Datasheet, Climate Change, p. 254
- Math Support, p. 261
- Math Practice, p. 262
- Additional INVESTIGATION, Modeling El Niño, A, B, & C, pp. 272–281

READING AND REINFORCEMENT

- Choose Your Own Strategy, B18–27
- Main Idea and Detail Notes, C37
- Daily Vocabulary Scaffolding, H1–8

 UNIT RESOURCE BOOK
- Vocabulary Practice, pp. 258–259
- Decoding Support, p. 260
- Summarizing the Chapter, pp. 282–283

 Audio Readings CD
Listen to Pupil Edition.

Audio Readings in Spanish CD
Listen to Pupil Edition in Spanish.

UNIT RESOURCE BOOK
- Reading Study Guide, A & B, pp. 226–229
- Spanish Reading Study Guide, pp. 230–231
- Challenge and Extension, p. 232
- Reinforcing Key Concepts, p. 234

UNIT RESOURCE BOOK
- Reading Study Guide, A & B, pp. 237–240
- Spanish Reading Study Guide, pp. 241–242
- Challenge and Extension, p. 243
- Reinforcing Key Concepts, p. 244

UNIT RESOURCE BOOK
- Reading Study Guide, A & B, pp. 247–250
- Spanish Reading Study Guide, pp. 251–252
- Challenge and Extension, p. 253
- Reinforcing Key Concepts, p. 255
- Challenge Reading, pp. 256–257

ASSESSMENT

- Chapter Review, p.141–142
- Standardized Test Practice, p. 143

 UNIT ASSESSMENT BOOK
- Diagnostic Test, pp. 61–62
- Chapter Test, A, B, & C, pp. 66–77
- Alternative Assessment, pp. 78–79
- Unit Test, A, B, & C, pp. 80–91

- Spanish Chapter Test, pp. 185–188
- Spanish Unit Test, pp. 189–192

 Test Generator CD-ROM
Generate customized tests.

Lab Generator CD-ROM
Rubrics for Labs

 Ongoing Assessment, pp. 117–118, 120–122

 Section 4.1 Review, p. 123

 UNIT ASSESSMENT BOOK
Section 4.1 Quiz, p. 63

Ongoing Assessment, pp. 126–128

Section 4.2 Review, p. 129

UNIT ASSESSMENT BOOK
Section 4.2 Quiz, p. 64

 Ongoing Assessment, pp. 132, 134, 136–137

 Section 4.3 Review, p. 138

UNIT ASSESSMENT BOOK
Section 4.3 Quiz, p. 65

STANDARDS

National Standards
A.2–8, A.9.a–c, A.9.e–f, D.1.f, D.1.j, D.2.a, F.5.b–c

See p. 114 for the standards.

National Standards
A.2–8, A.9.a–c, A.9.e–f, D.1.f, D.1.j, F.5.b–c

National Standards
A.2–8, A.9.a–c, A.9.e–f, D.1.f, D.1.j

National Standards
A.2–8, A.9.a–c, A.9.e–f,

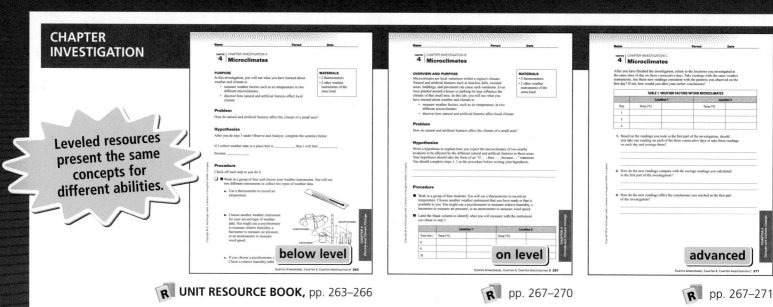

Leveled resources present the same concepts for different abilities.

below level

on level

advanced

 **UNIT RESOURCE BOOK,** pp. 263–266   pp. 267–270   pp. 267–271

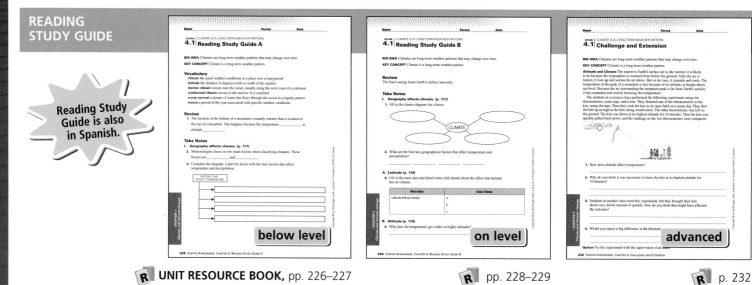

Reading Study Guide is also in Spanish.

below level

on level

advanced

UNIT RESOURCE BOOK, pp. 226–227   pp. 228–229   p. 232

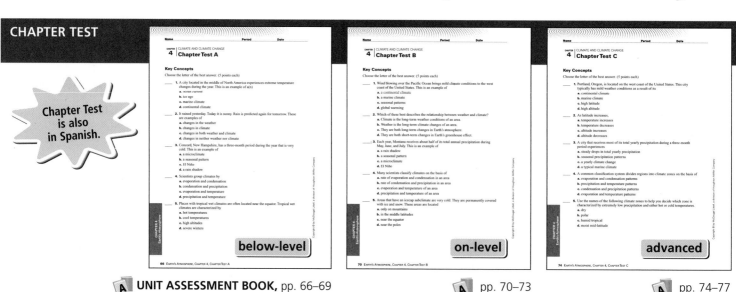

Chapter Test is also in Spanish.

below-level

on-level

advanced

UNIT ASSESSMENT BOOK, pp. 66–69   pp. 70–73   pp. 74–77

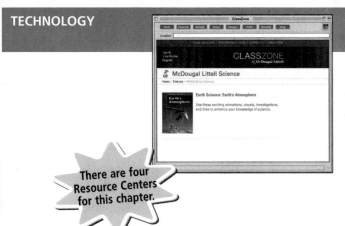

There are four Resource Centers for this chapter.

 **CLASSZONE.COM**

 CD/CD-ROMS

 **CLASSZONE.COM**

VISUAL CONTENT

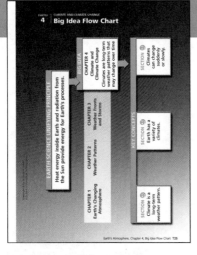

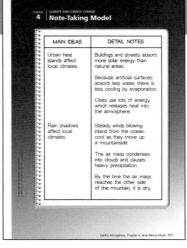

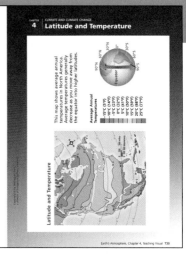

T **UNIT TRANSPARENCY BOOK,** p. T25

T p. T27

T p. T30

MORE SUPPORT

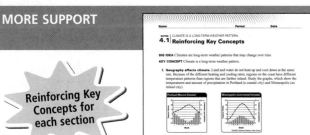

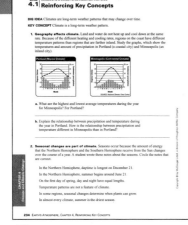

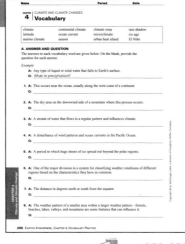

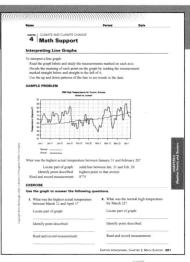

Reinforcing Key Concepts for each section

R **UNIT RESOURCE BOOK,** p. 234

R pp. 258–259

R p. 261

INTRODUCE

the **BIG** idea

Have students look at the photograph of the elephants and discuss how the question in the box links to the Big Idea:

- What clues indicate that more than one climate is shown?

- Would you expect cold or warm temperatures on the flat plain on which the elephants are walking?

- What kind of temperatures would you expect on the mountain peak in the distance? Why?

- Do you think the land on which the elephants live is wet or dry? Why?

National Science Education Standards

Content

D.1.j Global patterns of atmospheric movement influence local weather.

D.2.a Today's Earth processes are similar to those of the past. Earth history is influenced by occasional catastrophes, such as the impact of an asteroid.

Process

A.2–8 Design and conduct an investigation; use tools to gather and interpret data; use evidence to describe, predict, explain, model; think critically to make relationships between evidence and explanation; recognize different explanations and predictions; communicate scientific procedures and explanations; use mathematics.

A.9.a–c, A.9.e–f Understand scientific inquiry by using different investigations, methods, mathematics, and explanations based on logic, evidence, and skepticism.

F.5.b–c Science and technology in society

CHAPTER

Climate and Climate Change

the **BIG** idea

Climates are long-term weather patterns that may change over time.

Key Concepts

SECTION
(4.1) **Climate is a long-term weather pattern.**
Learn about the main factors that affect climate and about seasons.

SECTION
(4.2) **Earth has a variety of climates.**
Learn about different categories of climate.

SECTION
(4.3) **Climates can change suddenly or slowly.**
Learn about climate changes caused by natural events and human activity.

Internet Preview

CLASSZONE.COM
Chapter 4 online resources: Content Review, Simulation, four Resource Centers, Math Tutorial, Test Practice

> **What evidence of different types of climate can you see in this photo?**

INTERNET PREVIEW

CLASSZONE.COM For student use with the following pages:

Review and Practice
- Content Review, pp. 116, 140
- Math Tutorial: Interpreting Line Graphs, p. 139
- Test Practice, p. 143

Activities and Resources
- Internet Activity: El Niño, p. 115
- Simulation: Latitude and Altitude, p. 119
- Resource Centers: Climate Zones, p. 125; Climate Change, p. 134; Global Warming, p. 138

scilinks.org

What is Climate?
Code: MDL012

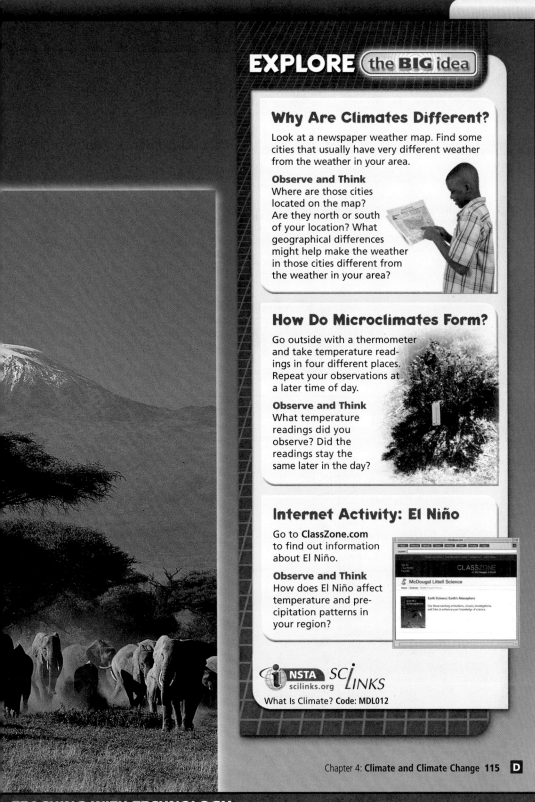

EXPLORE (the BIG idea)

Why Are Climates Different?

Look at a newspaper weather map. Find some cities that usually have very different weather from the weather in your area.

Observe and Think
Where are those cities located on the map? Are they north or south of your location? What geographical differences might help make the weather in those cities different from the weather in your area?

How Do Microclimates Form?

Go outside with a thermometer and take temperature readings in four different places. Repeat your observations at a later time of day.

Observe and Think
What temperature readings did you observe? Did the readings stay the same later in the day?

Internet Activity: El Niño

Go to **ClassZone.com** to find out information about El Niño.

Observe and Think
How does El Niño affect temperature and precipitation patterns in your region?

NSTA
scilinks.org
SCI LINKS
What Is Climate? Code: MDL012

Chapter 4: **Climate and Climate Change 115** **D**

EXPLORE (the BIG idea)

These inquiry-based activities are appropriate for use at home or as a supplement to classroom instruction.

Why Are Climates Different?

PURPOSE To introduce students to the concept of climate variations. Students locate different cities on a newspaper weather map to observe geographical effects on weather.

TIP *10 min.* Students should locate cities as far away from their own as possible.

Answers will vary.

REVISIT after p. 127

How Do Microclimates Form?

PURPOSE To introduce students to the concept of microclimates. Students will take temperature readings in four nearby places and notice varying temperatures.

TIP *10 min.* Have students take their second temperature readings at least eight hours after their first temperature readings.

Answers will vary.

REVISIT after p. 128

Internet Activity: El Niño

PURPOSE To introduce students to the concept of El Niño affecting weather patterns. Students will use the Internet to find out how El Niño affects their region's temperature and precipitation.

TIP *20 min.* Students will want to define the term *El Niño* before they research it.

Answers will vary.

REVISIT after p. 136.

TEACHING WITH TECHNOLOGY

Video Camera In this chapter you might want to film short clips of students as they take weather measurements for the Chapter Investigation, p. 130. Play these clips during an open house or during wait time at parent conferences.

CBL and Probeware If students have probeware, they may want to use a temperature probe for the investigations on pp. 117, 119, 130–131, 133. Other probeware, such as a relative humidity sensor or barometer, may be appropriate for the Chapter Investigation on pp. 130–131.

PREPARE

◯ CONCEPT REVIEW
Activate Prior Knowledge

- Ask students if they have ever been in a tightly closed room where someone was smoking for a while.

- Ask what would happen to the air in the room over time in such a scenario.

- Ask what impact the smoking would have on other people in the room.

- Have students compare the closed system of the room to Earth's atmosphere, which is also a closed system. Relate the scenario to the concepts in the concept review.

▶ TAKING NOTES

Main Idea and Detail Notes

Charting main ideas and details will help students practice outlining skills. Using a two-column format, students categorize facts as main ideas or details.

Choose Your Own Strategy

Having students choose their own note-taking strategies will allow them to use the strategies that personally fit them best. It is also a good review of the strategies already presented, such as frame games, description wheels, and word triangles.

Vocabulary and Note-Taking Resources

- Vocabulary Practice, pp. 258–259
- Decoding Support, p. 260

- Daily Vocabulary Scaffolding, p. T26
- Note-Taking Model, p. T27

- Choose Your Own Strategy, B18–27
- Main Idea and Detail Notes, C37
- Daily Vocabulary Scaffolding, H1–8

◯ CONCEPT REVIEW

- Earth's atmosphere supports life.
- In a system that consists of many parts, the parts usually influence one another.
- Human activities are increasing greenhouse gases.

◀ VOCABULARY REVIEW

altitude p. 10
greenhouse gas p. 24
weather p. 47
precipitation p. 57

CONTENT REVIEW
CLASSZONE.COM
Review concepts and vocabulary.

▶ TAKING NOTES

MAIN IDEA AND DETAIL NOTES

Make a two-column chart. Write the main ideas, such as those in the blue headings, in the column on the left. Write details about each of those main ideas in the column on the right.

CHOOSE YOUR OWN STRATEGY

Take notes about new vocabulary terms, using one or more of the strategies from earlier chapters—**frame game, description wheel,** or **word triangle.** Feel free to mix and match the strategies, or use an entirely different vocabulary strategy.

See the Note-Taking Handbook on pages R45–R51.

SCIENCE NOTEBOOK

MAIN IDEAS	DETAIL NOTES
1. Latitude affects climate.	1. Places close to the equator are usually warmer than places close to the poles.
	1. Latitude has the same effect in both hemispheres.
2. Altitude affects climate.	2. Temperature decreases with altitude.
	2. Altitude can overcome the effect of latitude on temperature.

Word Triangle

DESCRIPTION WHEEL

Frame Game

CHECK READINESS

Administer the Diagnostic Test to determine students' readiness for new science content and their mastery of requisite math skills.

  Diagnostic Test, pp. 61–62

Technology Resources

Students needing content and math skills should visit **ClassZone.com.**

- **CONTENT REVIEW**
- **MATH TUTORIAL**

  CONTENT REVIEW CD-ROM

4.1

KEY CONCEPT

Climate is a long-term weather pattern.

◀ **BEFORE, you learned**

- The Sun's energy heats Earth's surface unevenly
- The atmosphere's temperature changes with altitude
- Oceans affect wind flow

▶ **NOW, you will learn**

- How climate is related to weather
- What factors affect climate
- About seasonal patterns of temperature and precipitation

VOCABULARY

climate p. 117
latitude p. 118
marine climate p. 120
continental climate p. 120
ocean current p. 121
season p. 122

EXPLORE Solar Energy

How does the angle of light affect heating?

PROCEDURE

1. Tape a black square over the bulb of each thermometer. Then tape the thermometers to the cardboard tube as shown.

2. Place the arrangement on a sunny windowsill or under a lamp. One square should directly face the light. Record the temperatures.

3. Wait 10 minutes. Record the temperature changes.

WHAT DO YOU THINK?

- How did the temperature readings change?
- How did the angle of light affect the amount of heat absorbed?

MATERIALS

- tape
- 2 black paper squares
- 2 thermometers
- 1 cardboard tube from a paper towel roll
- sunny windowsill or lamp

VOCABULARY
You could use a frame game diagram to take notes about the term *climate*.

Geography affects climate.

You can check your current local weather simply by looking out a window. Weather conditions may not last very long; they can change daily or even hourly. In contrast, the climate of your area changes over much longer periods of time. **Climate** is the characteristic weather conditions in a place over a long period. Climate influences the kind of clothes you own, the design of your home, and even the sports you play.

All parts of weather make up climate, including wind, humidity, and sunshine. However, meteorologists usually focus on patterns of temperature and precipitation when they classify climates. Four key geographical factors affect temperature and precipitation: latitude, altitude, distance from large bodies of water, and ocean currents.

Chapter 4: **Climate and Climate Change** 117 **D**

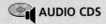

4.1 FOCUS

▶ **Set Learning Goals**

Students will

- Explain how climate is related to weather.
- Identify factors that affect climate.
- Define and describe seasons.
- Compare heating and cooling rates of soil and water in an experiment.

◀ **3-Minute Warm-Up**

Display Transparency 28 or copy this exercise on the board:
Fill in the blank to complete the sentence.

1. Uneven _____ of Earth's surface causes differences in air pressure. *heating*

2. Differences in _____ set air in motion. *air pressure*

3. _____ blow over Earth's surface for thousands of kilometers in steady patterns. *global winds*

T 3-Minute Warm-Up, p. T28

4.1 MOTIVATE

EXPLORE Solar Energy

PURPOSE To introduce the concept that the angle of light affects the heating of an object

TIP *15 min.* Explain that the purpose of the black squares is to absorb light on a flat surface.

WHAT DO YOU THINK? *Answers will vary, but the square directly facing the light should be warmer. More heat is absorbed when the light strikes a surface directly.*

Ongoing Assessment

Explain how climate is related to weather.

Ask: What is the relationship between climate and weather? *The term* climate *refers to average weather conditions over a long period.*

Teach from Visuals

Point out that the map is a flat representation of part of the curved surface on the globe. To help students relate the map to the globe, have them match latitudes represented on the right side of the map with latitudes on the globe.

To help students interpret the visual, ask:

• How are the degree measurements on the land part of the map different from the degree measurements on the far right and left sides of the map? *Degree measurements on the land part are temperature measurements in degrees Celsius. Degree measurements on the far right and left sides of the map (over water) are measurements of latitude.*

• In addition to degrees Celsius, in what unit is air temperature sometimes measured? *degrees Fahrenheit, or F*

This visual is also available as T30 in the Unit Transparency Book.

Develop Geometry Skills

Explain to students that the globe is a sphere, or circle in three dimensions.

Ask students to observe the image of the globe on this page. Point out that a line running between the poles would meet the equator at a right angle, which is 90°. The angle would cover one quarter of the globe's circumference.

Have students determine mathematically how many degrees are in the total sphere. *(90° · 4 = 360°)*

Summarize that a circle or sphere has 360 total degrees, that each half has 180 degrees, and each quarter has 90 degrees.

Ongoing Assessment

 *Answer: Temperatures generally decrease as latitude increases.*

Latitude and Temperature

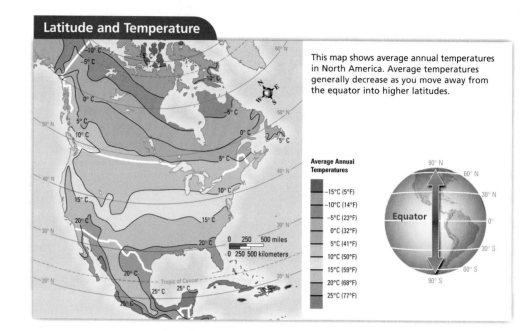

This map shows average annual temperatures in North America. Average temperatures generally decrease as you move away from the equator into higher latitudes.

Average Annual Temperatures

■	–15°C (5°F)
■	–10°C (14°F)
■	–5°C (23°F)
■	0°C (32°F)
■	5°C (41°F)
■	10°C (50°F)
■	15°C (59°F)
■	20°C (68°F)
■	25°C (77°F)

0   250   500 miles
0   250 500 kilometers

Latitude

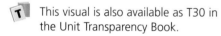 **READING TiP**
Notice on the globe in the illustration that latitude numbers get higher as you move away from the equator.

One factor that affects temperature is latitude. **Latitude** is the distance in degrees north or south of the equator, which is 0°. Each degree equals 1/360 of the distance around the world.

As you read in Chapter 2, the Sun heats Earth's curved surface unevenly. Sunlight strikes Earth's surface directly near the equator. Near the poles, sunlight strikes the surface at a lower angle, so it is more spread out. In addition, the polar regions receive little or no solar energy during winter.

Because of this pattern of uneven heating, average annual temperatures generally decrease as you move closer to the poles. For example, Belém, Brazil, which is almost on the equator, has an average temperature of about 26°C (79°F). Qaanaaq, Greenland, located close to the North Pole, has an average temperature of only –11°C (12°F).

Latitude has the same effect on temperature in both hemispheres. Suppose one city is located at 45° N and another city is located at 45° S. The first city is in the Northern Hemisphere, and the second is in the Southern Hemisphere. However, they are both nearly 5000 kilometers (3100 mi) from the equator, so they would receive about the same amount of sunlight over a year.

 CHECK YOUR READING What is the connection between latitude and temperature?

DIFFERENTIATE INSTRUCTION

? More Reading Support

A What word means "distance in degrees north or south of the equator"? *latitude*

B Is sunlight more concentrated at the equator or at the poles? *equator*

English Learners Readers are often asked to imagine a situation and consider its implications. For example, *Suppose one city is located at 45° N and another city is located at 45° S* (p.118), or *If you rode a cable car up a mountain . . .* (p. 119). These sentences require the reader to imagine a hypothetical scenario. This is not always clear to English learners due to their uncertainty of the language. When this occurs, be sure that English learners understand that the situations are hypothetical.

Altitude

Altitude, the height above sea level, is another geographical factor that affects temperature. If you rode a cable car up a mountain, the temperature would decrease by about 6.5°C (11.7°F) for every kilometer you rose in altitude. Why does it get colder as you move higher up? The troposphere is mainly warmed from below by Earth's surface. As convection lifts the warmed air to higher altitudes, the air expands and cools.

Altitude increases can overcome the effect of lower latitudes on temperature. The temperature at the peak of a tall mountain is low regardless of the mountain's latitude. One example is Mount Stanley, near the border of Uganda and the Democratic Republic of the Congo in central Africa. Although it lies just a short distance from the equator, Mount Stanley has ice sheets and a permanent covering of snow. Notice in the illustration how one mountain can have several types of climates.

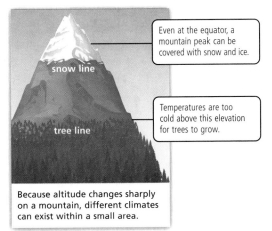

Even at the equator, a mountain peak can be covered with snow and ice.

Temperatures are too cold above this elevation for trees to grow.

Because altitude changes sharply on a mountain, different climates can exist within a small area.

SIMULATION
CLASSZONE.COM

Explore the effects of latitude and altitude.

INVESTIGATE Heating and Cooling Rates

How quickly do soil and water heat and cool?

PROCEDURE

1. Mark a line 3 centimeters from the top of each cup. Fill one cup to the line with water and the other with soil. Place a thermometer into the contents of each cup. Wait 2 minutes. Record the temperature in each cup.

2. Place the cups side by side in bright sunlight or under a lamp. Wait 10 minutes. Record the temperature in each cup.

3. Move the cups into a shaded area to cool. Wait 10 minutes. Record the temperature in each cup.

WHAT DO YOU THINK?

- Which heats up faster, soil or water?
- Which cools faster?
- How might the heating and cooling rates of inland areas compare with those of coastal areas?

CHALLENGE Will adding gravel to the soil change your results? Repeat the activity to test your prediction.

SKILL FOCUS
Comparing

MATERIALS
- 2 cups
- ruler
- soil
- water at room temperature
- 2 thermometers
- sunlight or lamp

TIME
25 minutes

Chapter 4: **Climate and Climate Change** 119 **D**

Teach from Visuals

Tell students that the visual of how oceans affect climate is a composite, or combination, of several different visual elements.

To help students interpret the visual, ask:

• What map do you see in the visual? *part of North America or part of the United States*

• What kind of graphs do you see in the visual? *combination bar and line graphs*

• On the graph for Portland, what represents temperature? *the plots on the line graph* What represents precipitation? *the bars in the bar graph*

Real World Example

We use water's ability to hold and slowly disperse heat in a number of practical ways. Gardeners use water-holding plastic "sleeves" or "tepees" to surround tender plants on cold spring nights. During the day, sunlight warms the water in folds or hollows inside the plastic; then the warm water radiates that heat during the cold night, protecting the plants from frost.

Develop Critical Thinking

APPLY Have students consider the climates of two U.S. cities at similar latitude: San Diego, Calif., and Topeka, Kan. On a wall map of the United States, point out the locations of these cities. Ask students which city is near a major body of water. *San Diego* Ask which is in the middle of a huge landmass. *Topeka* Ask students: Which city is more likely to have a marine climate? *San Diego*

Ongoing Assessment

CHECK YOUR READING *Answer: Marine climates have mild temperatures compared to continental climates at the same latitude, and marine climates also generally receive steady precipitation.*

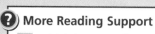

How Oceans Affect Climate

Regions near oceans have milder temperatures than inland regions at the same latitudes.

45° N

Portland: Latitude: 45.6° N

Minneapolis: Latitude: 44.9° N

35° N

PACIFIC OCEAN

Portland (Marine Climate)

Degrees Celsius / Centimeters precipitation / Month

Minneapolis (Continental Climate)

Degrees Celsius / Centimeters precipitation / Month

SOURCE: National Climatic Data Center

READING VISUALS The bars in the graphs show average precipitation, and the lines show average temperature. Compare each of these patterns in the two cities.

Large Bodies of Water

 E

Land heats up and cools off faster than water. Because oceans and large lakes slow down heating and cooling of the air, coastal regions tend to have milder temperatures than areas far inland. Large bodies of water also affect precipitation. Climates influenced by these factors are called marine and continental climates.

• **Marine climates** occur near the ocean, usually along the west coasts of continents. Temperatures do not drop very far at night. Summers and winters are mild. Many marine climates receive steady precipitation because winds blowing off the ocean bring moisture to the atmosphere. Large lakes can have a similar effect on the climates near their shores.

 F

• **Continental climates** occur in the interior of continents. Weather patterns vary in the different types of continental climates. However, most have large differences between daytime and nighttime temperatures because they lack the influence of nearby oceans. For the same reason, winter months are usually much colder than summer months.

CHECK YOUR READING How are marine climates different from continental climates?

DIFFERENTIATE INSTRUCTION

? More Reading Support

E Which heats up faster, land or water? *land*

F Which type of climate has more extreme temperatures, marine or continental? *continental*

Below Level Encourage students to look at the shape formed by each line in the graphs. Explain that graphs allow us to absorb lots of information by viewing data as a visual element. Ask: How might you compare the two lines by describing them as roller coasters? *Portland line: "baby" roller coaster with a gentle slope; Minneapolis line: a more challenging roller coaster with a steep slope.* Ask: How does the roller coaster imagery help you understand the climate comparison between the two cities? *It helps clarify that Minneapolis has more extreme temperature changes than Portland.*

Ocean Currents

? **G**

Ocean currents are streams of water that flow through oceans in regular patterns. They influence climates by transferring energy from one part of an ocean to another. In general, warm-water currents carry warmth from the tropics to higher latitudes, where they help keep coastal regions warm. Cold-water currents have the opposite effect. They cool coastal regions by carrying cold water from polar regions toward the equator.

? **H**

The illustration below shows the paths of ocean currents in the North Atlantic. Find the Gulf Stream on the illustration. The Gulf Stream is a major warm-water current. As the waters that feed the Gulf Stream pass near the Caribbean Sea and the Gulf of Mexico, the concentrated solar rays that strike there warm its water. Water flowing in the Gulf Stream can be 6°C to 10°C (11–18°F) warmer than the surrounding water. The Gulf Stream warms the winds that blow over it. In turn, those winds warm coastal regions.

Like altitude, ocean currents can overcome the effects of latitude. For example, London, England, has an average annual temperature of nearly 11°C (52°F). Natashquan, a town in eastern Canada at about the same latitude and altitude, has an average annual temperature of only 1°C (34°F). London's milder climate is the result of an ocean current carrying warm water to Europe's west coast.

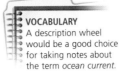

VOCABULARY
A description wheel would be a good choice for taking notes about the term *ocean current*.

Ocean Currents

Ocean currents can cause two places at the same latitude to have different climates.

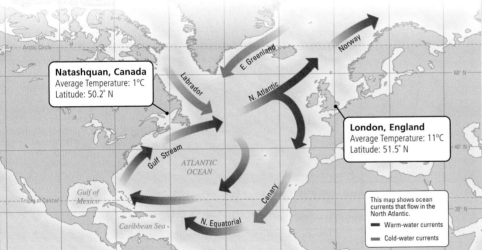

Natashquan, Canada
Average Temperature: 1°C
Latitude: 50.2° N

London, England
Average Temperature: 11°C
Latitude: 51.5° N

This map shows ocean currents that flow in the North Atlantic.
— Warm-water currents
— Cold-water currents

Teach Difficult Concepts

Some students may have a hard time understanding how streams of water, or currents, can flow within larger bodies of water. Explain that surface currents are mainly driven by global winds. Tell students that ocean currents move through the ocean the same way liquid moves when you blow across a bowl of soup to cool it.

Teach from Visuals

To help students interpret the "Ocean Currents" visual, ask:

• What do you see in the visual? *a map*

• What continents and oceans do you see on the map? *North America, Europe, and northern Africa, with the Atlantic Ocean in the middle*

• On the map, what do the arrows represent? *ocean currents*

Point out that ocean currents follow fairly regular paths along coastlines and into and across oceans.

Ongoing Assessment

Identify factors that affect climate.

Ask: What factors, in addition to latitude, affect climate? *altitude, distance from large bodies of water, and ocean currents*

DIFFERENTIATE INSTRUCTION

? **More Reading Support**

G What are streams of water that flow through oceans in a pattern called? *ocean currents*

H Name an important warm-water current in the Atlantic Ocean. *the Gulf Stream*

Advanced Have interested students choose a city with a marine climate and another city with a continental climate. Direct students to use a national news source to keep track of the temperatures in these two cities for two weeks. Have students use this temperature data to make a line graph showing the temperature changes. Make sure their graphs have two lines—one for each city. Students can also write a short paragraph comparing the two climates based on the graph data.

R Challenge and Extension, p. 232

Address Misconceptions

IDENTIFY Ask: Is the amount of daylight the same or varied in every part of North America right now? If students answer "the same," they may hold the misconception that length of daylight does not vary by locale, but only by season.

CORRECT Point out that Earth's polar regions have 24-hour daylight at midsummer and 24-hour darkness at midwinter. Make the point that other regions of the globe have different amounts of daylight and darkness compared with these polar extremes, even on the same day.

REASSESS On a world map or globe, point out two distinct locations in the Northern Hemisphere, one in the high latitudes and one in the tropics. Ask students to contrast the balance of daylight and darkness in the locales at a particular time, such as late December.

Teach from Visuals

To help students interpret the graph of temperatures, ask:

- What type of graph is at the bottom of the page? *a line graph*

- Why are there two lines on the line graph? *because the graph includes data for two towns—Half Moon Bay, CA, and Bloomington, IN.*

- On which side of the graph do you find a scale for degrees Celsius? *left side* On which side do you find a scale for degrees Fahrenheit? *right side*

Ongoing Assessment

Define and describe seasons.

Ask: Explain how extreme heat and heavy snowfall can occur in one place during the same year. *Extreme heat occurs during summer, and heavy snowfall occurs in winter.*

CHECK YOUR READING *Answer: longest—summer, shortest—winter*

Seasonal changes are part of climate.

What marks the change of seasons where you live? In the Midwest and New England, there are four distinct seasons. Mild spring and autumn months come between hotter summers and colder winters. In Florida and other southern states, the seasonal changes are much less extreme. **Seasons** are periods of the year associated with specific weather conditions, such as cold temperatures or frequent rain. These periods are part of the overall pattern that makes up a climate.

Temperature Patterns

MAIN IDEA AND DETAILS Record in your notes the important details about seasonal changes.

Seasons occur because the amounts of energy that the Northern Hemisphere and the Southern Hemisphere receive from the Sun change over the course of a year. Winter begins in the Northern Hemisphere around December 21, when the daytime is shortest. Summer begins around June 21, when the daytime is longest. Spring begins around March 21, and autumn begins around September 22. On the first day of spring and of autumn, day and night are equal in length. There are 12 hours of daylight and 12 hours of darkness.

CHECK YOUR READING Which seasons have the longest and the shortest periods of daytime?

Temperature patterns are an important feature of climate. The graph below shows the average monthly temperatures in Half Moon Bay, California, and Bloomington, Indiana. Each city has an average annual temperature of about 12°C (54°F). However, Bloomington has hot summers and cold winters, while Half Moon Bay has mild weather all year. Although their average annual temperatures are the same, they have different climates.

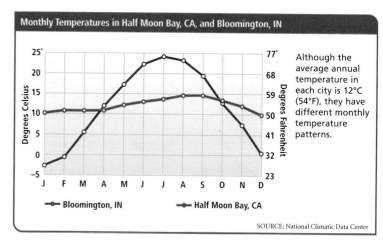

Monthly Temperatures in Half Moon Bay, CA, and Bloomington, IN

Although the average annual temperature in each city is 12°C (54°F), they have different monthly temperature patterns.

● Bloomington, IN   ● Half Moon Bay, CA

SOURCE: National Climatic Data Center

DIFFERENTIATE INSTRUCTION

More Reading Support

I What do most of the days in a season have in common? *similar weather patterns*

J What is the source of the energy that causes seasons? *sunlight*

Alternative Assessment Ask students to think about the climate in which they live. Have them consider whether it is more like that of Bloomington, Indiana, or Half Moon Bay, California. Encourage them to consider how different the seasons are from one another, how hot and cold it gets at different times of the year, and what kinds of clothes they wear during different seasons. Have students share their conclusions with one another.

Dry Season

Wet Season

INDIA

These photos show the same rice fields in India at different times of the year.

Precipitation Patterns

Like temperature patterns, seasonal patterns of precipitation vary among different climates. For example, Connecticut's precipitation is distributed fairly evenly throughout the year. In contrast, nearly half of Montana's precipitation falls during May, June, and July. Many tropical regions have wet and dry seasons. These regions stay warm all year long, but certain months are much rainier than other months.

The seasonal pattern of precipitation can determine the types of plants that grow in a region and the length of the growing season. Although Montana is a fairly dry state, much of its precipitation falls during the growing season. This pattern allows the state to be a major grain producer.

4.1 Review

KEY CONCEPTS

1. Explain the difference between climate and weather.

2. Make a chart showing how latitude, altitude, large bodies of water, and ocean currents affect climate.

3. How does the length of daytime change with each season?

CRITICAL THINKING

4. **Predict** How would a region's climate change if a cold-water ocean current stopped flowing past it?

5. **Identify Cause** What geographical factors might cause a region to have a narrow temperature range and mild weather all year?

◌ CHALLENGE

6. **Infer** Suggest specific climate characteristics that might make the owners of a vacation resort decide to advertise the average annual temperature rather than provide temperature averages for each month or season.

ANSWERS

1. weather: atmospheric conditions that last up to a few weeks; climate: weather conditions over a long period

2. latitude: increase makes temperatures decrease; altitude: increase makes temperatures decrease; large bodies of water: moderate

temperatures in coastal regions; ocean currents: move energy from tropics toward polar regions

3. daytime is longest in summer, shortest in winter

4. probably become warmer

5. nearby ocean and a warm-water ocean current

6. If the resort were located in an area with extreme temperature ranges the owners would suggest a mild year-round climate by advertising the average annual temperature.

INCLUSION Color-blind students may not be able to tell the difference in color between the two photographs of the rice fields. Ask students to suggest other ways to contrast the photographs. For example, lines in the ground are harder to see in the wet season photograph, perhaps because more vegetation is covering the ground than in the dry season.

Reinforce (the BIG idea)

Have students relate the section to the Big Idea.

 Reinforcing Key Concepts, p. 234

4.1 ASSESS & RETEACH

Assess

 Section 4.1 Quiz, p. 63

Reteach

Divide the class into four teams, and select one member of each team to be recorder. Assign each team one of the the four factors identified in the lesson as affecting climate (pp. 118–121):

• latitude
• altitude
• distance from large bodies of water
• ocean currents

Instruct team members to read the section about their factor and decide how the factor affects climate. The recorder will write down the team's conclusions.

On the board, draw a description wheel with "Climate" at the center and four spokes. Have a member from each team report to the class. Fill in the description wheel with the climate factors reported. Add any overlooked information. Have students record the filled-in description wheel as a study aid.

Technology Resources

Have students visit **ClassZone.com** for reaching of Key Concepts.

 CONTENT REVIEW

 CONTENT REVIEW CD-ROM

Set Learning Goal

To understand why architects need to incorporate knowledge about climate in their designs for buildings

Present the Science

Remind students that one of the major purposes of buildings is to give people protection from the elements. They should understand that requirements for various features of buildings differ according to climate. Make sure students know that architects design all aspects of buildings.

SNOW Structural elements such as roofs must be strong enough to bear the weight of frozen precipitation such as snow, sleet, hail, and glaze.

FLOODS In regions of extremely heavy rainfall, flooding is not the only concern that impacts construction. Architects must design roofs, gutters, and drains that quickly carry water away from the structure.

HEAT Avoiding extreme heat is a critical factor in health and comfort. Where sunlight is direct and intense, carelessly placed windows might magnify sunlight, increasing the heat inside a building. Likewise, some metals concentrate heat.

Discussion Question

Ask: Suppose an architect who has worked for many years in the northern United States moves his or her business to the Southwest. How do you think the architect should prepare to meet clients' needs in the new locale? *The architect should study climate conditions in the new locale. He or she should pay special attention to climate extremes, including frequency and duration of hot spells.*

Close

Ask: How does an architect design a building to provide protection from the elements? *An architect designs structures and systems that resist extreme weather conditions.*

SCIENCE on the JOB

ARCHITECT

Climate and Architecture

When architects design houses, office towers, and other buildings, they think about how the climate will affect the structures and the people who will use them. For example, when planning a house for a cold climate, an architect will consider ways to keep warm air inside. He or she might call for energy-efficient glass in the windows, thick insulation in walls, and an extra set of inside doors to close off entryways.

Snow

Snow is very heavy. Because of snow's weight, architects usually design slanted roofs on houses built in snowy climates. The sharper the slant, the easier snow slides off. This church was built in Norway around 1150.

Heat

In the 1960s, Houston wanted to get a major league baseball team. City officials asked architects to design a stadium suitable for Houston's hot, rainy climate. They created the first domed, air-conditioned ballpark, the Astrodome.

Floods

Intense rains and high winds combine to make floods common in many places. To protect themselves, some people who live on the shores of large rivers, lakes, and oceans build their homes on stilts. This home is in the Northern Territory of Australia. It was designed by the architect Glenn Murcutt and completed in 1994.

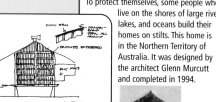

EXPLORE

1. **ANALYZING** Bring to class photos of buildings located in various climate regions. Discuss whether the architecture reflects the influence of the climate.

2. **CHALLENGE** Use building blocks to make a model of a house for a warm climate in which the wind usually blows from the west. Place doors, windows, and walls to get the best flow of air through the house. To check the airflow, dust your model with a light powder. Blow lightly and note how much powder moves.

EXPLORE

1. ANALYZING Answers will vary, but they should reflect an understanding of how climate influences design. If feasible, you might want to help students pinpoint the locales from which the pictures come.

2. CHALLENGE Models should have windows and doors on the western and eastern sides of the house. Before students do the activity, you might prompt them to recall a warm, breezy spring or summer day at home. Did they or other family members open up windows to get air flowing through the house? What was the path of that air flow? Students should come to the conclusion that to obtain the best circulation, they need openings on more than one face, or side, of the house.

KEY CONCEPT

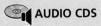

4.2 Earth has a variety of climates.

◀ **BEFORE, you learned**

- The main factors that affect climate are latitude, altitude, distance from large bodies of water, and ocean currents
- Seasonal changes in temperature and precipitation are part of climate

▶ **NOW, you will learn**

- How scientists classify climates
- About the characteristics of different climate zones
- How natural features and human activity affect climate

VOCABULARY

climate zone p. 125
microclimate p. 128
urban heat island p. 128
rain shadow p. 129

THINK ABOUT

What does ground cover reveal about climate?

For trees and bushes to grow, they must have enough precipitation and at least a few months of mild temperatures each year. Lichens and some small plants can grow in harsher climates. The photograph shows typical ground cover along Greenland's rocky coast. What does the ground cover tell you about Greenland's long-term weather patterns?

Scientists have identified six major climate zones.

RESOURCE CENTER
CLASSZONE.COM

Find out more about climate zones.

Classification systems can help you see patterns. For example, communities are often classified as cities, towns, and villages. This classification system organizes communities on the basis of size. Two cities in different parts of a country might have more in common than a village and a nearby city.

To show patterns in climate data, scientists have developed systems for classifying climates. A **climate zone** is one of the major divisions in a system for classifying the climates of different regions based on characteristics they have in common. The most widely used system groups climates by temperature and precipitation. The six major climate zones of this classification system are (1) humid tropical, (2) dry, (3) moist mid-latitude with mild winters, (4) moist mid-latitude with severe winters, (5) polar, and (6) highland.

Chapter 4: **Climate and Climate Change** 125 **D**

RESOURCES FOR DIFFERENTIATED INSTRUCTION

Below Level
UNIT RESOURCE BOOK
- Reading Study Guide A, pp. 237–238
- Decoding Support, p. 260

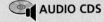 **AUDIO CDS**

Advanced
UNIT RESOURCE BOOK
Challenge and Extension, p. 243

English Learners
UNIT RESOURCE BOOK
Spanish Reading Study Guide, pp. 241–242

AUDIO CDS

- Audio Readings in Spanish
- Audio Readings (English)

○ **Set Learning Goals**

Students will

- Explain how scientists classify climates.
- Identify characteristics of different climate zones.
- Explain how natural features and human activity affect climate.

◐ **3-Minute Warm-Up**

Display Transparency 28 or copy this exercise on the board:

- City X: hot and dry in summer; mild and rainy in winter.
- City Y: hot and rainy in summer; mild and rainy in winter.
- City Z: cool and rainy all year.

Ask: How are these climates similar to and different from each other? *City X and City Y have similar winter climates. City Y has much more rain in the summer than does City X. City Z is different from both Cities X and Y because it is cool all year rather than hot and mild. City Z is similar to City X in that its summers are rainy.*

T 3-Minute Warm-Up, p. T28

4.2 MOTIVATE

THINK ABOUT

PURPOSE Students think about what different types of ground cover reveal about particular climates.

DISCUSS Tell students that lichens are one of the few organisms that can survive long periods of no precipitation. Ask: How does this compare to the ground cover in a rain forest? *Rain forests have more vegetation.* What does this suggest about the amount of precipitation in rain forests? *There is more than in areas with lots of lichens.*

Answer: Greenland's coast has a harsh climate.

Teach from Visuals

Help students view the "World Climates" map in two different ways. (1) Take a macro view; that is, view the map as a whole and think what the broad bands of color suggest. (2) Take a micro view; find each color in the key and point to instances of that color (climate zone) on the map. Remind students that the chart on the lower left with the color boxes is the map key.

To help students interpret the visual, ask:

- Using clues from the map, what do you think the bands of color stand for? *They stand for climates of the world.*

- Where on the map do you find tundra? *in the high latitudes, close to the poles*

Develop Critical Thinking

APPLY Ask students: If you lived in an area that is close to a line separating two climate zones on this map, how would you classify your climate from the map? *by mixing characteristics of both zones*

Ongoing Assessment

Explain how scientists classify climates.

Ask: What are the two most important factors that scientists consider when identifying climate zones? *temperature and precipitation*

READING VISUALS *Answer: 10 subclimates*

The chart on page 127 summarizes information about the different climate zones. Each climate zone has a specific set of characteristics. For example, humid tropical climates are hot and rainy. Many areas close to the equator have this type of climate.

A

Notice that most of the climate zones are further divided into subclimates. When scientists identify a subclimate, they choose one characteristic that makes it different from other subclimates within the same climate zone. For example, the humid tropical climate zone includes tropical wet climates and tropical wet and dry climates. The difference between them is that tropical wet climates have abundant rainfall every month, while tropical wet and dry climates have a few months of dry weather.

READING TIP
The colors on the map below correspond to the colors in the chart on page 127. As you read descriptions on the chart, look back to the map to find examples.

The climate map below shows that many regions scattered throughout the world have similar climates. When you use the map, keep in mind that climates do not change suddenly at the borders of the colored areas. Instead, each climate gradually blends into neighboring ones.

World Climates

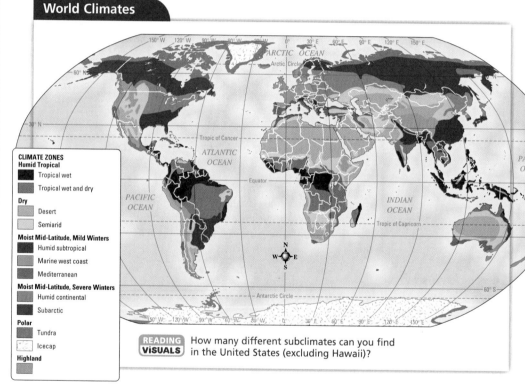

CLIMATE ZONES

Humid Tropical
- Tropical wet
- Tropical wet and dry

Dry
- Desert
- Semiarid

Moist Mid-Latitude, Mild Winters
- Humid subtropical
- Marine west coast
- Mediterranean

Moist Mid-Latitude, Severe Winters
- Humid continental
- Subarctic

Polar
- Tundra
- Icecap

Highland

READING VISUALS How many different subclimates can you find in the United States (excluding Hawaii)?

DIFFERENTIATE INSTRUCTION

? **More Reading Support**

A What can climate zones be subdivided into? *subclimates*

English Learners Have English learners write the definitions of *climate zone, microclimate, urban heat island,* and *rain shadow* in their Science Word Dictionaries. Students may not have prior knowledge of lichens on p. 125. Other languages may organize information in ways not commonly used in English. Be sure English learners understand how to read the Climate Classification chart on p. 127.

Climate Classification

Climate Zone	Subclimate	Description
Humid tropical	**Tropical wet** Example: Amazon rain forest in South America	Temperatures remain high throughout the year. Rising hot, humid air causes heavy cloud cover and abundant rainfall, with no dry season. Annual rainfall usually is more than 2.5 meters (8 ft).
	Tropical wet and dry Example: Miami, Florida	Like tropical wet climates, these climates are hot and rainy, but they have a dry season in winter.
Dry	**Desert** Example: Phoenix, Arizona	Precipitation is infrequent and scanty—usually less than 20 centimeters (8 in.) per year. Deserts include the hottest places on Earth, but they can be cool, especially at night. In most deserts high daytime temperatures lead to rapid evaporation, which increases the dryness.
	Semiarid Example: Denver, Colorado	These regions are found next to deserts. They have wider temperature ranges than deserts and are not as dry. Most of the Great Plains region in North America is semiarid.
Moist mid-latitude with mild winters	**Humid subtropical** Example: Charlotte, North Carolina	Summers are hot and muggy. Winters are usually mild. Precipitation is fairly even throughout the year.
	Marine west coast Example: Seattle, Washington	These regions have mild temperatures year-round and steady precipitation. Low clouds and fog are common.
	Mediterranean Example: San Francisco, California	Dry summers and mild, wet winters are typical of these regions. Some coastal areas have cool summers and frequent fog.
Moist mid-latitude with severe winters	**Humid continental** Example: Des Moines, Iowa	These regions have hot summers and cold winters. Precipitation is fairly even throughout the year. Snow covers the ground for 1 to 4 months in winter.
	Subarctic Example: Fairbanks, Alaska	Temperatures usually stay below freezing for 6 to 8 months each year. Summers are brief and cool. The amount of precipitation is low, but snow remains on the ground for long periods because of the cold.
Polar	**Tundra** Example: Barrow, Alaska	The average temperature of the warmest month is below 10°C (50°F). A deep layer of soil is frozen year-round. During summer a shallow layer at the surface thaws out and turns muddy.
	Icecap Example: Antarctica	The surface is permanently covered with ice and snow. Temperatures rarely rise above freezing, even in summer.
Highland	**Highland** Example: Rocky Mountains	Because temperature drops as altitude increases, mountain regions can contain many climates. Tall mountains may have a year-round covering of ice and snow at their peaks.

Tropical wet

Desert

Marine west coast

Humid continental

Tundra

127 D

Teach from Visuals

To help students interpret the "Climate Classification" visual, ask:

- Is the information in the chart more detailed on the right or left side? *right*
- Does each Climate Zone category have an accompanying photo? *yes*
- What do the colors in the Subclimate column represent? *subclimates* Where have you seen this color code before? *on the map on p. 126*

EXPLORE (the **BIG** idea)

Revisit "Why Are Climates Different?" on p. 115. Have students share the information that they found about climate.

Ongoing Assessment
Identify characteristics of different climate zones.

Ask: Using the chart, describe precipitation in a desert subclimate. *Precipitation in a desert subclimate is infrequent and scanty.*

DIFFERENTIATE INSTRUCTION

Inclusion Have students with cognitive disabilities deconstruct the Climate Classification chart. Give each student a photocopy of the chart, scissors, tape, and six blank sheets of paper. Have students cut out blocks from the Climate Zone column and tape each block near the top center of a blank page. Beside each block, have students write a simple definition of the climate zone name. For example, they might write "hot, rains a lot" for *Humid tropical* or "doesn't rain much" for *Dry*. Help students with words they don't know.

Integrate the Sciences

One reason green plants such as trees create microclimates is because of transpiration. When the area around a plant becomes warm, the plant will release water through its leaves in a process called transpiration. The nearby area then cools down due to the extra moisture in the air.

Real World Example

Home gardeners know they have microclimates right in their yards. They plant flowering shrubs that can't take strong, bitter winter winds in protected places. A protected place might be an east-facing stoop with thick, high bushes nearby. The stoop and shrubs stop howling winds in winter, which usually blow from west to east or north to south. Gardeners may put plants that tolerate hot, dry conditions at the southwest corner of the house. In summer, heat builds up to a maximum in mid-afternoon when sunlight shines on the western walls of buildings.

EXPLORE (the **BIG** idea)

Revisit "How Do Microclimates Form?" on p. 115. Have students share their observations.

Ongoing Assessment

Explain how natural features and human activity affect climate.

Ask: How does a city's microclimate compare to the climate of surrounding rural areas? *Cities tend to have microclimates that are warmer than surrounding areas.*

 Answer: by releasing heat from the use of energy

Natural features and human activity can affect local climates.

The climate map on page 126 shows three subclimates in Madagascar, a large island off the east coast of Africa. But if you went to Madagascar, you would probably notice a greater variety of climates. A meadow might be warmer than a nearby wooded area, and a city block might be warmer than a meadow.

READING **TiP**

You can use word parts to help you recall the meaning of climate terms. The prefix *sub-* can indicate a part of a larger unit. The prefix *micro-* means "very small."

The climates of smaller areas within a subclimate are called **microclimates.** The area of a microclimate can be as large as a river valley or smaller than a garden. Forests, beaches, lakes, valleys, hills, and mountains are some of the features that influence local climates. For example, sea breezes often make beaches cooler than nearby inland areas on warm afternoons.

Shade from the tree produces a cooler microclimate where snow takes longer to melt.

Urban Heat Islands

Humans create artificial surfaces that can also affect local climates. Cities are usually warmer than surrounding rural areas. The warmer body of air over a city is called an **urban heat island.** At certain times the air temperature may be as much as 12°C (22°F) higher in a large city than in the nearby countryside. The following factors contribute to this effect:

- During the day, buildings and streets absorb more solar energy than do grass, trees, and soil. These artificial surfaces release the additional stored energy at night, which warms the air over a city.
- Evaporation of moisture helps cool areas. Because artificial surfaces absorb less water than most natural surfaces, there is less cooling from evaporation in cities than in rural areas.
- Cities use a lot of energy for cooling, transportation, and other activities. The use of energy releases heat into the atmosphere.

 CHECK YOUR READING How do cities influence local temperature?

DIFFERENTIATE INSTRUCTION

More Reading Support

B What is the climate of a small area called? *microclimate*

C What is the warmer body of air over a city called? *urban heat island*

Advanced Challenge students to explain why rain shadows of mountain ranges can affect subclimates as well as microclimates. *Rain shadows can be caused by a whole range of mountains affecting a large region, or single mountains affecting a small area.*

 Challenge and Extension, p. 243

How Rain Shadows Form

Air cools as it flows up the mountain, causing water vapor to condense into clouds that release precipitation.

After blowing over the mountain, the air is much drier.

Rain Shadows

Mountains have a strong effect on climate in places where steady winds blow inland from oceans. The illustration above shows how mountains can affect precipitation:

- Air is forced to rise as it flows over a mountain.
- As the air rises and cools, it condenses into clouds. Areas near the side of a mountain that faces wind may get heavy precipitation.
- After passing over the mountain, the air is much drier because it has lost moisture through condensation and precipitation.

The dry area on the downwind side of a mountain where this process occurs is called a **rain shadow.** Mountains do not affect only local climates. Many dry climate zones that extend over large regions are found in the rain shadows of mountain ranges.

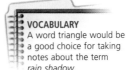

VOCABULARY
A word triangle would be a good choice for taking notes about the term *rain shadow*.

4.2 Review

KEY CONCEPTS

1. What two weather characteristics do meteorologists usually focus on when they determine climate zones?

2. Why do highland climate zones contain more than one climate?

3. How do mountains affect precipitation patterns?

CRITICAL THINKING

4. **Compare and Contrast** How are tundra and icecap subclimates similar? How are they different?

5. **Infer** In which climates would you expect to find the most vacation resorts? Explain.

CHALLENGE

6. **Apply** What is the subclimate of the region where you live? What microclimates exist in your local area?

ANSWERS

1. They focus on temperature and precipitation.

2. Altitude rises sharply on a mountain, and temperature decreases as altitude rises.

3. More precipitation falls on the windward side of a mountain than on the downwind side.

4. They are both polar subclimates. Icecaps are permanently covered with ice and snow. Tundra regions have summers with enough warmth to thaw out a shallow layer of soil at the surface.

5. Possible responses: humid subtropical, tropical wet and

dry, and Mediterranean because of their mild winters; highland climates because of skiing.

6. Answers will vary.

Teach from Visuals

Make sure students understand that the illustration shows a cross-section of a mountain.

To help students interpret the visual, ask:

- What do the arrows represent? *wind that is blowing in the direction indicated by the arrow tips*
- What is shown on the left side of the mountain peak, near the top? *precipitation falling from clouds*

Reinforce (the **BIG** idea)

Have students relate the section to the Big Idea.

 Reinforcing Key Concepts, p. 244

4.2 ASSESS & RETEACH

Assess

 Section 4.2 Quiz, p. 64

Reteach

Represent the climate chart on p. 127 as a branching tree structure. On the board, draw a large "trunk" at left extending vertically. To the right, draw six large, horizontal "branches." End on the right side of the board with another level of branching. On the trunk, write "Climates." On each of the six large branches, write one of the climate zone names. Finally, on the sub-branches, write subclimate names.

As you read text from the Description column on p. 127, have students identify the climate and subclimate for the description using the diagram on the board as an aid.

Technology Resources

Have students visit **ClassZone.com** for reteaching of Key Concepts.

 CONTENT REVIEW

 CONTENT REVIEW CD-ROM

Focus

PURPOSE Students will learn how natural and artificial features affect microclimate, or local climate.

OVERVIEW Students will

- take weather measurements of various kinds at contrasting sites in a locale;
- compare data from the contrasting sites to evaluate their hypothesis.

Lab Preparation

- Materials: Gather two of the same instruments from this list: psychrometers and a table to determine relative humidity; barometers to measure air pressure; or anemometers to measure wind speed.
- Prior to the investigation, have students read through the investigation and prepare their data tables. Or you may wish to copy and distribute datasheets and rubrics.

 UNIT RESOURCE BOOK, pp. 263–271

 SCIENCE TOOLKIT, F14

Lab Management

- Group students by fours and pair the students within the groups.
- Help groups select their weather data-gathering sites; approve the sites.
- If students use an anemometer such as the one shown, have them count the number of times the marked cup rotates during a period of one minute to calculate average wind speed. If they choose a psychrometer, advise them to take wet-bulb and dry-bulb readings outside and then check a relative humidity table inside.

SAFETY Keep students away from sites with traffic or other potential dangers; tell them to use instruments carefully.

Teaching with Technology

If probeware is available, students can use appropriate probes.

CHAPTER INVESTIGATION

Microclimates

OVERVIEW AND PURPOSE Microclimates are local variations within a region's climate. Natural and artificial features such as beaches, hills, wooded areas, buildings, and pavement can cause such variations. Even trees planted around a house or parking lot may influence the climate of that small area. In this lab, you will use what you have learned about weather and climate to

- measure weather factors, such as air temperature, in two different microclimates
- discover how natural and artificial features affect local climate

▶ Problem

How do natural and artificial features affect the climate of a small area?

▶ Hypothesize

Write a hypothesis to explain how you expect the microclimates of two nearby locations to be affected by the different natural and artificial features in those areas. Your hypothesis should take the form of an "If . . . , then . . . , because . . ." statement. You should complete steps 1–3 of the procedure before writing your hypothesis.

▶ Procedure

MATERIALS
- 2 thermometers
- 2 other weather instruments of the same kind

1. Work in a group of four students. You will use a thermometer to record air temperature. Choose another weather instrument that you have made or that is available to you. You might use a psychrometer to measure relative humidity, a barometer to measure air pressure, or an anemometer to measure wind speed.

2. Make data tables similar to the ones in the sample notebook page. The label in the second row of each table should identify what you will measure with the instrument you chose in step 1.

3. Go outside the school with your teacher, taking your instruments and notebook. Choose two locations near the school with different features for your group to study. For example, you might choose a grassy area and a paved area, or one area with trees and another area without trees.

D 130

INVESTIGATION RESOURCES

 CHAPTER INVESTIGATION, Microclimates
- Level A, pp. 263–266
- Level B, pp. 267–270
- Level C, p. 271

Advanced students should complete Levels B & C.

 Writing a Lab Report, D12–13

Technology Resources

Customize this student lab as needed or look for an alternative. Print rubrics to assess student lab reports.

 Lab Generator CD-ROM

4. Divide your group into two pairs. Each pair of students should have one thermometer and the other instrument you have chosen. You and your partner will study one location. The other pair will study the second location.

5. Decide ahead of time how you will control for variables. For example, both pairs might take measurements at a set height above the ground.

6. Draw pictures of the location you are studying in your notebook. Write a description of the natural and artificial features in this area.

7. Set up the instruments in your location. Record the air temperature. Take follow-up readings five and ten minutes later. Take a reading with the other weather instrument each time you take a temperature reading.

8. Record data gathered by the other two members of your group in your data table. Calculate the average temperature for each location. Then calculate the average reading for the other weather factor that you measured.

Observe and Analyze Write It Up

1. **IDENTIFY VARIABLES AND CONSTANTS** Identify the variables and constants in the investigation. List these factors in your **Science Notebook.**

2. **COMPARE AND CONTRAST** Which average measurements in the two locations were the same? What differences did your investigations reveal? For example, was one area cooler or less windy than the other?

Conclude Write It Up

1. **INFER** Answer the question posed in the problem.

2. **INTERPRET** Compare your results with your hypothesis. Did the results support your hypothesis? Did the natural and artificial features have the effects you expected?

3. **EVALUATE** What were the limitations of your instruments? What other sources of error could have affected the results?

4. **APPLY** How could you apply the results of your investigation to help you make landscaping or building decisions? For example, what could you do to make a picnic area more comfortable?

▶ INVESTIGATE Further

CHALLENGE Return to the locations you investigated at the same time of day on three consecutive days. Take readings with the same weather instruments that you used before. Are these new readings consistent with the patterns you observed on the first day? If not, how would you alter your earlier conclusions?

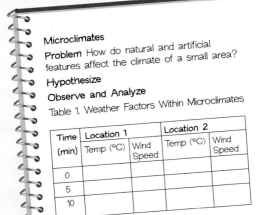

Microclimates

Problem How do natural and artificial features affect the climate of a small area?

Hypothesize

Observe and Analyze

Table 1. Weather Factors Within Microclimates

Time (min)	Location 1 Temp (°C)	Location 1 Wind Speed	Location 2 Temp (°C)	Location 2 Wind Speed
0				
5				
10				

Conclude

Chapter 4: **Climate and Climate Change** 131 **D**

▶ Observe and Analyze Write It Up

SAMPLE DATA Temperature readings at grassy site: 14°C, 14.5°C, 15.5°C; average temperature: 14.7°C.

Temperature readings at pavement site: 17.5°C, 19°C, 21°C; average temperature: 19.2°C.

1. *Constants will include weather instruments and time of day. Variables will include the natural and artificial features of the two different locations.*

2. *Average temperature at a paved site is higher than at a grassy site.*

▶ Conclude Write It Up

1. *Sample answer: Pavement raises the temperature; trees make an area less windy and cooler.*

2. *Answers will vary.*

3. *Answers will vary depending on instruments used. Other sources of error might include people or animals interfering with instruments.*

4. *Planting trees around a picnic table would make it more comfortable in summer by providing shade and more comfortable in winter by blocking wind.*

▶ INVESTIGATE Further

CHALLENGE Answers will vary.

Post-Lab Discussion

• Discuss with students how they controlled for variables in the investigation. (See step 5 in the Procedure.) Explain to students that if they had controlled for sunshine, other differences might emerge clearly. For example, a shady area near a stream or other source of water would probably be cooler than a drier shady area.

• **DIFFERENTIATION TIP** Have advanced students try to identify the independent and dependent variables in the investigation.

Chapter 4 **131** **D**

Set Learning Goals

Students will

- Explain how climates can cool when particles block sunlight.
- Recognize climate changes that repeat.
- Explain how climates may change due to global warming.
- Measure the temperature changes when sunlight is blocked in an experiment.

3-Minute Warm-Up

Display Transparency 29 or copy this exercise on the board:

Review the Climate Classification chart on p. 127. Ask students to describe the temperatures and precipitation of these climate types: humid tropical, polar, and dry.

 3-Minute Warm-Up, p. T29

 **MOTIVATE**

THINK ABOUT

PURPOSE Students think about how weather, sunlight, and climates are related.

DISCUSS Ask students to consider how particles that block sunlight might affect temperature. *They absorb sunlight and heat, making it cooler.*

Answer: volcanoes, the impact of huge space objects, and dust storms

Ongoing Assessment

Explain how climates can cool when particles block sunlight.

Ask: How can a volcano cause global cooling? *An eruption sends particles into the atmosphere; the particles spread out and block sunlight from Earth.*

CHECK YOUR READING *Answer: They can block solar energy to cause global cooling.*

KEY CONCEPT

4.3 Climates can change suddenly or slowly.

◀ **BEFORE, you learned**

- Earth absorbs and reflects solar energy
- Greenhouse gases help keep Earth warm
- Human activities are contributing to global warming

▶ **NOW, you will learn**

- How climates can cool when particles block sunlight
- About climate changes that repeat over time
- How climates may change because of global warming

VOCABULARY

ice age p. 135
El Niño p. 136

THINK ABOUT

How do particles affect light?

If you shine a light through foggy air, you may notice that the beam of light is dimmer than usual. The droplets, or liquid particles, that make up fog block some of the light from reaching objects in the beam's path. Which natural events can suddenly add many particles to the atmosphere?

Climates cool when particles block sunlight.

Our atmosphere contains many particulates—tiny solid and liquid particles mixed in with air. Particulates block some of the Sun's energy, preventing it from reaching Earth's surface. Occasionally a natural event will suddenly release enormous amounts of particulates. Such an event may cause a temporary change in climates around the world.

Large volcanic eruptions can send huge clouds of gas and dust into the stratosphere. When these clouds enter the stratosphere, they spread out and drift around the world. Volcanoes affect global climate mainly by releasing sulfur dioxide gas. The gas combines with water to form sulfuric acid droplets, which block sunlight. Because Earth absorbs less solar energy, average global temperatures may decrease for up to several years.

 CHECK YOUR READING How can a sudden release of particles affect climate?

D 132 Unit: Earth's Atmosphere

RESOURCES FOR DIFFERENTIATED INSTRUCTION

Below Level

UNIT RESOURCE BOOK

- Reading Study Guide A, pp. 247–248
- Decoding Support, p. 260

 AUDIO CDS

R **Additional INVESTIGATION,**
Modeling El Niño, A, B, & C, pp. 272–281; Teacher Instructions, pp. 284–285

Advanced

UNIT RESOURCE BOOK

- Challenge and Extension, p. 253
- Challenge Reading, pp. 256–257

English Learners

UNIT RESOURCE BOOK
Spanish Reading Study Guide, pp. 251–252

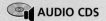 **AUDIO CDS**

- Audio Readings in Spanish
- Audio Readings (English)

In 1991, Mount Pinatubo erupted in the Philippines. The eruption, one of the largest of the last century, affected climates for about two years. During the summer of 1992, parts of North America were more than 3°C (5.4°F) cooler than usual. Over that entire year, global temperatures dropped by 0.5°C (0.9°F).

The impact of rocky objects from space can also release particles into the atmosphere. Earth is often hit by space objects. Most are too small to have much of an effect. However, objects 3 kilometers (2 mi) in diameter strike Earth about once every million years. These powerful collisions can suddenly change climates.

When a large space object strikes Earth, it explodes and leaves behind a crater, or pit, in the surface. The explosion throws dust into the atmosphere. The largest impacts may have raised so much dust that temperatures around the world dropped sharply for months. They may also have caused changes in the atmosphere by setting off forest fires. A space object that hit Earth 65 million years ago blasted out a crater about 200 kilometers (120 mi) in diameter in what is now Mexico. Many scientists think that climate changes following this impact led to the extinction of the dinosaurs and other species.

The eruption of Mount Pinatubo in 1991 affected temperatures around the world for about two years.

INVESTIGATE Climate Change

How does blocking sunlight affect temperature?

PROCEDURE

1. Tape the tissue paper to a window frame to cover one window. If you cannot cover the whole window, adjust the blinds or shade so that sunlight enters that window only through the tissue paper. Leave a second window on the same side of the room uncovered.

2. Adjust the shade or blinds of the uncovered window so that sunlight enters the room through equal areas of both windows. Place a thermometer in front of each window. Record the temperature for each window.

3. Wait 15 minutes. Record the temperature for each window.

WHAT DO YOU THINK?

- How did blocking one window with the tissue paper affect the temperature?
- What do you think caused this result?

CHALLENGE How would adding a second layer of tissue paper to the covered window affect the results? Add the second layer and repeat the activity to test your prediction.

SKILL FOCUS
Measuring

MATERIALS
- white tissue paper
- tape
- 2 thermometers

TIME
20 minutes

133 **D**

4.3 INSTRUCT

Teacher Demo

Use this demo to simulate the impact of a space object on Earth. Gather a small plate, cornstarch, and modeling clay.

Cover the plate with a layer of cornstarch. Mold a lump of clay into a ball. Have students infer what will happen when you drop the clay ball onto the plate. Have students describe what they observe. Careful observers should see a plume of tiny particles billowing up from the plate.

INVESTIGATE Climate Change

PURPOSE To measure temperatures in order to understand how blocking sunlight can affect temperature

TIPS *20 min.* Students could use two heat lamps as the energy source. Volunteers would hold the tissue paper between lamp and thermometer, being careful to position each heat lamp the same distance from the thermometer.

WHAT DO YOU THINK? *It lowered temperature. The tissue paper blocks some of the Sun's energy from reaching the thermometer.*

CHALLENGE *The second layer would lower the temperature further.*

R Datasheet, Climate Change, p. 254

Technology Resources

Customize this student lab as needed or look for an alternative. Print rubrics to assess student lab reports.

Lab Generator CD-ROM

Metacognitive Strategy

Have students write a paragraph explaining how "Investigate Climate Change" models the effect of excess particles in Earth's atmosphere. Remind them to use words and phrases of comparison, such as *like, in the same way, similar to,* and *also.*

Teach from Visuals

Point out that the landmasses look like pieces of a puzzle fitted together in the first map but have drifted apart in the second.

To help students interpret the visual, ask:

• What do the arrows on the second global map represent? *the directions in which the continents were moving 65 million years ago*

• Which is further in the past, 65 million years ago or 200 million years ago? *200 million years ago*

• Which map shows the continents more recently? *map 2*

Develop Critical Thinking

PREDICT Have students predict what the Earth's continental landmasses may look like millions of years from now. For example, some scientists believe the rift valley of East Africa will have widened so much 50 million years from now that it will have become an arm of the Indian Ocean slicing through the African continent.

Ongoing Assessment

CHECK YOUR READING *Answer: It causes continents to move into different latitudes, and it changes the paths of ocean currents and wind.*

Climates change as continents move.

Climates can change suddenly for brief periods after a volcanic eruption. In contrast, the movement of continents causes steady climate changes over many millions of years. The maps below show two stages of this movement in the distant past.

B

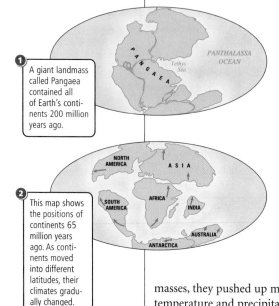

① A giant landmass called Pangaea contained all of Earth's continents 200 million years ago.

② This map shows the positions of continents 65 million years ago. As continents moved into different latitudes, their climates gradually changed.

① Earth's continents were once joined together in a gigantic landmass called Pangaea (pan-JEE-uh). This giant landmass began to break up about 200 million years ago.

② By 65 million years ago, the continents had moved closer to their present positions. As the continents moved, their climates gradually changed in different ways. Some continents cooled as they moved toward higher latitudes. Other continents grew warmer as they moved toward the equator.

The movement of continents had other effects on climate. As they drifted apart, the continents changed the paths of ocean currents that help warm coastal regions. When landmasses collided with other landmasses, they pushed up mountain ranges. Mountains influence temperature and precipitation patterns by altering the paths of winds.

CHECK YOUR READING How does the movement of continents change climate? Find three examples in the text above.

Some climate changes repeat over time.

In most climates, a cooler period regularly follows a warmer period each year. Some climate changes also occur in cycles. Ice ages and El Niño are two kinds of climate change that repeat over time.

Ice Ages

RESOURCE CENTER
CLASSZONE.COM

Learn more about climate change.

For much of Earth's history, the poles were free of ice because Earth was warmer than it is today. However, there have been about seven major periods of global cooling that lasted millions of years. Temperatures became low enough for ice to form year-round at the poles. The most recent of these periods began 2 million years ago and is still continuing.

DIFFERENTIATE INSTRUCTION

More Reading Support

B What causes very slow and steady climate change? *movement of the continents*

Inclusion Some students may have a hard time understanding continental drift. Make a photocopy of map 1. Mark heavy dashed lines on the borders between landmasses. Make and distribute photocopies of the altered map. Have students cut out the land "pieces" from the map. Tell them to put the pieces together, like a puzzle, on a smooth surface (desktop). Then have them slowly move the pieces apart so the pieces look like map 2.

How Ice Expands in an Ice Age

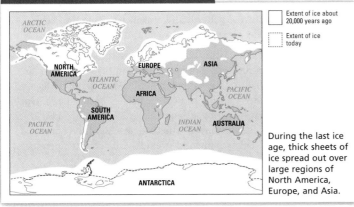

Extent of ice about 20,000 years ago

Extent of ice today

During the last ice age, thick sheets of ice spread out over large regions of North America, Europe, and Asia.

During major periods of global cooling, there are times when polar ice expands. **Ice ages** are periods in which huge sheets of ice spread out beyond the polar regions. The map above shows how far the ice sheets reached in the last ice age, which ended between 14,000 and 10,000 years ago. These sheets were several kilometers thick and covered nearly a third of Earth's land area.

Ice ages usually last tens of thousands of years. They are separated by warmer periods in which ice sheets shrink back toward the poles. We are living in one of these warmer periods. Average global temperatures are now 5°C to 10°C (9–18°F) higher than they were during the last ice age. Only Greenland and Antarctica have large ice sheets today.

Various sources of evidence show that ice ages occurred. Scientists study polar ice and the ocean floor to estimate past changes in temperature. Geological features that formed during ice ages, such as scratches on rocks, can reveal the movement of ice sheets. Some of the evidence also provides clues about what causes ice ages. Most scientists think that there are two main causes:

- Ice ages are closely linked to changes in how Earth moves around the Sun. These changes may have caused ice sheets to grow by altering the temperature patterns of the seasons.

- As you learned in Chapter 1, carbon dioxide is a greenhouse gas. Levels of carbon dioxide in the atmosphere dropped during ice ages. Lower carbon dioxide levels may have caused global cooling by weakening the greenhouse effect.

Other factors probably play a role in the development of ice ages. Scientists are still trying to understand how different factors work in combination to cause global cooling.

MAIN IDEA AND DETAILS
Record in your notes the important details about ice ages.

Teach from Visuals

To help students interpret the visual "How Ice Expands in an Ice Age," ask:

How do Earth's current ice sheets compare with the ice sheets of 20,000 years ago? *Today's ice sheets are confined to land near the poles. But 20,000 years ago, the ice sheets covered large regions of North America, Europe, and Asia.*

History of Science

In 1837, a Swiss scientist named Louis Agassiz made a startling announcement at a meeting of scientists. Agassiz said he believed that glaciers had once covered much of Europe in an ice age long ago. Most of the scientists rejected Agassiz's ideas. Agassiz was sure, however, that glaciers had once covered much of the European landscape. His study of rock formations in Switzerland revealed many clues of glacial action. In 1840, Agassiz published a book explaining his theory of a past ice age. Slowly, the world's scientists came to accept the concept of ice ages in Earth's distant past.

Integrate the Sciences

Huge masses of ice weighing millions of tons can build up in glaciers because of the way crystals in solid matter behave. When water is a liquid, its molecules slide over each other so easily that water tends to flow from high places to low. However, when water molecules lose enough energy—that is, get cold enough—they lock into specific patterns. These patterns in ice are rigid, so the molecules cannot slip and slide easily. This is why ice can pile up on land, rather than flowing away like water.

DIFFERENTIATE INSTRUCTION

? More Reading Support

C How long do ice ages usually last? *tens of thousands of years*

D What samples can scientists study to learn more about ice ages? *polar ice and ocean floor*

Below Level For students who struggle with metric conversions, remind them that even though Celsius and Fahrenheit numbers are different, the actual physical temperature is the same. Point out that the freezing point in Celsius is 0°, while in Fahrenheit it is 32°. Regardless of the system used to express the temperature of water, water will still freeze at the same point.

Point out that the two numbered visuals are diagrams showing a view of a part of Earth.

To help students interpret the visual depicting how El Niño forms, ask:

• How is the small map on the right related to diagrams 1 and 2? *It shows a bigger view of where diagrams 1 and 2 are located on Earth.*

• Which shows a cross-section perspective, the small map, or diagrams 1 and 2? *diagrams 1 and 2*

• Which direction is east on diagrams 1 and 2? *to the right*

EXPLORE (the **BIG** idea)

Revisit "Internet Activity: El Niño" on p. 115. Have students explain their answers.

Ongoing Assessment

Recognize climate changes that repeat over time.

Ask: How are ice ages and El Niño alike? *they repeat after intervals of contrasting climate*

El Niño

The oceans are closely connected to climate. **El Niño** (ehl NEEN-yoh) is a disturbance of wind patterns and ocean currents in the Pacific Ocean. It usually occurs every 3 to 7 years and lasts for 12 to 18 months.

El Niño causes temporary climate changes in many parts of the world. It can cause unusually dry conditions in the western Pacific region and unusually heavy rainfall in South America. In the United States, El Niño tends to bring heavier rainfall to the Southeast. During winter, storms may be stronger than usual in California, and temperatures are often milder in some northern states. All of these unusual conditions follow changes in wind strength and ocean temperatures.

① **Normal Year** Strong trade winds normally push warm water toward the western Pacific, where an area of low pressure develops. The rising warm air condenses into clouds that release heavy rain. Cooler water flows near the west coast of South America.

② **El Niño Year** Weak trade winds allow warm water to flow back toward the central and eastern Pacific. The clouds and heavy rain also shift eastward, toward South America. The effects of El Niño vary, depending on how much warming occurs in the eastern Pacific.

How El Niño Forms

Weak trade winds during El Niño cause changes in ocean temperature and precipitation.

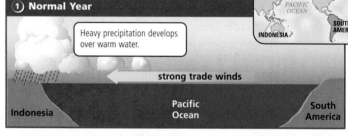

① **Normal Year**

Heavy precipitation develops over warm water.

strong trade winds

Indonesia   Pacific Ocean   South America

② **El Niño Year**

Precipitation and warm water move eastward.

weak trade winds

Indonesia   Pacific Ocean   South America

READING TiP
In the diagrams, color is used to show ocean temperature. **Red** means warmer water. **Blue** means cooler water.

DIFFERENTIATE INSTRUCTION

? **More Reading Support**

E What ocean does El Niño affect? *the Pacific Ocean*

F Is El Niño associated with stronger or weaker trade winds than usual? *weaker*

Advanced

R Challenge and Extension, p. 253

Have students who are interested in learning more about El Niño read the following article:

R Challenge Reading, pp. 256–257

1983  **2002**

This ice sheet on a mountain in Peru has shrunk 820 meters (2690 ft) in 19 years.

Human activities are changing climate.

Most climate experts predict that by 2100, there will be a rise in global temperature of 1.4°C to 5.8°C (2.5–10.4°F). As you read in Chapter 1, human activities release greenhouse gases. Higher levels of greenhouse gases in the atmosphere cause global warming. Earth hasn't warmed so rapidly at any time in at least the last 10,000 years. Even a small temperature increase could have a great impact on climate.

> **REMINDER**
>
> Remember that greenhouse gases are gases that absorb infrared energy.

Predictions of Climate Change

Although scientists expect all land areas to warm up by 2100, the rate of warming will be uneven. The greatest warming is expected to occur in the high latitudes of the Northern Hemisphere. The increase in Greenland's temperature, for example, may be two or three times the global average. Higher temperatures have recently started to melt the ice sheet that covers much of Greenland. Ice is also melting in the Arctic Ocean and on mountains in many parts of the world.

The effects of global warming on precipitation will also vary. Scientists predict an overall increase in precipitation, because more water will evaporate from Earth's warmer surface. Precipitation will tend to fall more heavily in short periods of time, which will increase flooding. However, some areas where water is already scarce may get even less precipitation. Lower precipitation in those areas will make droughts more frequent and severe.

CHECK YOUR READING 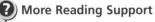 Summarize how global warming is expected to affect temperature and precipitation.

Teach from Visuals

To help students interpret the photographs of the ice sheet, ask:

- What text describes the two photographs? *the caption*
- To what "19 years" does the caption refer? *the 19-year period (1983 to 2002) between the two photographs*
- Why does dramatic shrinking of a glacier offer evidence of global warming? *The shrinking of the glacier indicates that temperatures have become warmer over the 19-year period between the photographs.*

Teach Difficult Concepts

Some students may have a hard time understanding the phrase "high latitudes of the Northern Hemisphere." Show students a globe or world map. Remind students that the horizontal lines are lines of latitude. The equator and nearby lines of latitude can be described as "low latitudes." Ask students what they think "high latitudes" might refer to. *lines of latitude near the poles*

Ongoing Assessment

Explain how climates may change due to global warming.

Ask: How does global warming cause overall precipitation to become heavier? *Precipitation becomes heavier because more water will evaporate from Earth's warmer surface.*

CHECK YOUR READING *Answer: Temperatures will rise unevenly; the greatest warming will occur in the northern high latitudes. Precipitation will increase in most areas but will decrease in dry areas.*

DIFFERENTIATE INSTRUCTION

? More Reading Support

G How much of an increase in global temperature do scientists predict by the year 2100? *1.4° to 5.8°C, or 2.5° to 10.4°F.*

Inclusion Students with visual impairments may not be able to see the dramatic difference between the 1983 photograph and the 2002 photo. If appropriate, have a volunteer describe the 1983 photograph, then describe the 2002 photograph, comparing it with the former.

Integrate the Sciences

A carbon dioxide (CO_2) molecule is made up of one carbon atom and two oxygen atoms. A small amount of carbon dioxide in Earth's atmosphere is needed to maintain life. Plants take in carbon dioxide to produce food, and animals give off carbon dioxide as a waste product. However, an increase in carbon dioxide in the atmosphere may be partly responsible for global warming. When fuels such as gasoline and coal are burned for energy, they give off carbon dioxide. Increasing levels of carbon dioxide may hold heat in Earth's atmosphere and change climates around the world.

Reinforce (the BIG idea)

Have students relate the section to the Big Idea.

 Reinforcing Key Concepts, p. 255

4.3 ASSESS & RETEACH

Assess

 Section 4.3 Quiz, p. 65

Reteach

Have students work together to make a three-column chart to summarize this lesson's content. Tell them to use these headings: Climate Event, Time Factor, Effects on World Climates.

Students should identify the following climate events: volcano (pp. 132–133), space object impact (p. 133), motion of continents (p. 134), ice ages (pp. 134–135), El Niño (p. 136), and global warming today (pp. 137–138).

Technology Resources

Have students visit **ClassZone.com** for reteaching of Key Concepts.

 CONTENT REVIEW

 CONTENT REVIEW CD-ROM

MAIN IDEA AND DETAILS
Record in your notes the important details about the impact of global warming.

RESOURCE CENTER
CLASSZONE.COM
Find out more about the effects of global warming.

Impact of Global Warming

Global warming affects many of Earth's systems. Because these systems work together in complex ways, it is difficult to predict the full impact of global warming. Most climate scientists predict that global warming will probably cause the following changes.

Sea Levels As temperatures warm, the oceans will expand. They will also gain additional water from melting ice. Scientists expect the average sea level to rise 9 to 88 centimeters (4–35 in.) over the next century. Higher sea levels will damage coastal regions and increase flooding. These problems could be severe in small island nations.

Wildlife Global warming will endanger many plant and animal species by altering natural habitats. Some species will die out or move to cooler areas. Other species, such as warm-water fishes, will benefit from an expansion of their habitats.

Agriculture Changes in temperature and precipitation can affect crops and livestock. If Earth warms more than a few degrees Celsius, most of the world's agriculture will be harmed. More moderate warming will help agriculture in some regions by lengthening the growing season. However, even moderate warming will harm agriculture in other regions.

Human Health Warmer temperatures could increase heat-related deaths and deaths from some diseases, such as malaria, especially in areas near the equator. On the other hand, deaths caused by extreme cold could decrease at higher latitudes.

Some scientists predict more dangerous changes beyond 2100 if humans continue to add greenhouse gases to the atmosphere at current levels. However, the harmful effects of global warming can be limited if we reduce emissions of greenhouse gases.

4.3 Review

KEY CONCEPTS

1. How can volcanic eruptions and impacts of large objects from space change climate?

2. What changes in climate occur during an ice age?

3. Give two examples of ways in which global warming will probably affect life on Earth.

CRITICAL THINKING

4. **Connect** What is the connection between latitude, the movement of continents, and climate change?

5. **Compare and Contrast** Compare and contrast the effects of El Niño and ice ages on climate.

⚫ CHALLENGE

6. **Infer** Discuss why some countries might be more reluctant than others to take steps to reduce levels of greenhouse gases.

ANSWERS

1. The sudden release of enormous amounts of liquid and solid particles into the atmosphere can block enough solar energy to cause global cooling.

2. Global temperatures cool, and ice sheets cover large areas of land.

3. Sea levels will rise; species will migrate or die out.

4. Because latitude has a strong influence on climate, the climates of the continents will change as they move into different latitudes.

5. They occur in cycles. El Niño repeats every few years; ice ages repeat after tens of thousands of years.

6. The impacts may be less extreme or even partly beneficial.

MATH in SCIENCE

MATH TUTORIAL

Click on Math Tutorial for more help with interpreting line graphs.

SKILL: INTERPRETING LINE GRAPHS

Carbon Dioxide Levels

Since the 1950s, carbon dioxide levels have been measured in air samples collected at the Mauna Loa Observatory in Hawaii. The graphs below show the carbon dioxide data plotted in two different ways. In the graph on the left, the scale showing carbon dioxide levels starts at 0 parts per million (ppm) and goes up to 400 ppm. The graph on the right offers a close-up view of the same data. The scale on the right-hand graph is broken to focus on the values from 310 ppm to 380 ppm.

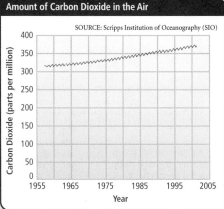

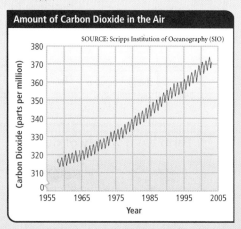

Use the graphs to answer the following questions.

1. What was the carbon dioxide level at the beginning of 1995?

2. The data show a 17 percent increase in the carbon dioxide level in the air from 1958 through 2001. Which graph shows this increase more clearly? Why?

3. In both graphs, the line that shows carbon dioxide levels is jagged, because carbon dioxide levels rise and fall regularly as the seasons change. In some years, the seasonal rise and fall is greater than in other years. Which graph emphasizes these variations more? Why?

CHALLENGE The carbon dioxide level in the air starts falling in May or June each year and continues to fall through October. What do you think causes this change to occur?

Chapter 4: **Climate and Climate Change** 139 **D**

MATH IN SCIENCE
Math Skills Practice for Science

Set Learning Goal

To interpret data of carbon dioxide levels plotted on a line graph

Present the Science

Carbon dioxide (CO_2) is one of a number of substances—mostly gases—in the atmosphere. It is measured in parts per million (ppm).

Develop Graphing Skills

Make sure students understand that plotting data on a line graph requires two axes, the x-axis (horizontal, bottom) and the y-axis (vertical, left side). In these graphs, the data show change over time.

Emphasize that the two graphs present exactly the same data, but in different views. The graph on the right truncates the y-axis to display only the range of CO_2 concentration that is covered by the data in the given 50-year range. Explain that the breaks in the line at several points in the 1950s and 1960s are due to the fact that data was unavailable for several months in these periods.

Close

Ask: How would a line graph showing global warming and the line graphs on this page be similar? *The data plotted would show a line rising from left to right.*

- Math Support, p. 261
- Math Practice, p. 262

Technology Resources

Students can visit **ClassZone.com** for practice with interpreting line graphs.

MATH TUTORIAL

ANSWERS

1. *360 parts per million*

2. *left graph; the unbroken scale on the y-axis starts at 0.*

3. *right graph; It has a shorter y-axis scale, which causes the line to rise and fall more steeply with the seasons each year.*

CHALLENGE *In the Northern Hemisphere, the CO_2 level falls in springtime, when plants that were dormant during the winter begin photosynthesis again, drawing CO_2 from the atmosphere.*

BACK TO

the **BIG** idea

Have students explain how the words *long-term* and *patterns* distinguish the definition of climate from that of weather. *Long-term indicates that climate is concerned with long periods of time; by contrast, weather can include observations made at any moment. Patterns suggest features that can be grouped by differences or similarities, suggesting observations over periods of time and/or distances.*

◉ KEY CONCEPTS SUMMARY

SECTION 4.1
Ask: What parts of the globe are associated with cooler weather patterns? What part is associated with warmer weather patterns? *The high latitudes, or regions closer to the poles, are associated with cooler patterns. Regions near the equator are associated with warmer patterns.*

SECTION 4.2
Ask: What could you assume about the temperature and precipitation patterns for two cities within the same band of color on the map? Why? *You could assume they have similar precipitation and temperature patterns, because they are in the same climate zone.*

SECTION 4.3
Ask: What clue in the photograph suggests how this natural event will affect climate? *The volcano is spewing out huge clouds of dust. The dust particles will block out some sunlight and therefore exert a cooling influence.*

Review Concepts

- Big Idea Flow Chart, p. T25
- Chapter Outline, pp. T31–T32

 Chapter Review

the **BIG** idea

Climates are long-term weather patterns that may change over time.

ℹ **CONTENT REVIEW**
CLASSZONE.COM

◉ KEY CONCEPTS SUMMARY

4.1 **Climate is a long-term weather pattern.**

The main factors that influence climate are
- latitude
- altitude
- distance from large bodies of water
- ocean currents

Seasonal changes are also part of climate patterns.

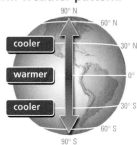

Temperatures usually decrease as latitude increases.

VOCABULARY
climate p. 117
latitude p. 118
marine climate p. 120
continental climate p. 120
ocean current p. 121
season p. 122

4.2 **Earth has a variety of climates.**

Each color on the map shows a different subclimate.

Scientists usually group climates by temperature and precipitation. There are six major climate zones. Climate zones can be divided into subclimates. Microclimates are smaller areas within subclimates.

VOCABULARY
climate zone p. 125
microclimate p. 128
urban heat island p. 128
rain shadow p. 129

4.3 **Climates can change suddenly or slowly.**

Natural events, such as eruptions of volcanoes, can change climate. Human activities that release greenhouse gases are also changing climate.

VOCABULARY
ice age p. 135
El Niño p. 136

D 140 Unit: **Earth's Atmosphere**

Technology Resources

Have students visit **ClassZone.com** or use the CD-ROM for a cumulative review of concepts.

 CONTENT REVIEW

 CONTENT REVIEW CD-ROM

Engage students in a whole-class interactive review of Key Concepts. Edit content as you wish.

 POWER PRESENTATIONS

Reviewing Vocabulary

Make a magnet word diagram for each of the vocabulary terms listed below. Write the term in the magnet. Write other terms or ideas related to it on the lines around the magnet.

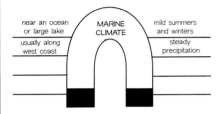

near an ocean or large lake — MARINE CLIMATE — mild summers and winters

usually along west coast — steady precipitation

1. continental climate
2. ocean current
3. microclimate
4. urban heat island
5. rain shadow
6. ice age

Reviewing Key Concepts

Multiple Choice *Choose the letter of the best answer.*

7. Compared with weather patterns, climate patterns are more
   a. severe   **c.** local
   b. long-term   **d.** unusual

8. Climates are usually classified by
   a. plant cover and animal life
   b. altitude and latitude
   c. bodies of water and ocean currents
   d. temperature and precipitation

9. Which latitude receives the least amount of solar energy?
   a. 30° N   **c.** 30° S
   b. 0°   **d.** 90° S

10. What is El Niño?
    a. a change in wind patterns and ocean currents
    b. an increase in carbon dioxide levels
    c. a decrease in global temperature
    d. a change in solar energy

11. Which effect is a likely result of global warming?
    a. fewer droughts
    b. lower sea levels
    c. more flooding
    d. more cold-related deaths

12. Volcanoes can cool the climate by
    a. increasing wind speeds
    b. using up Earth's energy
    c. releasing gas and particles
    d. raising air pressure

13. A large coastal city probably has cooler summers than a city at the same latitude that is
    a. on a mountain   **c.** near a volcano
    b. much smaller   **d.** far inland

14. Which carries warmth from the tropics toward the polar regions?
    a. urban heat islands
    b. warm-water currents
    c. cold-water currents
    d. trade winds

15. Several different climates can exist within a small area in
    a. marine climates
    b. continental climates
    c. polar climates
    d. highland climates

16. Day and night are equal in length on the first day of
    a. spring   **c.** winter
    b. summer   **d.** El Niño

Short Answer *Write a short answer to each question.*

17. How can changes caused by the movement of continents affect climate?

18. Identify the two main causes of ice ages.

19. Describe how a space object might have helped kill off the dinosaurs.

20. How is the climate of a city usually different from the climate of a nearby rural area?

Reviewing Vocabulary

1. Sample answer: <u>continental climate</u>—in interior of continents, no influence from oceans, daytime and nighttime temperatures vary, winter much colder than summer

2. Sample answer: <u>ocean currents</u>—patterned streams of ocean water, warm-water currents go from tropics to higher latitudes, cold-water currents go from higher latitudes to tropics

3. Sample answer: <u>microclimate</u>—within subclimates, size varies, beaches, lakes, valleys, mountains

4. Sample answer: <u>urban heat island</u>—warm air over a city, artificial surfaces absorb solar energy, artificial surfaces release heat energy, energy used to run cities adds heat to air

5. Sample answer: <u>rain shadow</u>—dry area, on downwind side of mountain, can be large area

6. Sample answer: <u>ice age</u>—huge ice sheets spread beyond polar regions, caused by changing movement of Earth around Sun, caused by low carbon dioxide levels

Reviewing Key Concepts

7. b	11. c	15. d
8. d	12. c	16. a
9. d	13. d	
10. a	14. b	

17. Climates cool or warm, depending on whether the land is moving toward or away from the equator. Ocean currents change and mountains are created, which influence climate.

18. Changes in Earth's rotation and movement around the sun can affect how solar energy is distributed over Earth, and lower CO_2 levels can decrease global temperature, causing ice ages.

19. A large space object that struck Earth 65 million years ago might have thrown so much dust into the atmosphere that Earth's temperature plunged for months, killing off dinosaurs.

20. Cities are usually warmer than surrounding countryside.

Thinking Critically

21. Location 1 has a summer dry season, in contrast to Location 2, which gets its heaviest precipitation in the summer.

22. Location 1 has mild temperatures all year round. Location 2 has cold winters and warm summers.

23. Distance from large bodies of water, because location 1 has more constant temperatures indicative of a marine climate. Location 2 is probably a continental climate.

24. Location 1 would be a better choice because average temperatures stay well above freezing all year. Location 2 has many cold months.

25. The city would become cooler because the grass would absorb less solar energy during the day and release less heat at night.

26. The mountain at 10°N would have a greater variety of climates because it is at a lower altitude; hence lower elevations may have warmer temperatures than the same elevations of the mountain at 65° N.

27. Both the water and the land absorb solar energy during the day.

28. Since Kathmandu is at a higher elevation, it is probably colder. Since Fuzhou is near the ocean, its climate is probably more moderate.

29. Student answers should reflect understanding of climate and global warming effects.

the BIG idea

30. Student answers should indicate an understanding of the different types of climate.

31. Student answers should reflect personal preferences and comprehension of how the indicated factors influence climate.

Thinking Critically

Use the climate graphs to answer the next four questions.

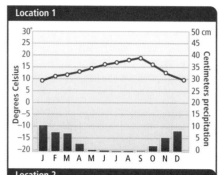

Location 1

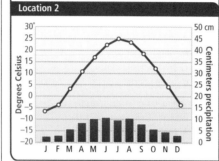

Location 2

21. **COMPARE AND CONTRAST** Compare and contrast the seasonal precipitation patterns shown in the graphs.

22. **COMPARE AND CONTRAST** Contrast the seasonal temperature patterns shown in the graphs.

23. **HYPOTHESIZE** Which of the four main geographical factors that affect climate is the most likely cause of the difference in temperature patterns in the two locations? Explain.

24. **SYNTHESIZE** Suppose you want to plant a crop that requires a long growing season. Which location would you choose? Why?

25. **IDENTIFY EFFECTS** Describe the effect on the microclimate of a city if people planted grass lawns on the roofs of buildings.

26. **SYNTHESIZE** Would you expect to find a greater variety of climates on a tall mountain at 10° N or at 65° N? Explain.

27. **APPLY** In the evening after a hot summer day, the temperature at a beach stays warmer longer than it does farther inland. Explain why this happens.

28. **APPLY** Both Kathmandu, Nepal, and Fuzhou, China, are located at about 25° N. Kathmandu is far inland and high in the mountains. Fuzhou is a seaport. How would you expect their climates to differ?

29. **PREDICT** What might be the impact of global warming in the area where you live?

the BIG idea

30. Look again at the photograph on pages 114–115. Now that you have finished the chapter, how would you change your response to the question on the photograph?

31. **EVALUATE** Describe a place that has what you consider to be a perfect climate. Explain how the following geographical factors affect the climate of that place:
    - latitude
    - altitude
    - distance from large bodies of water
    - ocean currents

UNIT PROJECTS

Evaluate all the data, results, and information in your project folder. Prepare to present your project.

MONITOR AND RETEACH

If students have difficulty evaluating factors of climate in questions 21–31, present the following scenario.

Suppose you plan to visit a distant place that you know nothing about. What factors would you try to identify about the place to help you decide what kind of wardrobe to pack? Make a list of the factors.

Students may benefit from summarizing one or more sections of the chapter.

R Summarizing the Chapter, pp. 282–283

Standardized Test Practice

Analyzing Data

The following tables show the average temperatures in four cities and the temperature characteristics of four climate zones. Use the information in the tables to answer the questions below.

City	Avg. Temperature in Coldest Month	Avg. Temperature in Warmest Month
Miami, Florida	20°C	29°C
Minneapolis, Minnesota	–11°C	23°C
Little Rock, Arkansas	4°C	28°C
Barrow, Alaska	–26°C	4°C

Climate Zone	Characteristics
Polar	Average temperature of warmest month is below 10°C.
Moist mid-latitude with severe winters	Average temperature of coldest month is below –2°C.
Moist mid-latitude with mild winters	Average temperature of coldest month is between –2°C and 18°C.
Humid tropical	Average temperature of every month is greater than 18°C.

1. What is the average temperature in Miami in the coldest month?
- **a.** –11°C
- **b.** 4°C
- **c.** 20°C
- **d.** 29°C

2. What is the average temperature in Little Rock in the warmest month?
- **a.** 4°C
- **b.** 23°C
- **c.** 28°C
- **d.** 29°C

3. Which city has a moist mid-latitude climate with mild winters?
- **a.** Miami
- **b.** Minneapolis
- **c.** Little Rock
- **d.** Barrow

4. Which city has a humid tropical climate?
- **a.** Miami
- **b.** Minneapolis
- **c.** Little Rock
- **d.** Barrow

5. Which city has a moist mid-latitude climate with severe winters?
- **a.** Miami
- **b.** Minneapolis
- **c.** Little Rock
- **d.** Barrow

6. In which climate zone would Little Rock be if its average temperature in the coldest month were 10° colder?
- **a.** polar
- **b.** moist mid-latitude with severe winters
- **c.** moist mid-latitude with mild winters
- **d.** humid tropical

Extended Response

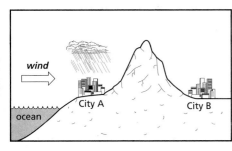

Use information in the diagram to answer the two questions below in detail.

7. City A receives 165 centimeters of rain each year. Explain why its climate is so moist. Use the words *wind, evaporate, condense,* and *precipitation* in your answer.

8. City B receives an average of 22 centimeters of rain each year. Explain why city B is much drier than city A. Use the term *rain shadow* in your answer.

Chapter 4: **Climate and Climate Change** 143 **D**

Analyzing Data

1. c	*4. a*
2. c	*5. b and d are both correct*
3. c	*6. b*

Extended Response

7. RUBRIC

4 points for a response that correctly answers the question and uses the following terms accurately:
- wind
- evaporate
- condense
- precipitation

Sample: The <u>wind</u> coming in from the ocean rises as it moves up the mountain. This air cools and <u>condenses</u> into clouds. The clouds produce lots of <u>precipitation</u>. The rain that reaches the ground then <u>evaporates</u> and the rain clouds build again. City A has a moist climate because of this process.

3 points for a response that uses three terms accurately

2 points for a response that correctly answers the question and uses two terms accurately

1 point for a response that correctly answers the question, but does not use the terms

8. RUBRIC

4 points for a response that correctly answers the question and uses the following terms accurately:
- rain shadow
- wind
- precipitation

Sample: After <u>wind</u> passes over the mountain, the air is dry because it already released <u>precipitation</u> on the other side of the mountain. The dry area on this side of the mountain is called a <u>rain shadow</u>. Since City B is located in the rain shadow, this means it will be drier than City A.

3 points for a response that uses all terms accurately

2 points for a response that correctly answers the question and uses two terms accurately

1 point for a response that correctly answers the question, but does not use the terms

---

METACOGNITIVE ACTIVITY

Have students answer the following questions in their **Science Notebook:**

1. Which actions in your daily routine contribute to climate change?
2. How do the concepts in this chapter relate to your life?
3. How would you change your Unit Project, now that you have finished the unit "Earth's Atmosphere"?

Student Resource Handbooks

Making Observations

An **observation** is an act of noting and recording an event, characteristic, behavior, or anything else detected with an instrument or with the senses.

Observations allow you to make informed hypotheses and to gather data for experiments. Careful observations often lead to ideas for new experiments. There are two categories of observations:

- **Quantitative observations** can be expressed in numbers and include records of time, temperature, mass, distance, and volume.

- **Qualitative observations** include descriptions of sights, sounds, smells, and textures.

EXAMPLE

A student dissolved 30 grams of Epsom salts in water, poured the solution into a dish, and let the dish sit out uncovered overnight. The next day, she made the following observations of the Epsom salt crystals that grew in the dish.

> To determine the mass, the student found the mass of the dish before and after growing the crystals and then used subtraction to find the difference.

> The student measured several crystals and calculated the mean length. (To learn how to calculate the mean of a data set, see page R36.)

Table 1. Observations of Epsom Salt Crystals

Quantitative Observations	Qualitative Observations
• mass = 30 g	• Crystals are clear.
• mean crystal length = 0.5 cm	• Crystals are long, thin, and rectangular.
• longest crystal length = 2 cm	• White crust has formed around edge of dish.

> Photographs or sketches are useful for recording qualitative observations.

 Epsom salt crystals

MORE ABOUT OBSERVING

- Make quantitative observations whenever possible. That way, others will know exactly what you observed and be able to compare their results with yours.

- It is always a good idea to make qualitative observations too. You never know when you might observe something unexpected.

Predicting and Hypothesizing

A **prediction** is an expectation of what will be observed or what will happen. A **hypothesis** is a tentative explanation for an observation or scientific problem that can be tested by further investigation.

EXAMPLE

Suppose you have made two paper airplanes and you wonder why one of them tends to glide farther than the other one.

1. Start by asking a question.

2. Make an educated guess. After examination, you notice that the wings of the airplane that flies farther are slightly larger than the wings of the other airplane.

3. Write a prediction based upon your educated guess, in the form of an "If . . . , then . . ." statement. Write the independent variable after the word *if*, and the dependent variable after the word *then*.

4. To make a hypothesis, explain why you think what you predicted will occur. Write the explanation after the word *because*.

1. Why does one of the paper airplanes glide farther than the other?

2. The size of an airplane's wings may affect how far the airplane will glide.

3. Prediction: If I make a paper airplane with larger wings, then the airplane will glide farther.

To read about independent and dependent variables, see page R30.

4. Hypothesis: If I make a paper airplane with larger wings, then the airplane will glide farther, because the additional surface area of the wing will produce more lift.

Notice that the part of the hypothesis after *because* adds an explanation of why the airplane will glide farther.

MORE ABOUT HYPOTHESES

• The results of an experiment cannot prove that a hypothesis is correct. Rather, the results either support or do not support the hypothesis.

• Valuable information is gained even when your hypothesis is not supported by your results. For example, it would be an important discovery to find that wing size is not related to how far an airplane glides.

• In science, a hypothesis is supported only after many scientists have conducted many experiments and produced consistent results.

Inferring

An **inference** is a logical conclusion drawn from the available evidence and prior knowledge. Inferences are often made from observations.

EXAMPLE

A student observing a set of acorns noticed something unexpected about one of them. He noticed a white, soft-bodied insect eating its way out of the acorn.

The student recorded these observations.

Observations

- There is a hole in the acorn, about 0.5 cm in diameter, where the insect crawled out.
- There is a second hole, which is about the size of a pinhole, on the other side of the acorn.
- The inside of the acorn is hollow.

Here are some inferences that can be made on the basis of the observations.

Inferences

- The insect formed from the material inside the acorn, grew to its present size, and ate its way out of the acorn.
- The insect crawled through the smaller hole, ate the inside of the acorn, grew to its present size, and ate its way out of the acorn.
- An egg was laid in the acorn through the smaller hole. The egg hatched into a larva that ate the inside of the acorn, grew to its present size, and ate its way out of the acorn.

When you make inferences, be sure to look at all of the evidence available and combine it with what you already know.

MORE ABOUT INFERENCES

Inferences depend both on observations and on the knowledge of the people making the inferences. Ancient people who did not know that organisms are produced only by similar organisms might have made an inference like the first one. A student today might look at the same observations and make the second inference. A third student might have knowledge about this particular insect and know that it is never small enough to fit through the smaller hole, leading her to the third inference.

Identifying Cause and Effect

In a **cause-and-effect relationship,** one event or characteristic is the result of another. Usually an effect follows its cause in time.

There are many examples of cause-and-effect relationships in everyday life.

Cause	Effect
Turn off a light.	Room gets dark.
Drop a glass.	Glass breaks.
Blow a whistle.	Sound is heard.

Scientists must be careful not to infer a cause-and-effect relationship just because one event happens after another event. When one event occurs after another, you cannot infer a cause-and-effect relationship on the basis of that information alone. You also cannot conclude that one event caused another if there are alternative ways to explain the second event. A scientist must demonstrate through experimentation or continued observation that an event was truly caused by another event.

EXAMPLE

Make an Observation

Suppose you have a few plants growing outside. When the weather starts getting colder, you bring one of the plants indoors. You notice that the plant you brought indoors is growing faster than the others are growing. You cannot conclude from your observation that the change in temperature was the cause of the increased plant growth, because there are alternative explanations for the observation. Some possible explanations are given below.

- The humidity indoors caused the plant to grow faster.

- The level of sunlight indoors caused the plant to grow faster.

- The indoor plant's being noticed more often and watered more often than the outdoor plants caused it to grow faster.

- The plant that was brought indoors was healthier than the other plants to begin with.

To determine which of these factors, if any, caused the indoor plant to grow faster than the outdoor plants, you would need to design and conduct an experiment.

See pages R28–R35 for information about designing experiments.

Recognizing Bias

Television, newspapers, and the Internet are full of experts claiming to have scientific evidence to back up their claims. How do you know whether the claims are really backed up by good science?

Bias is a slanted point of view, or personal prejudice. The goal of scientists is to be as objective as possible and to base their findings on facts instead of opinions. However, bias often affects the conclusions of researchers, and it is important to learn to recognize bias.

When scientific results are reported, you should consider the source of the information as well as the information itself. It is important to critically analyze the information that you see and read.

SOURCES OF BIAS

There are several ways in which a report of scientific information may be biased. Here are some questions that you can ask yourself:

1. Who is sponsoring the research?

   Sometimes, the results of an investigation are biased because an organization paying for the research is looking for a specific answer. This type of bias can affect how data are gathered and interpreted.

2. Is the research sample large enough?

   Sometimes research does not include enough data. The larger the sample size, the more likely that the results are accurate, assuming a truly random sample.

3. In a survey, who is answering the questions?

   The results of a survey or poll can be biased. The people taking part in the survey may have been specifically chosen because of how they would answer. They may have the same ideas or lifestyles. A survey or poll should make use of a random sample of people.

4. Are the people who take part in a survey biased?

   People who take part in surveys sometimes try to answer the questions the way they think the researcher wants them to answer. Also, in surveys or polls that ask for personal information, people may be unwilling to answer questions truthfully.

SCIENTIFIC BIAS

It is also important to realize that scientists have their own biases because of the types of research they do and because of their scientific viewpoints. Two scientists may look at the same set of data and come to completely different conclusions because of these biases. However, such disagreements are not necessarily bad. In fact, a critical analysis of disagreements is often responsible for moving science forward.

Identifying Faulty Reasoning

Faulty reasoning is wrong or incorrect thinking. It leads to mistakes and to wrong conclusions. Scientists are careful not to draw unreasonable conclusions from experimental data. Without such caution, the results of scientific investigations may be misleading.

EXAMPLE

Scientists try to make generalizations based on their data to explain as much about nature as possible. If only a small sample of data is looked at, however, a conclusion may be faulty. Suppose a scientist has studied the effects of the El Niño and La Niña weather patterns on flood damage in California from 1989 to 1995. The scientist organized the data in the bar graph below.

The scientist drew the following conclusions:

1. The La Niña weather pattern has no effect on flooding in California.

2. When neither weather pattern occurs, there is almost no flood damage.

3. A weak or moderate El Niño produces a small or moderate amount of flooding.

4. A strong El Niño produces a lot of flooding.

Flood and Storm Damage in California

Estimated damage (millions of dollars)

- Weak–moderate El Niño
- Strong El Niño

Starting year of season
(July 1–June 30)

SOURCE: *Governor's Office of Emergency Services, California*

For the six-year period of the scientist's investigation, these conclusions may seem to be reasonable. However, a six-year study of weather patterns may be too small of a sample for the conclusions to be supported. Consider the following graph, which shows information that was gathered from 1949 to 1997.

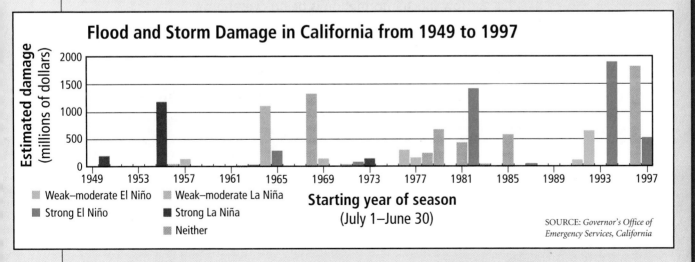

Flood and Storm Damage in California from 1949 to 1997

Estimated damage (millions of dollars)

- Weak–moderate El Niño
- Strong El Niño
- Weak–moderate La Niña
- Strong La Niña
- Neither

Starting year of season
(July 1–June 30)

SOURCE: *Governor's Office of Emergency Services, California*

The only one of the conclusions that all of this information supports is number 3: a weak or moderate El Niño produces a small or moderate amount of flooding. By collecting more data, scientists can be more certain of their conclusions and can avoid faulty reasoning.

Analyzing Statements

To **analyze** a statement is to examine its parts carefully. Scientific findings are often reported through media such as television or the Internet. A report that is made public often focuses on only a small part of research. As a result, it is important to question the sources of information.

Evaluate Media Claims

To **evaluate** a statement is to judge it on the basis of criteria you've established. Sometimes evaluating means deciding whether a statement is true.

Reports of scientific research and findings in the media may be misleading or incomplete. When you are exposed to this information, you should ask yourself some questions so that you can make informed judgments about the information.

1. **Does the information come from a credible source?**

   Suppose you learn about a new product and it is stated that scientific evidence proves that the product works. A report from a respected news source may be more believable than an advertisement paid for by the product's manufacturer.

2. **How much evidence supports the claim?**

   Often, it may seem that there is new evidence every day of something in the world that either causes or cures an illness. However, information that is the result of several years of work by several different scientists is more credible than an advertisement that does not even cite the subjects of the experiment.

3. **How much information is being presented?**

   Science cannot solve all questions, and scientific experiments often have flaws. A report that discusses problems in a scientific study may be more believable than a report that addresses only positive experimental findings.

4. **Is scientific evidence being presented by a specific source?**

   Sometimes scientific findings are reported by people who are called experts or leaders in a scientific field. But if their names are not given or their scientific credentials are not reported, their statements may be less credible than those of recognized experts.

Differentiate Between Fact and Opinion

Sometimes information is presented as a fact when it may be an opinion. When scientific conclusions are reported, it is important to recognize whether they are based on solid evidence. Again, you may find it helpful to ask yourself some questions.

1. **What is the difference between a fact and an opinion?**

   A **fact** is a piece of information that can be strictly defined and proved true. An **opinion** is a statement that expresses a belief, value, or feeling. An opinion cannot be proved true or false. For example, a person's age is a fact, but if someone is asked how old they feel, it is impossible to prove the person's answer to be true or false.

2. **Can opinions be measured?**

   Yes, opinions can be measured. In fact, surveys often ask for people's opinions on a topic. But there is no way to know whether or not an opinion is the truth.

HOW TO DIFFERENTIATE FACT FROM OPINION

Human Activities and the Environment

Opinions

Notice words or phrases that express beliefs or feelings. The words *unfortunately* and *careless* show that opinions are being expressed.

Unfortunately, human use of fossil fuels is one of the most significant developments of the past few centuries. Humans rely on fossil fuels, a non-renewable energy resource, for more than 90 percent of their energy needs.

Facts

Statements that contain statistics tend to be facts. Writers often use facts to support their opinions.

Opinion

Look for statements that speculate about events. These statements are opinions, because they cannot be proved.

This careless misuse of our planet's resources has resulted in pollution, global warming, and the destruction of fragile ecosystems. For example, oil pipelines carry more than one million barrels of oil each day across tundra regions. Transporting oil across such areas can only result in oil spills that poison the land for decades.

Lab Handbook

Safety Rules

Before you work in the laboratory, read these safety rules twice. Ask your teacher to explain any rules that you do not completely understand. Refer to these rules later on if you have questions about safety in the science classroom.

Directions

- Read all directions and make sure that you understand them before starting an investigation or lab activity. If you do not understand how to do a procedure or how to use a piece of equipment, ask your teacher.
- Do not begin any investigation or touch any equipment until your teacher has told you to start.
- Never experiment on your own. If you want to try a procedure that the directions do not call for, ask your teacher for permission first.
- If you are hurt or injured in any way, tell your teacher immediately.

Dress Code

goggles

apron

gloves

- Wear goggles when
  — using glassware, sharp objects, or chemicals
  — heating an object
  — working with anything that can easily fly up into the air and hurt someone's eye
- Tie back long hair or hair that hangs in front of your eyes.
- Remove any article of clothing—such as a loose sweater or a scarf—that hangs down and may touch a flame, chemical, or piece of equipment.
- Observe all safety icons calling for the wearing of eye protection, gloves, and aprons.

Heating and Fire Safety

fire safety

heating safety

- Keep your work area neat, clean, and free of extra materials.
- Never reach over a flame or heat source.
- Point objects being heated away from you and others.
- Never heat a substance or an object in a closed container.
- Never touch an object that has been heated. If you are unsure whether something is hot, treat it as though it is. Use oven mitts, clamps, tongs, or a test-tube holder.
- Know where the fire extinguisher and fire blanket are kept in your classroom.
- Do not throw hot substances into the trash. Wait for them to cool or use the container your teacher puts out for disposal.

Electrical Safety

electrical
safety

- Never use lamps or other electrical equipment with frayed cords.
- Make sure no cord is lying on the floor where someone can trip over it.
- Do not let a cord hang over the side of a counter or table so that the equipment can easily be pulled or knocked to the floor.
- Never let cords hang into sinks or other places where water can be found.
- Never try to fix electrical problems. Inform your teacher of any problems immediately.
- Unplug an electrical cord by pulling on the plug, not the cord.

Chemical Safety

chemical
safety

poison

fumes

- If you spill a chemical or get one on your skin or in your eyes, tell your teacher right away.
- Never touch, taste, or sniff any chemicals in the lab. If you need to determine odor, waft. Wafting consists of holding the chemical in its container 15 centimeters (6 in.) away from your nose, and using your fingers to bring fumes from the container to your nose.
- Keep lids on all chemicals you are not using.
- Never put unused chemicals back into the original containers. Throw away extra chemicals where your teacher tells you to.
- Pour chemicals over a sink or your work area, not over the floor.
- If you get a chemical in your eye, use the eyewash right away.
- Always wash your hands after handling chemicals, plants, or soil.

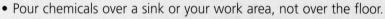

Wafting

LAB HANDBOOK

Glassware and Sharp-Object Safety

sharp
objects

- If you break glassware, tell your teacher right away.
- Do not use broken or chipped glassware. Give these to your teacher.
- Use knives and other cutting instruments carefully. Always wear eye protection and cut away from you.

Animal Safety

- Never hurt an animal.
- Touch animals only when necessary. Follow your teacher's instructions for handling animals.
- Always wash your hands after working with animals.

Cleanup

disposal

- Follow your teacher's instructions for throwing away or putting away supplies.
- Clean your work area and pick up anything that has dropped to the floor.
- Wash your hands.

Using Lab Equipment

Different experiments require different types of equipment. But even though experiments differ, the ways in which the equipment is used are the same.

Beakers

- Use beakers for holding and pouring liquids.
- Do not use a beaker to measure the volume of a liquid. Use a graduated cylinder instead. (See page R16.)
- Use a beaker that holds about twice as much liquid as you need. For example, if you need 100 milliliters of water, you should use a 200- or 250-milliliter beaker.

Test Tubes

- Use test tubes to hold small amounts of substances.
- Do not use a test tube to measure the volume of a liquid.
- Use a test tube when heating a substance over a flame. Aim the mouth of the tube away from yourself and other people.
- Liquids easily spill or splash from test tubes, so it is important to use only small amounts of liquids.

Test-Tube Holder

- Use a test-tube holder when heating a substance in a test tube.
- Use a test-tube holder if the substance in a test tube is dangerous to touch.
- Make sure the test-tube holder tightly grips the test tube so that the test tube will not slide out of the holder.
- Make sure that the test-tube holder is above the surface of the substance in the test tube so that you can observe the substance.

Test-Tube Rack

- Use a test-tube rack to organize test tubes before, during, and after an experiment.

- Use a test-tube rack to keep test tubes upright so that they do not fall over and spill their contents.

- Use a test-tube rack that is the correct size for the test tubes that you are using. If the rack is too small, a test tube may become stuck. If the rack is too large, a test tube may lean over, and some of its contents may spill or splash.

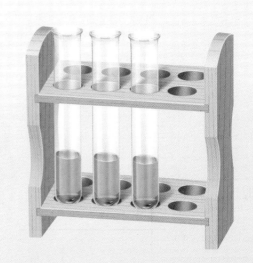

Forceps

- Use forceps when you need to pick up or hold a very small object that should not be touched with your hands.

- Do not use forceps to hold anything over a flame, because forceps are not long enough to keep your hand safely away from the flame. Plastic forceps will melt, and metal forceps will conduct heat and burn your hand.

Hot Plate

- Use a hot plate when a substance needs to be kept warmer than room temperature for a long period of time.

- Use a hot plate instead of a Bunsen burner or a candle when you need to carefully control temperature.

- Do not use a hot plate when a substance needs to be burned in an experiment.

- Always use "hot hands" safety mitts or oven mitts when handling anything that has been heated on a hot plate.

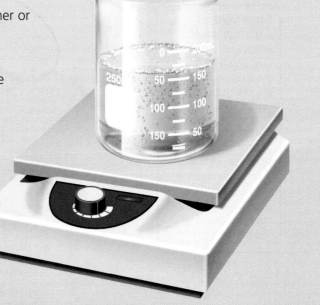

Microscope

Scientists use microscopes to see very small objects that cannot easily be seen with the eye alone. A microscope magnifies the image of an object so that small details may be observed. A microscope that you may use can magnify an object 400 times—the object will appear 400 times larger than its actual size.

Body The body separates the lens in the eyepiece from the objective lenses below.

Nosepiece The nosepiece holds the objective lenses above the stage and rotates so that all lenses may be used.

High-Power Objective Lens This is the largest lens on the nosepiece. It magnifies an image approximately 40 times.

Stage The stage supports the object being viewed.

Diaphragm The diaphragm is used to adjust the amount of light passing through the slide and into an objective lens.

Mirror or Light Source Some microscopes use light that is reflected through the stage by a mirror. Other microscopes have their own light sources.

Eyepiece Objects are viewed through the eyepiece. The eyepiece contains a lens that commonly magnifies an image 10 times.

Coarse Adjustment This knob is used to focus the image of an object when it is viewed through the low-power lens.

Fine Adjustment This knob is used to focus the image of an object when it is viewed through the high-power lens.

Low-Power Objective Lens This is the smallest lens on the nosepiece. It magnifies an image approximately 10 times.

Arm The arm supports the body above the stage. Always carry a microscope by the arm and base.

Stage Clip The stage clip holds a slide in place on the stage.

Base The base supports the microscope.

VIEWING AN OBJECT

1. Use the coarse adjustment knob to raise the body tube.

2. Adjust the diaphragm so that you can see a bright circle of light through the eyepiece.

3. Place the object or slide on the stage. Be sure that it is centered over the hole in the stage.

4. Turn the nosepiece to click the low-power lens into place.

5. Using the coarse adjustment knob, slowly lower the lens and focus on the specimen being viewed. Be sure not to touch the slide or object with the lens.

6. When switching from the low-power lens to the high-power lens, first raise the body tube with the coarse adjustment knob so that the high-power lens will not hit the slide.

7. Turn the nosepiece to click the high-power lens into place.

8. Use the fine adjustment knob to focus on the specimen being viewed. Again, be sure not to touch the slide or object with the lens.

MAKING A SLIDE, OR WET MOUNT

① Place the specimen in the center of a clean slide.

② Place a drop of water on the specimen.

③ Place a cover slip on the slide. Put one edge of the cover slip into the drop of water and slowly lower it over the specimen.

④ Remove any air bubbles from under the cover slip by gently tapping the cover slip.

⑤ Dry any excess water before placing the slide on the microscope stage for viewing.

Spring Scale (Force Meter)

- Use a spring scale to measure a force pulling on the scale.
- Use a spring scale to measure the force of gravity exerted on an object by Earth.
- To measure a force accurately, a spring scale must be zeroed before it is used. The scale is zeroed when no weight is attached and the indicator is positioned at zero.
- Do not attach a weight that is either too heavy or too light to a spring scale. A weight that is too heavy could break the scale or exert too great a force for the scale to measure. A weight that is too light may not exert enough force to be measured accurately.

Graduated Cylinder

- Use a graduated cylinder to measure the volume of a liquid.
- Be sure that the graduated cylinder is on a flat surface so that your measurement will be accurate.
- When reading the scale on a graduated cylinder, be sure to have your eyes at the level of the surface of the liquid.
- The surface of the liquid will be curved in the graduated cylinder. Read the volume of the liquid at the bottom of the curve, or meniscus (muh-NIHS-kuhs).
- You can use a graduated cylinder to find the volume of a solid object by measuring the increase in a liquid's level after you add the object to the cylinder.

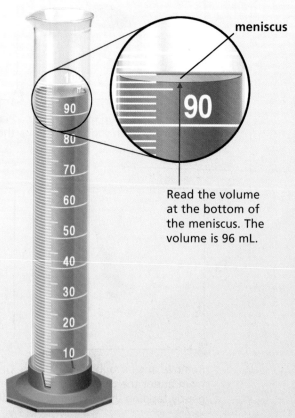

meniscus

Read the volume at the bottom of the meniscus. The volume is 96 mL.

Metric Rulers

- Use metric rulers or meter sticks to measure objects' lengths.

- Do not measure an object from the end of a metric ruler or meter stick, because the end is often imperfect. Instead, measure from the 1-centimeter mark, but remember to subtract a centimeter from the apparent measurement.

- Estimate any lengths that extend between marked units. For example, if a meter stick shows centimeters but not millimeters, you can estimate the length that an object extends between centimeter marks to measure it to the nearest millimeter.

- **Controlling Variables** If you are taking repeated measurements, always measure from the same point each time. For example, if you're measuring how high two different balls bounce when dropped from the same height, measure both bounces at the same point on the balls—either the top or the bottom. Do not measure at the top of one ball and the bottom of the other.

EXAMPLE

How to Measure a Leaf

1. Lay a ruler flat on top of the leaf so that the 1-centimeter mark lines up with one end. Make sure the ruler and the leaf do not move between the time you line them up and the time you take the measurement.

2. Look straight down on the ruler so that you can see exactly how the marks line up with the other end of the leaf.

3. Estimate the length by which the leaf extends beyond a marking. For example, the leaf below extends about halfway between the 4.2-centimeter and 4.3-centimeter marks, so the apparent measurement is about 4.25 centimeters.

4. Remember to subtract 1 centimeter from your apparent measurement, since you started at the 1-centimeter mark on the ruler and not at the end. The leaf is about 3.25 centimeters long (4.25 cm – 1 cm = 3.25 cm).

Triple-Beam Balance

This balance has a pan and three beams with sliding masses, called riders. At one end of the beams is a pointer that indicates whether the mass on the pan is equal to the masses shown on the beams.

1. Make sure the balance is zeroed before measuring the mass of an object. The balance is zeroed if the pointer is at zero when nothing is on the pan and the riders are at their zero points. Use the adjustment knob at the base of the balance to zero it.

2. Place the object to be measured on the pan.

3. Move the riders one notch at a time away from the pan. Begin with the largest rider. If moving the largest rider one notch brings the pointer below zero, begin measuring the mass of the object with the next smaller rider.

4. Change the positions of the riders until they balance the mass on the pan and the pointer is at zero. Then add the readings from the three beams to determine the mass of the object.

300 g	position of largest rider
90 g	position of middle rider
+ 3 g	position of smallest rider
393 g	mass of beaker

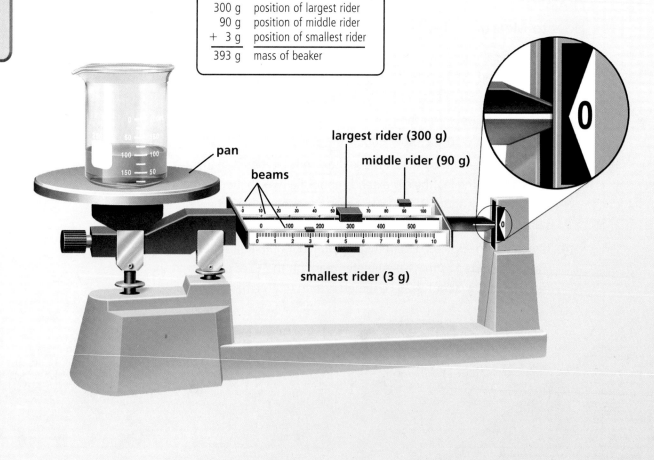

Double-Pan Balance

This type of balance has two pans. Between the pans is a pointer that indicates whether the masses on the pans are equal.

1. Make sure the balance is zeroed before measuring the mass of an object. The balance is zeroed if the pointer is at zero when there is nothing on either of the pans. Many double-pan balances have sliding knobs that can be used to zero them.

2. Place the object to be measured on one of the pans.

3. Begin adding standard masses to the other pan. Begin with the largest standard mass. If this adds too much mass to the balance, begin measuring the mass of the object with the next smaller standard mass.

4. Add standard masses until the masses on both pans are balanced and the pointer is at zero. Then add the standard masses together to determine the mass of the object being measured.

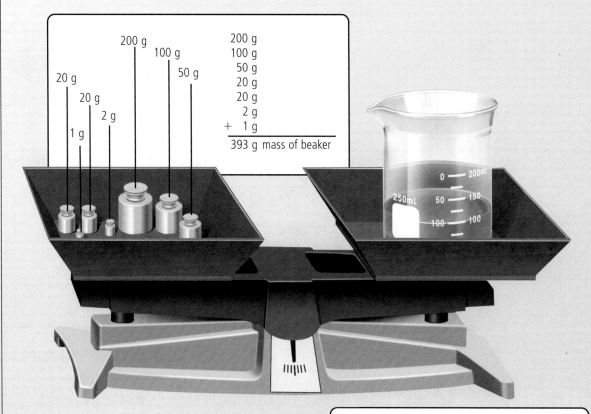

```
200 g
100 g
 50 g
 20 g
 20 g
  2 g
+ 1 g
─────
393 g  mass of beaker
```

Never place chemicals or liquids directly on a pan. Instead, use the following procedure:

1 Determine the mass of an empty container, such as a beaker.

2 Pour the substance into the container, and measure the total mass of the substance and the container.

3 Subtract the mass of the empty container from the total mass to find the mass of the substance.

The Metric System and SI Units

Scientists use International System (SI) units for measurements of distance, volume, mass, and temperature. The International System is based on multiples of ten and the metric system of measurement.

Basic SI Units		
Property	**Name**	**Symbol**
length	meter	m
volume	liter	L
mass	kilogram	kg
temperature	kelvin	K

SI Prefixes		
Prefix	**Symbol**	**Multiple of 10**
kilo-	k	1000
hecto-	h	100
deca-	da	10
deci-	d	$0.1 \left(\frac{1}{10}\right)$
centi-	c	$0.01 \left(\frac{1}{100}\right)$
milli-	m	$0.001 \left(\frac{1}{1000}\right)$

Changing Metric Units

You can change from one unit to another in the metric system by multiplying or dividing by a power of 10.

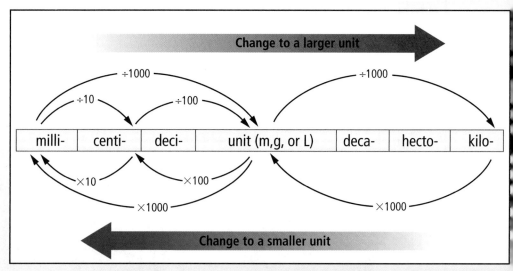

Example

Change 0.64 liters to milliliters.

(1) Decide whether to multiply or divide.

(2) Select the power of 10.

ANSWER 0.64 L = 640 mL

Change to a smaller unit by multiplying.

mL ⟵ × 1000 ⟶ L

0.64 × 1000 = **640.**

Example

Change 23.6 grams to kilograms.

(1) Decide whether to multiply or divide.

(2) Select the power of 10.

ANSWER 23.6 g = 0.0236 kg

Change to a larger unit by dividing.

g ⟶ ÷ 1000 ⟶ kg

23.6 ÷ 1000 = **0.0236**

Temperature Conversions

Even though the kelvin is the SI base unit of temperature, the degree Celsius will be the unit you use most often in your science studies. The formulas below show the relationships between temperatures in degrees Fahrenheit (°F), degrees Celsius (°C), and kelvins (K).

$$°C = \frac{5}{9} (°F - 32)$$

$$°F = \frac{9}{5} °C + 32$$

$$K = °C + 273$$

See page R42 for help with using formulas.

Examples of Temperature Conversions

Condition	Degrees Celsius	Degrees Fahrenheit
Freezing point of water	0	32
Cool day	10	50
Mild day	20	68
Warm day	30	86
Normal body temperature	37	98.6
Very hot day	40	104
Boiling point of water	100	212

Converting Between SI and U.S. Customary Units

Use the chart below when you need to convert between SI units and U.S. customary units.

SI Unit	From SI to U.S. Customary			From U.S. Customary to SI		
Length	When you know	multiply by	to find	When you know	multiply by	to find
kilometer (km) = 1000 m	kilometers	0.62	miles	miles	1.61	kilometers
meter (m) = 100 cm	meters	3.28	feet	feet	0.3048	meters
centimeter (cm) = 10 mm	centimeters	0.39	inches	inches	2.54	centimeters
millimeter (mm) = 0.1 cm	millimeters	0.04	inches	inches	25.4	millimeters
Area	When you know	multiply by	to find	When you know	multiply by	to find
square kilometer (km^2)	square kilometers	0.39	square miles	square miles	2.59	square kilometers
square meter (m^2)	square meters	1.2	square yards	square yards	0.84	square meters
square centimeter (cm^2)	square centimeters	0.155	square inches	square inches	6.45	square centimeters
Volume	When you know	multiply by	to find	When you know	multiply by	to find
liter (L) = 1000 mL	liters	1.06	quarts	quarts	0.95	liters
	liters	0.26	gallons	gallons	3.79	liters
	liters	4.23	cups	cups	0.24	liters
	liters	2.12	pints	pints	0.47	liters
milliliter (mL) = 0.001 L	milliliters	0.20	teaspoons	teaspoons	4.93	milliliters
	milliliters	0.07	tablespoons	tablespoons	14.79	milliliters
	milliliters	0.03	fluid ounces	fluid ounces	29.57	milliliters
Mass	When you know	multiply by	to find	When you know	multiply by	to find
kilogram (kg) = 1000 g	kilograms	2.2	pounds	pounds	0.45	kilograms
gram (g) = 1000 mg	grams	0.035	ounces	ounces	28.35	grams

Precision and Accuracy

When you do an experiment, it is important that your methods, observations, and data be both precise and accurate.

low precision

precision, but not accuracy

precision and accuracy

LAB HANDBOOK

Precision

In science, **precision** is the exactness and consistency of measurements. For example, measurements made with a ruler that has both centimeter and millimeter markings would be more precise than measurements made with a ruler that has only centimeter markings. Another indicator of precision is the care taken to make sure that methods and observations are as exact and consistent as possible. Every time a particular experiment is done, the same procedure should be used. Precision is necessary because experiments are repeated several times and if the procedure changes, the results will change.

EXAMPLE

Suppose you are measuring temperatures over a two-week period. Your precision will be greater if you measure each temperature at the same place, at the same time of day, and with the same thermometer than if you change any of these factors from one day to the next.

Accuracy

In science, it is possible to be precise but not accurate. **Accuracy** depends on the difference between a measurement and an actual value. The smaller the difference, the more accurate the measurement.

EXAMPLE

Suppose you look at a stream and estimate that it is about 1 meter wide at a particular place. You decide to check your estimate by measuring the stream with a meter stick, and you determine that the stream is 1.32 meters wide. However, because it is hard to measure the width of a stream with a meter stick, it turns out that you didn't do a very good job. The stream is actually 1.14 meters wide. Therefore, even though your estimate was less precise than your measurement, your estimate was actually more accurate.

Making Data Tables and Graphs

Data tables and graphs are useful tools for both recording and communicating scientific data.

Making Data Tables

You can use a **data table** to organize and record the measurements that you make. Some examples of information that might be recorded in data tables are frequencies, times, and amounts.

EXAMPLE

Suppose you are investigating photosynthesis in two elodea plants. One sits in direct sunlight, and the other sits in a dimly lit room. You measure the rate of photosynthesis by counting the number of bubbles in the jar every ten minutes.

1. Title and number your data table.
2. Decide how you will organize the table into columns and rows.
3. Any units, such as seconds or degrees, should be included in column headings, not in the individual cells.

Table 1. Number of Bubbles from Elodea

Time (min)	Sunlight	Dim Light
0	0	0
10	15	5
20	25	8
30	32	7
40	41	10
50	47	9
60	42	9

> Always number and title data tables.

The data in the table above could also be organized in a different way.

Table 1. Number of Bubbles from Elodea

Light Condition	Time (min)						
	0	10	20	30	40	50	60
Sunlight	0	15	25	32	41	47	42
Dim light	0	5	8	7	10	9	9

> Put units in column heading.

Making Line Graphs

You can use a **line graph** to show a relationship between variables. Line graphs are particularly useful for showing changes in variables over time.

EXAMPLE

Suppose you are interested in graphing temperature data that you collected over the course of a day.

Table 1. Outside Temperature During the Day on March 7

	Time of Day						
	7:00 A.M.	9:00 A.M.	11:00 A.M.	1:00 P.M.	3:00 P.M.	5:00 P.M.	7:00 P.M.
Temp (°C)	8	9	11	14	12	10	6

1. Use the vertical axis of your line graph for the variable that you are measuring—temperature.

2. Choose scales for both the horizontal axis and the vertical axis of the graph. You should have two points more than you need on the vertical axis, and the horizontal axis should be long enough for all of the data points to fit.

3. Draw and label each axis.

4. Graph each value. First find the appropriate point on the scale of the horizontal axis. Imagine a line that rises vertically from that place on the scale. Then find the corresponding value on the vertical axis, and imagine a line that moves horizontally from that value. The point where these two imaginary lines intersect is where the value should be plotted.

5. Connect the points with straight lines.

Be sure to add a number and a title to your graph.

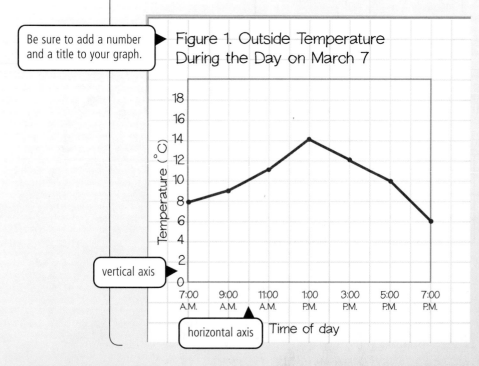

Figure 1. Outside Temperature During the Day on March 7

vertical axis

horizontal axis

Making Circle Graphs

You can use a **circle graph**, sometimes called a pie chart, to represent data as parts of a circle. Circle graphs are used only when the data can be expressed as percentages of a whole. The entire circle shown in a circle graph is equal to 100 percent of the data.

EXAMPLE

Suppose you identified the species of each mature tree growing in a small wooded area. You organized your data in a table, but you also want to show the data in a circle graph.

1. To begin, find the total number of mature trees.

    56 + 34 + 22 + 10 + 28 = 150

2. To find the degree measure for each sector of the circle, write a fraction comparing the number of each tree species with the total number of trees. Then multiply the fraction by 360°.

    Oak: $\frac{56}{150} \times 360° = 134.4°$

3. Draw a circle. Use a protractor to draw the angle for each sector of the graph.

4. Color and label each sector of the graph.

5. Give the graph a number and title.

Table 1. Tree Species in Wooded Area

Species	Number of Specimens
Oak	56
Maple	34
Birch	22
Willow	10
Pine	28

Figure 1. Tree Species in Wooded Area

Instead of labeling each sector, you could make a color key.

- Oak 56
- Maple 34
- Pine 28
- Birch 22
- Willow 10

Bar Graph

A **bar graph** is a type of graph in which the lengths of the bars are used to represent and compare data. A numerical scale is used to determine the lengths of the bars.

EXAMPLE

To determine the effect of water on seed sprouting, three cups were filled with sand, and ten seeds were planted in each. Different amounts of water were added to each cup over a three-day period.

Table 1. Effect of Water on Seed Sprouting

Daily Amount of Water (mL)	Number of Seeds That Sprouted After 3 Days in Sand
0	1
10	4
20	8

1. Choose a numerical scale. The greatest value is 8, so the end of the scale should have a value greater than 8, such as 10. Use equal increments along the scale, such as increments of 2.

2. Draw and label the axes. Mark intervals on the vertical axis according to the scale you chose.

3. Draw a bar for each data value. Use the scale to decide how long to make each bar.

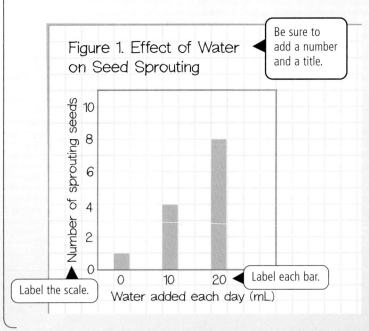

Figure 1. Effect of Water on Seed Sprouting

Be sure to add a number and a title.

Label the scale.

Label each bar.

Double Bar Graph

A **double bar graph** is a bar graph that shows two sets of data. The two bars for each measurement are drawn next to each other.

EXAMPLE

The same seed-sprouting experiment was repeated with potting soil. The data for sand and potting soil can be plotted on one graph.

1. Draw one set of bars, using the data for sand, as shown below.
2. Draw bars for the potting-soil data next to the bars for the sand data. Shade them a different color. Add a key.

Table 2. Effect of Water and Soil on Seed Sprouting

Daily Amount of Water (mL)	Number of Seeds That Sprouted After 3 Days in Sand	Number of Seeds That Sprouted After 3 Days in Potting Soil
0	1	2
10	4	5
20	8	9

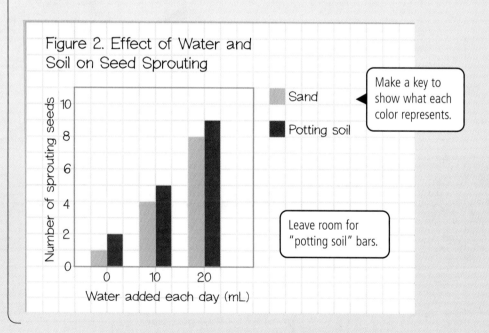

Figure 2. Effect of Water and Soil on Seed Sprouting

Make a key to show what each color represents.

Leave room for "potting soil" bars.

Designing an Experiment

Use this section when designing or conducting an experiment.

Determining a Purpose

You can find a purpose for an experiment by doing research, by examining the results of a previous experiment, or by observing the world around you. An **experiment** is an organized procedure to study something under controlled conditions.

1. Write the purpose of your experiment as a question or problem that you want to investigate.

2. Write down research questions and begin searching for information that will help you design an experiment. Consult the library, the Internet, and other people as you conduct your research.

> Don't forget to learn as much as possible about your topic before you begin.

EXAMPLE

Middle school students observed an odor near the lake by their school. They also noticed that the water on the side of the lake near the school was greener than the water on the other side of the lake. The students did some research to learn more about their observations. They discovered that the odor and green color in the lake came from algae. They also discovered that a new fertilizer was being used on a field nearby. The students inferred that the use of the fertilizer might be related to the presence of the algae and designed a controlled experiment to find out whether they were right.

Problem
How does fertilizer affect the presence of algae in a lake?

Research Questions
- Have other experiments been done on this problem? If so, what did those experiments show?
- What kind of fertilizer is used on the field? How much?
- How do algae grow?
- How do people measure algae?
- Can fertilizer and algae be used safely in a lab? How?

> **Research**
> As you research, you may find a topic that is more interesting to you than your original topic, or learn that a procedure you wanted to use is not practical or safe. It is OK to change your purpose as you research.

Writing a Hypothesis

A **hypothesis** is a tentative explanation for an observation or scientific problem that can be tested by further investigation. You can write your hypothesis in the form of an "If . . . , then . . . , because . . ." statement.

Hypothesis

If the amount of fertilizer in lake water is increased, then the amount of algae will also increase, because fertilizers provide nutrients that algae need to grow.

> **Hypotheses**
> For help with hypotheses, refer to page R3.

Determining Materials

Make a list of all the materials you will need to do your experiment. Be specific, especially if someone else is helping you obtain the materials. Try to think of everything you will need.

Materials

- 1 large jar or container
- 4 identical smaller containers
- rubber gloves that also cover the arms
- sample of fertilizer-and-water solution
- eyedropper
- clear plastic wrap
- scissors
- masking tape
- marker
- ruler

Determining Variables and Constants

EXPERIMENTAL GROUP AND CONTROL GROUP

An experiment to determine how two factors are related always has two groups—a control group and an experimental group.

1. Design an experimental group. Include as many trials as possible in the experimental group in order to obtain reliable results.

2. Design a control group that is the same as the experimental group in every way possible, except for the factor you wish to test.

> **Experimental Group:** two containers of lake water with one drop of fertilizer solution added to each
>
> **Control Group:** two containers of lake water with no fertilizer solution added

Go back to your materials list and make sure you have enough items listed to cover both your experimental group and your control group.

VARIABLES AND CONSTANTS

Identify the variables and constants in your experiment. In a controlled experiment, a **variable** is any factor that can change. **Constants** are all of the factors that are the same in both the experimental group and the control group.

Hypothesis
If the amount of fertilizer in lake water is increased, then the amount of algae will also increase, because fertilizers provide nutrients that algae need to grow.

1. Read your hypothesis. The **independent variable** is the factor that you wish to test and that is manipulated or changed so that it can be tested. The independent variable is expressed in your hypothesis after the word *if*. Identify the independent variable in your laboratory report.

2. The **dependent variable** is the factor that you measure to gather results. It is expressed in your hypothesis after the word *then*. Identify the dependent variable in your laboratory report.

> Table 1. Variables and Constants in Algae Experiment
>
> | Independent Variable | Dependent Variable | Constants |
> |---|---|---|
> | Amount of fertilizer in lake water | Amount of algae that grow | • Where the lake water is obtained
• Type of container used
• Light and temperature conditions where water will be stored |

Set up your experiment so that you will test only one variable.

MEASURING THE DEPENDENT VARIABLE

Before starting your experiment, you need to define how you will measure the dependent variable. An **operational definition** is a description of the one particular way in which you will measure the dependent variable.

Your operational definition is important for several reasons. First, in any experiment there are several ways in which a dependent variable can be measured. Second, the procedure of the experiment depends on how you decide to measure the dependent variable. Third, your operational definition makes it possible for other people to evaluate and build on your experiment.

EXAMPLE 1

An operational definition of a dependent variable can be qualitative. That is, your measurement of the dependent variable can simply be an observation of whether a change occurs as a result of a change in the independent variable. This type of operational definition can be thought of as a "yes or no" measurement.

Table 2. Qualitative Operational Definition of Algae Growth

Independent Variable	Dependent Variable	Operational Definition
Amount of fertilizer in lake water	Amount of algae that grow	Algae grow in lake water

A qualitative measurement of a dependent variable is often easy to make and record. However, this type of information does not provide a great deal of detail in your experimental results.

EXAMPLE 2

An operational definition of a dependent variable can be quantitative. That is, your measurement of the dependent variable can be a number that shows how much change occurs as a result of a change in the independent variable.

Table 3. Quantitative Operational Definition of Algae Growth

Independent Variable	Dependent Variable	Operational Definition
Amount of fertilizer in lake water	Amount of algae that grow	Diameter of largest algal growth (in mm)

A quantitative measurement of a dependent variable can be more difficult to make and analyze than a qualitative measurement. However, this type of data provides much more information about your experiment and is often more useful.

Writing a Procedure

Write each step of your procedure. Start each step with a verb, or action word, and keep the steps short. Your procedure should be clear enough for someone else to use as instructions for repeating your experiment.

> If necessary, go back to your materials list and add any materials that you left out.

> **Controlling Variables**
> The same amount of fertilizer solution must be added to two of the four containers.

> **Controlling Variables**
> All four containers must receive the same amount of light.

Procedure

1. Put on your gloves. Use the large container to obtain a sample of lake water.

2. Divide the sample of lake water equally among the four smaller containers.

3. Use the eyedropper to add one drop of fertilizer solution to two of the containers.

4. Use the masking tape and the marker to label the containers with your initials, the date, and the identifiers "Jar 1 with Fertilizer," "Jar 2 with Fertilizer," "Jar 1 without Fertilizer," and "Jar 2 without Fertilizer."

5. Cover the containers with clear plastic wrap. Use the scissors to punch ten holes in each of the covers.

6. Place all four containers on a window ledge. Make sure that they all receive the same amount of light.

7. Observe the containers every day for one week.

8. Use the ruler to measure the diameter of the largest clump of algae in each container, and record your measurements daily.

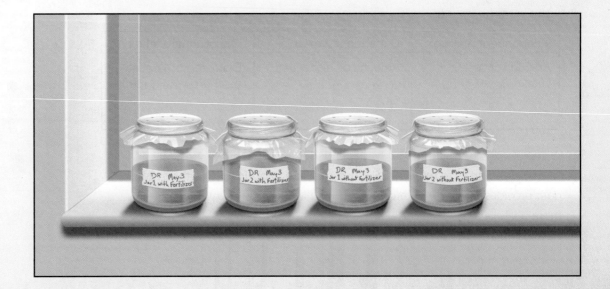

Recording Observations

Once you have obtained all of your materials and your procedure has been approved, you can begin making experimental observations. Gather both quantitative and qualitative data. If something goes wrong during your procedure, make sure you record that too.

> **Observations**
> For help with making qualitative and quantitative observations, refer to page R2.

> For more examples of data tables, see page R23.

Table 4. Fertilizer and Algae Growth

Date and Time	Experimental Group		Control Group		
	Jar 1 with Fertilizer (diameter of algae in mm)	Jar 2 with Fertilizer (diameter of algae in mm)	Jar 1 without Fertilizer (diameter of algae in mm)	Jar 2 without Fertilizer (diameter of algae in mm)	Observations
5/3 4:00 P.M.	0	0	0	0	condensation in all containers
5/4 4:00 P.M.	0	3	0	0	tiny green blobs in jar 2 with fertilizer
5/5 4:15 P.M.	4	5	0	3	green blobs in jars 1 and 2 with fertilizer and jar 2 without fertilizer
5/6 4:00 P.M.	5	6	0	4	water light green in jar 2 with fertilizer
5/7 4:00 P.M.	8	10	0	6	water light green in jars 1 and 2 with fertilizer and in jar 2 without fertilizer
5/8 3:30 P.M.	10	18	0	6	cover off jar 2 with fertilizer
5/9 3:30 P.M.	14	23	0	8	drew sketches of each container

> Notice that on the sixth day, the observer found that the cover was off one of the containers. It is important to record observations of unintended factors because they might affect the results of the experiment.

> Use technology, such as a microscope, to help you make observations when possible.

Drawings of Samples Viewed Under Microscope on 5/9 at 100x

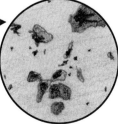
Jar 1 with Fertilizer

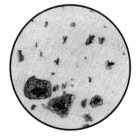
Jar 2 with Fertilizer

Jar 1 without Fertilizer

Jar 2 without Fertilizer

Summarizing Results

To summarize your data, look at all of your observations together. Look for meaningful ways to present your observations. For example, you might average your data or make a graph to look for patterns. When possible, use spreadsheet software to help you analyze and present your data. The two graphs below show the same data.

EXAMPLE 1

Always include a number and a title with a graph.

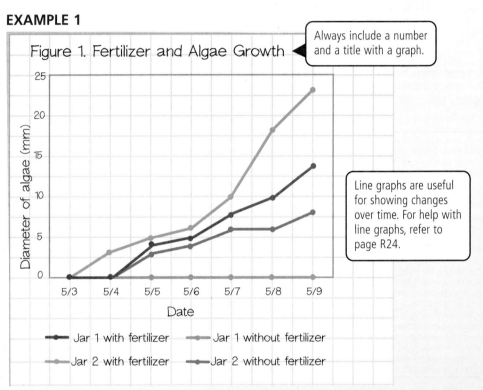

Line graphs are useful for showing changes over time. For help with line graphs, refer to page R24.

EXAMPLE 2

Bar graphs are useful for comparing different data sets. This bar graph has four bars for each day. Another way to present the data would be to calculate averages for the tests and the controls, and to show one test bar and one control bar for each day.

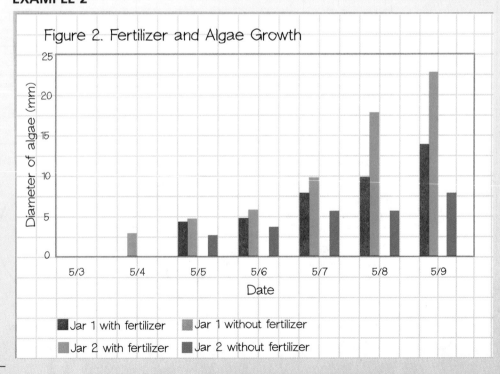

LAB HANDBOOK

Drawing Conclusions

RESULTS AND INFERENCES

To draw conclusions from your experiment, first write your results. Then compare your results with your hypothesis. Do your results support your hypothesis? Be careful not to make inferences about factors that you did not test.

> For help with making inferences, see page R4.

Results and Inferences

The results of my experiment show that more algae grew in lake water to which fertilizer had been added than in lake water to which no fertilizer had been added. My hypothesis was supported. I infer that it is possible that the growth of algae in the lake was caused by the fertilizer used on the field.

> Notice that you cannot conclude from this experiment that the presence of algae in the lake was due only to the fertilizer.

QUESTIONS FOR FURTHER RESEARCH

Write a list of questions for further research and investigation. Your ideas may lead you to new experiments and discoveries.

Questions for Further Research

- What is the connection between the amount of fertilizer and algae growth?
- How do different brands of fertilizer affect algae growth?
- How would algae growth in the lake be affected if no fertilizer were used on the field?
- How do algae affect the lake and the other life in and around it?
- How does fertilizer affect the lake and the life in and around it?
- If fertilizer is getting into the lake, how is it getting there?

Math Handbook

Describing a Set of Data

Means, medians, modes, and ranges are important math tools for describing data sets such as the following widths of fossilized clamshells.

13 mm   25 mm   14 mm   21 mm   16 mm   23 mm   14 mm

Mean

The **mean** of a data set is the sum of the values divided by the number of values.

Example

To find the mean of the clamshell data, add the values and then divide the sum by the number of values.

$$\frac{13 \text{ mm} + 25 \text{ mm} + 14 \text{ mm} + 21 \text{ mm} + 16 \text{ mm} + 23 \text{ mm} + 14 \text{ mm}}{7} = \frac{126 \text{ mm}}{7} = 18 \text{ mm}$$

ANSWER The mean is 18 mm.

Median

The **median** of a data set is the middle value when the values are written in numerical order. If a data set has an even number of values, the median is the mean of the two middle values.

Example

To find the median of the clamshell data, arrange the values in order from least to greatest. The median is the middle value.

13 mm   14 mm   14 mm   16 mm   21 mm   23 mm   25 mm

ANSWER The median is 16 mm.

Mode

The **mode** of a data set is the value that occurs most often.

> ### Example
>
> To find the mode of the clamshell data, arrange the values in order from least to greatest and determine the value that occurs most often.
>
> 13 mm   14 mm   14 mm   16 mm   21 mm   23 mm   25 mm
>
> **ANSWER** The mode is 14 mm.

A data set can have more than one mode or no mode. For example, the following data set has modes of 2 mm and 4 mm:

2 mm   2 mm   3 mm   4 mm   4 mm

The data set below has no mode, because no value occurs more often than any other.

2 mm   3 mm   4 mm   5 mm

Range

The **range** of a data set is the difference between the greatest value and the least value.

> ### Example
>
> To find the range of the clamshell data, arrange the values in order from least to greatest.
>
> 13 mm   14 mm   14 mm   16 mm   21 mm   23 mm   25 mm
>
> Subtract the least value from the greatest value.
>
> 13 mm is the least value.
> 25 mm is the greatest value.
>
> 25 mm − 13 mm = 12 mm
>
> **ANSWER** The range is 12 mm.

Using Ratios, Rates, and Proportions

You can use ratios and rates to compare values in data sets. You can use proportions to find unknown values.

Ratios

A **ratio** uses division to compare two values. The ratio of a value a to a nonzero value b can be written as $\frac{a}{b}$.

Example

The height of one plant is 8 centimeters. The height of another plant is 6 centimeters. To find the ratio of the height of the first plant to the height of the second plant, write a fraction and simplify it.

$$\frac{8 \text{ cm}}{6 \text{ cm}} = \frac{4 \times \overset{1}{\cancel{2}}}{3 \times \underset{1}{\cancel{2}}} = \frac{4}{3}$$

ANSWER The ratio of the plant heights is $\frac{4}{3}$.

You can also write the ratio $\frac{a}{b}$ as "a to b" or as $a : b$. For example, you can write the ratio of the plant heights as "4 to 3" or as $4 : 3$.

Rates

A **rate** is a ratio of two values expressed in different units. A unit rate is a rate with a denominator of 1 unit.

Example

A plant grew 6 centimeters in 2 days. The plant's rate of growth was $\frac{6 \text{ cm}}{2 \text{ days}}$. To describe the plant's growth in centimeters per day, write a unit rate.

Divide numerator and denominator by 2: $\quad \frac{6 \text{ cm}}{2 \text{ days}} = \frac{6 \text{ cm} \div 2}{2 \text{ days} \div 2}$

> You divide 2 days by 2 to get 1 day, so divide 6 cm by 2 also.

Simplify: $\quad = \frac{3 \text{ cm}}{1 \text{ day}}$

ANSWER The plant's rate of growth is 3 centimeters per day.

Proportions

A **proportion** is an equation stating that two ratios are equivalent. To solve for an unknown value in a proportion, you can use cross products.

Example

If a plant grew 6 centimeters in 2 days, how many centimeters would it grow in 3 days (if its rate of growth is constant)?

Write a proportion:	$\dfrac{6 \text{ cm}}{2 \text{ days}} = \dfrac{x \text{ cm}}{3 \text{ days}}$
Set cross products:	$6 \cdot 3 = 2x$
Multiply 6 and 3:	$18 = 2x$
Divide each side by 2:	$\dfrac{18}{2} = \dfrac{2x}{2}$
Simplify:	$9 = x$

ANSWER The plant would grow 9 centimeters in 3 days.

Using Decimals, Fractions, and Percents

Decimals, fractions, and percentages are all ways of recording and representing data.

Decimals

A **decimal** is a number that is written in the base-ten place value system, in which a decimal point separates the ones and tenths digits. The values of each place is ten times that of the place to its right.

Example

A caterpillar traveled from point *A* to point *C* along the path shown.

A   **36.9 cm**   **B**   **52.4 cm**   C

ADDING DECIMALS To find the total distance traveled by the caterpillar, add the distance from *A* to *B* and the distance from *B* to *C*. Begin by lining up the decimal points. Then add the figures as you would whole numbers and bring down the decimal point.

```
  36.9 cm
+ 52.4 cm
  89.3 cm
```

ANSWER The caterpillar traveled a total distance of 89.3 centimeters.

Example *continued*

SUBTRACTING DECIMALS To find how much farther the caterpillar traveled on the second leg of the journey, subtract the distance from *A* to *B* from the distance from *B* to *C*.

$$
\begin{array}{r}
52.4 \text{ cm} \\
- 36.9 \text{ cm} \\
\hline
15.5 \text{ cm}
\end{array}
$$

ANSWER The caterpillar traveled 15.5 centimeters farther on the second leg of the journey.

Example

A caterpillar is traveling from point *D* to point *F* along the path shown. The caterpillar travels at a speed of 9.6 centimeters per minute.

D **E** **33.6 cm** F

MULTIPLYING DECIMALS You can multiply decimals as you would whole numbers. The number of decimal places in the product is equal to the sum of the number of decimal places in the factors.

For instance, suppose it takes the caterpillar 1.5 minutes to go from *D* to *E*. To find the distance from *D* to *E*, multiply the caterpillar's speed by the time it took.

> Align as shown.

$$
\begin{array}{rl}
9.6 & \quad 1 \quad \text{decimal place} \\
\times 1.5 & \quad +1 \quad \text{decimal place} \\
\hline
480 & \\
96 & \\
\hline
14.40 & \quad 2 \quad \text{decimal places}
\end{array}
$$

ANSWER The distance from *D* to *E* is 14.4 centimeters.

DIVIDING DECIMALS When you divide by a decimal, move the decimal points the same number of places in the divisor and the dividend to make the divisor a whole number.

For instance, to find the time it will take the caterpillar to travel from *E* to *F*, divide the distance from *E* to *F* by the caterpillar's speed.

$$
9.6\overline{)33.6}
$$

> Move each decimal point one place to the right.

$$
\begin{array}{r}
3.5 \\
96\overline{)336.} \\
\underline{288} \\
480 \\
\underline{480} \\
0
\end{array}
$$

> Line up decimal points.

ANSWER The caterpillar will travel from *E* to *F* in 3.5 minutes.

Fractions

A **fraction** is a number in the form $\frac{a}{b}$, where b is not equal to 0. A fraction is in **simplest form** if its numerator and denominator have a greatest common factor (GCF) of 1. To simplify a fraction, divide its numerator and denominator by their GCF.

Example

A caterpillar is 40 millimeters long. The head of the caterpillar is 6 millimeters long. To compare the length of the caterpillar's head with the caterpillar's total length, you can write and simplify a fraction that expresses the ratio of the two lengths.

Write the ratio of the two lengths:	$\dfrac{\text{Length of head}}{\text{Total length}} = \dfrac{6 \text{ mm}}{40 \text{ mm}}$
Write numerator and denominator as products of numbers and the GCF:	$= \dfrac{3 \times 2}{20 \times 2}$
Divide numerator and denominator by the GCF:	$= \dfrac{3 \times \overset{1}{\cancel{2}}}{20 \times \underset{1}{\cancel{2}}}$
Simplify:	$= \dfrac{3}{20}$

ANSWER In simplest form, the ratio of the lengths is $\frac{3}{20}$.

Percents

A **percent** is a ratio that compares a number to 100. The word *percent* means "per hundred" or "out of 100." The symbol for *percent* is %.

For instance, suppose 43 out of 100 caterpillars are female. You can represent this ratio as a percent, a decimal, or a fraction.

Percent	Decimal	Fraction
43%	0.43	$\dfrac{43}{100}$

Example

In the preceding example, the ratio of the length of the caterpillar's head to the caterpillar's total length is $\frac{3}{20}$. To write this ratio as a percent, write an equivalent fraction that has a denominator of 100.

Multiply numerator and denominator by 5:	$\dfrac{3}{20} = \dfrac{3 \times 5}{20 \times 5}$
	$= \dfrac{15}{100}$
Write as a percent:	$= 15\%$

ANSWER The caterpillar's head represents 15 percent of its total length.

Using Formulas

A mathematical **formula** is a statement of a fact, rule, or principle. It is usually expressed as an equation.

In science, a formula often has a word form and a symbolic form. The formula below expresses Ohm's law.

The term *variable* is also used in science to refer to a factor that can change during an experiment.

Word Form

$$\text{Current} = \frac{\text{voltage}}{\text{resistance}}$$

Symbolic Form

$$I = \frac{V}{R}$$

In this formula, I, V, and R are variables. A mathematical **variable** is a symbol or letter that is used to represent one or more numbers.

Example

Suppose that you measure a voltage of 1.5 volts and a resistance of 15 ohms. You can use the formula for Ohm's law to find the current in amperes.

Write the formula for Ohm's law: $\quad I = \dfrac{V}{R}$

Substitute 1.5 volts for V and 15 ohms for R: $\quad I = \dfrac{1.5 \text{ volts}}{15 \text{ ohms}}$

Simplify: $\quad I = 0.1 \text{ amp}$

ANSWER The current is 0.1 ampere.

If you know the values of all variables but one in a formula, you can solve for the value of the unknown variable. For instance, Ohm's law can be used to find a voltage if you know the current and the resistance.

Example

Suppose that you know that a current is 0.2 amperes and the resistance is 18 ohms. Use the formula for Ohm's law to find the voltage in volts.

Write the formula for Ohm's law: $\quad I = \dfrac{V}{R}$

Substitute 0.2 amp for I and 18 ohms for R: $\quad 0.2 \text{ amp} = \dfrac{V}{18 \text{ ohms}}$

Multiply both sides by 18 ohms: $\quad 0.2 \text{ amp} \cdot 18 \text{ ohms} = V$

Simplify: $\quad 3.6 \text{ volts} = V$

ANSWER The voltage is 3.6 volts.

MATH HANDBOOK

Finding Areas

The area of a figure is the amount of surface the figure covers.

Area is measured in square units, such as square meters (m²) or square centimeters (cm²). Formulas for the areas of three common geometric figures are shown below.

Area = (side length)²
$A = s^2$

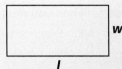

Area = length × width
$A = lw$

Area = $\frac{1}{2}$ × base × height

$A = \frac{1}{2} bh$

Example

Each face of a halite crystal is a square like the one shown. You can find the area of the square by using the steps below.

3 mm

3 mm

Write the formula for the area of a square: $A = s^2$

Substitute 3 mm for s: $= (3 \text{ mm})^2$

Simplify: $= 9 \text{ mm}^2$

ANSWER The area of the square is 9 square millimeters.

Finding Volumes

The volume of a solid is the amount of space contained by the solid.

Volume is measured in cubic units, such as cubic meters (m³) or cubic centimeters (cm³). The volume of a rectangular prism is given by the formula shown below.

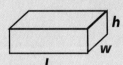

Volume = length × width × height
$V = lwh$

Example

A topaz crystal is a rectangular prism like the one shown. You can find the volume of the prism by using the steps below.

10 mm

12 mm

20 mm

Write the formula for the volume of a rectangular prism: $V = lwh$

Substitute dimensions: $= 20 \text{ mm} \times 12 \text{ mm} \times 10 \text{ mm}$

Simplify: $= 2400 \text{ mm}^3$

ANSWER The volume of the rectangular prism is 2400 cubic millimeters.

Using Significant Figures

The **significant figures** in a decimal are the digits that are warranted by the accuracy of a measuring device.

When you perform a calculation with measurements, the number of significant figures to include in the result depends in part on the number of significant figures in the measurements. When you multiply or divide measurements, your answer should have only as many significant figures as the measurement with the fewest significant figures.

Example

Using a balance and a graduated cylinder filled with water, you determined that a marble has a mass of 8.0 grams and a volume of 3.5 cubic centimeters. To calculate the density of the marble, divide the mass by the volume.

Write the formula for density: $\text{Density} = \dfrac{\text{mass}}{\text{Volume}}$

Substitute measurements: $= \dfrac{8.0 \text{ g}}{3.5 \text{ cm}^3}$

Use a calculator to divide: $\approx 2.285714286 \text{ g/cm}^3$

ANSWER Because the mass and the volume have two significant figures each, give the density to two significant figures. The marble has a density of 2.3 grams per cubic centimeter.

Using Scientific Notation

Scientific notation is a shorthand way to write very large or very small numbers. For example, 73,500,000,000,000,000,000,000 kg is the mass of the Moon. In scientific notation, it is 7.35×10^{22} kg.

Example

You can convert from standard form to scientific notation.

Standard Form	Scientific Notation
720,000	7.2×10^5
5 decimal places left	Exponent is 5.
0.000291	2.91×10^{-4}
4 decimal places right	Exponent is −4.

You can convert from scientific notation to standard form.

Scientific Notation	Standard Form
4.63×10^7	46,300,000
Exponent is 7.	7 decimal places right
1.08×10^{-6}	0.00000108
Exponent is −6.	6 decimal places left

Note-Taking Handbook

Note-Taking Strategies

Taking notes as you read helps you understand the information. The notes you take can also be used as a study guide for later review. This handbook presents several ways to organize your notes.

Content Frame

1. Make a chart in which each column represents a category.
2. Give each column a heading.
3. Write details under the headings.

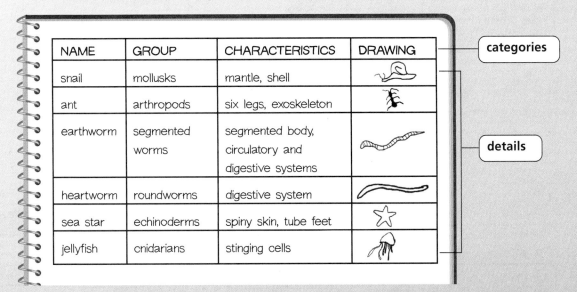

NAME	GROUP	CHARACTERISTICS	DRAWING
snail	mollusks	mantle, shell	
ant	arthropods	six legs, exoskeleton	
earthworm	segmented worms	segmented body, circulatory and digestive systems	
heartworm	roundworms	digestive system	
sea star	echinoderms	spiny skin, tube feet	
jellyfish	cnidarians	stinging cells	

categories

details

Combination Notes

1. For each new idea or concept, write an informal outline of the information.
2. Make a sketch to illustrate the concept, and label it.

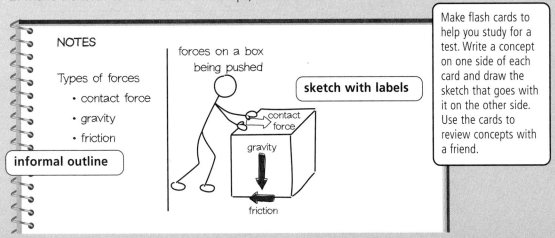

NOTES

Types of forces
- contact force
- gravity
- friction

informal outline

forces on a box being pushed

sketch with labels

contact force

gravity

friction

Make flash cards to help you study for a test. Write a concept on one side of each card and draw the sketch that goes with it on the other side. Use the cards to review concepts with a friend.

Main Idea and Detail Notes

1. In the left-hand column of a two-column chart, list main ideas. The blue headings express main ideas throughout this textbook.

2. In the right-hand column, write details that expand on each main idea.

You can shorten the headings in your chart. Be sure to use the most important words.

When studying for tests, cover up the detail notes column with a sheet of paper. Then use each main idea to form a question—such as "How does latitude affect climate?" Answer the question, and then uncover the detail notes column to check your answer.

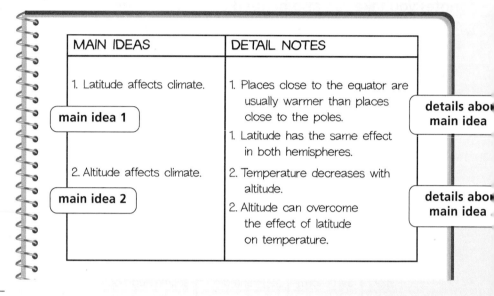

MAIN IDEAS	DETAIL NOTES
1. Latitude affects climate.	1. Places close to the equator are usually warmer than places close to the poles.
main idea 1	1. Latitude has the same effect in both hemispheres.
2. Altitude affects climate.	2. Temperature decreases with altitude.
main idea 2	2. Altitude can overcome the effect of latitude on temperature.

details abo
main idea

details abo
main idea

Main Idea Web

1. Write a main idea in a box.

2. Add boxes around it with related vocabulary terms and important details.

You can find definitions near highlighted terms.

definition of *work*
Work is the use of force to move an object.

formula
Work = force · distance

main idea
Force is necessary to do work.

The joule is the unit used to measure work.
definition of *joule*

Work depends on the size of a force.
important detail

NOTE-TAKING HANDBOOK

Mind Map

1. Write a main idea in the center.
2. Add details that relate to one another and to the main idea.

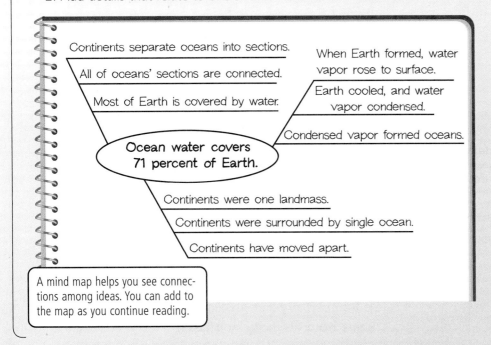

Continents separate oceans into sections.

All of oceans' sections are connected.

Most of Earth is covered by water.

When Earth formed, water vapor rose to surface.

Earth cooled, and water vapor condensed.

Condensed vapor formed oceans.

Ocean water covers 71 percent of Earth.

Continents were one landmass.

Continents were surrounded by single ocean.

Continents have moved apart.

A mind map helps you see connections among ideas. You can add to the map as you continue reading.

Supporting Main Ideas

1. Write a main idea in a box.
2. Add boxes underneath with information—such as reasons, explanations, and examples—that supports the main idea.

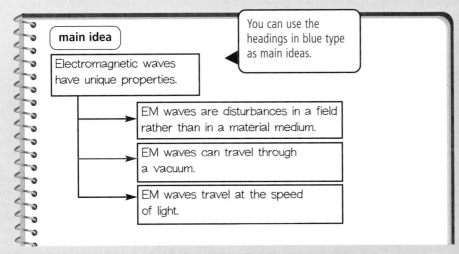

main idea

Electromagnetic waves have unique properties.

You can use the headings in blue type as main ideas.

EM waves are disturbances in a field rather than in a material medium.

EM waves can travel through a vacuum.

EM waves travel at the speed of light.

Outline

1. Copy the chapter title and headings from the book in the form of an outline.

2. Add notes that summarize in your own words what you read.

Cell Processes

[1st key idea]

I. Cells capture and release energy. **[1st subpoint of I]**

   A. All cells need energy.

   B. Some cells capture light energy. **[2nd subpoint of I]**

      1. Process of photosynthesis **[1st detail about B]**

      2. Chloroplasts (site of photosynthesis) **[2nd detail about B]**

      3. Carbon dioxide and water as raw materials

      4. Glucose and oxygen as products

   C. All cells release energy.

      1. Process of cellular respiration

      2. Fermentation of sugar to carbon dioxide

      3. Bacteria that carry out fermentation

II. Cells transport materials through membranes.

   A. Some materials move by diffusion.

      1. Particle movement from higher to lower concentrations

      2. Movement of water through membrane (osmosis)

   B. Some transport requires energy.

      1. Active transport

      2. Examples of active transport

Correct Outline Form
Include a title.

Arrange key ideas, subpoints, and details as shown.

Indent the divisions of the outline as shown.

Use the same grammatical form for items of the same rank. For example, if A is a sentence, B must also be a sentence.

You must have at least two main ideas or subpoints. That is, every A must be followed by a B, and every 1 must be followed by a 2.

Concept Map

1. Write an important concept in a large oval.

2. Add details related to the concept in smaller ovals.

3. Write linking words on arrows that connect the ovals.

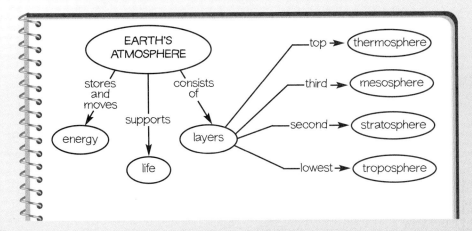

The main ideas or concepts can often be found in the blue headings. An example is "The atmosphere stores and moves energy." Use nouns from these concepts in the ovals, and use the verb or verbs on the lines.

Venn Diagram

1. Draw two overlapping circles, one for each item that you are comparing.

2. In the overlapping section, list the characteristics that are shared by both items.

3. In the outer sections, list the characteristics that are peculiar to each item.

4. Write a summary that describes the information in the Venn diagram.

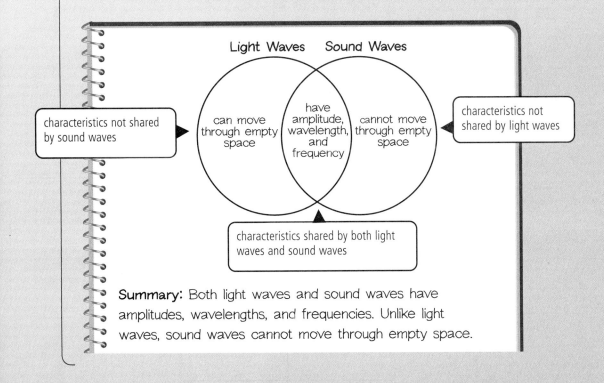

Summary: Both light waves and sound waves have amplitudes, wavelengths, and frequencies. Unlike light waves, sound waves cannot move through empty space.

Vocabulary Strategies

Important terms are highlighted in this book. A definition of each term can be found in the sentence or paragraph where the term appears. You can also find definitions in the Glossary. Taking notes about vocabulary terms helps you understand and remember what you read.

Description Wheel

1. Write a term inside a circle.
2. Write words that describe the term on "spokes" attached to the circle.

When studying for a test with a friend, read the phrases on the spokes one at a time until your friend identifies the correct term.

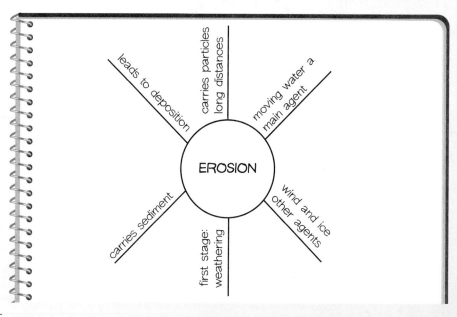

Four Square

1. Write a term in the center.
2. Write details in the four areas around the term.

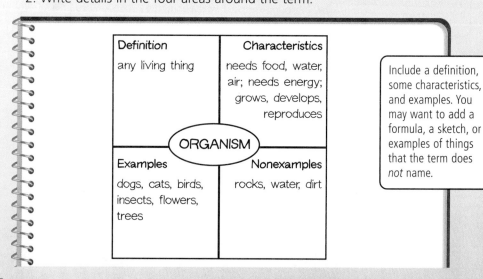

Include a definition, some characteristics, and examples. You may want to add a formula, a sketch, or examples of things that the term does *not* name.

Frame Game

1. Write a term in the center.

2. Frame the term with details.

> Include examples, descriptions, sketches, or sentences that use the term in context. Change the frame to fit each new term.

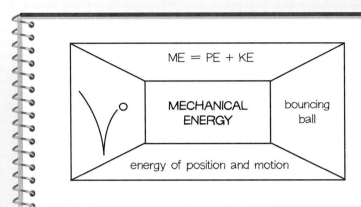

Magnet Word

1. Write a term on the magnet.

2. On the lines, add details related to the term.

> You can also use phrases or sentences on the lines.

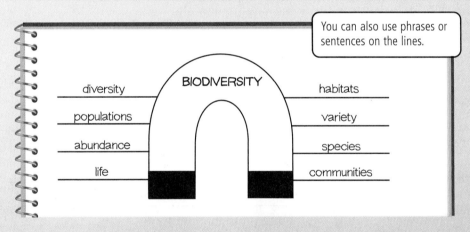

Word Triangle

1. Write a term and its definition in the bottom section.

2. In the middle section, write a sentence in which the term is used correctly.

3. In the top section, draw a small picture to illustrate the term.

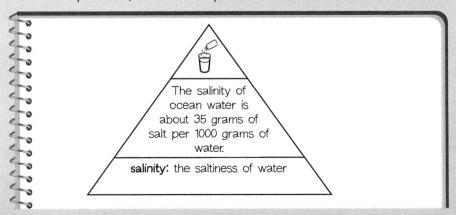

NOTE-TAKING HANDBOOK

Appendix

Station Symbols

Meteorologists use station symbols to condense the weather data they receive from ground stations. The symbols are displayed on maps. The information in a station symbol can be understood by the meteorologists of any country.

In the symbol, air pressure readings are shortened by omitting the initial 9 or 10 and the decimal point. For numbers greater than 500, place a 9 to the left of the number and divide by 10 to get the air pressure in millibars. For numbers less than 500, place a 10 to the left and then divide by 10.

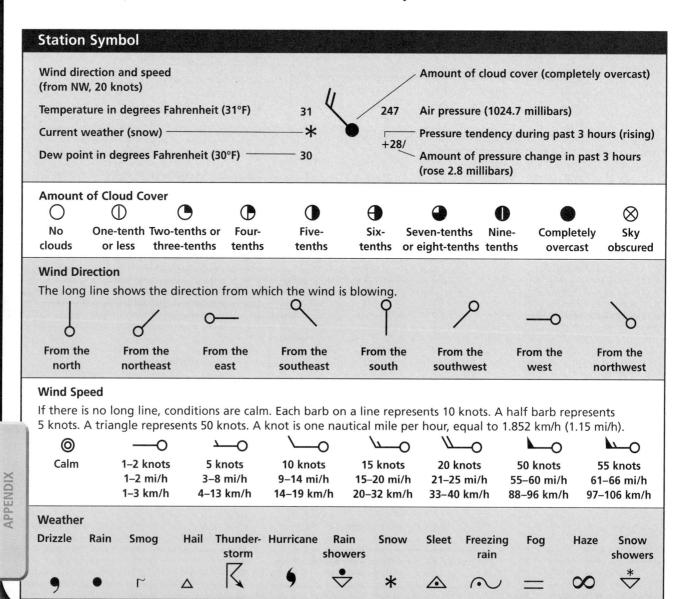

Station Symbol

Wind direction and speed (from NW, 20 knots)	**Amount of cloud cover** (completely overcast)
Temperature in degrees Fahrenheit (31°F) — 31	247 — **Air pressure** (1024.7 millibars)
Current weather (snow) — ✳	**Pressure tendency during past 3 hours** (rising)
Dew point in degrees Fahrenheit (30°F) — 30	+28/ — **Amount of pressure change in past 3 hours** (rose 2.8 millibars)

Amount of Cloud Cover

No clouds	One-tenth or less	Two-tenths or three-tenths	Four-tenths	Five-tenths	Six-tenths	Seven-tenths or eight-tenths	Nine-tenths	Completely overcast	Sky obscured

Wind Direction

The long line shows the direction from which the wind is blowing.

From the north	From the northeast	From the east	From the southeast	From the south	From the southwest	From the west	From the northwest

Wind Speed

If there is no long line, conditions are calm. Each barb on a line represents 10 knots. A half barb represents 5 knots. A triangle represents 50 knots. A knot is one nautical mile per hour, equal to 1.852 km/h (1.15 mi/h).

Calm	1–2 knots 1–2 mi/h 1–3 km/h	5 knots 3–8 mi/h 4–13 km/h	10 knots 9–14 mi/h 14–19 km/h	15 knots 15–20 mi/h 20–32 km/h	20 knots 21–25 mi/h 33–40 km/h	50 knots 55–60 mi/h 88–96 km/h	55 knots 61–66 mi/h 97–106 km/h

Weather

Drizzle	Rain	Smog	Hail	Thunderstorm	Hurricane	Rain showers	Snow	Sleet	Freezing rain	Fog	Haze	Snow showers

Relative Humidity

You can find the relative humidity by calculating the difference between the two readings on a psychrometer. First look up the dry-bulb temperature in the left-hand column of the relative humidity chart. Then find in the top line the difference between the wet-bulb temperature and the dry-bulb temperature.

Relative Humidity (%)

Dry-Bulb Temperature (°C)	Difference Between Wet-Bulb and Dry-Bulb Temperatures (°C)															
	0	1	2	3	4	5	6	7	8	9	10	11	12	13	14	15
−20	100	28														
−18	100	40														
−16	100	48														
−14	100	55	11													
−12	100	61	23													
−10	100	66	33													
−8	100	71	41	13												
−6	100	73	48	20												
−4	100	77	54	32	11											
−2	100	79	58	37	20	1										
0	100	81	63	45	28	11										
2	100	83	67	51	36	20	6									
4	100	85	70	56	42	27	14									
6	100	86	72	59	46	35	22	10								
8	100	87	74	62	51	39	28	17	6							
10	100	88	76	65	54	43	33	24	13	4						
12	100	88	78	67	57	48	38	28	19	10	2					
14	100	89	79	69	60	50	41	33	25	16	8	1				
16	100	90	80	71	62	54	45	37	29	21	14	7	1			
18	100	91	81	72	64	56	48	40	33	26	19	12	6			
20	100	91	82	74	66	58	51	44	36	30	23	17	11	5		
22	100	92	83	75	68	60	53	46	40	33	27	21	15	10	4	
24	100	92	84	76	69	62	55	49	42	36	30	25	20	14	9	4
26	100	92	85	77	70	64	57	51	45	39	34	28	23	18	13	9
28	100	93	86	78	71	65	59	53	47	42	36	31	26	21	17	12
30	100	93	86	79	72	66	61	55	49	44	39	34	29	25	20	16

Wind Speeds

Descriptive names, such as *fresh gale,* were used by sailors and other people to describe the strength of winds. Later, ranges of wind speeds were determined. The table below lists the wind speeds and conditions you might observe around you on land.

Beaufort Number	Wind Speed	Description
	Beaufort Scale of Wind Speeds	
0	0 km/h (0 mi/h)	**Calm or Still** Smoke will rise vertically
1	2–5 km/h (1–3 mi/h)	**Light Air** Rising smoke drifts, weather vane is inactive
2	6–12 km/h (4–7 mi/h)	**Light Breeze** Leaves rustle, can feel wind on your face, weather vane moves
3	13–20 km/h (8–12 mi/h)	**Gentle Breeze** Leaves and twigs move around, lightweight flags extend
4	21–30 km/h (13–18 mi/h)	**Moderate Breeze** Thin branches move, dust and paper raised
5	31–40 km/h (19–24 mi/h)	**Fresh Breeze** Small trees sway
6	41–50 km/h (25–31 mi/h)	**Strong Breeze** Large tree branches move, open wires (such as telegraph wires) begin to "whistle," umbrellas are difficult to keep under control
7	51–61 km/h (32–38 mi/h)	**Moderate Gale** Large trees begin to sway, noticeably difficult to walk
8	62–74 km/h (39–46 mi/h)	**Fresh Gale** Twigs and small branches are broken from trees, walking into the wind is very difficult
9	75–89 km/h (47–54 mi/h)	**Strong Gale** Slight damage occurs to buildings, shingles are blown off of roofs
10	90–103 km/h (55–63 mi/h)	**Whole Gale** Large trees are uprooted, building damage is considerable
11	104–119 km/h (64–72 mi/h)	**Storm** Extensive, widespread damage. These typically occur only at sea, rarely inland.
12	120 km/h or more (74 mi/h or more)	**Hurricane** Extreme damage, very rare inland

Tornado Intensities

The Fujita scale describes the strength of a tornado based on the damage it does. The scale is useful for classifying tornadoes even though it is not exact. For example, a tornado can strengthen and then weaken before it dies out. The wind speeds are estimates of the strongest winds near the ground. Most tornadoes are F0 or F1. One-quarter to one-third of tornadoes are F2 or F3. Only a few percent of tornadoes are F4 or F5.

Fujita Scale for Tornadoes

F-Scale	Wind Speed	Type of Damage
F0	64–116 km/h (40–72 mi/h)	**Light Damage** Some damage to chimneys; branches broken off trees; shallow-rooted trees pushed over; sign boards damaged
F1	117–180 km/h (73–112 mi/h)	**Moderate Damage** Surface peeled off roofs; mobile homes pushed off foundations or overturned; moving autos blown off roads
F2	181–253 km/h (113–157 mi/h)	**Considerable Damage** Roofs torn off frame houses; mobile homes demolished; boxcars overturned; large trees snapped or uprooted; light-object missiles generated; cars lifted off ground
F3	254–332 km/h (158–206 mi/h)	**Severe Damage** Roofs and some walls torn off well-constructed houses; trains overturned; most trees in forest uprooted; heavy cars lifted off the ground and thrown
F4	333–418 km/h (207–260 mi/h)	**Devastating Damage** Well-constructed houses leveled; structures with weak foundations blown away some distance; cars thrown and large missiles generated
F5	419–512 km/h (261–318 mi/h)	**Incredible Damage** Strong frame houses leveled off foundations and swept away; automobile-sized missiles fly through the air in excess of 100 meters (109 yds); trees debarked; incredible phenomena will occur

Glossary

A

acid rain
Rain that has become more acidic than normal due to pollution. (p. 70)

lluvia ácida Lluvia que se ha vuelto más ácida de lo normal debido a la contaminación.

air mass
A large volume of air that has nearly the same temperature and humidity at different locations at the same altitude. (p. 79)

masa de aire Un gran volumen de aire que tiene casi la misma temperatura y humedad en distintos puntos a la misma altitud.

air pollution
Harmful materials added to the air that can cause damage to living things and the environment. (p. 27)

contaminación de aire Materiales nocivos añadidos al aire que pueden causar daño a los seres vivos y al medio ambiente.

air pressure
The force of air molecules pushing on an area. (p. 43)

presión de aire La fuerza de las moléculas de aire empujando sobre un área.

altitude
The distance above sea level. (p. 10)

altitud La distancia sobre el nivel del mar.

atmosphere
The outer layer of gases of a large body in space, such as a planet or star; the mixture of gases that surrounds the solid Earth; one of the four parts of the Earth system. (p. 9)

atmósfera La capa externa de gases de un gran cuerpo que se encuentra en el espacio, como un planeta o una estrella; la mezcla de gases que rodea la Tierra sólida; una de las cuatro partes del sistema terrestre.

atom
The smallest particle of an element that has the chemical properties of that element. (p. xvii)

átomo La partícula más pequeña de un elemento que tiene las propiedades químicas del elemento.

B

barometer
An instrument that measures air pressure in the atmosphere. (p. 46)

barómetro Un instrumento que mide la presión del aire en la atmósfera.

biosphere (BY-uh-SFEER)
All living organisms on Earth in the air, on the land, and in the waters; one of the four parts of the Earth system. (p. xix)

biosfera Todos los organismos vivos de la Tierra, en el aire, en la tierra y en las aguas; una de las cuatro partes del sistema de la Tierra.

blizzard
A blinding snowstorm with winds of at least 56 kilometers per hour (35 mi/h), usually with temperatures below −7°C (20°F). (p. 90)

ventisca Una cegadora tormenta de nieve con vientos de por lo menos 56 kilómetros por hora (35 mi/h), usualmente con temperaturas menores a −7°C (20°F).

C

climate
The characteristic weather conditions in an area over a long period of time. (p. 117)

clima Las condiciones meteorológicas características de un lugar durante un largo período de tiempo.

climate zone
One of the major divisions in a system for classifying the climates of different regions based on characteristics they have in common. (p. 125)

zona climática Una de las mayores divisiones en un sistema de clasificación de climas de diferentes regiones, basado en las características que tienen en común.

compound
A substance made up of two or more different types of atoms bonded together.

compuesto Una sustancia formada por dos o más diferentes tipos de átomos enlazados.

condensation

The process by which a gas changes into a liquid. (p. 56)

condensación El proceso por el cual un gas se transforma en líquido.

conduction

The transfer of heat energy from one substance to another through direct contact without obvious motion. (p. 18)

conducción La transferencia de energía calorífica de una sustancia a otra a través de contacto directo, sin que haya movimiento obvio.

continental climate

A climate that occurs in the interior of a continent, with large temperature differences between seasons. (p. 120)

clima continental El clima que se presenta en el interior de un continente, con grandes diferencias de temperatura entre estaciones.

convection

The transfer of energy from place to place by the motion of heated gas or liquid; in Earth's mantle, convection is thought to transfer energy by the motion of solid rock, which when under great heat and pressure can move like a liquid. (p. 19)

convección La transferencia de energía de un lugar a otro por el movimiento de un líquido o gas calentado; se piensa que en el manto terrestre la convección transfiere energía mediante el movimiento de roca sólida, la cual puede moverse como un líquido cuando está muy caliente y bajo alta presión.

Coriolis effect (KAWR-ee-OH-lihs)

The influence of Earth's rotation on objects that move over Earth. (p. 49)

efecto Coriolis La influencia de la rotación de la Tierra sobre objetos que se mueven sobre la Tierra.

cycle

n. A series of events or actions that repeat themselves regularly; a physical and/or chemical process in which one material continually changes locations and/or forms. Examples include the water cycle, the carbon cycle, and the rock cycle.

v. To move through a repeating series of events or actions.

ciclo *s.* Una serie de eventos o acciones que se repiten regularmente; un proceso físico y/o químico en el cual un material cambia continuamente de lugar y/o forma. Ejemplos: el ciclo del agua, el ciclo del carbono y el ciclo de las rocas.

D

data

Information gathered by observation or experimentation that can be used in calculating or reasoning. *Data* is a plural word; the singular is *datum*.

datos Información reunida mediante observación o experimentación y que se puede usar para calcular o para razonar.

density

A measure of the amount of matter packed into a unit volume; the density of an object is equal to its mass divided by its volume. (p. 10)

densidad Una medida de la cantidad de materia contenida en una unidad de volumen; la densidad de un objeto es igual a su masa dividida por su volumen.

dew point

The temperature at which air with a given amount of water vapor will reach saturation. (p. 58)

punto de rocío La temperatura a la cual el aire con una cantidad determinada de vapor de agua alcanzará la saturación.

E

element

A substance that cannot be broken down into a simpler substance by ordinary chemical changes. An element consists of atoms of only one type.

elemento Una sustancia que no puede descomponerse en otra sustancia más simple por medio de cambios químicos normales. Un elemento consta de átomos de un solo tipo.

El Niño (ehl NEEN-yoh)

A disturbance of wind patterns and ocean currents in the Pacific Ocean that causes temporary climate changes in many parts of the world. (p. 136)

El Niño Un disturbio en los patrones de viento y las corrientes oceánicas del océano Pacifico que causa cambios climáticos temporales en muchas partes del mundo.

energy
The ability to do work or to cause a change. For example, the energy of a moving bowling ball knocks over pins; energy from food allows animals to move and to grow; and energy from the Sun heats Earth's surface and atmosphere, which causes air to move. (p. xv)

energía La capacidad para trabajar o causar un cambio. Por ejemplo, la energía de una bola de boliche en movimiento tumba los pinos; la energía proveniente de su alimento permite a los animales moverse y crecer; la energía del Sol calienta la superficie y la atmósfera de la Tierra, lo que ocasiona que el aire se mueva.

evaporation
The process by which liquid changes into gas. (p. 56)

evaporación El proceso por el cual un líquido se transforma en gas.

experiment
An organized procedure to study something under controlled conditions. (p. xxiv)

experimento Un procedimiento organizado para estudiar algo bajo condiciones controladas.

F

force
A push or a pull; something that changes the motion of an object. (p. xvii)

fuerza Un empuje o un jalón; algo que cambia el movimiento de un objeto.

fossil
A trace or the remains of a once-living thing from long ago. (p. xxi)

fósil Un rastro o los restos de un organismo que vivió hace mucho tiempo.

fossil fuels
Fuels formed from the remains of prehistoric organisms that are burned for energy. (p. 28)

combustibles fósiles Combustibles formados a partir de los restos de organismos prehistóricos que son consumidos para obtener energía.

freezing rain
Rain that freezes when it hits the ground or another surface and coats the surface with ice. (p. 68)

lluvia helada Lluvia que se congela cuando cae a la tierra o cualquier otra superficie y cubre la superficie con hielo.

friction
A force that resists the motion between two surfaces in contact. (p. xxi)

fricción Una fuerza que resiste el movimiento entre dos superficies en contacto.

front
The boundary between air masses. (p. 82)

frente El limite entre masas de aire.

G

gas
A state of matter different from liquid and solid, with no definite volume and no definite shape.

gas Un estado de la material, que no es sólido ni líquido, en el cual la sustancia se puede expandir o contraer para llenar un recipiente.

geosphere (JEE-uh-SFEER)
All the features on Earth's surface—continents, islands, and seafloor—and everything below the surface—the inner and outer core and the mantle; one of the four parts of the Earth system. (p. xix)

geosfera Todas las características de la superficie de la Tierra, es decir, continentes, islas y el fondo marino, y de todo bajo la superficie, es decir, el núcleo externo e interno y el manto; una de las cuatro partes del sistema de la Tierra.

global winds
Winds that travel long distances in steady patterns over several weeks. (p. 48)

vientos globales Vientos que viajan grandes distancias en patrones fijos por varias semanas.

gravity
The force that objects exert on each other because of their mass. (p. xvii)

gravedad La fuerza que los objetos ejercen entre sí debido a su masa.

greenhouse effect
The process by which certain gases in a planet's atmosphere absorb and emit infrared radiation, resulting in an increase in surface temperature. (p. 24)

efecto invernadero El proceso mediante el cual ciertos gases en la atmósfera de un planeta absorben y emiten radiación infrarroja, resultando en un incremento de la temperatura superficial del planeta.

greenhouse gases
Gases, such as carbon dioxide and methane, that absorb and give off infrared radiation as part of the greenhouse effect. (p. 24)

gases invernadero Gases, como el dióxido de carbono y el metano, que absorben y emiten radiación infrarroja como parte del efecto invernadero.

H

hail
Layered lumps or balls of ice that fall from cumulonimbus clouds. (p. 68)

granizo Trozos de hielo que caen de nubes cumulonimbos.

high-pressure system
A generally calm and clear weather system that occurs when air sinks down in a high-pressure center and spreads out toward areas of lower pressure as it nears the ground. (p. 84)

sistema de alta presión Un sistema climático generalmente claro y calmo que se presenta cuando el aire desciende en un centro de alta presión y se esparce hacia áreas de baja presión conforme se acerca al suelo.

humidity
The amount of water vapor in air. (p. 58)

humedad La cantidad de vapor de agua en el aire.

hurricane (HUR-ih-KAYN)
A tropical low-pressure system with sustained winds of 120 kilometers per hour (74 mi/h) or more. (p. 87)

huracán Un sistema tropical de baja presión con vientos sostenidos de 120 kilómetros por hora (74 mi/h) o más.

hydrosphere (HY-druh-SFEER)
All water on Earth—in the atmosphere and in the oceans, lakes, glaciers, rivers, streams, and underground reservoirs; one of the four parts of the Earth system. (p. xix)

hidrosfera Toda el agua de la Tierra: en la atmósfera y en los océanos, lagos, glaciares, ríos, arroyos y depósitos subterráneos; una de las cuatro partes del sistema de la Tierra.

hypothesis
A tentative explanation for an observation or phenomenon. A hypothesis is used to make testable predictions. (p. xxiv)

hipótesis Una explicación provisional de una observación o de un fenómeno. Una hipótesis se usa para hacer predicciones que se pueden probar.

I

ice age
A period of time during which surface temperatures drop significantly and huge ice sheets spread out beyond the polar regions. (p. 135)

edad de hielo Un período de tiempo durante el cual las temperaturas superficiales disminuyen significativamente y grandes capas de hielo se extienden más allá de las regiones polares.

infrared radiation (IHN-fruh-REHD RAY-dee-AY-shuhn)
Radiation of lower frequencies than visible light. (p. 23)

radiación infrarroja Radiación de frecuencia más baja que la luz visible.

isobar (EYE-suh-BAHR)
A line on a weather map connecting places that have the same air pressure. (p. 101)

isobara Una línea en un mapa climático que conecta lugares que tienen la misma presión de aire.

J, K

jet stream
A wind that flows in the upper troposphere from west to east over vast distances at great speeds. (p. 52)

corriente de chorro Un viento que sopla vastas distancias en la troposfera superior de oeste a este a grandes velocidades.

L

latitude
The distance in degrees north or south from the equator. (p. 118)

latitud La distancia en grados norte o sur a partir del ecuador.

law
In science, a rule or principle describing a physical relationship that always works in the same way under the same conditions. The law of conservation of energy is an example.

ley En las ciencias, una regla o un principio que describe una relación física que siempre funciona de la misma manera bajo las mismas condiciones. La ley de la conservación de la energía es un ejemplo.

lightning
A discharge of electricity from one part of a cloud to another or between a cloud and the ground, causing a bright flash of light. (p. 92)

relámpago Una descarga eléctrica de una parte de una nube a otra o entre una nube y la tierra que causa un brillante rayo de luz.

low-pressure system
A large and often stormy weather system that occurs when air moves around and into a low-pressure center, then moves up to higher altitudes. (p. 85)

sistema de baja presión Un sistema climático grande y usualmente lluvioso que se presenta cuando el aire se mueve alrededor de y hacia un centro de baja presión, y luego se mueve hacia mayores altitudes.

M, N

marine climate
A climate influenced by a nearby ocean, with generally mild temperatures and steady precipitation. (p. 120)

clima marino El clima influido por un océano cercano, y que generalmente tiene temperaturas moderadas y precipitación poco variable.

mass
A measure of how much matter an object is made of.

masa Una medida de la cantidad de materia de la que está compuesto un objeto.

matter
Anything that has mass and volume. Matter exists ordinarily as a solid, a liquid, or a gas. (p. xvii)

materia Todo lo que tiene masa y volumen. Generalmente la materia existe como sólido, líquido o gas.

meteorologist (MEE-tee-uh-RAHL-uh-jihst)
A scientist who studies weather. (p. 98)

meteorólogo Un científico que estudia el clima.

microclimate
The climate of a smaller area within a subclimate. (p. 128)

microclima El clima de un área más pequeña dentro de un subclima.

molecule
A group of atoms that are held together by covalent bonds so that they move as a single unit.

molécula Un grupo de átomos que están unidos mediante enlaces covalentes de tal manera que se mueven como una sola unidad.

monsoon
A wind that changes direction with the seasons. (p. 54)

monzón Un viento que cambia de dirección con las estaciones.

O

ocean current
A stream of water that flows through the ocean in a regular pattern. (p. 121)

corriente oceánica Un flujo de agua que se mueve a través del océano de una forma regular.

ozone
A gas molecule that consists of three oxygen atoms. (p. 23)

ozono Una molécula de gas que consiste en tres átomos de oxígeno.

P, Q

particulates
Tiny particles or droplets, such as dust, dirt, and pollen, that are mixed in with air. (p. 28)

particulados Diminutas partículas o gotas, como por ejemplo de polvo, tierra o polen, que están mezcladas con el aire.

precipitation
Any type of liquid or solid water that falls to Earth's surface, such as rain, snow, or hail. (p. 57)

precipitación Cualquier tipo de agua líquida o sólida que cae a la superficie de la Tierra, como por ejemplo lluvia, nieve o granizo.

R

radiation (RAY-dee-AY-shuhn)
Energy that travels across distances as certain types of waves. (p. 17)

radiación Energía que viaja a través de la distancia en forma de ciertos tipos de ondas.

rain shadow
An area on the downwind side of a mountain that gets less precipitation than the side that faces the wind. (p. 129)

sombra de lluvia Un área viento abajo de una montaña que recibe menos precipitación que el lado de la montaña que hace frente al viento.

relative humidity

The comparison of the amount of water vapor in air with the maximum amount of water vapor that can be present in air at that temperature. (p. 58)

humedad relativa La comparación entre la cantidad de vapor de agua en el aire y la cantidad máxima de vapor de agua que puede estar presente en el aire a esa temperatura.

S

saturation

A condition of the atmosphere in which the rates of evaporation and condensation are equal. (p. 58)

saturación Una condición de la atmósfera en la cual las tasas de evaporación y condensación son iguales.

seasons

Periods of the year associated with specific weather conditions. (p. 122)

estaciones Los períodos del año asociados a condiciones climáticas específicas.

sleet

Small pellets of ice that form when rain passes through a layer of cold air and freezes before hitting the ground. (p. 68)

aguanieve Pequeñas bolitas de hielo que se forman cuando la lluvia pasa a través de una capa de aire frío y se congela antes de caer al suelo.

smog

The combination of smoke and fog; a type of air pollution that occurs when sunlight causes unburnt fuels, fumes, and other gases to react chemically, often seen as a brownish haze. (p. 28)

smog La combinación de humo y neblina; un tipo de contaminación de aire que se presenta cuando la luz solar provoca la reacción química de combustibles no consumidos, humos y otros gases, que a menudo se ve como una bruma parda.

storm surge

A rapid rise in water level in a coastal area that occurs when a hurricane pushes a huge mass of ocean water, often leading to flooding and widespread destruction. (p. 89)

marea de tormenta Un rápido aumento del nivel del agua en un área costera que ocurre cuando un huracán empuja una gran masa de agua oceánica, muchas veces provocando inundaciones y destrucción extensa.

system

A group of objects or phenomena that interact. A system can be as simple as a rope, a pulley, and a mass. It also can be as complex as the interaction of energy and matter in the four parts of the Earth system.

sistema Un grupo de objetos o fenómenos que interactúan. Un sistema puede ser algo tan sencillo como una cuerda, una polea y una masa. También puede ser algo tan complejo como la interacción de la energía y la materia en las cuatro partes del sistema de la Tierra.

T

technology

The use of scientific knowledge to solve problems or engineer new products, tools, or processes.

tecnología El uso de conocimientos científicos para resolver problemas o para diseñar nuevos productos, herramientas o procesos.

theory

In science, a set of widely accepted explanations of observations and phenomena. A theory is a well-tested explanation that is consistent with all available evidence.

teoría En las ciencias, un conjunto de explicaciones de observaciones y fenómenos que es ampliamente aceptado. Una teoría es una explicación bien probada que es consecuente con la evidencia disponible.

thunder

The sound wave created by intensely heated air around a lightning bolt. (p. 92)

trueno La onda sonora creada por el aire calentado intensamente alrededor de un relámpago.

thunderstorm

A storm with lightning and thunder. (p. 92)

tormenta eléctrica Una tormenta con relámpagos y truenos.

tornado

A violently rotating column of air stretching from a cloud to the ground. (p. 95)

tornado Una columna de aire que gira violentamente y se extiende desde una nube hasta el suelo.

tropical storm (TRAHP-ih-kuhl)

A low-pressure system that starts in the tropics with winds of at least 65 kilometers per hour (40 mi/h) but less than 120 kilometers per hour (74 mi/h). (p. 87)

tormenta tropical Un sistema de baja presión que inicia en los trópicos con vientos de por lo menos 65 kilómetros por hora (40 mi/h) pero menores a 120 kilómetros por hora (74 mi/h).

U

ultraviolet radiation (UHL-truh-VY-uh-liht RAY-dee-AY-shuhn)
Radiation of higher frequencies than visible light, which can cause sunburn and other types of damage. (p. 23)

> **radiación ultravioleta** Radiación de frecuencia más alta que la luz visible que puede causar quemaduras de sol y otros tipos de daño.

urban heat island
The warmer body of air over a city. (p. 128)

> **isla de calor urbana** La masa de aire más cálida que se encuentra sobre una ciudad.

V

variable
Any factor that can change in a controlled experiment, observation, or model. (p. R30)

> **variable** Cualquier factor que puede cambiar en un experimento controlado, en una observación o en un modelo.

volume
An amount of three-dimensional space, often used to describe the space that an object takes up.

> **volumen** Una cantidad de espacio tridimensional; a menudo se usa este término para describir el espacio que ocupa un objeto.

W, X, Y, Z

weather
The condition of Earth's atmosphere at a particular time and place. (p. 47)

> **estado del tiempo** La condición de la atmósfera terrestre en un lugar y momento particular.

wind
The horizontal movement of air caused by differences in air pressure. (p. 47)

> **viento** El movimiento horizontal de aire provocado por diferencias en la presión de aire.

Index

Page numbers for definitions are printed in **boldface** type.
Page numbers for illustrations, maps, and charts are printed in *italics*.

coal. *See* fossil fuels.

computers
  global warming models and, 31
  weather forecasting and, 100–103

contact force, xvii

condensation, **56,** *56,* 72. *See also* dew point.
  cloud formation and, *57, 59, 72,* 82, *83*
  energy released by, 93
  mountains' effect on, *129*
  water cycle and, 12, *13, 57*

conduction, **18,** *18, 36*

Connecticut, precipitation patterns in, 123

constants, **R30**

continental drift, 134

continents. *See also* land.
  movement of and climate, *134*

control group, R30

convection, **xv,** *18,* **19,** 21, *36,* 119
  Earth's interior, xv
  thunderstorm formation and, *93*

coral, *4,* 5

Coriolis effect, **49,** *49,* 50, *51, 72,* 84, *85,* 87

critical analysis, R8
  of statements, R8–R9

cumulonimbus clouds, *61, 62, 71,* 82, *83, 88,* 89, *93*

cumulus clouds, *60, 61, 62,* 93, *93*

current. *See* ocean currents.

cycles, **12,** *13. See also* carbon cycle; nitrogen cycle; water cycle.

cyclones, 87

D

data, analyzing, xxv

data tables, making, R23

decay, 12, *13*

decimals, **R39,** R40
  adding, R39
  dividing, R40
  multiplying, R40
  subtracting, R40

density, **10,** 44

desert subclimate, *126, 127*

design, technological, xxvi–xxvii

dew point, **58,** *58, 59. See also* condensation.

measurement of, *100*
  role in cloud formation, *59*

dinosaurs, extinction of, 133

doldrums (region), 50, *51*

Doppler radar, used to track precipitation, 68, *99, 100,* 101, 112

downdraft, 93

drizzle. *See* rain.

dropsonde, xxvii, *xxvii*

droughts, 137

dry bulb temperature, R53

dry climate zone, 125, *126, 127,* 129

dust
  in atmosphere, 2–5, *3,* 11, *14, 28,* 132–133
  environmental impact of, 3–5

dust storm, 4, 5, *14*

E

Earth
  change over time, xx, 132–138
  gravity and, xvii
  heat of, xiv–xv
  interior, xiv–xv, xix
  magnetic field of, xvii
  processes, xiv–xv, 12–14
  rotation of and wind patterns, *49, 51*
  solar radiation and surface of, 16, *17,* 48
  surface, xxi, 16, *17*
  system, xviii–xix, 9

earthquake, xv, xxi

Earth science, xiii.
  unifying principles of, xiii–xxi

easterlies (winds), 50, *51*

East Greenland Current (ocean), *121*

El Niño (climate event), 134, **136,** *136*
  Internet activity, 115

energy, xviii–xix
  Earth system and, xix
  heat, xiv, xv, xix
  movement of in atmosphere, *18,* 18–21

Environmental Protection Agency (U.S.), 29

greenhouse gases, **24,** 24–25, *25, 30,* 30–33, *36,* 111, 112, 135, 137, *139,* 140
    efforts to reduce, *32*
    natural sources of, 30–31
    production by human activities, *30,* 30–31, 137, 138
Greenland, effects of global warming on, 137
ground stations, *99,* 100
growing season, global warming and, 138
Gulf of Mexico
    ocean currents in, 121
    tornado formation and, 95
Gulf Stream (ocean current), *121*

H

hail, 57, **68,** *69, 72,* 94
    damage caused by, 68, 94
    formation of, 68, *69*
    largest recorded, 68
Half Moon Bay, CA, *122*
Halley, Edmund, 110
heat. *See also* energy.
    Earth's, xiv, xv
highland climate zone, 125, *126, 127*
high-pressure systems, **84,** *84,* 100, *101*
Himalayan mountains, xxi
horse latitudes, 50, *51*
human health, effects of global warming on, 138
humid continental subclimate, *126, 127*
humidity, **58**
    relative, **58,** 64, R53
humid subtropical subclimate, *126, 127*
humid tropical climate zone, 125, *126, 127*
hurricanes, *xxvii,* **87,** 87–89, *88, 89, 106, 112*
    effects of, *89*
    eye, *88,* 89
    eye wall, *88,* 89
    Floyd, *88*
    formation of, 87–89, *88*
    Fran, *89*
    safety in, *89*
    season in eastern U.S., 88
    structure of, *88,* 89
    technology and, xxvi–xxvii

hurricane warning, 89
hurricane watch, 89
hydrosphere, **xix**
hypothesis, **xxiv,** xxv, **R3,** R29

I

ice, 57, 66, 90–91
    in clouds, 60, 93
    growth of crystals, 67
    role in precipitation, 67, 68, *69*
ice ages, 134–135, **135,** *135*
    evidence of past, 135
icecap subclimate, *126, 127*
ice sheets, retreat of, *135, 137*
ice storms, 68, *91. See also* winter storms.
India, seasonal precipitation in, *123*
Indian Ocean, storms in, 87
inference, **R4,** R35
infrared radiation, 18, **23,** *36*
    role in greenhouse effect, 24, *25*
    satellite images, *102*
International System of Units, R20–R21
islands, effects of global warming on, 138
isobars, *100,* **101,** *101*

J

jet stream, **52,** *52, 55*
    influence on weather, 52
    movement of air masses by, 81
    polar, *52*
    subtropical, *52*

K

Kyoto Protocol (international agreement), 32
    See also greenhouse gases.

INDEX

S

INDEX

U

ultraviolet radiation, **23,** 32, *36*
    absorption of, *20,* 21, *23,* 32, *36*
    ozone and, *20,* 21, *23,* 32, *36*
    skin cancer and, *23*
United States
    government action to limit pollution, 29, 32, 33
    greenhouse gas production of, 32
    weather of, during El Niño years, 136
units of measurement, R20–R21
    air pressure, 101
universe, xvi, xvii
urban heat islands, **128**

V

valley breezes, 53
variables, **R30,** R31, R32
    controlling, R17
    dependent, **R30,** R31
    independent, **R30**
visible light, 16, *17,* 22, *102*
vocabulary strategies, R50–R51
    description wheel, 42, 116, R50, *R50*
    four square, R50, *R50*
    frame game, 8, 116, R51, *R51*
    magnet word, R51, *R51*
    word triangle, 78, 116, R51, *R51*
volcanic eruptions
    atmosphere and, 14, *28,* 30
    gases released by, 132
    global climate's effect on, 132, *133,* 140
volcanoes, xiv–xv, *xiv,* xxi
volume, **R43**

W, X, Y, Z

water, xix
    bodies of and climate, 117, *120,* 140
    hydrosphere, xix
    radiation and, xv

water cycle, 12, *13, 57. See also* condensation; evaporation; precipitation.
water pollution, 70
waterspouts, 95. *See also* tornadoes.
water vapor, *11,* 12, *13,* 24, 31, *56, 57, 58, 59*
    in clouds, 60, 63, 66, 69, *72*
    role in formation of acid rain, 70
waves, xv
weather, 43–70, **47.** *See also* climate; meteorology; weather systems; wind.
    compared to climate, 117
    forecasting, 110–113
    Sun and, xix
weather balloons, *99*
weather buoys, *99*
weather data
    maps and, *100, 101, 102, 103*
    tools for collection of, *99,* 106
weather forecasting, 103. *See also* meteorology.
weather maps, *83, 84, 85,* 100, *101, 102, 103,* R52
    reading station symbols on, *100,* R52,
weather safety, *89, 91, 94, 96*
    Internet activity, 77
weather station, 112
    technology and, 110, 112
weather systems, 76–106
    high-pressure, **84,** *84,* 100, 101
    low-pressure, *84,* **85,** *100, 101,* 106
westerlies (winds), 50, *51*
wet bulb temperature, R53
wet mount, making a, R15, *R15*
wildlife, global warming's effects on, 138
wind, xv, **47,** 47–54, *51, 55. See also* jet stream.
    Beaufort scale, R54
    dust and, 3–4
    formation of, *48*
    global, **48,** 48–52, *49, 51,* 72, 81, 85
    Internet activity, 41
    latitude and, *48,* 48–52, *51, 52*
    local, *53*
    measurement of, *100,* R54
    Sun's energy and, 110
    temperature and, 47–48, *48*
    thunderstorms and, 94
    trade, 50, *51,* 110
    travel affected by, 52

Acknowledgments

Photography

Cover © Bill Ross/Corbis; **i** © Bill Ross/Corbis; **iii** *left (top to bottom)* Photograph of James Trefil by Evan Cantwell; Photograph of Rita Ann Calvo by Joseph Calvo; Photograph of Linda Carnine by Amilcar Cifuentes; Photograph of Sam Miller by Samuel Miller; *right (top to bottom)* Photograph of Kenneth Cutler by Kenneth A. Cutler; Photograph of Donald Steely by Marni Stamm; Photograph of Vicky Vachon by Redfern Photographics; **vi** © Catherine Karnow/Corbis; **vii** AP/WideWorld Photos; **ix** Photographs by Sharon Hoogstraten; **xiv–xv** Doug Scott/age fotostock; **xvi–xvii** © AFLO FOTO Agency; **xviii–ix** © Tim Fitzharris/Masterfile; **xx–xxi** AP/WideWorld Photos; **xxii** © Vince Streano/Corbis; **xxiii** © Roger Ressmeyer/Corbis; **xxiv** top University of Florida Lightning Research Laboratory; *center* © Roger Ressmeyer/Corbis; **xxv** *center* © Mauro Fermariello/Science Researchers; *bottom right* © Alfred Pasieka/Photo Researchers; **xxvi–xxvii** © Stocktrek/Corbis; **xxvi–xxvii** NOAA; **xxvii** © Alan Schein Photography/Corbis; **xxvii** Vaisala Oyj, Finland; **xxxii** © The Chedd-Angier Production Company; **2–3** © Bruce Byers/Getty Images; **3** © D. Faulkner/Photo Researchers; **4** *top left* Luiz C. Marigo/Peter Arnold, Inc.; *top center* Image courtesy Norman Kuring, SeaWiFS Project/NASA; *top right* Norbert Wu; *bottom center* © The Chedd-Angier Production Company; **6–7** © Peter Griffith/Masterfile; **7** *top, center* Photographs by Sharon Hoogstraten; **10** *top* © Didrik Johnck/Corbis Sygma; *bottom* Photograph by Sharon Hoogstraten; **11** NASA; **13** © Michael K. Nichols/NGS Image Collection; **14** *top left, top right* Provided by the SeaWiFS Project, NASA/Goddard Space Flight Center, and ORBIMAGE; **15** M. Thonig/Robertstock.com; **16** David Young-Wolff/PhotoEdit; **17** Photograph by Sharon Hoogstraten; **19** © Gerald and Buff Corsi/Visuals Unlimited, Inc.; **22, 24** Photographs by Sharon Hoogstraten; **26** *top, bottom* PhotoDisc/Getty Images; *background* © Pulse Productions/SuperStock/PictureQuest; **27** Photograph by Sharon Hoogstraten; **28** © P.G. Adam/Publiphoto/Photo Researchers; **29** AP/WideWorld Photos; **30** *background, center left* PhotoDisc/Getty Images; *center right* © Corbis/PictureQuest; **32** © Mug Shots/Corbis; **33** *top left, bottom left* NASA/Goddard Space Flight Center; **34** *top left* © Still Pictures/Peter Arnold, Inc.; *left, right* Photographs by Sharon Hoogstraten; **36** NASA; **37** © Tom Branch/Photo Researchers; **40–41** © Catherine Karnow/Corbis; **41, 45, 47** Photographs by Sharon Hoogstraten; **54** *top left, top right* Earth Vistas; **55** *top* NASA/Corbis; *background* © Lester Lefkowitz/Corbis; **56** *center right* Photograph by Sharon Hoogstraten; *bottom right* © Japack Company/Corbis; **57** © Kristi Bressert/Index Stock Imagery/PictureQuest; **59** Photograph by Sharon Hoogstraten; **60** Grant Heilman/Grant Heilman Photography, Inc.; **62** *top* © John Mead/Photo Researchers; *center* © Royalty-free/Corbis; *bottom* Fred Whitehead/Animals Animals/Earth Scenes; **63** © Tom Till; **64** *top* © Gunter Marx Photography/Corbis; *bottom left, bottom right, center* Photographs by Sharon Hoogstraten; **66** © Stockbyte/PictureQuest; **67** Photograph by Sharon Hoogstraten; **69** *bottom left* © Larry West/Photo Researchers; *bottom right* © Astrid & Hanns-Frieder Michler/Photo Researchers; **70** © Will McIntyre/Photo Researchers; **71** © 1990 Warren Faidley/Weatherstock; **74** © Dorling Kindersley; **76–77** AP/WideWorld Photos; **77, 81** Photographs by Sharon Hoogstraten; **83** © PhotoDisc/Getty Images; **84** Provided by Space Science and Engineering Center, University of Wisconsin-Madison; **86** © Stephen J. Krasemann/Photo Researchers; **87** Photograph by Sharon Hoogstraten; **88** Image by Marit Jentoft-Nilsen/NASA GSFC; **89** *top, center* Courtesy of U.S. Geological Survey; **90** Photograph by Sharon Hoogstraten; **91** AP/WideWorld Photos; **92, 94** *top* Photographs by Sharon Hoogstraten; *bottom left* © PhotoDisc/Getty Images; **95** *left, center, right* © David K. Hoadley; **96** © Reuters/New Media/Corbis; **97** *background* © Waite Air Photos, Inc.; *top left, top right* © Fletcher & Baylis/Photo Researchers; **98** Used with permission © January 9, 2003 Chicago Tribune Company, Chicago, Illinois. Photograph by Sharon Hoogstraten; **101** Provided by Space Science & Engineering Center, University of Wisconsin-Madison; **102** WSBT-TV, South Bend, Indiana; **104** *top left* Mary Kate Denny/PhotoEdit, Inc.; *center left, bottom right* Photographs by Sharon Hoogstraten; **105** Photograph by Sharon Hoogstraten; **106** Image by Marit Jentoft-Nilsen/NASA GSFC; **108** Used with permission © January 9, 2003 Chicago Tribune Company, Chicago, Illinois. Photograph by Sharon Hoogstraten; **110** *top right* © Joel W. Rogers/Corbis; *bot-*

tom © Dorling Kindersley; **111** *top left* © Snark/Art Resource, New York; *top right* Matthew Oldfield, Scubazoo/Photo Researchers; *bottom* National Museum of American History, Smithsonian Institution; **112** *top left* © Mark A. Schneider/Photo Researchers; *top right* © Bettmann/Corbis; *right center* © Roger Ressmeyer/Corbis; *bottom* © Corbis; **113** NASA; **114–115** © Ferrero-Labat/Auscape International; **115** *top, center,* **117, 119** Photographs by Sharon Hoogstraten; **120** *left* Tony Freeman/PhotoEdit, Inc.; *right* © Duomo/Corbis; **123** *top left, top right* Steve McCurry/Magnum Photos; **124** *top left* © Dave G. Houser/Corbis; *center right* AP/WideWorld Photos; *center left, bottom* Glenn Murcutt; **125** © The Image Bank/Getty Images; **127** *center left* © Rick Schafer/Index Stock Imagery/PictureQuest; *top left* © Gerald D. Tang; *bottom* © Photodisc/Getty Images; *center right* © Willard Clay; *top right* © Bill Ross/Corbis; *bottom left* © John Conrad/Corbis; **130** *top left* © Mark Lewis/Pictureque/ PictureQuest; *center left* Photograph by Sharon Hoogstraten; **132** Johner/Photonica; **133** *top right* © Photodisc/Getty Images; *bottom right* Photograph by Sharon Hoogstraten; **137** Lonnie G. Thompson, Ohio State University; **139** Simon Fraser/Mauna Loa Observatory/ Photo Researchers; **140, R28** Photodisc/Getty Images.

Illustrations and Maps

Accurate Art Inc. **75, 109**
Argosy **46, 119**
Richard Bonson/Wildlife Art Ltd. **44, 72**
Peter Bull/Wildlife Art, Ltd. **99, 106**
Stephen Durke **17, 18, 25, 36**
Chris Forsey MCA **129**
Gary Hincks **20, 36, 48, 51**
MapQuest.com, Inc. **3, 14, 49, 52, 54, 55, 80, 83, 85, 86, 88, 89, 93, 97, 118, 120, 121, 123, 126, 133, 134, 135, 136, 140, 143**
Precision Graphics **53, 59, 72**
Mike Saunders **61, 69, 72**
Dan Stuckenschneider **R11–R19, R22, R32**
Space Science and Engineering Center, University of Wisconsin-Madison **84, 100, 101, 102, 106**
Raymond Turvey **83, 106**

Content Standards: 5–8

A. Science as Inquiry

As a result of activities in grades 5–8, all students should develop

Abilities Necessary to do Scientific Inquiry

A.1 Identify questions that can be answered through scientific investigations. Students should develop the ability to refine and refocus broad and ill-defined questions. An important aspect of this ability consists of students' ability to clarify questions and inquiries and direct them toward objects and phenomena that can be described, explained, or predicted by scientific investigations. Students should develop the ability to identify their questions with scientific ideas, concepts, and quantitative relationships that guide investigation.

A.2 Design and conduct a scientific investigation. Students should develop general abilities, such as systematic observation, making accurate measurements, and identifying and controlling variables. They should also develop the ability to clarify their ideas that are influencing and guiding the inquiry, and to understand how those ideas compare with current scientific knowledge. Students can learn to formulate questions, design investigations, execute investigations, interpret data, use evidence to generate explanations, propose alternative explanations, and critique explanations and procedures.

A.3 Use appropriate tools and techniques to gather, analyze, and interpret data. The use of tools and techniques, including mathematics, will be guided by the question asked and the investigations students design. The use of computers for the collection, summary, and display of evidence is part of this standard. Students should be able to access, gather, store, retrieve, and organize data, using hardware and software designed for these purposes.

A.4 Develop descriptions, explanations, predictions, and models using evidence. Students should base their explanation on what they observed, and as they develop cognitive skills, they should be able to differentiate explanation from description—providing causes for effects and establishing relationships based on evidence and logical argument. This standard requires a subject matter knowledge base so the students can effectively conduct investigations, because developing explanations establishes connections between the content of science and the contexts within which students develop new knowledge.

A.5 Think critically and logically to make the relationships between evidence and explanations. Thinking critically about evidence includes deciding what evidence should be used and accounting for anomalous data. Specifically, students should be able to review data from a simple experiment, summarize the data, and form a logical argument about the cause-and-effect relationships in the experiment. Students should begin to state some explanations in terms of the relationship between two or more variables.

A.6 Recognize and analyze alternative explanations and predictions. Students should develop the ability to listen to and respect the explanations proposed by other students. They should remain open to and acknowledge different ideas and explanations, be able to accept the skepticism of others, and consider alternative explanations.

A.7 Communicate scientific procedures and explanations. With practice, students should become competent at communicating experimental methods, following instructions, describing observations, summarizing the results of other groups, and telling other students about investigations and explanations.

A.8 Use mathematics in all aspects of scientific inquiry. Mathematics is essential to asking and answering questions about the natural world. Mathematics can be used to ask questions; to gather, organize, and present data; and to structure convincing explanations.

Understandings about Scientific Inquiry

A.9.a Different kinds of questions suggest different kinds of scientific investigations. Some investigations involve observing and describing objects, organisms, or events; some involve collecting specimens; some involve experiments; some involve seeking more information; some involve discovery of new objects and phenomena; and some involve making models.

A.9.b Current scientific knowledge and understanding guide scientific investigations. Different scientific domains employ different methods, core theories, and standards to advance scientific knowledge and understanding.

A.9.c Mathematics is important in all aspects of scientific inquiry.

A.9.d Technology used to gather data enhances accuracy and allows scientists to analyze and quantify results of investigations.

A.9.e Scientific explanations emphasize evidence, have logically consistent arguments, and use scientific principles, models, and theories. The scientific community accepts and uses such explanations until displaced by better scientific ones. When such displacement occurs, science advances.

A.9.f Science advances through legitimate skepticism. Asking questions and querying other scientists' explanations is part of scientific inquiry. Scientists evaluate the explanations proposed by other scientists by examining evidence, comparing evidence, identifying faulty reasoning, pointing out statements that go beyond the evidence, and suggesting alternative explanations for the same observations.

A.9.g Scientific investigations sometimes result in new ideas and phenomena for study, generate new methods or procedures for an investigation, or develop new technologies to improve the collection of data. All of these results can lead to new investigations.

B. Physical Science

As a result of their activities in grades 5–8, all students should develop an understanding of

Properties and Changes of Properties in Matter

B.1.a A substance has characteristic properties, such as density, a boiling point, and solubility, all of which are independent of the amount of the sample. A mixture of substances often can be separated into the original substances using one or more of the characteristic properties.

B.1.b Substances react chemically in characteristic ways with other substances to form new substances (compounds) with different characteristic properties. In chemical reactions, the total mass is conserved. Substances often are placed in categories or groups if they react in similar ways; metals is an example of such a group.

B.1.c Chemical elements do not break down during normal laboratory reactions involving such treatments as heating, exposure to electric current, or reaction with acids. There are more than 100 known elements that combine in a multitude of ways to produce compounds, which account for the living and nonliving substances that we encounter.

Motions and Forces

B.2.a The motion of an object can be described by its position, direction of motion, and speed. That motion can be measured and represented on a graph.

B.2.b An object that is not being subjected to a force will continue to move at a constant speed and in a straight line.

B.2.c If more than one force acts on an object along a straight line, then the forces will reinforce or cancel one another, depending on their direction and magnitude. Unbalanced forces will cause changes in the speed or direction of an object's motion.

Transfer of Energy

B.3.a Energy is a property of many substances and is associated with heat, light, electricity, mechanical motion, sound, nuclei, and the nature of a chemical. Energy is transferred in many ways.

B.3.b Heat moves in predictable ways, flowing from warmer objects to cooler ones, until both reach the same temperature.

B.3.c Light interacts with matter by transmission (including refraction), absorption, or scattering (including reflection). To see an object, light from that object—emitted by or scattered from it—must enter the eye.

B.3.d Electrical circuits provide a means of transferring electrical energy when heat, light, sound, and chemical changes are produced.

B.3.e In most chemical and nuclear reactions, energy is transferred into or out of a system. Heat, light, mechanical motion, or electricity might all be involved in such transfers.

B.3.f The sun is a major source of energy for changes on the earth's surface. The sun loses energy by emitting light. A tiny fraction of that light reaches the earth, transferring energy from the sun to the earth. The sun's energy arrives as light with a range of wavelengths, consisting of visible light, infrared, and ultraviolet radiation.

C. Life Science

As a result of their activities in grades 5–8, all students should develop understanding of

Structure and Function in Living Systems

C.1.a   Living systems at all levels of organization demonstrate the complementary nature of structure and function. Important levels of organization for structure and function include cells, organs, tissues, organ systems, whole organisms, and ecosystems.

C.1.b   All organisms are composed of cells—the fundamental unit of life. Most organisms are single cells; other organisms, including humans, are multicellular.

C.1.c   Cells carry on the many functions needed to sustain life. They grow and divide, thereby producing more cells. This requires that they take in nutrients, which they use to provide energy for the work that cells do and to make the materials that a cell or an organism needs.

C.1.d   Specialized cells perform specialized functions in multicellular organisms. Groups of specialized cells cooperate to form a tissue, such as a muscle. Different tissues are in turn grouped together to form larger functional units, called organs. Each type of cell, tissue, and organ has a distinct structure and set of functions that serve the organism as a whole.

C.1.e   The human organism has systems for digestion, respiration, reproduction, circulation, excretion, movement, control, and coordination, and for protection from disease. These systems interact with one another.

C.1.f   Disease is a breakdown in structures or functions of an organism. Some diseases are the result of intrinsic failures of the system. Others are the result of damage by infection by other organisms.

Reproduction and Heredity

C.2.a   Reproduction is a characteristic of all living systems; because no individual organism lives forever, reproduction is essential to the continuation of every species. Some organisms reproduce asexually. Other organisms reproduce sexually.

C.2.b   In many species, including humans, females produce eggs and males produce sperm. Plants also reproduce sexually—the egg and sperm are produced in the flowers of flowering plants. An egg and sperm unite to begin development of a new individual. That new individual receives genetic information from its mother (via the egg) and its father (via the sperm). Sexually produced offspring never are identical to either of their parents.

C.2.c   Every organism requires a set of instructions for specifying its traits. Heredity is the passage of these instructions from one generation to another.

C.2.d   Hereditary information is contained in genes, located in the chromosomes of each cell. Each gene carries a single unit of information. An inherited trait of an individual can be determined by one or by many genes, and a single gene can influence more than one trait. A human cell contains many thousands of different genes.

C.2.e   The characteristics of an organism can be described in terms of a combination of traits. Some traits are inherited and others result from interactions with the environment.

Regulation and Behavior

C.3.a All organisms must be able to obtain and use resources, grow, reproduce, and maintain stable internal conditions while living in a constantly changing external environment.

C.3.b Regulation of an organism's internal environment involves sensing the internal environment and changing physiological activities to keep conditions within the range required to survive.

C.3.c Behavior is one kind of response an organism can make to an internal or environmental stimulus. A behavioral response requires coordination and communication at many levels, including cells, organ systems, and whole organisms. Behavioral response is a set of actions determined in part by heredity and in part from experience.

C.3.d An organism's behavior evolves through adaptation to its environment. How a species moves, obtains food, reproduces, and responds to danger are based in the species' evolutionary history.

Populations and Ecosystems

C.4.a A population consists of all individuals of a species that occur together at a given place and time. All populations living together and the physical factors with which they interact compose an ecosystem.

C.4.b Populations of organisms can be categorized by the function they serve in an ecosystem. Plants and some microorganisms are producers—they make their own food. All animals, including humans, are consumers, which obtain food by eating other organisms. Decomposers, primarily bacteria and fungi, are consumers that use waste materials and dead organisms for food. Food webs identify the relationships among producers, consumers, and decomposers in an ecosystem.

C.4.c For ecosystems, the major source of energy is sunlight. Energy entering ecosystems as sunlight is transferred by producers into chemical energy through photosynthesis. That energy then passes from organism to organism in food webs.

C.4.d The number of organisms an ecosystem can support depends on the resources available and abiotic factors, such as quantity of light and water, range of temperatures, and soil composition. Given adequate biotic and abiotic resources and no disease or predators, populations (including humans) increase at rapid rates. Lack of resources and other factors, such as predation and climate, limit the growth of populations in specific niches in the ecosystem.

Diversity and Adaptations of Organisms

C.5.a Millions of species of animals, plants, and microorganisms are alive today. Although different species might look dissimilar, the unity among organisms becomes apparent from an analysis of internal structures, the similarity of their chemical processes, and the evidence of common ancestry.

C.5.b Biological evolution accounts for the diversity of species developed through gradual processes over many generations. Species acquire many of their unique characteristics through biological adaptation, which involves the selection of naturally occurring variations in populations. Biological adaptations include changes in structures, behaviors, or physiology that enhance survival and reproductive success in a particular environment.

C.5.c Extinction of a species occurs when the environment changes and the adaptive characteristics of a species are insufficient to allow its survival. Fossils indicate that many organisms that lived long ago are extinct. Extinction of species is common; most of the species that have lived on the earth no longer exist.

D. Earth and Space Science

As a result of their activities in grades 5–8, all students should develop an understanding of

Structure of the Earth System

D.1.a   The solid earth is layered with a lithosphere; hot, convecting mantle; and dense, metallic core.

D.1.b   Lithospheric plates on the scales of continents and oceans constantly move at rates of centimeters per year in response to movements in the mantle. Major geological events, such as earthquakes, volcanic eruptions, and mountain building, result from these plate motions.

D.1.c   Land forms are the result of a combination of constructive and destructive forces. Constructive forces include crustal deformation, volcanic eruption, and deposition of sediment, while destructive forces include weathering and erosion.

D.1.d   Some changes in the solid earth can be described as the "rock cycle." Old rocks at the earth's surface weather, forming sediments that are buried, then compacted, heated, and often recrystallized into new rock. Eventually, those new rocks may be brought to the surface by the forces that drive plate motions, and the rock cycle continues.

D.1.e   Soil consists of weathered rocks and decomposed organic material from dead plants, animals, and bacteria. Soils are often found in layers, with each having a different chemical composition and texture.

D.1.f   Water, which covers the majority of the earth's surface, circulates through the crust, oceans, and atmosphere in what is known as the "water cycle." Water evaporates from the earth's surface, rises and cools as it moves to higher elevations, condenses as rain or snow, and falls to the surface where it collects in lakes, oceans, soil, and in rocks underground.

D.1.g   Water is a solvent. As it passes through the water cycle it dissolves minerals and gases and carries them to the oceans.

D.1.h   The atmosphere is a mixture of nitrogen, oxygen, and trace gases that include water vapor. The atmosphere has different properties at different elevations.

D.1.i   Clouds, formed by the condensation of water vapor, affect weather and climate.

D.1.j   Global patterns of atmospheric movement influence local weather. Oceans have a major effect on climate, because water in the oceans holds a large amount of heat.

D.1.k   Living organisms have played many roles in the earth system, including affecting the composition of the atmosphere, producing some types of rocks, and contributing to the weathering of rocks.

Earth's History

D.2.a   The earth processes we see today, including erosion, movement of lithospheric plates, and changes in atmospheric composition, are similar to those that occurred in the past. Earth history is also influenced by occasional catastrophes, such as the impact of an asteroid or comet.

D.2.b   Fossils provide important evidence of how life and environmental conditions have changed.

Earth in the Solar System

D.3.a The earth is the third planet from the sun in a system that includes the moon, the sun, eight other planets and their moons, and smaller objects, such as asteroids and comets. The sun, an average star, is the central and largest body in the solar system.

D.3.b Most objects in the solar system are in regular and predictable motion. Those motions explain such phenomena as the day, the year, phases of the moon, and eclipses.

D.3.c Gravity is the force that keeps planets in orbit around the sun and governs the rest of the motion in the solar system. Gravity alone holds us to the earth's surface and explains the phenomena of the tides.

D.3.d The sun is the major source of energy for phenomena on the earth's surface, such as growth of plants, winds, ocean currents, and the water cycle. Seasons result from variations in the amount of the sun's energy hitting the surface, due to the tilt of the earth's rotation on its axis and the length of the day.

E. Science and Technology

As a result of activities in grades 5–8, all students should develop

Abilities of Technological Design

E.1 Identify appropriate problems for technological design. Students should develop their abilities by identifying a specified need, considering its various aspects, and talking to different potential users or beneficiaries. They should appreciate that for some needs, the cultural backgrounds and beliefs of different groups can affect the criteria for a suitable product.

E.2 Design a solution or product. Students should make and compare different proposals in the light of the criteria they have selected. They must consider constraints—such as cost, time, trade-offs, and materials needed—and communicate ideas with drawings and simple models.

E.3 Implement a proposed design. Students should organize materials and other resources, plan their work, make good use of group collaboration where appropriate, choose suitable tools and techniques, and work with appropriate measurement methods to ensure adequate accuracy.

E.4 Evaluate completed technological designs or products. Students should use criteria relevant to the original purpose or need, consider a variety of factors that might affect acceptability and suitability for intended users or beneficiaries, and develop measures of quality with respect to such criteria and factors; they should also suggest improvements and, for their own products, try proposed modifications.

E.5 Communicate the process of technological design. Students should review and describe any completed piece of work and identify the stages of problem identification, solution design, implementation, and evaluation.

Understandings about Science and Technology

E.6.a   Scientific inquiry and technological design have similarities and differences. Scientists propose explanations for questions about the natural world, and engineers propose solutions relating to human problems, needs, and aspirations. Technological solutions are temporary; technologies exist within nature and so they cannot contravene physical or biological principles; technological solutions have side effects; and technologies cost, carry risks, and provide benefits.

E.6.b   Many different people in different cultures have made and continue to make contributions to science and technology.

E.6.c   Science and technology are reciprocal. Science helps drive technology, as it addresses questions that demand more sophisticated instruments and provides principles for better instrumentation and technique. Technology is essential to science, because it provides instruments and techniques that enable observations of objects and phenomena that are otherwise unobservable due to factors such as quantity, distance, location, size, and speed. Technology also provides tools for investigations, inquiry, and analysis.

E.6.d   Perfectly designed solutions do not exist. All technological solutions have trade-offs, such as safety, cost, efficiency, and appearance. Engineers often build in back-up systems to provide safety. Risk is part of living in a highly technological world. Reducing risk often results in new technology.

E.6.e   Technological designs have constraints. Some constraints are unavoidable, for example, properties of materials, or effects of weather and friction; other constraints limit choices in the design, for example, environmental protection, human safety, and aesthetics.

E.6.f   Technological solutions have intended benefits and unintended consequences. Some consequences can be predicted, others cannot.

F. Science in Personal and Social Perspectives

As a result of activities in grades 5–8, all students should develop understanding of

Personal Health

F.1.a   Regular exercise is important to the maintenance and improvement of health. The benefits of physical fitness include maintaining healthy weight, having energy and strength for routine activities, good muscle tone, bone strength, strong heart/lung systems, and improved mental health. Personal exercise, especially developing cardiovascular endurance, is the foundation of physical fitness.

F.1.b   The potential for accidents and the existence of hazards imposes the need for injury prevention. Safe living involves the development and use of safety precautions and the recognition of risk in personal decisions. Injury prevention has personal and social dimensions.

F.1.c   The use of tobacco increases the risk of illness. Students should understand the influence of short-term social and psychological factors that lead to tobacco use, and the possible long-term detrimental effects of smoking and chewing tobacco.

F.1.d   Alcohol and other drugs are often abused substances. Such drugs change how the body functions and can lead to addiction.

F.1.e   Food provides energy and nutrients for growth and development. Nutrition requirements vary with body weight, age, sex, activity, and body functioning.

F.1.f   Sex drive is a natural human function that requires understanding. Sex is also a prominent means of transmitting diseases. The diseases can be prevented through a variety of precautions.

F.1.g   Natural environments may contain substances (for example, radon and lead) that are harmful to human beings. Maintaining environmental health involves establishing or monitoring quality standards related to use of soil, water, and air.

Populations, Resources, and Environments

F.2.a   When an area becomes overpopulated, the environment will become degraded due to the increased use of resources.

F.2.b   Causes of environmental degradation and resource depletion vary from region to region and from country to country.

Natural Hazards

F.3.a   Internal and external processes of the earth system cause natural hazards, events that change or destroy human and wildlife habitats, damage property, and harm or kill humans. Natural hazards include earthquakes, landslides, wildfires, volcanic eruptions, floods, storms, and even possible impacts of asteroids.

F.3.b   Human activities also can induce hazards through resource acquisition, urban growth, land-use decisions, and waste disposal. Such activities can accelerate many natural changes.

F.3.c   Natural hazards can present personal and societal challenges because misidentifying the change or incorrectly estimating the rate and scale of change may result in either too little attention and significant human costs or too much cost for unneeded preventive measures.

Risks and Benefits

F.4.a   Risk analysis considers the type of hazard and estimates the number of people that might be exposed and the number likely to suffer consequences. The results are used to determine the options for reducing or eliminating risks.

F.4.b   Students should understand the risks associated with natural hazards (fires, floods, tornadoes, hurricanes, earthquakes, and volcanic eruptions), with chemical hazards (pollutants in air, water, soil, and food), with biological hazards (pollen, viruses, bacterial, and parasites), social hazards (occupational safety and transportation), and with personal hazards (smoking, dieting, and drinking).

F.4.c   Individuals can use a systematic approach to thinking critically about risks and benefits. Examples include applying probability estimates to risks and comparing them to estimated personal and social benefits.

F.4.d   Important personal and social decisions are made based on perceptions of benefits and risks.

Science and Technology in Society

F.5.a   Science influences society through its knowledge and world view. Scientific knowledge and the procedures used by scientists influence the way many individuals in society think about themselves, others, and the environment. The effect of science on society is neither entirely beneficial nor entirely detrimental.

F.5.b   Societal challenges often inspire questions for scientific research, and social priorities often influence research priorities through the availability of funding for research.

F.5.c   Technology influences society through its products and processes. Technology influences the quality of life and the ways people act and interact. Technological changes are often accompanied by social, political, and economic changes that can be beneficial or detrimental to individuals and to society. Social needs, attitudes, and values influence the direction of technological development.

F.5.d   Science and technology have advanced through contributions of many different people, in different cultures, at different times in history. Science and technology have contributed enormously to economic growth and productivity among societies and groups within societies.

F.5.e   Scientists and engineers work in many different settings, including colleges and universities, businesses and industries, specific research institutes, and government agencies.

F.5.f   Scientists and engineers have ethical codes requiring that human subjects involved with research be fully informed about risks and benefits associated with the research before the individuals choose to participate. This ethic extends to potential risks to communities and property. In short, prior knowledge and consent are required for research involving human subjects or potential damage to property.

F.5.g   Science cannot answer all questions and technology cannot solve all human problems or meet all human needs. Students should understand the difference between scientific and other questions. They should appreciate what science and technology can reasonably contribute to society and what they cannot do. For example, new technologies often will decrease some risks and increase others.

G. History and Nature of Science

As a result of activities in grades 5–8, all students should develop understanding of

Science as a Human Endeavor

G.1.a   Women and men of various social and ethnic backgrounds—and with diverse interests, talents, qualities, and motivations—engage in the activities of science, engineering, and related fields such as the health professions. Some scientists work in teams, and some work alone, but all communicate extensively with others.

G.1.b   Science requires different abilities, depending on such factors as the field of study and type of inquiry. Science is very much a human endeavor, and the work of science relies on basic human qualities, such as reasoning, insight, energy, skill, and creativity—as well as on scientific habits of mind, such as intellectual honesty, tolerance of ambiguity, skepticism, and openness to new ideas.

Nature of Science

G.2.a Scientists formulate and test their explanations of nature using observation, experiments, and theoretical and mathematical models. Although all scientific ideas are tentative and subject to change and improvement in principle, for most major ideas in science, there is much experimental and observational confirmation. Those ideas are not likely to change greatly in the future. Scientists do and have changed their ideas about nature when they encounter new experimental evidence that does not match their existing explanations.

G.2.b In areas where active research is being pursued and in which there is not a great deal of experimental or observational evidence and understanding, it is normal for scientists to differ with one another about the interpretation of the evidence or theory being considered. Different scientists might publish conflicting experimental results or might draw different conclusions from the same data. Ideally, scientists acknowledge such conflict and work towards finding evidence that will resolve their disagreement.

G.2.c It is part of scientific inquiry to evaluate the results of scientific investigations, experiments, observations, theoretical models, and the explanations proposed by other scientists. Evaluation includes reviewing the experimental procedures, examining the evidence, identifying faulty reasoning, pointing out statements that go beyond the evidence, and suggesting alternative explanations for the same observations. Although scientists may disagree about explanations of phenomena, about interpretations of data, or about the value of rival theories, they do agree that questioning, response to criticism, and open communication are integral to the process of science. As scientific knowledge evolves, major disagreements are eventually resolved through such interactions between scientists.

History of Science

G.3.a Many individuals have contributed to the traditions of science. Studying some of these individuals provides further understanding of scientific inquiry, science as a human endeavor, the nature of science, and the relationships between science and society.

G.3.b In historical perspective, science has been practiced by different individuals in different cultures. In looking at the history of many peoples, one finds that scientists and engineers of high achievement are considered to be among the most valued contributors to their culture.

G.3.c Tracing the history of science can show how difficult it was for scientific innovators to break through the accepted ideas of their time to reach the conclusions that we currently take for granted.

1. The Nature of Science

By the end of the 8th grade, students should know that

1.A The Scientific World View

1.A.1 When similar investigations give different results, the scientific challenge is to judge whether the differences are trivial or significant, and it often takes further studies to decide. Even with similar results, scientists may wait until an investigation has been repeated many times before accepting the results as correct.

1.A.2 Scientific knowledge is subject to modification as new information challenges prevailing theories and as a new theory leads to looking at old observations in a new way.

1.A.3 Some scientific knowledge is very old and yet is still applicable today.

1.A.4 Some matters cannot be examined usefully in a scientific way. Among them are matters that by their nature cannot be tested objectively and those that are essentially matters of morality. Science can sometimes be used to inform ethical decisions by identifying the likely consequences of particular actions but cannot be used to establish that some action is either moral or immoral.

1.B Scientific Inquiry

1.B.1 Scientists differ greatly in what phenomena they study and how they go about their work. Although there is no fixed set of steps that all scientists follow, scientific investigations usually involve the collection of relevant evidence, the use of logical reasoning, and the application of imagination in devising hypotheses and explanations to make sense of the collected evidence.

1.B.2 If more than one variable changes at the same time in an experiment, the outcome of the experiment may not be clearly attributable to any one of the variables. It may not always be possible to prevent outside variables from influencing the outcome of an investigation (or even to identify all of the variables), but collaboration among investigators can often lead to research designs that are able to deal with such situations.

1.B.3 What people expect to observe often affects what they actually do observe. Strong beliefs about what should happen in particular circumstances can prevent them from detecting other results. Scientists know about this danger to objectivity and take steps to try and avoid it when designing investigations and examining data. One safeguard is to have different investigators conduct independent studies of the same questions.

1.C The Scientific Enterprise

1.C.1 Important contributions to the advancement of science, mathematics, and technology have been made by different kinds of people, in different cultures, at different times.

1.C.2 Until recently, women and racial minorities, because of restrictions on their education and employment opportunities, were essentially left out of much of the formal work of the science establishment; the remarkable few who overcame those obstacles were even then likely to have their work disregarded by the science establishment.

1.C.3 No matter who does science and mathematics or invents things, or when or where they do it, the knowledge and technology that result can eventually become available to everyone in the world.

1.C.4 Scientists are employed by colleges and universities, business and industry, hospitals, and many government agencies. Their places of work include offices, classrooms, laboratories, farms, factories, and natural field settings ranging from space to the ocean floor.

1.C.5 In research involving human subjects, the ethics of science require that potential subjects be fully informed about the risks and benefits associated with the research and of their right to refuse to participate. Science ethics also demand that scientists must not knowingly subject coworkers, students, the neighborhood, or the community to health or property risks without their prior knowledge and consent. Because animals cannot make informed choices, special care must be taken in using them in scientific research.

1.C.6 Computers have become invaluable in science because they speed up and extend people's ability to collect, store, compile, and analyze data, prepare research reports, and share data and ideas with investigators all over the world.

1.C.7 Accurate record-keeping, openness, and replication are essential for maintaining an investigator's credibility with other scientists and society.

3. The Nature of Technology

By the end of the 8th grade, students should know that

3.A Technology and Science

3.A.1 In earlier times, the accumulated information and techniques of each generation of workers were taught on the job directly to the next generation of workers. Today, the knowledge base for technology can be found as well in libraries of print and electronic resources and is often taught in the classroom.

3.A.2 Technology is essential to science for such purposes as access to outer space and other remote locations, sample collection and treatment, measurement, data collection and storage, computation, and communication of information.

3.A.3 Engineers, architects, and others who engage in design and technology use scientific knowledge to solve practical problems. But they usually have to take human values and limitations into account as well.

3.B Design and Systems

3.B.1 Design usually requires taking constraints into account. Some constraints, such as gravity or the properties of the materials to be used, are unavoidable. Other constraints, including economic, political, social, ethical, and aesthetic ones, limit choices.

3.B.2 All technologies have effects other than those intended by the design, some of which may have been predictable and some not. In either case, these side effects may turn out to be unacceptable to some of the population and therefore lead to conflict between groups.

3.B.3 Almost all control systems have inputs, outputs, and feedback. The essence of control is comparing information about what is happening to what people want to happen and then making appropriate adjustments. This procedure requires sensing information, processing it, and making changes. In almost all modern machines, microprocessors serve as centers of performance control.

3.B.4 Systems fail because they have faulty or poorly matched parts, are used in ways that exceed what was intended by the design, or were poorly designed to begin with. The most common ways to prevent failure are pretesting parts and procedures, overdesign, and redundancy.

3.C Issues in Technology

3.C.1 The human ability to shape the future comes from a capacity for generating knowledge and developing new technologies—and for communicating ideas to others.

3.C.2 Technology cannot always provide successful solutions for problems or fulfill every human need.

3.C.3 Throughout history, people have carried out impressive technological feats, some of which would be hard to duplicate today even with modern tools. The purposes served by these achievements have sometimes been practical, sometimes ceremonial.

3.C.4 Technology has strongly influenced the course of history and continues to do so. It is largely responsible for the great revolutions in agriculture, manufacturing, sanitation and medicine, warfare, transportation, information processing, and communications that have radically changed how people live.

3.C.5 New technologies increase some risks and decrease others. Some of the same technologies that have improved the length and quality of life for many people have also brought new risks.

3.C.6 Rarely are technology issues simple and one-sided. Relevant facts alone, even when known and available, usually do not settle matters entirely in favor of one side or another. That is because the contending groups may have different values and priorities. They may stand to gain or lose in different degrees, or may make very different predictions about what the future consequences of the proposed action will be.

3.C.7 Societies influence what aspects of technology are developed and how these are used. People control technology (as well as science) and are responsible for its effects.

4. The Physical Setting

By the end of the 8th grade, students should know that

4.A The Universe

4.A.1   The sun is a medium-sized star located near the edge of a disk-shaped galaxy of stars, part of which can be seen as a glowing band of light that spans the sky on a very clear night. The universe contains many billions of galaxies, and each galaxy contains many billions of stars. To the naked eye, even the closest of these galaxies is no more than a dim, fuzzy spot.

4.A.2   The sun is many thousands of times closer to the earth than any other star. Light from the sun takes a few minutes to reach the earth, but light from the next nearest star takes a few years to arrive. The trip to that star would take the fastest rocket thousands of years. Some distant galaxies are so far away that their light takes several billion years to reach the earth. People on earth, therefore, see them as they were that long ago in the past.

4.A.3   Nine planets of very different size, composition, and surface features move around the sun in nearly circular orbits. Some planets have a great variety of moons and even flat rings of rock and ice particles orbiting around them. Some of these planets and moons show evidence of geologic activity. The earth is orbited by one moon, many artificial satellites, and debris.

4.A.4   Large numbers of chunks of rock orbit the sun. Some of those that the earth meets in its yearly orbit around the sun glow and disintegrate from friction as they plunge through the atmosphere—and sometimes impact the ground. Other chunks of rocks mixed with ice have long, off-center orbits that carry them close to the sun, where the sun's radiation (of light and particles) boils off frozen material from their surfaces and pushes it into a long, illuminated tail.

4.B The Earth

4.B.1   We live on a relatively small planet, the third from the sun in the only system of planets definitely known to exist (although other, similar systems may be discovered in the universe).

4.B.2   The earth is mostly rock. Three-fourths of its surface is covered by a relatively thin layer of water (some of it frozen), and the entire planet is surrounded by a relatively thin blanket of air. It is the only body in the solar system that appears able to support life. The other planets have compositions and conditions very different from the earth's.

4.B.3   Everything on or anywhere near the earth is pulled toward the earth's center by gravitational force.

4.B.4   Because the earth turns daily on an axis that is tilted relative to the plane of the earth's yearly orbit around the sun, sunlight falls more intensely on different parts of the earth during the year. The difference in heating of the earth's surface produces the planet's seasons and weather patterns.

4.B.5   The moon's orbit around the earth once in about 28 days changes what part of the moon is lighted by the sun and how much of that part can be seen from the earth—the phases of the moon.

4.B.6   Climates have sometimes changed abruptly in the past as a result of changes in the earth's crust, such as volcanic eruptions or impacts of huge rocks from space. Even relatively small changes in atmospheric or ocean content can have widespread effects on climate if the change lasts long enough.

4.B.7   The cycling of water in and out of the atmosphere plays an important role in determining climatic patterns. Water evaporates from the surface of the earth, rises and cools, condenses into rain or snow, and falls again to the surface. The water falling on land collects in rivers and lakes, soil, and porous layers of rock, and much of it flows back into the ocean.

4.B.8   Fresh water, limited in supply, is essential for life and also for most industrial processes. Rivers, lakes, and groundwater can be depleted or polluted, becoming unavailable or unsuitable for life.

4.B.9   Heat energy carried by ocean currents has a strong influence on climate around the world.

4.B.10 Some minerals are very rare and some exist in great quantities, but—for practical purposes—the ability to recover them is just as important as their abundance. As minerals are depleted, obtaining them becomes more difficult. Recycling and the development of substitutes can reduce the rate of depletion but may also be costly.

4.B.11 The benefits of the earth's resources—such as fresh water, air, soil, and trees—can be reduced by using them wastefully or by deliberately or inadvertently destroying them. The atmosphere and the oceans have a limited capacity to absorb wastes and recycle materials naturally. Cleaning up polluted air, water, or soil or restoring depleted soil, forests, or fishing grounds can be very difficult and costly.

4.C Processes that Shape the Earth

4.C.1   The interior of the earth is hot. Heat flow and movement of material within the earth cause earthquakes and volcanic eruptions and create mountains and ocean basins. Gas and dust from large volcanoes can change the atmosphere.

4.C.2   Some changes in the earth's surface are abrupt (such as earthquakes and volcanic eruptions) while other changes happen very slowly (such as uplift and wearing down of mountains). The earth's surface is shaped in part by the motion of water and wind over very long times, which act to level mountain ranges.

4.C.3   Sediments of sand and smaller particles (sometimes containing the remains of organisms) are gradually buried and are cemented together by dissolved minerals to form solid rock again.

4.C.4   Sedimentary rock buried deep enough may be reformed by pressure and heat, perhaps melting and recrystallizing into different kinds of rock. These re-formed rock layers may be forced up again to become land surface and even mountains. Subsequently, this new rock too will erode. Rock bears evidence of the minerals, temperatures, and forces that created it.

4.C.5   Thousands of layers of sedimentary rock confirm the long history of the changing surface of the earth and the changing life forms whose remains are found in successive layers. The youngest layers are not always found on top, because of folding, breaking, and uplift of layers.

4.C.6   Although weathered rock is the basic component of soil, the composition and texture of soil and its fertility and resistance to erosion are greatly influenced by plant roots and debris, bacteria, fungi, worms, insects, rodents, and other organisms.

4.C.7   Human activities, such as reducing the amount of forest cover, increasing the amount and variety of chemicals released into the atmosphere, and intensive farming, have changed the earth's land, oceans, and atmosphere. Some of these changes have decreased the capacity of the environment to support some life forms.

4.D Structure of Matter

4.D.1 All matter is made up of atoms, which are far too small to see directly through a microscope. The atoms of any element are alike but are different from atoms of other elements. Atoms may stick together in well-defined molecules or may be packed together in large arrays. Different arrangements of atoms into groups compose all substances.

4.D.2 Equal volumes of different substances usually have different weights.

4.D.3 Atoms and molecules are perpetually in motion. Increased temperature means greater average energy, so most substances expand when heated. In solids, the atoms are closely locked in position and can only vibrate. In liquids, the atoms or molecules have higher energy, are more loosely connected, and can slide past one another; some molecules may get enough energy to escape into a gas. In gases, the atoms or molecules have still more energy and are free of one another except during occasional collisions.

4.D.4 The temperature and acidity of a solution influence reaction rates. Many substances dissolve in water, which may greatly facilitate reactions between them.

4.D.5 Scientific ideas about elements were borrowed from some Greek philosophers of 2,000 years earlier, who believed that everything was made from four basic substances: air, earth, fire, and water. It was the combinations of these "elements" in different proportions that gave other substances their observable properties. The Greeks were wrong about those four, but now over 100 different elements have been identified, some rare and some plentiful, out of which everything is made. Because most elements tend to combine with others, few elements are found in their pure form.

4.D.6 There are groups of elements that have similar properties, including highly reactive metals, less-reactive metals, highly reactive nonmetals (such as chlorine, fluorine, and oxygen), and some almost completely nonreactive gases (such as helium and neon). An especially important kind of reaction between substances involves combination of oxygen with something else—as in burning or rusting. Some elements don't fit into any of the categories; among them are carbon and hydrogen, essential elements of living matter.

4.D.7 No matter how substances within a closed system interact with one another, or how they combine or break apart, the total weight of the system remains the same. The idea of atoms explains the conservation of matter: If the number of atoms stays the same no matter how they are rearranged, then their total mass stays the same.

4.E Energy Transformations

4.E.1 Energy cannot be created or destroyed, but only changed from one form into another.

4.E.2 Most of what goes on in the universe—from exploding stars and biological growth to the operation of machines and the motion of people—involves some form of energy being transformed into another. Energy in the form of heat is almost always one of the products of an energy transformation.

4.E.3 Heat can be transferred through materials by the collisions of atoms or across space by radiation. If the material is fluid, currents will be set up in it that aid the transfer of heat.

4.E.4 Energy appears in different forms. Heat energy is in the disorderly motion of molecules; chemical energy is in the arrangement of atoms; mechanical energy is in moving bodies or in elastically distorted shapes; gravitational energy is in the separation of mutually attracting masses.

4.F Motion

4.F.1   Light from the sun is made up of a mixture of many different colors of light, even though to the eye the light looks almost white. Other things that give off or reflect light have a different mix of colors.

4.F.2   Something can be "seen" when light waves emitted or reflected by it enter the eye—just as something can be "heard" when sound waves from it enter the ear.

4.F.3   An unbalanced force acting on an object changes its speed or direction of motion, or both. If the force acts toward a single center, the object's path may curve into an orbit around the center.

4.F.4   Vibrations in materials set up wavelike disturbances that spread away from the source. Sound and earthquake waves are examples. These and other waves move at different speeds in different materials.

4.F.5   Human eyes respond to only a narrow range of wavelengths of electromagnetic radiation— visible light. Differences of wavelength within that range are perceived as differences in color.

4.G Forces of Nature

4.G.1   Every object exerts gravitational force on every other object. The force depends on how much mass the objects have and on how far apart they are. The force is hard to detect unless at least one of the objects has a lot of mass.

4.G.2   The sun's gravitational pull holds the earth and other planets in their orbits, just as the planets' gravitational pull keeps their moons in orbit around them.

4.G.3   Electric currents and magnets can exert a force on each other.

5. The Living Environment

By the end of the 8th grade, students should know that

5.A Diversity of Life

5.A.1 One of the most general distinctions among organisms is between plants, which use sunlight to make their own food, and animals, which consume energy-rich foods. Some kinds of organisms, many of them microscopic, cannot be neatly classified as either plants or animals.

5.A.2 Animals and plants have a great variety of body plans and internal structures that contribute to their being able to make or find food and reproduce.

5.A.3 Similarities among organisms are found in internal anatomical features, which can be used to infer the degree of relatedness among organisms. In classifying organisms, biologists consider details of internal and external structures to be more important than behavior or general appearance.

5.A.4 For sexually reproducing organisms, a species comprises all organisms that can mate with one another to produce fertile offspring.

5.A.5 All organisms, including the human species, are part of and depend on two main interconnected global food webs. One includes microscopic ocean plants, the animals that feed on them, and finally the animals that feed on those animals. The other web includes land plants, the animals that feed on them, and so forth. The cycles continue indefinitely because organisms decompose after death to return food material to the environment.

5.B Heredity

5.B.1 In some kinds of organisms, all the genes come from a single parent, whereas in organisms that have sexes, typically half of the genes come from each parent.

5.B.2 In sexual reproduction, a single specialized cell from a female merges with a specialized cell from a male. As the fertilized egg, carrying genetic information from each parent, multiplies to form the complete organism with about a trillion cells, the same genetic information is copied in each cell.

5.B.3 New varieties of cultivated plants and domestic animals have resulted from selective breeding for particular traits.

5.C Cells

5.C.1 All living things are composed of cells, from just one to many millions, whose details usually are visible only through a microscope. Different body tissues and organs are made up of different kinds of cells. The cells in similar tissues and organs in other animals are similar to those in human beings but differ somewhat from cells found in plants.

5.C.2 Cells repeatedly divide to make more cells for growth and repair. Various organs and tissues function to serve the needs of cells for food, air, and waste removal.

5.C.3 Within cells, many of the basic functions of organisms—such as extracting energy from food and getting rid of waste—are carried out. The way in which cells function is similar in all living organisms.

5.C.4 About two-thirds of the weight of cells is accounted for by water, which gives cells many of their properties.

5.D Interdependence of Life

5.D.1   In all environments—freshwater, marine, forest, desert, grassland, mountain, and others—organisms with similar needs may compete with one another for resources, including food, space, water, air, and shelter. In any particular environment, the growth and survival of organisms depend on the physical conditions.

5.D.2   Two types of organisms may interact with one another in several ways: They may be in a producer/consumer, predator/prey, or parasite/host relationship. Or one organism may scavenge or decompose another. Relationships may be competitive or mutually beneficial. Some species have become so adapted to each other that neither could survive without the other.

5.E Flow of Matter and Energy

5.E.1   Food provides molecules that serve as fuel and building material for all organisms. Plants use the energy in light to make sugars out of carbon dioxide and water. This food can be used immediately for fuel or materials or it may be stored for later use. Organisms that eat plants break down the plant structures to produce the materials and energy they need to survive. Then they are consumed by other organisms.

5.E.2   Over a long time, matter is transferred from one organism to another repeatedly and between organisms and their physical environment. As in all material systems, the total amount of matter remains constant, even though its form and location change.

5.E.3   Energy can change from one form to another in living things. Animals get energy from oxidizing their food, releasing some of its energy as heat. Almost all food energy comes originally from sunlight.

5.F Evolution of Life

5.F.1   Small differences between parents and offspring can accumulate (through selective breeding) in successive generations so that descendants are very different from their ancestors.

5.F.2   Individual organisms with certain traits are more likely than others to survive and have offspring. Changes in environmental conditions can affect the survival of individual organisms and entire species.

5.F.3   Many thousands of layers of sedimentary rock provide evidence for the long history of the earth and for the long history of changing life forms whose remains are found in the rocks. More recently deposited rock layers are more likely to contain fossils resembling existing species.

6. The Human Organism

By the end of the 8th grade, students should know that

6.A Human Identity

6.A.1 Like other animals, human beings have body systems for obtaining and providing energy, defense, reproduction, and the coordination of body functions.

6.A.2 Human beings have many similarities and differences. The similarities make it possible for human beings to reproduce and to donate blood and organs to one another throughout the world. Their differences enable them to create diverse social and cultural arrangements and to solve problems in a variety of ways.

6.A.3 Fossil evidence is consistent with the idea that human beings evolved from earlier species.

6.A.4 Specialized roles of individuals within other species are genetically programmed, whereas human beings are able to invent and modify a wider range of social behavior.

6.A.5 Human beings use technology to match or excel many of the abilities of other species. Technology has helped people with disabilities survive and live more conventional lives.

6.A.6 Technologies having to do with food production, sanitation, and disease prevention have dramatically changed how people live and work and have resulted in rapid increases in the human population.

6.B Human Development

6.B.1 Fertilization occurs when sperm cells from a male's testes are deposited near an egg cell from the female ovary, and one of the sperm cells enters the egg cell. Most of the time, by chance or design, a sperm never arrives or an egg isn't available.

6.B.2 Contraception measures may incapacitate sperm, block their way to the egg, prevent the release of eggs, or prevent the fertilized egg from implanting successfully.

6.B.3 Following fertilization, cell division produces a small cluster of cells that then differentiate by appearance and function to form the basic tissues of an embryo. During the first three months of pregnancy, organs begin to form. During the second three months, all organs and body features develop. During the last three months, the organs and features mature enough to function well after birth. Patterns of human development are similar to those of other vertebrates.

6.B.4 The developing embryo—and later the newborn infant—encounters many risks from faults in its genes, its mother's inadequate diet, her cigarette smoking or use of alcohol or other drugs, or from infection. Inadequate child care may lead to lower physical and mental ability.

6.B.5 Various body changes occur as adults age. Muscles and joints become less flexible, bones and muscles lose mass, energy levels diminish, and the senses become less acute. Women stop releasing eggs and hence can no longer reproduce. The length and quality of human life are influenced by many factors, including sanitation, diet, medical care, sex, genes, environmental conditions, and personal health behaviors.

6.C Basic Functions

6.C.1 Organs and organ systems are composed of cells and help to provide all cells with basic needs.

6.C.2 For the body to use food for energy and building materials, the food must first be digested into molecules that are absorbed and transported to cells.

6.C.3 To burn food for the release of energy stored in it, oxygen must be supplied to cells, and carbon dioxide removed. Lungs take in oxygen for the combustion of food and they eliminate the carbon dioxide produced. The urinary system disposes of dissolved waste molecules, the intestinal tract removes solid wastes, and the skin and lungs rid the body of heat energy. The circulatory system moves all these substances to or from cells where they are needed or produced, responding to changing demands.

6.C.4 Specialized cells and the molecules they produce identify and destroy microbes that get inside the body.

6.C.5 Hormones are chemicals from glands that affect other body parts. They are involved in helping the body respond to danger and in regulating human growth, development, and reproduction.

6.C.6 Interactions among the senses, nerves, and brain make possible the learning that enables human beings to cope with changes in their environment.

6.D Learning

6.D.1 Some animal species are limited to a repertoire of genetically determined behaviors; others have more complex brains and can learn a wide variety of behaviors. All behavior is affected by both inheritance and experience.

6.D.2 The level of skill a person can reach in any particular activity depends on innate abilities, the amount of practice, and the use of appropriate learning technologies.

6.D.3 Human beings can detect a tremendous range of visual and olfactory stimuli. The strongest stimulus they can tolerate may be more than a trillion times as intense as the weakest they can detect. Still, there are many kinds of signals in the world that people cannot detect directly.

6.D.4 Attending closely to any one input of information usually reduces the ability to attend to others at the same time.

6.D.5 Learning often results from two perceptions or actions occurring at about the same time. The more often the same combination occurs, the stronger the mental connection between them is likely to be. Occasionally a single vivid experience will connect two things permanently in people's minds.

6.D.6 Language and tools enable human beings to learn complicated and varied things from others.

6.E Physical Health

6.E.1 The amount of food energy (calories) a person requires varies with body weight, age, sex, activity level, and natural body efficiency. Regular exercise is important to maintain a healthy heart/lung system, good muscle tone, and bone strength.

6.E.2 Toxic substances, some dietary habits, and personal behavior may be bad for one's health. Some effects show up right away, others may not show up for many years. Avoiding toxic substances, such as tobacco, and changing dietary habits to reduce the intake of such things as animal fat increases the chances of living longer.

6.E.3 Viruses, bacteria, fungi, and parasites may infect the human body and interfere with normal body functions. A person can catch a cold many times because there are many varieties of cold viruses that cause similar symptoms.

6.E.4 White blood cells engulf invaders or produce antibodies that attack them or mark them for killing by other white cells. The antibodies produced will remain and can fight off subsequent invaders of the same kind.

6.E.5 The environment may contain dangerous levels of substances that are harmful to human beings. Therefore, the good health of individuals requires monitoring the soil, air, and water and taking steps to keep them safe.

6.F Mental Health

6.F.1 Individuals differ greatly in their ability to cope with stressful situations. Both external and internal conditions (chemistry, personal history, values) influence how people behave.

6.F.2 Often people react to mental distress by denying that they have any problem. Sometimes they don't know why they feel the way they do, but with help they can sometimes uncover the reasons.

8. The Designed World

By the end of the 8th grade, students should know that

8.A Agriculture

8.A.1 Early in human history, there was an agricultural revolution in which people changed from hunting and gathering to farming. This allowed changes in the division of labor between men and women and between children and adults, and the development of new patterns of government.

8.A.2 People control the characteristics of plants and animals they raise by selective breeding and by preserving varieties of seeds (old and new) to use if growing conditions change.

8.A.3 In agriculture, as in all technologies, there are always trade-offs to be made. Getting food from many different places makes people less dependent on weather in any one place, yet more dependent on transportation and communication among far-flung markets. Specializing in one crop may risk disaster if changes in weather or increases in pest populations wipe out that crop. Also, the soil may be exhausted of some nutrients, which can be replenished by rotating the right crops.

8.A.4 Many people work to bring food, fiber, and fuel to U.S. markets. With improved technology, only a small fraction of workers in the United States actually plant and harvest the products that people use. Most workers are engaged in processing, packaging, transporting, and selling what is produced.

8.B Materials and Manufacturing

8.B.1 The choice of materials for a job depends on their properties and on how they interact with other materials. Similarly, the usefulness of some manufactured parts of an object depends on how well they fit together with the other parts.

8.B.2 Manufacturing usually involves a series of steps, such as designing a product, obtaining and preparing raw materials, processing the materials mechanically or chemically, and assembling, testing, inspecting, and packaging. The sequence of these steps is also often important.

8.B.3 Modern technology reduces manufacturing costs, produces more uniform products, and creates new synthetic materials that can help reduce the depletion of some natural resources.

8.B.4 Automation, including the use of robots, has changed the nature of work in most fields, including manufacturing. As a result, high-skill, high-knowledge jobs in engineering, computer programming, quality control, supervision, and maintenance are replacing many routine, manual-labor jobs. Workers therefore need better learning skills and flexibility to take on new and rapidly changing jobs.

8.C Energy Sources and Use

8.C.1 Energy can change from one form to another, although in the process some energy is always converted to heat. Some systems transform energy with less loss of heat than others.

8.C.2 Different ways of obtaining, transforming, and distributing energy have different environmental consequences.

8.C.3 In many instances, manufacturing and other technological activities are performed at a site close to an energy source. Some forms of energy are transported easily, others are not.

8.C.4 Electrical energy can be produced from a variety of energy sources and can be transformed into almost any other form of energy. Moreover, electricity is used to distribute energy quickly and conveniently to distant locations.

8.C.5 Energy from the sun (and the wind and water energy derived from it) is available indefinitely. Because the flow of energy is weak and variable, very large collection systems are needed. Other sources don't renew or renew only slowly.

8.C.6 Different parts of the world have different amounts and kinds of energy resources to use and use them for different purposes.

8.D Communication

8.D.1 Errors can occur in coding, transmitting, or decoding information, and some means of checking for accuracy is needed. Repeating the message is a frequently used method.

8.D.2 Information can be carried by many media, including sound, light, and objects. In this century, the ability to code information as electric currents in wires, electromagnetic waves in space, and light in glass fibers has made communication millions of times faster than is possible by mail or sound.

8.E Information Processing

8.E.1   Most computers use digital codes containing only two symbols, 0 and 1, to perform all operations. Continuous signals (analog) must be transformed into digital codes before they can be processed by a computer.

8.E.2   What use can be made of a large collection of information depends upon how it is organized. One of the values of computers is that they are able, on command, to reorganize information in a variety of ways, thereby enabling people to make more and better uses of the collection.

8.E.3   Computer control of mechanical systems can be much quicker than human control. In situations where events happen faster than people can react, there is little choice but to rely on computers. Most complex systems still require human oversight, however, to make certain kinds of judgments about the readiness of the parts of the system (including the computers) and the system as a whole to operate properly, to react to unexpected failures, and to evaluate how well the system is serving its intended purposes.

8.E.4   An increasing number of people work at jobs that involve processing or distributing information. Because computers can do these tasks faster and more reliably, they have become standard tools both in the workplace and at home.

8.F Health Technology

8.F.1   Sanitation measures such as the use of sewers, landfills, quarantines, and safe food handling are important in controlling the spread of organisms that cause disease. Improving sanitation to prevent disease has contributed more to saving human life than any advance in medical treatment.

8.F.2   The ability to measure the level of substances in body fluids has made it possible for physicians to make comparisons with normal levels, make very sophisticated diagnoses, and monitor the effects of the treatments they prescribe.

8.F.3   It is becoming increasingly possible to manufacture chemical substances such as insulin and hormones that are normally found in the body. They can be used by individuals whose own bodies cannot produce the amounts required for good health.

9. The Mathematical World

By the end of the 8th grade, students should know that

9.A Numbers

9.A.1   There have been systems for writing numbers other than the Arabic system of place values based on tens. The very old Roman numerals are now used only for dates, clock faces, or ordering chapters in a book. Numbers based on 60 are still used for describing time and angles.

9.A.2   A number line can be extended on the other side of zero to represent negative numbers. Negative numbers allow subtraction of a bigger number from a smaller number to make sense, and are often used when something can be measured on either side of some reference point (time, ground level, temperature, budget).

9.A.3   Numbers can be written in different forms, depending on how they are being used. How fractions or decimals based on measured quantities should be written depends on how precise the measurements are and how precise an answer is needed.

9.A.4   The operations + and – are inverses of each other—one undoes what the other does; likewise x and ÷ .

9.A.5   The expression a/b can mean different things: a parts of size 1/b each, a divided by b, or a compared to b.

9.A.6   Numbers can be represented by using sequences of only two symbols (such as 1 and 0, on and off); computers work this way.

9.A.7   Computations (as on calculators) can give more digits than make sense or are useful.

9.B Symbolic Relationships

9.B.1   An equation containing a variable may be true for just one value of the variable.

9.B.2   Mathematical statements can be used to describe how one quantity changes when another changes. Rates of change can be computed from differences in magnitudes and vice versa.

9.B.3   Graphs can show a variety of possible relationships between two variables. As one variable increases uniformly, the other may do one of the following: increase or decrease steadily, increase or decrease faster and faster, get closer and closer to some limiting value, reach some intermediate maximum or minimum, alternately increase and decrease indefinitely, increase or decrease in steps, or do something different from any of these.

9.C Shapes

9.C.1   Some shapes have special properties: triangular shapes tend to make structures rigid, and round shapes give the least possible boundary for a given amount of interior area. Shapes can match exactly or have the same shape in different sizes.

9.C.2   Lines can be parallel, perpendicular, or oblique.

9.C.3   Shapes on a sphere like the earth cannot be depicted on a flat surface without some distortion.

9.C.4   The graphic display of numbers may help to show patterns such as trends, varying rates of change, gaps, or clusters. Such patterns sometimes can be used to make predictions about the phenomena being graphed.

9.C.5   It takes two numbers to locate a point on a map or any other flat surface. The numbers may be two perpendicular distances from a point, or an angle and a distance from a point.

9.C.6   The scale chosen for a graph or drawing makes a big difference in how useful it is.

9.D Uncertainty

9.D.1   How probability is estimated depends on what is known about the situation. Estimates can be based on data from similar conditions in the past or on the assumption that all the possibilities are known.

9.D.2   Probabilities are ratios and can be expressed as fractions, percentages, or odds.

9.D.3   The mean, median, and mode tell different things about the middle of a data set.

9.D.4   Comparison of data from two groups should involve comparing both their middles and the spreads around them.

9.D.5   The larger a well-chosen sample is, the more accurately it is likely to represent the whole. But there are many ways of choosing a sample that can make it unrepresentative of the whole.

9.D.6   Events can be described in terms of being more or less likely, impossible, or certain.

9.E Reasoning

9.E.1   Some aspects of reasoning have fairly rigid rules for what makes sense; other aspects don't. If people have rules that always hold, and good information about a particular situation, then logic can help them to figure out what is true about it. This kind of reasoning requires care in the use of key words such as if, and, not, or, all, and some. Reasoning by similarities can suggest ideas but can't prove them one way or the other.

9.E.2   Practical reasoning, such as diagnosing or troubleshooting almost anything, may require many-step, branching logic. Because computers can keep track of complicated logic, as well as a lot of information, they are useful in a lot of problem-solving situations.

9.E.3   Sometimes people invent a general rule to explain how something works by summarizing observations. But people tend to overgeneralize, imagining general rules on the basis of only a few observations.

9.E.4   People are using incorrect logic when they make a statement such as "If A is true, then B is true; but A isn't true, therefore B isn't true either."

9.E.5   A single example can never prove that something is always true, but sometimes a single example can prove that something is not always true.

9.E.6   An analogy has some likenesses to but also some differences from the real thing.

10. Historical Perspectives

By the end of the 8th grade, students should know that

10.A Displacing the Earth from the Center of the Universe

10.A.1 The motion of an object is always judged with respect to some other object or point and so the idea of absolute motion or rest is misleading.

10.A.2 Telescopes reveal that there are many more stars in the night sky than are evident to the unaided eye, the surface of the moon has many craters and mountains, the sun has dark spots, and Jupiter and some other planets have their own moons.

10.F Understanding Fire

10.F.1 From the earliest times until now, people have believed that even though millions of different kinds of material seem to exist in the world, most things must be made up of combinations of just a few basic kinds of things. There has not always been agreement, however, on what those basic kinds of things are. One theory long ago was that the basic substances were earth, water, air, and fire. Scientists now know that these are not the basic substances. But the old theory seemed to explain many observations about the world.

10.F.2 Today, scientists are still working out the details of what the basic kinds of matter are and of how they combine, or can be made to combine, to make other substances.

10.F.3 Experimental and theoretical work done by French scientist Antoine Lavoisier in the decade between the American and French revolutions led to the modern science of chemistry.

10.F.4 Lavoisier's work was based on the idea that when materials react with each other many changes can take place but that in every case the total amount of matter afterward is the same as before. He successfully tested the concept of conservation of matter by conducting a series of experiments in which he carefully measured all the substances involved in burning, including the gases used and those given off.

10.F.5 Alchemy was chiefly an effort to change base metals like lead into gold and to produce an elixir that would enable people to live forever. It failed to do that or to create much knowledge of how substances react with each other. The more scientific study of chemistry that began in Lavoisier's time has gone far beyond alchemy in understanding reactions and producing new materials.

10.G Splitting the Atom

10.G.1 The accidental discovery that minerals containing uranium darken photographic film, as light does, led to the idea of radioactivity.

10.G.2 In their laboratory in France, Marie Curie and her husband, Pierre Curie, isolated two new elements that caused most of the radioactivity of the uranium mineral. They named one radium because it gave off powerful, invisible rays, and the other polonium in honor of Madame Curie's country of birth. Marie Curie was the first scientist ever to win the Nobel prize in two different fields—in physics, shared with her husband, and later in chemistry.

10.I Discovering Germs

10.I.1 Throughout history, people have created explanations for disease. Some have held that disease has spiritual causes, but the most persistent biological theory over the centuries was that illness resulted from an imbalance in the body fluids. The introduction of germ theory by Louis Pasteur and others in the 19th century led to the modern belief that many diseases are caused by microorganisms—bacteria, viruses, yeasts, and parasites.

10.I.2 Pasteur wanted to find out what causes milk and wine to spoil. He demonstrated that spoilage and fermentation occur when microorganisms enter from the air, multiply rapidly, and produce waste products. After showing that spoilage could be avoided by keeping germs out or by destroying them with heat, he investigated animal diseases and showed that microorganisms were involved. Other investigators later showed that specific kinds of germs caused specific diseases.

10.I.3 Pasteur found that infection by disease organisms—germs—caused the body to build up an immunity against subsequent infection by the same organisms. He then demonstrated that it was possible to produce vaccines that would induce the body to build immunity to a disease without actually causing the disease itself.

10.I.4 Changes in health practices have resulted from the acceptance of the germ theory of disease. Before germ theory, illness was treated by appeals to supernatural powers or by trying to adjust body fluids through induced vomiting, bleeding, or purging. The modern approach emphasizes sanitation, the safe handling of food and water, the pasteurization of milk, quarantine, and aseptic surgical techniques to keep germs out of the body; vaccinations to strengthen the body's immune system against subsequent infection by the same kind of microorganisms; and antibiotics and other chemicals and processes to destroy microorganisms.

10.I.5 In medicine, as in other fields of science, discoveries are sometimes made unexpectedly, even by accident. But knowledge and creative insight are usually required to recognize the meaning of the unexpected.

10.J Harnessing Power

10.J.1 Until the 1800s, most manufacturing was done in homes, using small, handmade machines that were powered by muscle, wind, or running water. New machinery and steam engines to drive them made it possible to replace craftsmanship with factories, using fuels as a source of energy. In the factory system, workers, materials, and energy could be brought together efficiently.

10.J.2 The invention of the steam engine was at the center of the Industrial Revolution. It converted the chemical energy stored in wood and coal, which were plentiful, into mechanical work. The steam engine was invented to solve the urgent problem of pumping water out of coal mines. As improved by James Watt, it was soon used to move coal, drive manufacturing machinery, and power locomotives, ships, and even the first automobiles.

11. Common Themes

By the end of the 8th grade, students should know that

11.A Systems

11.A.1 A system can include processes as well as things.

11.A.2 Thinking about things as systems means looking for how every part relates to others. The output from one part of a system (which can include material, energy, or information) can become the input to other parts. Such feedback can serve to control what goes on in the system as a whole.

11.A.3 Any system is usually connected to other systems, both internally and externally. Thus a system may be thought of as containing subsystems and as being a subsystem of a larger system.

11.B Models

11.B.1 Models are often used to think about processes that happen too slowly, too quickly, or on too small a scale to observe directly, or that are too vast to be changed deliberately, or that are potentially dangerous.

11.B.2 Mathematical models can be displayed on a computer and then modified to see what happens.

11.B.3 Different models can be used to represent the same thing. What kind of a model to use and how complex it should be depends on its purpose. The usefulness of a model may be limited if it is too simple or if it is needlessly complicated. Choosing a useful model is one of the instances in which intuition and creativity come into play in science, mathematics, and engineering.

11.C Constancy and Change

11.C.1 Physical and biological systems tend to change until they become stable and then remain that way unless their surroundings change.

11.C.2 A system may stay the same because nothing is happening or because things are happening but exactly counterbalance one another.

11.C.3 Many systems contain feedback mechanisms that serve to keep changes within specified limits.

11.C.4 Symbolic equations can be used to summarize how the quantity of something changes over time or in response to other changes.

11.C.5 Symmetry (or the lack of it) may determine properties of many objects, from molecules and crystals to organisms and designed structures.

11.C.6 Cycles, such as the seasons or body temperature, can be described by their cycle length or frequency, what their highest and lowest values are, and when these values occur. Different cycles range from many thousands of years down to less than a billionth of a second.

11.D Scale

11.D.1 Properties of systems that depend on volume, such as capacity and weight, change out of proportion to properties that depend on area, such as strength or surface processes.

11.D.2 As the complexity of any system increases, gaining an understanding of it depends increasingly on summaries, such as averages and ranges, and on descriptions of typical examples of that system.

12. Habits of Mind

By the end of the 8th grade, students should know that

12.A Values and Attitudes

12.A.1 Know why it is important in science to keep honest, clear, and accurate records.

12.A.2 Know that hypotheses are valuable, even if they turn out not to be true, if they lead to fruitful investigations.

12.A.3 Know that often different explanations can be given for the same evidence, and it is not always possible to tell which one is correct.

12.B Computation and Estimation

12.B.1 Find what percentage one number is of another and figure any percentage of any number.

12.B.2 Use, interpret, and compare numbers in several equivalent forms such as integers, fractions, decimals, and percents.

12.B.3 Calculate the circumferences and areas of rectangles, triangles, and circles, and the volumes of rectangular solids.

12.B.4 Find the mean and median of a set of data.

12.B.5 Estimate distances and travel times from maps and the actual size of objects from scale drawings.

12.B.6 Insert instructions into computer spreadsheet cells to program arithmetic calculations.

12.B.7 Determine what unit (such as seconds, square inches, or dollars per tankful) an answer should be expressed in from the units of the inputs to the calculation, and be able to convert compound units (such as yen per dollar into dollar per yen, or miles per hour into feet per second).

12.B.8 Decide what degree of precision is adequate and round off the result of calculator operations to enough significant figures to reasonably reflect those of the inputs.

12.B.9 Express numbers like 100, 1,000, and 1,000,000 as powers of 10.

12.B.10 Estimate probabilities of outcomes in familiar situations, on the basis of history or the number of possible outcomes.

12.C Manipulation and Observation

12.C.1 Use calculators to compare amounts proportionally.

12.C.2 Use computers to store and retrieve information in topical, alphabetical, numerical, and key-word files, and create simple files of their own devising.

12.C.3 Read analog and digital meters on instruments used to make direct measurements of length, volume, weight, elapsed time, rates, and temperature, and choose appropriate units for reporting various magnitudes.

12.C.4 Use cameras and tape recorders for capturing information.

12.C.5 Inspect, disassemble, and reassemble simple mechanical devices and describe what the various parts are for; estimate what the effect that making a change in one part of a system is likely to have on the system as a whole.

12.D Communication Skills

12.D.1 Organize information in simple tables and graphs and identify relationships they reveal.

12.D.2 Read simple tables and graphs produced by others and describe in words what they show.

12.D.3 Locate information in reference books, back issues of newspapers and magazines, compact disks, and computer databases.

12.D.4 Understand writing that incorporates circle charts, bar and line graphs, two-way data tables, diagrams, and symbols.

12.D.5 Find and describe locations on maps with rectangular and polar coordinates.

12.E Critical-Response Skills

12.E.1 Question claims based on vague attributions (such as "Leading doctors say...") or on statements made by celebrities or others outside the area of their particular expertise.

12.E.2 Compare consumer products and consider reasonable personal trade-offs among them on the basis of features, performance, durability, and cost.

12.E.3 Be skeptical of arguments based on very small samples of data, biased samples, or samples for which there was no control sample.

12.E.4 Be aware that there may be more than one good way to interpret a given set of findings.

12.E.5 Notice and criticize the reasoning in arguments in which (1) fact and opinion are intermingled or the conclusions do not follow logically from the evidence given, (2) an analogy is not apt, (3) no mention is made of whether the control groups are very much like the experimental group, or (4) all members of a group (such as teenagers or chemists) are implied to have nearly identical characteristics that differ from those of other groups.